Loot

Loot

How Israel Stole Palestinian Property

Adam Raz

VERSO

London • New York

This book was translated into English thanks to the generous support of the Germanacos Family Foundation.

This English-language edition first published by Verso 2024
Translation © Philip Hollander 2024
First published as *Bizat ha-rekhush ha-'Arvi be-Milhemet ha-'Atsma'ut* [Looting of Arab property in the War of Independence] by Carmel Publishing House 2020
© Adam Raz 2020

1 3 5 7 9 10 8 6 4 2

Verso
UK: 6 Meard Street, London W1F 0EG
US: 388 Atlantic Avenue, Brooklyn, NY 11217
versobooks.com

Verso is the imprint of New Left Books

ISBN-13: 978-1-80429-515-1
ISBN-13: 978-1-80429-517-5 (UK EBK)
ISBN-13: 978-1-80429-518-2 (US EBK)

British Library Cataloguing in Publication Data
A catalogue record for this book is available from the British Library

Library of Congress Cataloging-in-Publication Data

Names: Raz, Adam, 1982- author.
Title: Loot : how Israel stole Palestinian property / Adam Raz.
Other titles: Bizat ha-rekhush ha-'Arvi be-Milḥemet ha-'Atsma'ut. English.
Description: English-language edition. | London ; Brooklyn, NY : Verso, 2024. | Includes bibliographical references and index.
Identifiers: LCCN 2024022656 (print) | LCCN 2024022657 (ebook) | ISBN 9781804295151 (hardback) | ISBN 9781804295182 (ebook)
Subjects: LCSH: Israel-Arab War, 1948-1949—Destruction and pillage. | Palestinian Arabs—Israel. | Abandonment of property—Israel. | Palestinian Nakba, 1947-1948.
Classification: LCC DS126.96.D47 R3913 2024 (print) | LCC DS126.96.D47 (ebook) | DDC 364.16095694—dc23/eng/20240524
LC record available at https://lccn.loc.gov/2024022656
LC ebook record available at https://lccn.loc.gov/2024022657

Typeset in Minion by Hewer Text UK Ltd, Edinburgh
Printed and bound by CPI Group (UK) Ltd, Croydon CR0 4YY

To Grandpa,
Simhah (Simi) Shiloni, Palmachnik

'Put one in the camel. It is a perfect target!' shouted the captain without a smile. I lowered the rifle from my shoulder and then I put it back. I knew I could not refuse . . . Only somebody who had killed *at least* one person could choose not to shoot a camel. Also, deep down I thought that I wanted to shoot a living being . . . 'Shoot it! Do not be so *sensitive*!' He turned to the lieutenant and said, 'Do not bother him. It is enemy property!' Again, I understood the meaning of the word . . . It seemed that I hit it this time, because the camel suddenly stuck out its neck and began to walk around in a circle with his soft legs twitching. He did not try to flee. He did not know where to go. He only knew that he needed to run. Hence, he ran aimlessly in circles until he slowly collapsed, as if he was obediently responding to his camel driver's staff by kneeling . . . Rather than drawing closer to God, I knew that I had distanced myself from him . . . 'The village has been conquered. They raised the white flag. Do you see?' said the lieutenant . . . 'Let us pass by the camel and see where you hit him,' [said the captain] . . . The camel was young and beautiful like the desert wind. It lay curled in upon itself. It legs were pressed up into its chest and its head was lying in the grass . . . I turned away from it and I began walking aimlessly just like it had until the camel rose for my back to see. It has been following me ever since.

Dan Ben-Amotz
'On the Camel and the Victory', in Efraim Talmi,
ed., *Pen and dagger: Stories of the Independence War*
[Hebrew] (Tel Aviv: M. Neuman, 1950)

Contents

Part II:
THE PLUNDER OF PALESTINIAN PROPERTY —
POLITICS AND SOCIETY

Archival Collections and Abbreviations

Ben-Gurion Archive, Sde Boker (BGA)
Beit Hameiri Archive, Safed (BHA)
Central Zionist Archives, Jerusalem (CZA)
Conflict Document Collection, Akevot Institute, Haifa
Haganah Historical Archives, Tel Aviv (HHA)
Haifa Municipal Archives, Haifa (HMA)
HaShomer Archive, Kfar Giladi (HAS)
Israel Defense Forces and Defense Establishment Archive, Tel Aviv
    (IDF)
Israel State Archives (ISA)
Jabotinsky Institute Archive, Tel Aviv (JIA)
Jerusalem Municipal Archives, Jerusalem (JMA)
Kibbutz Beit Hashita Archive, Beit Hashita
Kibbutz Mishmar HaNegev Archive, Mishmar HaNegev
Kibbutz HaZorea Archive, HaZorea (KHZ)
Knesset Archives, Jerusalem (KAJ)
Labor Party Archive, Beit Berl (LPA)
National Library of Israel Archives, Jerusalem
Oranim Group Archive, Oranim
Palmach Generation Association Archive, Tel Aviv (PGA)
Pinchas Lavon Institute for Labour Movement Research Archive, Tel
    Aviv (LMA)
Tel Aviv-Yafo Municipal Archives, Tel Aviv (TYA)

United Nations Archives, New York (documents in English)
Yad Tabenkin Archive, Ramat Efal (YTA)
Yad Yaari Research and Documentation Center Archives, Givat Haviva
  (YYA)
Yitzhak Rabin Center Archive, Tel Aviv (YRC)

All documents in these archives are in Hebrew unless otherwise specified.

Introduction

At its inception, the Zionist movement was not a movement of dispossession. In fact, even after the Independence War, it should not be viewed as one.[1] It would be more accurate to say that disagreements concerning the character of the Zionist project, its integration into the Arab domain, and its relations with the Land of Israel's Palestinian residents existed within the Zionist movement, more specifically in its leadership ranks. In the final months of 1947, crucial decisions were being made about Mandate Palestine. A vast international struggle between competing interests combined with numerous other factors to bring the area to a crossroads. As different leadership circles weighed the partition plan, regional leaders faced off against each other; they had decisive choices to make. Yet this did not necessarily mean that any single *group* of leaders was facing off against another, as historians commonly present it. It was first and foremost *within* each leadership circle that leaders were pitted against each other. The alternatives were clear: Would the area be divided through armed struggle – an option that made it highly likely that there would be population transfer? Or would a different choice be made – in this case a politically negotiated partition that would preserve economic unity and would proceed peacefully (in accordance with the basic framework of the partition plan)? Venomous

---

1   On this topic, see Yigal Wagner and Adam Raz, *Herzl: The conflicts of Zionism's founder with supporters and opponents* [Hebrew] (Jerusalem: Carmel, 2018).

Arab rhetoric convinced many fine people that the Arabs were united in their desire to fight a war to exterminate the Zionists. This was not actually the case. As venomous talk whose rhetoric closely paralleled that employed by the Nazis only a few years earlier dominated conversation, alliances were being forged and firm ties were being formed in the Yishuv, the body of Jewish residents in Palestine prior to the establishment of the State of Israel in 1948.[2]

In the Zionist leadership stratum, different and conflicting policy positions competed against one another: one favoured a long transition period between the British Mandate's conclusion and the declaration of two states, in accordance with the partition plan, seeing this as the most effective way to coordinate how the two entities that were about to emerge alongside each other in a twin sovereign act would interact in the governmental, economic, and political realms. This position emphasized that the Arabs were not all cut from the same cloth, and that there were alternatives to the reactionary politics of the mufti and the terrorism that accompanied it. Although political manipulation enabled it to achieve ascendancy, the second position was held by only a minority of leaders. It looked to radicalize the conflict, bring about war sooner, and resolve matters more quickly. Even during the civil war stage that started in November–December 1947 and lasted until the declaration of independence and the Arab nations' invasion of the Land of Israel, there were leaders, such as Chaim Weizmann, who supported the former position. In a letter to President Harry Truman written in April 1948, he declared that 'Palestine is inhabited by two peoples. These peoples have separate political aspirations and common economic interests.' Therefore, preservation of economic unity between the two entities during the partition's implementation assumed great importance.[3]

In any case, in contrast with the widespread view among historians, David Ben-Gurion, and the advocates of the latter's position, never intended to adopt the partition plan to the letter. Unlike the Israeli

---

2   Yoram Nimrod, 'Conservatism or change in the Arab world: Conflicting preferences in the Zionist administration (1946–1948)' [Hebrew], *Katedra* 67 (March 1993): 54–69.

3   Dr Chaim Weizmann to President Truman, 9 April 1948, Truman Papers, Official File, in *Foreign Relations of the United States*, 1948, vol. 5, part 2, *The Near East, South Asia, and Africa* (Washington, DC: Government Printing Office, 1976), Document 139, available at Office of the Historian, US Department of State, history.state.gov.

historian Benny Morris, for example, I do not view the Independence War as 'the almost inevitable result of more than half a century of Arab–Jewish friction and conflict'.[4] On the contrary, rational politicians on both sides of the barricades made the conscious decision to go to war.

This book constitutes part of a larger historiographical and historiosophic mosaic whose first pieces were set in place many years ago by friends, some of whom are no longer with us. For example, my conclusions accord with those of historian Yoram Nimrod, whose *War or peace? Formation of patterns in Israeli Arab relations, 1947–1950*, published after his death, pointed to a Zionist/Israeli policy that strove to use war as a means for inclusion of more land within Israeli territorial boundaries than had been allocated to it by the partition plan.[5] For this policy to succeed, things needed to be done to fortify the extremist Arab position. This position was not universally embraced, and it was pitted against a contradictory position held by members of the Zionist elite. Despite the time that has passed since its publication, Nimrod's book remains the most original and detailed study of how political struggles that took place before and during the war brought about diplomatic entanglements.

In a number of meticulous studies describing the major clashes that roiled the Israeli political elite, particularly the labour movement elite, historian Eyal Kafkafi demonstrated how battles presented to the public as grounded in ideological disagreements, such as the controversy over the Palmach's dismantlement, were merely camouflaged to appear this way.[6] In reality, they reflected skirmishes between groups possessing divergent political interests. For example, in her books *Truth or faith: Yitzhak Tabenkin as mentor of Hakibbutz Hameuhad* and *Pinchas Lavon: Anti-messiah*, Kafkafi shows that it was not differences of opinion concerning means that led to clashes. On the contrary, it was the divergence of social agendas, which could not be pursued simultaneously, that brought about conflict.[7] Similarly, in a long series of articles that

---

4   Benny Morris, *1948* (Tel Aviv: 'Am 'Oved, 2010), 15.

5   Yoram Nimrod, *War or peace? Formation of patterns in Israeli Arab relations, 1947–1950* [Hebrew] (Givat Haviva: Institute for Peace Research, 2000).

6   The Palmach (acronym for 'strike companies') was the elite fighting force of the underground army of the Yishuv during the period of the British Mandate for Palestine.

7   Eyal Kafkafi, *Truth or faith: Yitzhak Tabenkin as mentor of Hakibbutz Hameuhad* [Hebrew] (Jerusalem: Yad Izhak Ben-Zvi, 1992); Eyal Kafkafi, *Pinchas Lavon: Anti-messiah* [Hebrew] (Tel Aviv: 'Am 'Oved, 1998).

were posthumously published in the collection *One party, two paths*, Nimrod and Kafkafi's friend Benko Adar analysed the confrontation that took place during the Independence War between Ben-Gurion and Yisrael Galili, head of the National Command. Like Kafkafi, Adar did not see the forceful confrontation between the two men as a reflection of different ideological positions concerning particular issues, such as military–state relations, but as a reflection of divergent outlooks concerning the way that the war should be waged and, by extension, the way the war would conclude.[8]

Over the course of the last decade, I have published a number of studies that continue the historiographical and theoretical project of Kafkafi, Nimrod, Adar, and others. Two of them are particularly relevant to this book. *The Kafr Qasim massacre: A political biography* [Hebrew] (Jerusalem: Carmel, 2018) described and analysed the debate within the ruling Mapai party concerning the use of military rule to govern Israeli Arabs; it asserted that the segregationist policy Ben-Gurion enacted towards Israel's Palestinian residents reflected his broader social outlook and his ambitions for the future character of the Zionist project. In other words, security concerns did not necessitate military rule (as it has regularly been presented for decades). Instead, the policy was put in place to signal the direction in which Ben-Gurion wanted to take the Zionist project. Subsequently, I published *The iron fist regime: David Ben-Gurion, the statism debate, and the controversy over Israeli nuclear policy* [Hebrew] (Jerusalem: Carmel, 2019), the second instalment in a three-book series about the history of the Israeli nuclear programme. Building upon my earlier book, I used the first part of *The iron fist regime* to present Ben-Gurion's view of the Israeli Jewish community and the policies he considered in its best interest. I take issue with those who present Ben-Gurion as an exemplary democrat, and I point to how Ben-Gurion had little faith in democracy and employed a fundamentally anti-democratic political approach to pursue his agenda. Consequently, Ben-Gurion had a great deal in common with other contemporaneous world leaders who possessed a similar outlook.

In *The iron fist regime*, whose title is a direct reference to Ben-Gurion's approach, I demonstrate his possession of a well-formulated outlook concerning the Israeli commonwealth's social character. This outlook, I

---

8   Benko Adar, *One party, two paths* [Hebrew] (Oranim: Hug Oranim Press, 2004).

argue, stood at the heart of a major controversy that roiled the Israeli political elite. Although we cannot fully address it here, Ben-Gurion was usually found in the minority within his own party. One of this book's central claims is that Ben-Gurion viewed war as a tool for societal design. In April 1948, he explained that 'war will bring about beneficial internal changes in the make-up of the Yishuv', and he maintained that through war 'we will heal the Jewish body'.[9] Elsewhere he explained that the attack on Israel that took place during the Independence War was a "most hateful act that produced *the most blessed results*'.[10] According to Ben-Gurion, the Arab rulers did not understand that 'by putting pressure on Israel, [they] caused creativity and strength to *surge forth from the depths of the Jewish soul* that would have been otherwise inaccessible'. The prime minister argued that, despite the casualties and the heavy expenses incurred in the fight against the Arabs, 'the benefits outweighed the costs'.[11]

The iron fist regime considered statism at length, addressing it not as a concept or an ethereal idea but as a political concept employable for societal organization. In fact, the book asserted that Ben-Gurionist statism was advanced as an alternative to a movement-based approach. The struggle between these approaches voiced the opposition between two methods for organizing social relations and dividing political power in the nascent Israeli state. When you clear away the jargon and the ideological patches given to it over time, statism is revealed as something designed to camouflage how Ben-Gurion's governmental objectives ran counter to the aims of those who favoured the movement approach, like Yisrael Galili and Ya'akov Hazan of Mapam, Pinchas Lavon and Moshe Sharett of Mapai, and others. Under the cover of statism, Ben-Gurion strove to establish a 'strong state' at whose helm he would stand as a 'strong leader'. This is one of the reasons why he favoured the creation of a weak democracy with lax

9 Me'ir Avizohar and Avi Bareli, eds, *Now or never: Mapai deliberations in the final year of the British Mandate, Introductions and documents* [Hebrew], vol. 2 (Bet Berl: Hotza'at 'Ayanot, 1989), 346.

10 David Ben-Gurion, 'Our security and our status', in *Government annual* [Hebrew] ([Jerusalem]: Government Press Office, 1960), I, available at Israel State Archives (hereafter ISA), archives.gov.il, emphasis added.

11 David Ben-Gurion, 'Middle Eastern nation or eternal nation', in *Vision and way* [Hebrew], vol. 5 (Tel Aviv: 'Ayanot, 1957), 130–5, 133, emphasis added.

political oversight that allowed for a hierarchical political system and concentration of power.

This book is organized into two parts. The first provides a chronological description of the plunder of Arab property during the Independence War (1947–49), and it concludes, more or less, with the signing of the last ceasefire agreement in mid-1949. The second part discusses the plunder from a socio-political perspective. This book aims to shed light on an insufficiently understood aspect of history during these years: the involvement of large parts of the Israeli population – citizens and soldiers alike – in the plunder of property belonging to the Arab population. Yet, this is not just the story of this plunder. It is a political story, too. The plunder, I argue, was not just tolerated by specific people within the political and military establishments (particularly Prime Minister David Ben-Gurion); it also served a political role in the fashioning of Israeli society's appearance, the division of political power in the new state, and the shaping of wartime and post-war relations between Israel and the Arab world. I argue that the Jewish population's widespread participation in looting played an integral part in the implementation of the policy direction that Ben-Gurion and his political partners took in internal and external affairs.

To the best of my knowledge, this is the first book whose primary focus is the plunder of Arab property. Nonetheless, it is not the first book to deal with the theft of Arab property (indeed, use of the word 'theft' involves a value judgement). Before proceeding, it is useful to discuss the different ways that these two terms are employed. Usually, when scholars discuss what happened to Arab property in 1948 (some authors, like me, employ the term 'Independence War', others use 'Nakba' ('catastrophe' in Arabic), and still others refer to it by date: 'the 1948 War'), a significant issue that plays an ongoing role in discussions and negotiations dedicated to resolution of the conflict held from 1948 to the present, focus is given to the lands and buildings that the approximately 700,000 Arab inhabitants – Palestinian refugees – of the Land of Israel left behind when the war forced them into exile. A number of compelling scholarly works have tackled this weighty matter, but it is only tangentially related to the issues on which this book focuses.[12]

---

12 For two books that deal with land and only tangentially touch upon the matter of moveable assets, see Sami Hadawi, *Palestinian Rights and Losses in 1948* (London:

This study deals with the plunder of *moveable* property left behind by Arabs – in other words, the contents of tens of thousands of homes and stores, diverse agricultural produce, huge quantities of livestock, cars, a great deal of mechanical equipment, factory apparatuses, and many other things. From a financial perspective, this property's value was undoubtedly insignificant when compared with the value of the Arab-owned lands and structures expropriated by the State of Israel both during and after the war. (Consequently, in diplomatic discussions over the course of the last few decades, the moveable assets stolen from the refugees have proven a much less thorny topic than the issue of immovable property).[13] Nonetheless, important aspects of the plunder of moveable Arab assets are worthy of discussion.

Three principal criteria distinguish the plunder of *moveable* property from the theft of land and buildings during and after the war. *First,* it was not out of compliance with some political order from above that people looted. In contrast, the expropriation of Arab-owned lands and buildings, both during and after the war, was agreed upon by a handful of decision makers and carried out by the state. Like every political decision made by appropriate institutions, it was accepted in the halls of power, and the public was forced to accept it. For example, the passage of the 'Absentee Property Law' of 1950 – one of a series of draconian laws that allowed the state to seize control of immovable Arab property – enabled widespread theft of Arab lands and property, and shaped the political, economic, and social reality of the State of Israel. Yet, this law reflects a decision by politicians that the general public did not help make.[14] Meanwhile, the looting of

---

Saqi Books, 1998); Michael Fischbach, *Records of Dispossession: Palestinian Property and the Arab-Israeli Conflict* (New York: Columbia University Press, 2003).

13   There are those who do not differentiate between the plunder of movable assets during the war (that is to say, an illegal activity), wartime expropriation carried out for strategic purposes (in a legal way), and seizure of Arab-owned land and transfer of ownership to others. The whole approach of the Israeli Jewish community to Arab property and the practices that they employed in relationship to it are considered 'theft'. See, for example: Salim Tamari, 'Heard Nothing, Seen Nothing', *Journal of Palestine Studies* 34, no. 3 (2005): 89–91.

14   On the law and critical attitudes towards it within the political realm, see Adam Raz, *The Kafr Qasim Massacre: A Political Biography* (Jerusalem: Carmel, 2018), 45–8. Sabri Jiryis's book is still one of the most interesting ones about the series of laws that set up the seizure of immovable Arab property. Sabri Jiryis, *The Arabs in Israel 1948–1966*, trans. Meric Dobson (Beirut: Institute for Palestine Studies, 1969).

moveable assets was voluntary, and many people engaged in this criminal behaviour.

Second, since the looters were members of the general Jewish population acting as individuals and not as a sovereign entity, it influenced and shaped their attitudes (a) towards the Palestinian refugees and the Arabs that remained in the country, (b) towards themselves and their society, and (c) towards the way that the Israeli–Arab–Palestinian conflict as a whole should be resolved. In light of this, there was good reason for the widespread looting to disturb many people at the time, and decision makers, intellectuals, public figures, journalists, and many others viewed it as a serious affliction. There were even those who saw the prevalence of looting as something that extinguished Zionism's pioneering moral character. In the second half of the book, I address this issue at length.

Third, looting and theft during wartime is a historic phenomenon dating back millennia, of which the twentieth century provides abundant examples.[15] During the Vietnam War, American soldiers looted belongings from the Vietnamese, and during the conquest of Germany at the end of World War II, Allied soldiers pillaged civilian property. The present case is unique for one clear reason that is worth repeating: the looting population (the Jews) plundered the property of *neighbouring inhabitants* (the Arabs). These were not abstract 'enemies' who resided on the other side of the ocean. They were yesterday's neighbours.

The first part of this study begins with a description of the despoliation that took place throughout the war, beginning with the expulsion and flight of tens of thousands of Arabs from Mandate Palestine and concluding with the end of the Independence War. Since the objective here is to shed light specifically on the depredation, I forego rehearsal of the timeline of the war or the political or military discussion of how it was proceeding, about which a great deal has already been written. The second part offers a socio-political discussion grounded in the findings of the first, and it focuses on presentation of the various political positions taken concerning plunder, its effects, and its meaning that were exposed in Israel. I argue that individual pillaging enlisted the Jewish

---

15   Todd Gray, *Looting in Wartime Britain* (Exeter: Mint Press, 2009); Tuba Inal, *Looting and Rape in Wartime: Law and Change in International Relations* (Philadelphia: University of Pennsylvania Press, 2013), 28–58, 167–86.

population to support a policy that aimed to remove (and/or not return) Arab inhabitants at war's end.

There will be those who say that it would have been enough to argue that 'many Jews looted' or to describe the case of one city – let us say Tiberias, Haifa, Jerusalem, Jaffa, Acre, Safed, Beisan (Beit She'an), Ramle, Lydda, or Beersheba – or some village or another as an illustration (the village of Qisarya or Deir Yassin, for example), and not to describe the looting in each and every location. It is true that there is little difference in the way that Haifa and Jaffa were plundered, because the two cities were completely pillaged. Nonetheless, since this is the first one-volume study to narrate how the Jewish population looted Arab moveable property, I considered it best to include information about what happened in all the cities (among which there are, in fact, important differences).

Those interested in skipping over the first part of the book can try to get by with what Ben-Gurion told the Mapai central committee at a July 1948 meeting, after the young state's leaders had received a reasonably clear picture of the looting in Arab and mixed cities: 'It turns out that most Jews are thieves ... I say this simply and intentionally, because regretfully it is the truth.'[16]

Note to the reader: I often use the terms 'Arab' and 'Palestinian' interchangeably throughout the book. The predominant use of the word 'Arab' here is certainly not meant to erase Palestinianism but reflects the usage of the time period, when both Arabs and Jews used 'Arab' rather than 'Palestinian'.

All quotations translated from Hebrew-language source material, unless otherwise noted, are translated by the author.

---

16 Minutes of Mapai Central Committee [meeting], 24 July 1948, file: Protocols of the Party Central Committee, 2-23-1948-1949, Labor Party Archive (hereafter, LPA).

PART I

The Plunder of Palestinian Property – Chronicle of a Disappearance

The terrified flight of Arab residents in their multitudes, the massive relinquishment of property numbering in hundreds and thousands [of] apartments, stores, warehouses, and workshops, and the abandonment of crops in the field, and fruit in gardens, orchards, and vineyards, all this during the upheaval of war . . . placed a serious material temptation before the struggling and victorious Yishuv . . . The desire for vengeance, moral self-justification, and material temptation tripped up many, many people . . . Things on the ground went downhill without anything to hold them back.[1]

Dov Shafrir, Israeli state custodian of abandoned property

---

1 Dov Shafrir, 'Report on the activities of the custodian of absentees' property up until 31 March 1949', 18 April 1949, file: Office of the Custodian of Absentees' Property, Gimmel-5434/3, ISA. The office that they established in July 1948 was called 'The Custodian for Abandoned Property', and in January 1949 the name was changed to 'The Custodian for Absentee's Property'. This is the name commonly used up until the present. This study will employ the office's initial name.

On 29 November 1947, the United Nations General Assembly approved the Partition Plan for Palestine. The Independence War broke out immediately after, and fighting continued until the signing of a cease-fire agreement with Syria on 20 July 1949. Over the years, commentators have divided the war according to various periodizations, but most regard it as having two primary stages. The first, lasting from late November (or early December) 1947 until 14 May 1948, when independence was declared and the Arab armies invaded Israel, constitutes the *civil war stage*, when the two communities living in Mandate Palestine under British rule fought against each other. During this stage, characterized by guerrilla fighting and acts of terror by each side against the other, the Arab inhabitants were aided by a small volunteer force from Arab countries, along with the Arab Liberation Army. (This stage can also be divided into substages: during the first months, the Arab forces were on the offensive. Meanwhile, until the end of March, the Haganah – the main Zionist paramilitary organization that operated during the British Mandate – adopted a largely defensive posture. From the end of March until the middle of May, the Haganah adopted an offensive posture and routed Mandate Palestine's Palestinian community.) The second stage of the war (*the regional-war stage*) began with the invasion of the Arab armies of Syria, Egypt, Transjordan, and Iraq, as well as small expeditionary forces from additional countries, immediately after the Israeli Declaration of Independence and the end of the British Mandate.[1] In practice, hostilities ended in January 1949 (though, during the ceasefire negotiations, the war continued at a low level of intensity in the far south), and in mid-1949, the war officially came to an end.

During the war, there were two truces: the first was from 11 June to 8 July 1948; the second was from 19 July to 22 October 1948. The days of battle during the second part of the war, the regional-war stage, added up to only slightly more than two months. During the civil war stage, most of the fighting took place in territories that the partition plan had allocated to Israel (with the major exceptions of the city of Jerusalem and the Tel Aviv–Jerusalem corridor), and it was during this period that all of the mixed cities were conquered. In practice, from the moment the Haganah abandoned the defensive policy adopted during the first months of fighting (November 1947 through the end of March 1948) and assumed an offensive policy – from the beginning of April to the middle of May 1948 – it conquered Tiberias, Haifa, the West Jerusalem neighbourhoods, Jaffa, Acre, Safed, and Beisan (Beit She'an). During the ten days between the two truces that took place in the regional war period, the Haganah conquered Ramle and Lydda, and subsequently, towards the end of the fighting, Beersheba. It conquered hundreds of villages throughout the War.

The displacement of cities' and villages' Arab residents, whether due to forced evacuation, destruction of livelihoods, economic despoilment, or the like, forged a new reality. On the eve of the war, 1,970,000 people resided in the western Land of Israel. About a third of them, approximately 650,00, were Jews. About 826,000 of these people were Arabs living in territory that would become part of the State of Israel; about 650,000 people left Mandate Palestine and went into exile.[2] The emptying of this territory of its Arab residents did not take place at once but occurred in stages. If up until April 1948, thirty to forty thousand Arabs had left Mandate Palestine, during the major conquests of April and May more than 200,000 additional residents departed. In the coming months,

---

1   Motti Golani, *Last days: The mandatory government; Evacuation and war* [Hebrew] (Jerusalem: Zalman Shazar Center, 2008).

2   Avraham Sela, 'Palestinian Arabs in the 1948 War', in Moshe Ma'oz and Benjamin Kedar, eds, *The Palestinian national movement: From confrontation to acceptance?* [Hebrew] (Tel Aviv: Misrad ha-bitahon, 1996).

hundreds of thousands more Arabs left the country.[3] The overwhelming majority of these left their property behind, some a great deal and some very little, and went on to live in refugee camps for the rest of their lives. 'There was a war,' said Foreign Minister Moshe Sharett at a cabinet meeting held in November 1951. 'There are lots of inheritances. One of these inheritances [that needs to be dealt with] is the abandoned property.'[4]

There is no reliable data pertaining to the value or the extent of the moveable assets left behind in Israel. While it is possible to quantify, count, and estimate the value of lands and orchards (and, of course, there is a disagreement about the value of Arab-owned lands), it is impossible to do this with pianos, books, clothes, jewellery, tables, electronic equipment, cars, and various other forms of moveable property. Even the values of homes, some of which were destroyed during the fighting and others intentionally destroyed thereafter, are easy to estimate. Valuations – which, in any event, were in the tens of millions in 1940s Palestinian pounds – are necessary for those who need to estimate reparations, to make settlements, and to perform other similar tasks. Estimation of the looted property's value, however, is not directly relevant to this historical study, the primary objective of which is to illuminate how wide swathes of the Israeli population actively participated in the looting of Arab property. To achieve that goal, tables and statistics are not what is important; it is enough to look at photo albums of Haifa or Acre, Jaffa or Jerusalem, to get a sense of the great magnitude of property that the Arab residents left behind.[5] Nevertheless, for those who are interested, in November 1951, the United Nations Palestine Conciliation Commission estimated the value of moveable Arab property that was left behind at more than 18.6 million Palestine pounds.[6] I will discuss this more at the end of the chapter.

The war forcibly unravelled the existing relationships between the two nations – a development political scientist Menachem Klein

3   On this, see Benny Morris, The Birth of the Palestinian Refugee Problem, 1947–1949 (New York: Cambridge University Press, 1987).

4   Cabinet meeting minutes, 4 November 1951, ISA.

5   For data on the separate Arab and Jewish economies, as well as the areas where these two economies merged, see Joshua Ziman, The Revival of Palestine (New York: Sharon Press, 1946).

6   Progress Report of the United Nations Conciliation Commission for Palestine Covering the Period from 23 January to 19 November 1951, General Assembly Official Records: Sixth Session, 20 November 1951, UN Archives, archives.un.org.

captures in the spot-on title of his book on the subject, published in Hebrew as *Keshurim* ('Connected').[7] The communities, which had lived in neighbourly relations with one another, became enemies. There is no doubt that the Jewish population's plunder of Arab property played a role in shaping the two communities' subsequent relations.[8] Such an acknowledgement helps make sense of the long-standing Jewish silence about the looting.

Part I, organized chronologically, aims towards description rather than interpretation, describing succinctly the Jewish population's participation in the looting of Arab property in tens of cities and hundreds of villages over the course of the war. With the exception of Nazareth, which we will discuss in the second part of this book, all the Arab and mixed cities were completely looted, and their inhabitants departed, fled, or were expelled (frequently, the motivations behind departure were intertwined). An additional chapter dedicated to the looting that occurred in villages provides some representative examples of the plunder of property there. (Indeed, description of the looting of *every* village for which relevant documentary evidence exists would extend far beyond the needs of this study.) An additional chapter will be dedicated to the plunder of mosques, churches, and religious buildings – an activity that was also widespread during the war.

When the name of an Arab individual, an Arab village, or a holy site is mentioned, the Arabic form of the name will follow its English form in parentheses. In a large number of cases, when the names of Arabs or Arab villages are found in Hebrew documents, they are written inaccurately. This is the case not only with historical documents but with

---

7   Menachem Klein, *Connected: The story of the land's inhabitants* [Hebrew] (Tel Aviv: ha-Kibbutz ha-me'uhad, 2015). This book was first published in English as Menachem Klein, *Lives in Common: Arabs and Jews in Jerusalem, Jaffa, and Hebron*, trans. Haim Watzman (New York: Oxford University Press, 2014).

8   Arabs also looted and robbed during the war. Yet there was a significant difference between the looting undertaken by the different sides. First, most of the Arab looters were soldiers who had arrived from neighbouring countries (and their attitude to Mandate Palestine's Arab population was frequently violent and chastening). In other words, these were not native inhabitants. Second, the Arab soldiers looted light, mobile equipment because they travelled long distances. Third, the extent of the looting that the Arabs and the Jews undertook is not comparable. Fourth, sometimes (and perhaps these were most of the cases), the Arab residents who fled, or were expelled from their place of residence, settled in other places in the land and 'looted' the orchards and fields there. The Arab looting began several days after the partition plan's adoption.

archival file names. To make it easier for others to locate these files, I have in most cases left the names as they were originally written, even when this proves inaccurate, grating to the ear, and irritating to the eye. Every individual or site has a name, and it is fitting to be precise when writing their names. The disdainful way that various archives have written file names should be addressed.

Each chapter opens with 'the day after'; by design, there is no reference, beyond a general description, to how a given city (or village) was conquered. It should come as no surprise that scholars disagree about the nature of these conquests. The pillaging, it is important to stress, took place in spaces where the Arab residents were no longer present.

Tiberias

Tiberias was the first city conquered during the war. According to data from a population estimate, 5,310 Arabs and 6,130 Jews lived there in 1945.[1] In the months preceding the fall of Arab Tiberias, relations between the two communities were generally good. The al-Tabari (الطبري) family that led the city's Arab population was well known for the good relations that it maintained with its Jewish neighbours.[2] In the beginning of February, the Arab forces attacked the Jews. Only limited numbers of Arab combatants entered the city in the days to come. In March 1948, tensions rose following planned Haganah operations in the city and a number of gun battles between forces on both sides. Arab forces occasionally disrupted traffic on and around the city's main street. The escalation on the ground began to have an effect, damaging the system of checks and balances that city residents had in place. Yet,

---

1   *Village Statistics 1945: A Classification of Land and Area Ownership in Palestine* (Beirut: PLO Research Center, 1970), 73. *Village Statistics 1945* was prepared by the Office of Statistics and the Department of Lands of the British Mandate Government for the Anglo-American Committee of Inquiry on Palestine that operated in 1945. The Zionist movement subjected the study to critique. I refer to the 1970 edition throughout.

2   For a brief discussion of the Tabari family, see Oded Avishar, *Tiberias book: The Galilee city and its settlement through the ages* [Hebrew] (Jerusalem: Keter, 1973), 337–9. Also see Mustafa Abbasi, 'The Tabari family and leadership of the Arab community of Tiberias during the late Ottoman and British Mandate periods' [Hebrew], *Katedra* 120 (2006): 183–200.

during March, the civilian leaders from both national groups worked to reach an organized ceasefire in the city. That month, the two sides agreed to the 'Tiberian Peace' that reflected their desire to preserve neighbourly relations and the status quo. On April 8, the ceasefire lapsed, and the sides began to exchange fire again. Efforts to re-establish the ceasefire proved unsuccessful.[3]

On April 12, a company of the Israeli military's Golani Brigade attacked Nasser al-Din (ناصر الدين), a village a kilometre west of the city, killing twenty-two village residents. This provided fodder for the Arab public, which declared that the attack comprised a second Deir Yassin massacre – evoking the bloody events in the village of Deir Yassin (دير ياسين) three days earlier. Days later, on the night of 17 April, the Palmach's (Haganah's elite fighting force) Third Battalion and units from the Golani Brigade started attacking Arab residential areas in the city. Operations undertaken to conquer the city, including mortar fire, killed approximately eighty Arabs. A day later, Arab Tiberias fell. The Jewish forces demanded unconditional surrender, and the Arab notables decided, with British encouragement, to vacate the city.[4] The next day, on 18 April, with British aid and urging, the Palestinian residents of Tiberias were transported out of the city in long convoys.[5] After the war, they would be prohibited from returning.

The massive Arab exodus completely shocked the Haganah military leadership. 'Nobody had imagined this before,' Nahum Av, the Haganah commander of the old city of Tiberias, subsequently wrote. On the day the Arabs departed, armed guards were placed at the entrance to the old city to prevent the Jewish residents from bursting into the Arab neighbourhoods and breaking into Arab homes. Soldiers, who had just ceased fighting, stood 'opposite Jews, [armed] with weapons, who tried to forcibly enter the city with the express goal of plundering and looting'. These efforts did not prevent looting from taking place on a

3 Tamir Goren, 'The war for the mixed cities in the North', in Alon Kadish, ed., *Israel's War of Independence 1948–1949*, vol. 1 [Hebrew] (Ramat Efal: Galili Association for Defense Force Research, 2004), 171–205, esp. 172–9.

4 Benny Morris, *1948* (Tel Aviv: 'Am 'Oved, 2010), 160–1; Yoav Gelber, *Independence versus Nakba* [Hebrew] (Or Yehudah: Dvir, 2004), 163–4; Binyamin Etzioni, ed., *Tree and dagger: The battle path of the Golani Brigade* [Hebrew] (Tel Aviv: Ma'arakhot, 1951), 106–18.

5 Morris, *1948*, 160–1. See also 'Why the Arabs left Tiberias', April 1948, file: 128/1951-18, Israel Defense Forces and Defense Establishment Archive (hereafter, IDF).

scale unprecedented in a war that had only broken out a few months earlier. Civilians and residents began to penetrate into the Arab neighbourhood and made off with whatever they could get their hands on. In an effort to drive away the civilians, soldiers fired their weapons. The night after the city's conquest, in an effort to prevent Jewish residents' and fighters' ongoing destruction and looting of Arab neighbours' property, Av patrolled the alleys of the city. 'The next day', wrote Av, 'throughout the day, crowds mobbed the barriers that had been set up and tried to burst through them. The soldiers needed to use force to hold them back.'[6] One of the Palmach fighters charged with the prevention of looting explained that 'the residents of Tiberias descended on the homes like locusts . . . We needed to use batons and blows, to beat the looters and to force them to leave the possessions on the ground.'[7]

In practice, many soldiers 'did not stand around twiddling their thumbs and decided to join the "party"'.[8] The day after the city's conquest, the commander issued a proclamation outlawing despoliation and strictly prohibiting soldiers from coming into contact with Arab property. The local emergency committee issued a proclamation that placed similar restrictions on the city's inhabitants.[9] In practice, soldiers had begun plundering days before the city emptied, bursting into stores that had been closed due to the fighting.[10] Yosef Nahmani, one of the founders of 'Hashomer', a Tiberias resident and a Jewish National Fund official, described in the secrecy of his diary how 'the Jewish masses pounced on the stores and began to rob them'. He wrote: 'It was a strong blow to the morality of our struggle . . . Disgusting . . . what a moral failure.'[11] Nahmani wanted to protect Arab property, and not just for moral

6   Nahum Av (Ebo), *The battle for Tiberias* [Hebrew] (Tel Aviv: Defense Ministry Press, 1991), 211.

7   Hayyim Kremer (Negev Brigade), interview, May–June 1986, file: 16-12/52/66, Yad Tabenkin Archive (hereafter, YTA).

8   Av, *Battle for Tiberias*, 211, 215.

9   See 'Proclamation declaring independent military rule in the city', a complete photo of which is found in Av, *Battle for Tiberias*, 214. Also see *Forty days in the campaign to liberate Tiberias: A collection of testimonies* [Hebrew] (Tel Aviv: Defense Ministry Press 1993), 44, 51. The emergency committee's proclamation can be found as Proclamation no. 624, IDF.

10   Yosef Nahmani diary, 16 April 1948, HaShomer Archive (hereafter, HAS).

11   Nahmani diary, 18 April 1948.

reasons. 'From a political perspective, it is also extremely important that the property be looked after, and that when [the Arab residents] return they will find that it is safe. It will also make a positive impression on the outside world.'[12] As has been previously noted, the city's Arab residents would become refugees, never to return home.

Less than a day after the city had been conquered, Tiberias looked like 'a war had taken place there'.[13] To a certain extent, Av chose to downplay the soldiers' role in the pillaging; on 18 April, he wrote in his diary: 'Homes full of property and no signs of life. Full stores and no buyers. A tremendous quantity of property abandoned. Our soldiers walked through the alleys and they could not believe their eyes.'[14] Unlike Av, Netiva Ben-Yehuda, a Palmach fighter and writer who participated in the Battle of Tiberias, wrote frankly about how her comrades in arms looted the city: 'These scenes were familiar to me, but I was always used to associating them with what others did to us during the Holocaust, during the world wars, and during all the pogroms. Oy, how we knew those scenes so well. And here – here we were doing these horrible things to others.'[15]

Ben-Yehuda did not just address the plunder; she also discussed the removal of the city's residents. The city's Arab residents were not physically expelled. Yet, in the days prior to the evacuation, Haganah activities in the area played a central role in spreading fear among the Arab population and intensifying their concerns about the future if they chose to remain.[16] Soldiers quickly set aside their moral inhibitions concerning despoliation, she wrote. 'I am not saying that we proved unable to ultimately overcome them.' Following its participation in the

---

12   Nahmani diary, 19 April 1948.

13   Ibid.

14   Av, *Battle for Tiberias*, 212.

15   Netiva Ben-Yehuda, *Through the binding ropes* [Hebrew] (Jerusalem: Domino Press, 1985), 162.

16   A report on migration asserted that Arab 'fear' was the reason behind the evacuation of Tiberias. See 'The migration of Palestinian Arabs in the period 1 December 1947 to 1 June 1948', 30 June 1948, file: Yosef Waschitz – personal archive, (3) 27.35-95, Yad Yaari Research and Documentation Center Archives (hereafter, YYA). For in-depth discussion of this report, its concealment, and its revelation, see Akevot Institute report [Hebrew], July 2019. For a critique of this migration report, see Shabtai Teveth, 'The Palestine Arab Refugee Problem and Its Origins', *Middle Eastern Studies* 26, no. 2 (April 1990): 214–49.

city's conquest, the Palmach's Third Battalion began loading up huge quantities of equipment and taking them out of the city. 'Our hands trembled severely as we loaded it onto the pickup truck. The weight of the load was not what made them shake. Even now my hands tremble from just writing about it. That is how we returned to Migdal.'[17] Looting was granted free rein, which created an environment of lawlessness and violent reprisal. For instance, a youth who stole a tire was shot and killed by a military policeman.[18]

De jure, depredation was forbidden, and it had been decided that Arab property should be protected. De facto, the dam was burst, and looting spread like floodwaters. In his diary entry from 22 April, four days after the city's conquest, Nahmani described what was happening there:

In the afternoon, I returned to Tiberias, and I found it in a wild state. Ten by ten, in groups, the Jews moved about and robbed Arab homes and stores. This made a very powerful impression on me. This behaviour was so ugly. It stained our flag. This pillaging began after the Jewish authorities' proclamation and after the warnings of the Jewish community council and the emergency committee not to harm Arab property or any other property. After participating in the pillaging and showing themselves to be poor role models, the Haganah soldiers proved unable to rein in the masses. There was a competition between the different Haganah platoons stationed in Migdal, Ginosar, Yavne'el, and Ein Gev, who arrived in cars and boats and loaded up all types of things [like:] refrigerators, beds, etc. They displayed permits from their company commanders showing that they had permission to take things. It is clear that the Jewish masses in Tiberias burst into action to be just like them. The soldiers assigned specifically to protect property ignored what was going on around them, and it is rumoured that they were accepting bribes. A moral collapse. If powerful means are not adopted, such things are liable to demoralize

17   Ben-Yehuda, *Binding of ropes*, 162. Cf. Shlomo Cohen, interview, Collection of the Galili Centre for Defence Studies, 23 September 1984, file: 12-3/42/23, YTA.

18   Zvi Inbar, *Scales of justice and the sword: Foundations of military law in Israel* [Hebrew] (Tel Aviv: Ma'arakhot, 2005), 617. On this incident, see Testimonies of Avraham Riklin and Yehudah Boneh, n.d., Palmach Generation Association Archive (hereafter, PGA).

those in our circles and to damage our capacity and ability to rule, as well as our ideals.[19]

On 3 May, people were appointed to a new committee for Arab assets in Tiberias whose purpose was to protect the Arab property that remained in the city after the Arab residents' rapid departure. During a 5 June meeting, Nahmani reported on how the committee had requested that the Jewish population return stolen property. Occasionally, Nahmani reported, the police would find stolen property and return it to the committee's warehouses. The mayor, Shimon Dahan, declared that only immovable assets remained in the city. 'Everything else has been taken.' He demanded that the city's two mosques and four churches be better protected. 'Extremely shameful things like the dirtying of holy sites and incidents of unjustified vandalism have occurred.'[20]

One could see people walking between the breached stores and taking stuff that remained after the shameful plunder . . . I toured the streets and beheld a city that had been more or less normal only a short time earlier. Behold, now it was a plundered ghost town whose stores were breached and whose homes were tenantless . . . people digging through the piles that remained after the great plunder proved the most shameful sight. In any case, I found what I saw to be humiliating. I pondered. How? We should not have let this happen.[21]

There were committee members who asserted that efforts to prevent looting began too late, and that efforts should now be focused on preserving the status quo. 'The personal belongings that have been stolen are already lost, and it is futile for us to try to return them to their owners.' A committee member said that Ze'ev Opatovsky, the Haganah-selected commander of the city after Av, 'demanded Arab property from the city for the [kibbutzim] Sha'ar HaGolan and Masada'.[22] (Months later, Opatovsky was put on trial. The indictment against him asserted that 'he presented fabricated receipts to the Golani Brigade paymaster that concealed money he had

---

19 Nahmani diary, 22 April 1948.

20 Meeting summary of the Committee for Arab Assets in Tiberias, 5 June 1948, file: Tiberias: Committee for Arab Affairs, Gimmel-29/310, ISA.

21 Av, *Battle for Tiberias*, 215.

22 Meeting summary of the Committee for Arab Assets in Tiberias, 5 June 1948.

pocketed for himself'. It appears that the trial ended when Opatovsky returned the stolen property. No additional actions were taken against him.)[23] The committee came to understand that soldiers had heavily pillaged the warehouses where the Arab property the authority had successfully saved from looting was concentrated. 'Soldiers emptied the warehouses, and, afterwards, the civilian residents did what they did,' said Ya'akov Abulafia, chairman of the city's Citizens' Committee. The agricultural settlements in the area also participated in the looting.[24]

Yitzhak Gevirtz, manager of the Arab Assets Department ('the first unit that was created in response to the need to protect minority property' during the period of the Provisional State Council, as Israeli minister of minorities Bechor-Shalom Sheetrit later wrote), opined that, with effort, it would be possible to return a portion of the stolen property.[25] He asserted that he could point to

tens of cases [throughout the country] where we have returned stolen or plundered property. This has had a positive effect. It was accomplished with the aid of the police, and now the military will begin to act more cautiously and will return property that was seized illegally.[26]

Nonetheless, several accessed sources indicate that almost no looted Tiberian property was returned. In any case, few people were put on trial for looting orphaned Arab property. According to a report on trials related to 'abandoned' property that took place between mid-March and mid-August 1948, four months after the conquest of Arab Tiberias, only ten trials had been conducted in the city and three more cases were still under investigation.[27] Two months after the city's conquest, the military police called Av back to Tiberias to make a statement about the events that took place in the days immediately after its conquest. 'The investigation branched out in numerous different directions, but suddenly the

---

23   Inbar, *Scales of justice*, 617–18.

24   Yitzhak Tager, interview, Collection of the Galili Centre for Defence Studies, 17 June 1983, file: 12-3/45/84, YTA.

25   Memorandum on activities of the Ministry of Minorities (May 1948 – January 1949), file: Memorandum on activities of the Ministry of Minorities, Gimmel-304/63, ISA.

26   Meeting summary of the Committee for Arab Assets in Tiberias, 5 June 1948.

27   'Statistics submitted by the police pertaining to abandoned property trials from 15 May 1948 to 12 August 1948', file: General, Gimmel-307/16, ISA.

case was closed, and they put an end to an affair that drew a lot of negative attention and left a bad taste in lots of people's mouths.'[28] This situation recurred in additional locations.

Alongside the despoliation, soldiers and residents did serious damage to buildings and moveable property. The new Israeli state's appointed minister of minorities, Bechor-Shalom Sheetrit, warned about the evil inclination that took hold of people during the conquest: 'The damage done to hotel buildings in Tiberias is dumbfounding.' In his opinion, it would have been possible to use these buildings for various purposes, and 'now thousands of liras would need to be spent [to repair them]'.[29] Antiquities were also looted.[30] Soldiers and/or civilians wreaked havoc in churches throughout the city.[31] Over weeks and months, it proved difficult to protect Arab property from the plundering masses, and the effort required resources. Thus, looting and destruction continued to impact the ancient mixed city without much being done to inhibit it. The French consul in Haifa visited Tiberias shortly after its conquest to clarify the status of French property in the city. The building where his representative resided had been damaged and plundered. At the consul's request, the military authorities promised to protect the remaining property. When the consul visited again in September, 'he found the home nearly irreparably damaged and almost none of [his representative's] possessions remained'.[32] More than once, ministers needed to get involved to protect property from looting and destruction or from confiscation by the Custodian of Abandoned Property's [Office].[33]

---

28 Av, *Battle for Tiberias*, 215.

29 Minutes of a meeting that took place at the Haifa municipal building, 6 June 1948, file: various reports, Gimmel-306/62, ISA.

30 Raz Kletter, *Just Past?: The Making of Israeli Archaeology* (New York: Routledge, 2006), 9.

31 Meeting summary of the Committee for Arab Assets in Tiberias, 5 June 1948.

32 H. Bilin to Walter Eytan, 30 September 1948, file: Office of Minister Bechor-Shalom Sheetrit, Gimmle Lamed-14820/2, ISA.

33 Yosef Malka resided in an apartment in Tiberias belonging to the Armenian judge Gaspar Aghajanian. The judge asked Malka to watch over his property while he was away. 'During the pillaging in Tiberias, people tried to break into the apartment, but I stood watch and I prevented it. Furthermore, I obtained documents from the city commander stating that the aforementioned property was not to be touched and that appointed me the property's caretaker and guard.' Subsequently, it turned out that the Custodian's Office wanted to confiscate it, but Minister of Minorities Sheetrit stepped in. See Yosef Malka to the minister of minorities, 6 October 1948, file: Aghajanian Gaspar, Gimmel-298/14, ISA.

Nahmani, who was an eyewitness, asserted that 'most of the city's residents participated in the pillaging and theft. Now one needs to deal with an uneducated population; it is necessary to take precautions when dealing with it to stave off physical resistance and potential harm.'[34] Tiberias, the first mixed city to be conquered, served as a model for what would happen over the coming months in Arab and mixed cities throughout Israel.

---

34   Nahmani diary, 4 April 1948.

Haifa

A few days after the looting of Arab Tiberias, Arab Haifa's turn arrived. Haifa – Mandate Palestine's northern capital and its central seaport – was almost equally divided between Arab and Jewish residents. According to a 1946 survey, out of a total population of 145,000, there were 74,000 Jews, 41,000 Muslims, and 30,000 Christians. Echoing the fall of Arab Tiberias, the British-sponsored exodus of its Arab inhabitants and the emptying out of the Arab villages near Kibbutz Mishmar HaEmek and in the Jordan Valley, which had begun in the previous days and weeks, sowed fear in the Arabs of the land's mixed, modern, and second-largest city. The violence the attackers and defenders rained down on each other led thousands of Arabs to abandon the city in the days before the bloody events of the latter half of April 1948.[1]

On 22 April, in the wake of Operation Bi'ur Hametz (The Burning of Leavened Products) that had begun the previous day, Arab Haifa surrendered. There had been stubborn fighting throughout the city. The combat tactics of Haganah forces under the command of Moshe Carmel, who oversaw the Carmeli Brigade, received criticism, especially from the British high commissioner of Palestine, Alan Gordon

---

1 On the fall of Arab Haifa, see Tamir Goren, *Arab Haifa in 1948: The intensity of the struggle and the dimensions of the collapse* [Hebrew] (Ben-Gurion Institute for Israel, Zionism, and Ben-Gurion's Legacy / Ben-Gurion University Press, 2006).

Cunningham, who considered the Jewish fighters' combat methods barbaric.[2] In the days following the Arab side's surrender, almost all the city's Arab residents abandoned it. There were no more than 3,500 Arabs in the city at the beginning of May, and there might have been far fewer.[3] The city's residents fled quickly. The shelling of the Arab-filled market square played a pivotal role in stoking fear and in encouraging flight.[4] Thousands quickly made their way to the port with the aid – and there are those who assert with the encouragement – of the British, abandoned their city and all their possessions, and headed towards Acre and more northerly points. A year after the war, Carmel wrote:

> How many destroyed homes and debris heaps piled high with crushed pieces of furniture . . . doors on both sides of the street breached. The sidewalks littered with prized possessions from the homes . . . On a threshold, a cradle leaning on its side. Beside it, a naked, somewhat crushed, doll lying face down. Where was the baby? Where had it been exiled? Where?[5]

The Arab inhabitants' abandonment of the city astounded the Jewish leadership. 'A dead city, a carcass of a city', Ben-Gurion wrote in his diary a few days after a visit to the city.

> Why did tens of thousands of people leave their city, their homes and their wealth in an insufficiently justified panic? . . . It is hard to believe that extremely wealthy people, really rich people who people in the know number among the country's wealthiest,

---

2   Benny Morris, *1948* (Tel Aviv: 'Am 'Oved, 2010), 166. In contrast, Moshe Carmel, who oversaw the Battle of Haifa for the Jewish side, wrote that after the cessation of fighting in Haifa, British general Hugh Charles Stockwell told him the following: 'We were surprised by how humane your military tactics were and how few Arab victims there were. There were only two hundred Arabs dead. If my army had been called upon to conquer this city and had encountered such resistance, five thousand Arabs would have been killed.' Moshe Carmel, *Northern battles* [Hebrew] ('En Harod: ha-Kibbutz ha-me'uhad, 1949), 100–11.

3   Memorandum on activities of the Ministry of Minorities.

4   On this event, see Shai Fogelman, 'The return to Haifa' [Hebrew], *Haaretz*, 27 May 2011.

5   Moshe Carmel, *Northern battles*, 112.

would leave all their wealth behind because somebody told them
to do so.[6]

Among the Arab communities of Mandate Palestine, the Haifa Arab
community was the richest and most modern; due to its hasty departure, the property that it left behind was prodigious. Many Arab inhabitants thought that once the Arab armies invaded, they would quickly
return accompanied by Arab soldiers and that they would recapture the
city. The looting began while fighting was still ongoing. A combat unit
commander wrote that 'great decisiveness was needed to overcome' the
urge to loot. On the one hand, the soldiers were fighting and conquering, but, on the other, they found time to steal things, such as sewing
machines, record players, and clothing.[7]

After Arab Haifa surrendered, the inclination to loot could be given
free rein. Tzadok Eshel, a member of the Carmeli Brigade, wrote:

People took whatever they could get their hands on. Subsequently,
people with an entrepreneurial spirit got involved. They broke into
abandoned stores and loaded the merchandise onto every vehicle
they could find. Anarchy reigned ... Alongside the joy of liberating
the city and the relief after months of bloodletting, it was shocking to
see the fervour of civilians looking to get something for nothing who
descended upon the homes of people who had been treated unkindly
by fate and turned into refugees.[8]

Yosef Nahmani (a founder of 'Hashomer' and Jewish National Fund official), who visited Haifa the day after its conquest, wrote in his diary that
looters were pillaging Arab homes undisturbed. Days earlier, he had
written about the looting of his hometown Tiberias:

Old people and women of all ages and religious observances took part
in the pillaging [in Haifa]. Nobody prevented them from doing so.

---

6   Quotes from diary entry for 1 May 1948. See David Ben-Gurion, *The War of
Independence* [Hebrew], ed. Gershon Rivlin and Elhanan Oren (Tel Aviv: Defense
Ministry Press, 1982), 381.

7   Zeʿev Yitzhaki, 'Operations report – Halisa (21–22 April 1948)', file: 7353/1949-46, IDF.

8   Tzadok Eshel, *Haganah battles in Haifa* [Hebrew] (Tel Aviv: Defense Ministry
Press, 1978), 378.

Shame and disgrace covered my face and I wanted to spit on the city and leave it . . . We will suffer for this, as will our efforts to educate children and youth. People have lost all sense of shame, and such acts damage the society's moral foundations. We need to apply pressure so that the means to stop these ugly acts and to return the stolen property to its owners are taken up.[9]

As in the case of Tiberias a few days earlier, the Haganah command in the Haifa district published an announcement prohibiting the looting of abandoned property. 'Unfortunately, I must point out,' wrote the Haganah commander in the area, 'that there are Jews, both individuals and small groups, who have been participating in looting. This is likely to bring disgrace upon the city's Jewish residents and our emergent independent government.' People were afraid that widespread looting would lead to renewed British involvement in the war after they had only just evacuated the city as part of the termination of the Mandate. 'On account of this, I have decided to put a stop to this criminal phenomenon immediately and completely,' stated the order.[10] Yet this Haganah announcement, the stationing of fire department and Civil Guard units outside the entrances to Arab neighbourhoods to prevent Jews from entering them, and roads and passageway closures did not significantly contribute to the prevention of pillaging. In fact, the Haganah commander's assertion that only 'individuals and small groups' participated in the looting proved inaccurate.

'These actions were undertaken too late,' wrote Mordecai Yacobovitz, a Haganah solider who participated in the occupation of the city, when criticizing Haganah activities there. 'The masses had already committed robbery; they had stolen and looted, plundered and taken everything they could get their hands on. They streamed in from throughout the city and from outside it; they came by foot and in vehicles.'[11] The city's police commander recalled a visit that he made to the lower city:

---

9   Yosef Nahmani diary, 23 April 1948, HAS.

10   'Haganah order to prevent theft in the Haifa District' [Hebrew], *Kol Ha'am*, 28 April 1948.

11   Mordecai Yacobovitz, *From Palmach to I.D.F.* [Hebrew] (Tel Aviv: Amihai, n. d.), 93.

It was desolate there. There were not a lot of inhabitants to be seen. There were only groups of Jewish whippersnappers wandering around Khamra Square, the market and the Arab mercantile centre. Lots of stores and homes had been ransacked and the alleys were littered with various household objects.[12]

The looting was so extensive that the military prosecutor for the Haifa district, Moshe Ben-Peretz, who accompanied the combat forces in Haifa, asserted that in mid-June 1948

> there was no longer anything to take from the Arabs. It was simply a pogrom. They shot at pictures – it was atrocious. The commanders, each one of them made excuses: 'I only arrived two weeks ago' etc. There was nobody to arrest. There was no way to know when the pillaging took place, and they replaced commanders daily.[13]

Officials of the Hebrew Office (now 'Chamber') of Commerce and Industry protested against the looting and how people were treating Arab property in the city. 'In the most recent meetings of our office council, we strongly censured the lust for plunder that arose with Haifa's conquest,' they wrote to the Haifa Emergency Committee that was charged with returning life to normal. Arab-owned stores and warehouses 'were emptied and a sizable portion of the merchandise – both essential and non-essential consumer products – was seized and stolen by organizations, companies, and individuals without anybody overseeing what was done or documenting what was taken'. The office noted:

> These actions do not accord with the official declarations directed towards the Arabs calling on them to return to Haifa and resume their lives. We are afraid that these actions constitute not only a moral stain but that the irregular and undocumented way that they were carried out will at some time lead the injured Arab parties to bring exorbitant lawsuits too.

---

12   Haifa police chief to the Haifa Emergency Committee, 1 May 1948, file: Jewish-Arab relations on the eve of the British departure, 3105/20, Haifa Municipal Archives (hereafter, HMA). Also see 'A bundle of documents', 9 May 1948, file: 244/1951-44, IDF.
13   Minutes of seminar of military prosecutors, 16 June 1948, file: 2294/1950-2882, IDF.

Office officials recalled the fine commercial relations that had existed between the two national groups residing in the city. They further noted their opposition 'to the types and forms of activities undertaken' to deal with Arab property. Their position, they noted despondently, was ignored. They concluded their letter with the following declaration: 'In the future, history will judge us for our actions.'[14]

In a long article, Israeli Communist Party member Ruth Lubitz addressed the looting at length, and she expressed a similar sentiment to that of the Commerce Office:

There was a historic opportunity to create bonds of understanding with progressive Arab circles . . . there was a historic opportunity to put into practice everything that so many leaders have written and said about guaranteeing total equality to the Jewish State's Arab inhabitants . . . Nobody acted on these opportunities.

Lubitz argued that the Yishuv leadership

did nothing to prevent part of the city's residents from acting on their basest instincts. It remained silent and tolerated the plague-like spread of pillaging. Haifa was plundered in a most disgraceful manner. They continue to despoil to this very day. Haifa's Arab residents fled. The Histadrut's executive committee's empty rhetoric will ring hollow to them . . . Many people and parties have criticized the mass pillage, but no institution has stepped up to stop it. We need to learn the lesson that Haifa has to teach us well, so that its history will not repeat itself elsewhere.[15]

A 10 May memorandum on conditions in Haifa submitted by the Communist Party Central Committee to the Jewish National Council and the Haganah Command referenced a 'campaign of looting, plunder, and theft of colossal proportions'. Less than two weeks had passed since the conquest, and 'almost all of the Arab residents' apartments have

---

14 Office of Hebrew Commerce and Industry (Haifa and the district) to the Emergency Committee, Haifa, 18 May 1948, file: The Emergency Committee adjacent to Haifa's Hebrew Community Council, Section 53, 00001/6, HMA.

15 Ruth Lubitz, 'On the purity of our war' [Hebrew], *Kol Ha'am*, 30 May 1948. Also see editorial [Hebrew], *Kol Ha'am*, 23 May 1948.

been emptied of everything of value, merchandise and consumer products have been pillaged from stores, and the machinery has been taken from workshops and factories'. According to the party committee, 'everything' was done 'in front of the eyes of Haganah authorities'.[16]

Yacobovitz wrote that Haganah members were less involved with the looting than others:

> We had whole streets available to us; countless buildings were under our protection; it was as if stores and emporiums were open in expectation of our arrival. Great wealth awaited us every step of the way. Yet we did not reach out and start grabbing things.

Yacobovitz's friend argued that they fought for months, 'were wounded and killed, and, in the end, all the shirkers and greedy people showed up to enjoy the fruits of our labour'.[17] However, the general prosecutor of the Carmeli Brigade asserted that the Haganah commanders simply did not report their subordinates' crimes.[18] After the conquest of Haifa, Ben-Gurion wrote in his diary that the Zionist paramilitary organization Irgun had arranged a complete and total plunder of the Wadi Nisnas neighbourhood and that robbers and thieves had joined them. He noted that members of the Haganah looted too:

> There were cases where Haganah members, including commanders, were found in possession of stolen property too. About ten of them are currently being held for this. They looked for Arabs, captured them, arrested them, beat them, and tortured them as well.[19]

16 'Conditions in Haifa: Two weeks after the Haganah's conquest of the Arab part of the city – A memorandum submitted to the Jewish National Council and the Haganah command by the Central Committee of the Communist Party of the Land of Israel', 10 May 1948, file: General 15-164/4, YTA.

17 Yacobovitz, From Palmach to I.D.F., 93.

18 Zvi Inbar, Scales of justice and the sword: Foundations of military law in Israel [Hebrew] (Tel Aviv: Ma'arakhot, 2005), 669.

19 Quotes from diary entry for 1 May 1948: Ben-Gurion, The War of Independence, 378. See the comments of Golda Meir too: 'In the first day or two [after the conquest] conditions in the conquered areas were bad, especially in the sector under Irgun control. They left nothing, selling it on the spot. Other parts of the city were not left in pristine condition either.' Minutes of Jewish Agency administration meeting, 6 May 1948, Ben-Gurion Archive (hereafter, BGA). Moshe Carmel ordered a curfew in the Arab neighbourhoods to prevent Irgun looting and told the public that the curfew had been

Not all combatants looted. Yet many soldiers did, sowing resentment among their peers. The newspaper *Al HaMishmar* (On Guard) reprinted an article that had previously appeared in *BaMivtza* (On Campaign), the Carmeli Brigade journal; it describes a meeting between soldiers and a military policeman stationed in the area:

The incident occurred at a roadblock on the way from Ayin to Haifa. A vehicle with ten young men in it was travelling on the road when it arrived at the checkpoint and was stopped. When the military police-man approached the vehicle, he saw a bounteous treasure: *Booty!* The military policeman, who in his abundant naivete thought that he had been stationed at the roadblock to seize all the plunder from passing automobiles, began to remove the booty from the car in a courteous manner. At that moment, a cry rose up from among those travelling in the vehicle. 'Did you fight the Ar[abs] like we did? We suffered and we have the right to plunder! Get out of here! If you do not . . .' With no other guard in the area, the military policeman was pushed off the vehicle's running board, and the courageous warriors and their vehi-cle continued on their way to the safe haven offered by the Haifa black market. This incident is documented. I saw it with my own eyes. It is just one of many such occurrences. Consequently, the need to restrain the thieves among us has become a crucial problem that needs to be addressed right now . . . Those among us who take the law into their own hands and espouse rights that nobody granted to them diminish our steadfastness from within. They seriously endanger us. We need to use the force of law and punishment to fight them. Comrades! I have spoken a lot about Zionist values, because there is one

---

instituted to prevent the infiltration of armed Arabs. See Moshe Carmel to Yisrael Galili, 24 April 1948, file: Operations with and contact between the Irgun and Lehi and the Haganah 15-185/2, YTA. See also Aharon Cohen to Mapam party secretariat, 28 April 1948, file: 10-(4)95.20, YYA. Elsewhere Cohen wrote: 'The Haganah commander's orders to prevent acts of looting were given after a large part of the work had already been done. It is hard to determine what subsequent effect the orders had. Irgun members organized and engaged in widescale plunder in one of Arab Haifa's richest neighbour-hoods, Wadi Nisnas. They only stopped when the Haganah gave them an ultimatum demanding that they leave the neighbourhood . . . Under the pretence of searching for weapons, stores, workshops, and residences were breached and looted.' Aharon Cohen, 'Our Arab policy during the war: Prolegomena to an investigation by public commis-sion', file: (4) 10-95.10, YYA.

fundamental problem. *The future character of our state* is currently at stake, and I am worried about what will become of it. What are we fighting for? Are we fighting for a state where brute force will rule and each person will take pride in being more thievish and exploitative than those around him, or are we fighting for a collaboratively established democratic state? Only through the forging of consciousness and the restraint of individual desire can a democratic state emerge in this land that has already been partially consumed by fascistic tendencies.[20]

For months after the city's conquest, such incidents continued to take place regularly. Sometimes, the military police succeeded in preventing the pillagers from making it to their desired destination. On 31 October 1948, for example, two vehicles 'loaded with huge quantities of leather, shoes, blankets, sugar, ammunition, and more' were captured. Their contents were seized because the soldiers did not have documents confirming that the merchandise was supposed to leave the city. An additional truck was stopped that day due to the establishment of road-blocks on the Acre–Haifa road.[21] In practice, even policeman pillaged.[22]

As mentioned above, after the conquest of Arab Haifa, Ben-Gurion visited the city. As he stood on the balcony of the Eden Hotel alongside the noted Arabist and Haganah intelligence officer Ezra Danin, the two men looked out onto the streets of the lower city and observed the mass looting. Danin, whom the Zionist institutions had placed in charge of abandoned property (the state had not yet been established), recalled in his memoirs how they saw 'organized and unorganized groups of Jews breaking into Arab stores'. Rumours spread that members of Nahalal (a moshav, or cooperative agricultural community) were plundering warehouses on their own behalf and that workers from the Solel Boneh

---

20   'Because the matter is in our souls' [Hebrew], *Al HaMishmar*, 15 June 1948. There are more than a few reports like this.

21   'The topic of discussion: Abandoned property', Haifa district military police, 29 November 1948, file: 710/1950-152, IDF.

22   One of the soldiers explained: 'We saw two Jewish policemen emerge from a taxi. They began loading radios into the taxi. It was right by the police station, and I immediately approached one of them. He said: "I am a policeman. Leave me alone." For the first time in his life, Ya'akov [Lublini] lost it and he punched him. The guy flew. He told him to drop the radio.' Maksim Cohen, interview, Collection of the Galili Centre for Defence Studies, 7 December 1983, file: 12-3/42/24, YTA.

construction company were stealing equipment in the port. Danin asked to speak with Ben-Gurion about what was happening. 'Ben Gurion dismissed me saying: if this property were to fall into private hands, would you be any happier? At least it is not private pillaging.'[23] Apparently Ben-Gurion did not view the looting as particularly troubling.

It was at this time that Ben-Gurion appointed Moshe Dayan to his first executive role: organization of the abandoned property in Haifa. While there is not a great deal of documentation about Dayan's activities during this period, his biographer Shabtai Teveth writes that

> he did not have well-formulated ideas about this topic. To prevent looting, he ordered that everything of use to the IDF [Israel Defense Forces] be transferred to its warehouses and that everything else, principally seeds, be sent to the Jewish agricultural settlements.

Teveth writes that the future Israeli prime minister Golda Meir, who participated in discussions about how to proceed, thought that this was the proper thing to do. It turns out that there were those who saw things differently, 'viewing this as a detrimental move to take. It was more a liquidation operation than a state seizure of enemy property.'[24]

Teveth does not mention the names of those who had different opinions about what to do with the abandoned property. Yet Gad Machnes, director of the young Israeli state's Ministry of Minorities, sharply criticized the measures that the authorities, particularly Ben-Gurion, took to prevent the looting of Arab Haifa. Prior to the Declaration of Independence, Yisrael Galili, head of the Haganah National Command, and David Horovitz from the Ministry of Finance had given Ministry of Minorities officials the authority to address abandoned-property issues, and they did so independently. 'We travelled to Haifa to deal with matters there and set them in order,' said Machnes in an internal Ministry of Minorities meeting.

> Yet, before we could do so, Ben-Gurion issued a contradictory order. *Consequently,* the people on site gave themselves permission to break

23   Ezra Danin, *Zionist at any price* [Hebrew], vol. 1, ed. Gershon Rivlin (Jerusalem: Kiddum Press, 1987), 218.

24   Shabtai Teveth, *Moshe Dayan: A biography* [Hebrew] (Jerusalem: Schocken, 1971), 251. Also see Moshe Carmel, interview by Oral History Department, 8 March 1978, 27, BGA.

into buildings and plunder Haifa. We wanted to quit immediately. Golda Meyerson (Meir) got involved and we arrived at some kind of agreement about what to do in Haifa.[25]

In his diary, Ben-Gurion wrote that Danin and his subordinates from the Arab Information Service (the intelligence and counter-espionage arm of the Haganah) 'are complaining about Moshe Dayan and his orders to empty the warehouses'.[26] Meir explained that, in practice, the army was not actively involved in prevention of looting in the city. 'All it did was set up a roadblock on the way up to the Carmel, but it is not even asking those who pass through for identity cards.'[27]

It is unclear what that 'contradictory order' that Ben-Gurion gave was. Yet a different order that Ben-Gurion gave at that time certainly contributed to the pillaging of property. During his visit to the city, Ben-Gurion ordered that the few Arab residents who remained in the city be moved from their places of residence and concentrated in two centres: Wadi Nisnas (for Christians) and Wadi Salib (for Muslims). At the end of June, in accordance with his orders, the Arabs began to be concentrated in the two wadis.

For a number of days, Arabs continued to depart the city through the port. Notably, there were Jewish residents who called on Haifa's Arabs to remain. Ben-Gurion opposed local Jewish leaders' attempts to convince them to stay. 'How many will there still be? If they want to go – why are you holding them back? Let them go!' he urged. Danin, who was present when this statement was made, wrote that this was the first time he had 'explicitly' heard they were supposed to let the Arabs leave. This stood 'in opposition to what Gad Machnes had previously told us on behalf of Yisrael Galili, the head of the National Command'.[28] The position that

---

25   Minutes of the second meeting of the Ministry of Minorities, 15 July 1948, file: Department head meetings, Gimmel-307/17, ISA, emphasis added.

26   Quote from diary entry for 1 May 1948: Ben-Gurion, *The War of Independence*, 382.

27   Meeting of the Jewish Agency executive, file: J1\3853, Central Zionist Archives (hereafter, CZA). Party Central Committee meeting, 11 May 1948, file: 2-23-1948-1949, LPA.

28   Danin, *Zionist at any price*, 218–19. In her book, Golda Meir wrote that Ben-Gurion told her, 'I want you to travel to Haifa at once . . . I also want you to try to persuade the Arabs on the beach to come back. You must get it into their heads that there is nothing to fear.' Golda Meir, *My Life* (New York: G. P. Putnam's Sons, 1975), 279.

Ben-Gurion offered in his diary was more moderate than the one he had expressed in Haifa: 'It is not our job to bring the Arabs back.'[29] Indeed, many people in Haifa tried to convince their Arab neighbours to remain in their places, but alliances and neighbourly relations built over the course of years crumbled. The Haifa Workers' Council published a public appeal and called for cooperation between the two national groups in the city:

> For years and years, we have lived together peacefully in Haifa, our city, and we have interacted with each other with understanding and as brothers . . . hostile elements . . . they are the ones that have sparked a quarrel between us and damaged our relationship.[30]

Benny Morris wrote that 'in the week following the conclusion of [military] clashes, the attitude and the behaviour of the assorted Jewish authorities towards the city's Arabs were ambiguous.'[31] Indeed, distribution of proclamations and calls for the Arabs to remain in the city (which certainly had to make some kind of impression) did not go hand in hand with the military's aggressive behaviour and mass participation in pillaging.

Ezra Danin saw the day Ben-Gurion visited Haifa as a 'decision day' vis-à-vis the policy to uproot the Arabs. Years after the war, he would state:

> [Before the conquest of Haifa] we worked to prevent the departure of Arabs from the country. For this reason, [Yehoshua] Palmon, Gad Machnes, and I met with Salim Abd al-Rahim (عبد الرحيم), one of the gang leaders in Tulkarm [in April 1948]. He told us about the Arab nations' decision to employ the fingers tactic when they invaded with

---

Yigal Elam refuted what Meir said about Ben-Gurion's order to her. Yigal Elam, *The executors* [Hebrew] (Jerusalem: Keter, 1991), 47–8. In fact, the purpose behind Meir's trip to Haifa was something completely different. Ben-Gurion wrote: 'I suggest that Golda establish relations between the civilian Jewish representatives and our command.' David Ben-Gurion to Yisrael Galili, 29 April 1948, file: General 15-164/3, YTA.

29   Quotes from diary entry for 1 May 1948: Ben-Gurion, *The War of Independence*, 382.

30   Public appeal made by the Haifa Workers Council, 28 April 1948, file: 481/1949-62, IDF.

31   Morris, *1948*, 168.

the coastal plan. As he explained, the Arabs were told to leave the area so that the army could employ artillery. Gad Machnes went to Galili [the Head of the National Command]. We received permission to travel along the coast to prevent the Arabs from departing ... we never thought that the Arabs would leave. For years, we ran a department for cultivating neighbourly relations, with all that went with it. Yet, on decision day, Ben-Gurion said that if they wanted to leave, they should leave.[32]

During his visit to the city, Ben-Gurion gave clear orders to command: first, it was forbidden for the number of the Arabs in the city to exceed 15,000; second, two-thirds of those who remained would be Christians and one-third would be Muslim; third, the Arab Christians would be concentrated in the Wadi Nisnas neighbourhood; fourth, the Arab Muslims would be concentrated in the Wadi Salib neighbourhood. In compliance with these orders, the remaining Arab residents were ordered to vacate their homes by 5 July 1948.[33] Yosef Waschitz, an Arab Department member from the left-wing political party Mapam, who was at the centre of what was going on in Haifa at the time, reported:

The speed with which things are being carried out has made it so people are brought into apartments filled with possessions before there is a chance to list what furniture, clothes, etc. are found in them. It is impossible to protect this property. *No preparations were made at all.* The apartments are as filthy as the streets, there is no water, there is no gas, and there are no locks on the doors. Not enough time has been allocated to properly organize apartment distribution.

Rumours spread among Haifa's beaten and frightened Arabs that people were going 'to slaughter them'. Members of the Arab left asserted that 'this was a racist political operation, rather than a military one, intended to create an Arab *ghetto* in Haifa'. Waschitz strongly opposed what he

---

32   Quoted in Yoram Nimrod, 'Creation of the patterns of Israel-Arab relations' [Hebrew], PhD diss., Hebrew University, 1985, 268–9.

33   See 'Conquered city headquarters, commander of the Arab city-permanent order', file: 7249/1949-126, IDF. For an expanded discussion of the concentration of Arabs in Haifa, see Tamir Goren, *From dependence to integration: Israeli rule and the Arabs of Haifa 1948-1950* [Hebrew] (Haifa: Haifa University Press, 1996), 36–42.

saw as neither a logical nor a strategic move. At the end of the memorandum, he wrote:

> It seems to me that this concentration is the most important [i.e.,
> dramatic] move that has been made in the State of Israel pertaining to
> Arab affairs. Here it will be determined if the State of Israel will be a
> democratic state or a feudal state with medieval customs and
> Nuremberg Laws.[34]

Similar ghettoes would be established in other cities.[35]

What the newspapers wrote about the vast pillaging and looting was
euphemistic and inaccurate. For example, one article in *ha-Boker* read:

> In practice, when Haganah forces acted decisively against the robbers,
> the pillaging in Arab areas of Haifa was brought to a conclusion . . . The
> city's governor declared a curfew around [the old mercantile centre]
> every evening from 7 o'clock at night until 6 o'clock [in the morning].[36]

In reality, the pillaging was not halted at all. Rather, after most of the
property of the Arab inhabitants who had left the city had already been
stolen, it assumed a different character. One can find numerous
complaints made by Haifa Arabs in files of the Ministry of Minorities
that testify to the events of that time. Here is an example: Rose Elias
Abdullah Kheir (عبدالله خير) requested the authorities' assistance. At the
time of the city's conquest, she was still in her home in Wadi Nisnas with
her children. It happened that a Haganah soldier stole the money and
jewellery that she had in a cashbox in her house.

> A few days later, [he] entered the home, thinking that nobody was
> there, and put the cashbox key [back]. When I asked him where he

---

34   On Ben-Gurion's visit and his orders, see Yosef Waschitz to the Mapam Central
Committee secretariat, 5 July 1948, file: Yosef Waschitz – personal archive [Hebrew], (4)
10-95.10, YYA. Also see Goren, *From dependence to integration*, 38–42, 65–72; Yfaat
Weiss, *Wadi Salib: The present and the absent* [Hebrew] (Tel Aviv: ha-Kibbutz
ha-me'uhad, 2007), 34–42.

35   On this see Adam Raz, 'Holding them in concentration camps is no more justified' [Hebrew], *Haaretz*, 28 June 2020.

36   'Curfew in a Haifa neighbourhood to prevent acts of robbery' [Hebrew],
ha-Boker, 10 June 1948.

got the key, he told me that it was none of my business. I responded
to him that I was . . . the owner of the home. He left and did not say
a word.[37]

Minister of Minorities Bechor-Shalom Sheetrit intervened on
behalf of Arabs who had remained in the city. He wrote the police
commissioner about soldiers who were breaking into the warehouses
of Arabs still in Haifa and who were treating the property contained
therein as their own. He told of an Arab merchant who had lodged a
complaint against two soldiers with the police. 'Subsequently, the two
soldiers came to his third-floor apartment at 1 Gefen Street and threatened to murder him in a rude and humiliating manner if he continued
to maintain or claim ownership to the aforementioned warehouse.'
The soldiers 'declared that they could not care less about governments
and authorizations.'[38]

Tzadok Eshel of the Carmeli Brigade wrote that one of the difficulties
faced by those attempting to stop the looting was that even though
guards were put in place, they were 'powerless when facing people who
appeared with notes and authorizations given to them by commanders
and designated authorities'.[39] The story of Yousef Khalil Meheshem
(مهيشم), an Arab merchant and resident of Haifa, illustrates this. As he
explained: 'a man named Nahum Gutman from the military police'
appeared at his home with 'a note written in Hebrew that I did not
understand, and he asserted that the note permitted him to take over a
room in my house'. Gutman got two men and they began to remove
'furniture from the room, and he forcibly and coercively took control of
the room'. As we will subsequently see, seizure of rooms in Arab homes
occurred frequently in Haifa. Meheshem wrote: 'I was forced to accept
the situation and I left him to do what he wanted with the room.' Only a
short time later, when Meheshem and his wife were not in their

37   Rose Elias Abdullah Kheir to the custodian of Arab property in Haifa, January
1949, file: Rose Elias Abdullah Kheir, Gimmel-1318/51, ISA; file: Rose Abdullah Kheir,
Gimmel-298/23, ISA.

38   Bechor-Shalom Sheetrit to the police commissioner, 19 December 1948, file:
Elias Beshara Rizk, Gimmel-1318/69, ISA. See also the story of Muhammad al-Sir Abd
al-Jalil (عبد الجليل) of Wadi Salib: file: Muhammad al-Sir Abd al-Jalil, Gimmel-298/60,
ISA.

39   Eshel, *Haganah battles*, 378.

'conquered' apartment, Gutman returned. This time, additional men accompanied him, and they broke down the doors to all the rooms and 'removed all the furniture' from them. Then Gutman 'ordered' Meheshem's wife 'not to touch anything'. Finally, after he had stolen all the furniture that he wanted, Gutman seized all the room keys from their legal owners.[40] 'Expropriations' from Arab residents still living in Haifa were accomplished in a variety of different ways, legal and otherwise, without explanations or permits.[41]

Alongside the plunder of private homes and stores, churches were also pillaged and seriously damaged.[42] A number of cases where 'churches in Haifa were desecrated' were reported to the Ministry of Minorities. 'Unknown' people broke through windows and doors and 'stole various things, including sacred objects' from churches throughout Haifa. People stole whatever they could get their hands on from the Greek Orthodox church near the market: priestly robes, furniture, lamps, a silver cross, a silver goblet, and more. Furniture, silver desk lamps, kitchen utensils, beds, mattresses, clothing, and sacred instruments were stolen from the Roman Catholic church in the Carmel Camp. The police found two armoires that had been stolen from the church in the homes of new immigrants. According to the report, the police were only able to catch the thieves once. The Catholic church in Wadi Jamal and the neighbouring rectory met a similar fate.[43] Original Bahá'í religious manuscripts were also

40   Yousef Khalil Meheshem to the director of the Ministry of Minorities in Haifa, 22 October 1948, file: Yousef Khalil Meheshem, Gimmel-1322/7, ISA.

41   There are many examples of this. 'Mr Ami Birnblum . . . in uniform, together with a small, uniformed military force, broke into my store and seized all of its contents . . . To my astonishment, I found the owner of the property, Mr Chaim Komornik, on site making use of my furniture as he saw fit.' George Salim Jarjura (جرجورة) to Bechor-Shalom Sheetrit, 12 October 1948, file: Jarjura, Gimmel-298/100, ISA.

42   H. Z. Hirschberg (director of the Department for Muslim Religious Affairs), report from reconnaissance on 24–25 August 1948, file: Conquered Israeli territories, Het Tzadi-2564/9, ISA.

43   Inspector Shani, Lower City Station to the Ministry of Minorities, 31 July 1948, file: Damage to holy sites in Haifa and their protection – general, Gimmel-309/61, ISA. Also see Tzvi Ayalon to Carmeli, 31 July 1948; Telegram of the director of Orthodox sacred property, 25 July 1948; file: Christian holy sites, Het Tzadi -2397/7, ISA. On the looting and the damage caused to Haifa's Terra Sancta Monastery, see file: The Terra Sancta Monastery, Gimmel-1321/27, ISA.

plundered. Subsequently, some of them were located in a store in the city.[44]

Available records show that squatters quickly invaded the homes of Arabs who remained; when it comes to invasions of the tens of thousands of Arab homes from which residents were expelled or fled, documentation is scare since there was nobody there to lodge complaints. Ben-Gurion's order designated Wadi Nisnas as an area for remaining Arabs to reside, and the neighbourhood's boundaries were set: Caesarea Street to the east, Huri Street to the north, and ha-Har Street to the west. Nonetheless, Jews began to invade the neighbourhood and forcibly expel its residents from their homes.[45] Moshe Yatah, director of the Ministry of Minorities branch office in Haifa, reported in September 1948 that

> with time 'apartment seekers' in uniform and in civilian dress began to arrive in the wadi. They broke into both empty apartments designated for Arabs and apartments that were already occupied by Arab families. After such invasive visits, the best-case scenario for the Arab residents is that they just need to fix some doors and locks and let the bruises that they received heal.

Quite often, as we have already seen above, the Arabs 'were forced' to relinquish part of their apartments after a 'compromise' had been reached. Frequently, the invaders successfully 'softened up' the Arab residents 'with harassment and the brandishing of firearms. [Things] that sometimes led them to flee their apartments.' These invasions further reduced the limited territory apportioned to Arabs.[46]

Yatakh wrote to the city commander in August because

---

44   On this affair, see file: Nair Afnan, Gimmel-1318/31, ISA.

45   We will not address the responses of Haifa's Arab residents to their concentration in Wadi Nisnas here. See, for example, Protest of the residents of the Wadi Jamal neighbourhood before the trustee of Arab property in Haifa, 19 August 1948; Residents of the Zaytun neighbourhood to the governor of the Haifa District, 22 August 1948; Ministry of Minorities to the Haifa city commander, 31 August 1948; file: Problems of Arab evacuation and housing in Haifa – general, Gimmel-1322/2, ISA.

46   'Concerning the problems of the Arab population of Haifa', memorandum no. 7, Haifa branch to the Ministry of Minorities in the Kiryah, 9 September 1948, file: Haifa, Gimmel-309/31, ISA. For example, see the case of Elias Sima'an Mansur (منصور), file: Elias Sima'an Mansur, Gimmel-1323/29, ISA.

the *movement* of Arabs from apartments that the command only settled them in a short time earlier and the authorized *seizures* in the areas that the command has established for them has led Arabs and the other minorities to lose respect for our institutions and what they say.[47]

It is clear that the combined protests of the Arabs and the Ministry of Minorities did not accomplish a great deal. In November, two months later, Yatakh continued to report that the Arabs who had been promised Jewish residences would not be permitted in the ghetto areas that the authorities had delineated for them. 'In fact, home invasions are being committed ceaselessly, and Arabs are being evicted by force or by the directive of Jewish institutions that are not authorized to give such orders.' Yatakh demanded that the integrity of the concentrated Arab areas be maintained, and that some kind of mechanism be created to keep home invaders away. He did not care if these roles were performed by the police, the city's military headquarters, or the military police.[48]

As chaos reigned, people in positions of authority were trying to profit from the situation. Examples abound. For instance, Yatakh wrote to the city commander about the apartment of Hana Yosef Haddad (حداد) in Wadi Nisnas that was invaded by a soldier and his family in late August. The Jewish family forcibly took possession of two of its rooms. The apartment owner turned to both the civilian and military police for help, and nothing was done. 'The invading soldier did not have a legal seizure order, but two military policemen demanded that the aforementioned Arab give him the two rooms.' As usual, Yatakh turned to the city commander and demanded that measures be taken to prevent invasions, 'both those self-initiated and those undertaken in accordance with authorized housing directives'.[49] The district commander responded succinctly to Yatakh: 'The soldier that entered the aforementioned apartment did not invade it. On the contrary, he moved in, because he had a

---

47   Moshe Yatah to the Haifa city commander, 31 August 1948, file: Concentration of Arabs in Wadi Nisnas, Gimmel-309/68, ISA.

48   Report of the Haifa branch to the Ministry of Minorities, 16 November 1948, file: Haifa, Gimmel-309/31, ISA.

49   Moshe Yatah to the Haifa city commander, 8 September 1948, file: Hana Yousef Haddad, Gimmel-310/7, ISA.

permit . . . a permit that was given in error.'[50] Whether the soldier knew that he had been given a permit erroneously or not, when he forcibly entered the apartment he told the apartment's Arab owner that it was 'none of his business' when he asked whether a directive had been issued allowing him to move into the apartment.[51]

The Ministry of Minorities and the Temporary Arab Committee (the Arab body representing the interests of Arabs who had remained in Haifa) saw eye to eye concerning what was going on with Arab property. The committee warned and complained 'about the anarchy and disorder existing in the Wadi Nisnas area', pointing out that the measures taken to bring order to the area had been ineffective and that things were only getting worse. The committee noted that the Jewish residents 'invade . . . in an organized manner and the committee cannot stop them, a situation that has created and continues to create an artificial housing crisis.'[52]

When power trumped rules of morality and decency, countless Palestinian apartments were handed out. Yosef Kushnir, director of the Assets Department in the Office of the Trustee of Arab Property in Haifa, quit his job over what he claimed to be the reckless management of 'matters [related to] assets and apartments in Haifa'. Kushnir wrote to the trustee of Arab Property, Naftali Lifshitz, and told him about 'the bedlam and lawlessness prevailing in the distribution of apartments' that he had encountered.[53] In turns out that 'there was no public oversight over the distribution of apartments' by those authorized to do so. The process of reappropriating apartments was not given

careful consideration, and clerks involved in the matter took apartments for themselves . . . [and] there was no oversight to ensure that

---

50   Haifa district commander to the Ministry of Minorities Haifa office, 14 September 1948, file: Hana Yousef Haddad, Gimmel-310/7, ISA.

51   Mordehai Lipkin (lawyer) to the city's military headquarters, 7 September 1948, file: Hana Yousef Haddad, Gimmel-310/7, ISA.

52   The Temporary Arab Committee, Haifa, to the director of the Ministry of Minorities in the Kiryah [Sheetrit], 14 November 1948, file: Office of Minister Bechor-Shalom Sheetrit 14280/9, ISA.

53   At the end of May 1948, Naftali Lifshitz was appointed by Ben-Gurion to oversee Arab property in Haifa. See Yosef Ya'akovson to Carmeli, 23 May 1948, file: Lifshitz, Naftali, Gimmel-300/87, ISA. 'Naftali Lifshitz is the only one who is authorized to remove Arab property from conquered territory': Commander of the Carmeli Brigade to his charges, 24 May 1948, file: 6680/1949-5, IDF.

those who received apartments had not been selling the apartments that they had previously owned . . . There were no available guidelines, and, at the very least, no guidelines had been distributed for how and why apartments were to be given out, something that made it possible for the clerks to deal with the matter as they saw fit and that raises concerns that not everything was done on a just basis and not everything was carried out properly.

Kushnir asserted that the administrative situation encouraged home invasions, eroded public trust, and led to 'a continuation of the lawlessness and bedlam that allowed private individuals and officials to grab apartments'. Kushnir criticized how appointments were made and protested against the appointment of one D. Sneh to oversee the management of apartments and assets in Haifa. Based on his conversations with the custodian of abandoned property, he understood that this appointment, as Custodian Dov Shafrir put it, was the 'result of a political complication'. Kushnir added: 'in other words, political intrigue'.[54] It was not stated who was behind this intrigue.

Sheetrit reported at length to the Knesset Presidium (which manages the order of debates in the Knesset, or Israeli parliament) about what was taking place in Haifa. Every day people were breaking into homes. Most of the invasions were of Arab homes, but sometimes Jewish homes were taken too. Warehouses where 'abandoned' property was stored were also the target of break-ins. Sometimes home invaders left after extorting a payment; sometimes they forcibly entered and prevented apartment residents from returning by changing the locks. In these cases, the police and the city's trustee of abandoned property became involved. Sheetrit wrote at length about what happened to George Mu'ammar (معمر), a Haifa lawyer who was harassed by soldiers who coveted his property. His story is only one of many documented in Ministry of Minorities files housed in the Israel State Archives. Soldiers burst into the home of Mu'ammar and demanded that he clear a room for them. Mu'ammar refused and called the police to have the invaders removed from his home. The soldiers returned several days later, Sheetrit continued:

54 Yosef Kushnir to Naftali Lifshitz, the trustee of Arab property in Haifa, September 1948, file: Kushnir, Gimmel-300/40, ISA.

[And] between twenty and thirty [men] jumped over the fence and approached Mu'ammar's house, where his servant Ibrahim Khalil Nasra (نصرا) was found. One of the wicked [soldiers] presented himself as a police officer and demanded that the servant open the door. He refused, and the wicked [soldiers] told him that if he did not open the door, they would break it down and he would meet a bitter end. He opened the door, and he asked the officer to wait for the homeowner to return. The scoundrels entered. The servant tried to make a call, but the officer did not let him do so. The men who entered began tearing the rugs off the wall, cutting the radio wires, and removing all the armoires and furniture from the rooms and piling them in the hallway and just outside the house. When the servant wanted to leave the home, the officer did not allow him to go. Meanwhile, advocate George Mu'ammar returned home. When he found that they had already removed the furniture from three rooms, he locked one of the other rooms. The home invaders broke the door down and burst into the room. Maiz, Mu'ammar's cousin, called the police from a different location, because the home invaders had cut the telephone line in the home. Four policemen arrived. Apparently, this force proved unable to remove the invaders from the home. They left and came back with Officer Shtiger and ten additional policemen. The police officer took the home invaders' leaders, including Sergeant Adler, to headquarters. The other home invaders remained on site, and they said to the Arabs, 'this is how you treat Jews in Iraq.'

The Haifa lawyer Ya'akov Salamon arrived to mediate between the two sides, telling Mu'ammar that if the soldiers 'left without a victory, they were liable to break in again, to misbehave, to shoot, etc.' Therefore, it was necessary to arrive at a solution that maintained the home invaders' honour. He suggested that one of the home invaders be allowed to stay. In fact, Mu'ammar agreed to this. The soldiers plundered valuable property, destroying numerous pieces of furniture in the apartment. Two officers among the home invaders explained that they could break into Arab apartments because 'the police will not shoot us'. Several days later, following Salamon's 'mediation', the home invaders apologized to Mu'ammar.[55] After Haifa's conquest, events like this occurred regularly there.

---

55 Bechor-Shalom Sheetrit to the Knesset Presidium, 3 April 1949, file: Military invasions of Arab homes, Gimmel-309/55, ISA.

Home invasions remained frequent, and numerous times, the Temporary Arab Committee in Haifa attempted, unsuccessfully, to meet with Ben-Gurion to discuss their situation.[56] In April 1949, however, the prime minister was forced to intervene after a company-sized group invaded homes.[57] At the beginning of the month, in an organized and blatantly illegal manner, about 200 soldiers invaded the homes of Arab residents on Abbas Street (the only street outside of Wadi Nisnas where Haifa's Arab Christians were legally permitted to live) and in Wadi Nisnas. The organizer of the mass invasion was David Yosef Adler, a soldier who had been discharged a month earlier and who chaired the Haifa District Committee for the Handicapped.[58] As opposed to earlier home invasions, which were conducted spontaneously by individuals or smaller groups, this was a highly coordinated operation.[59] The newspapers took note of it, with *Al HaMishmar* reporting: 'A sad spectacle played out in the streets. The invaders arrived in trucks carrying furniture. Arabs and their possession were taken outside. Screams were heard. Arab children were seen crying.' The newspaper reported that the Arab residents wondered 'whether there was Hitlerite rule here' after men, as well as their women and children, had been beaten, and their possessions had been broken after being thrown from their apartments.[60]

Learning quickly of the mass invasion, Sheetrit called on the prime minister to intervene immediately. This was one of the few occasions on

---

56   Moshe Yatah to Bechor-Shalom Sheetrit, 30 March 1949, file: Military invasions of Arab homes.

57   For example: 'Today Arabs living at 40 Abbas Street and the buildings surrounding it came and told us that military policemen and soldiers break into their apartments on a daily basis in attempts to take them over or to destroy property . . . We demand that an order be given to the military police and to the soldiers to stop these home invasions.' Moshe Yatah to the Haifa district commander et al., 10 December 1948 (and additional correspondence in the file), file: Soldiers' invasion of apartments, Gimmel-309/83, ISA.

58   See the Announcement of Adler David Yosef from 7 April 1949, file: 260/1951-64, IDF. Cf. Tom Segev, *1949: The First Israelis*, trans. Arlen Weinstein (New York: Free Press, 1986), 76.

59   'The topic of discussion: Invasions of residential Arab areas – Haifa', Haifa District military police, 7 April 1949, file: 260/1951-64, IDF.

60   'Tens of soldiers and demobilized soldiers invaded Arab-owned apartments in Haifa' [Hebrew], *Al HaMishmar*, 8 April 1948; 'Soldiers occupy Arab-owned homes in Haifa and expel their residents: The plot was foiled' [Hebrew], *Kol Ha'am*, 8 April 1949; 'Soldiers invade Arab-owned apartments in Haifa and are removed' [Hebrew], *ha-Boker*, 10 April 1949.

which Ben-Gurion intervened meaningfully in matters related to looting and plundering. In the wake of Sheetrit's petition, the prime minister's military adjutant announced that the invasion was not an operation
being carried out by the military or the government, and an explicit
order was given to stop it, 'to restore public order', and to prosecute the
guilty.[61]

Minister Sheetrit hurried to Haifa. Perhaps he did this because he
knew that without his ministerial presence, the mass invasion would not
be stopped.[62] Again, he wrote a detailed report about the apartment
invasions. About 200 armed soldiers arrived in military vehicles in the
early morning and invaded apartments on Abbas Street and in Wadi
Nisnas. Words can scarcely describe the horror that took place in the
coming hours; violence, chaos, destruction, and fear reigned in the
streets of Haifa. Only towards evening were most of the apartments on
the street cleared. According to Sheetrit, the police were helpless. The
apartment of Knesset member Tawfik Toubi (طوبي) of the Israeli
Communist Party was among those broken into that day. Sheetrit
summarized the event as follows:

> During the various home invasions, there were cases where the invad-
> ers used force, hit men and women, knocked down doors, gathered
> up the furniture that they removed from rooms, and took people
> from their homes and put them in the street. Until an order was
> received from Tel Aviv, the army did not offer [the residents] any
> assistance. It is clear that the home invasions were organized by army
> officers. There were officers among the invaders who removed their
> rank insignia, so that they would not be recognized. The police have
> the license plate numbers of about ten vehicles. The police are contin-
> uing to investigate. It believes that the home invasions will continue,
> and they will remain an issue until there are no longer available

---

61 Announcement received from Prime Minister Ben-Gurion through his adjutant major Nehemiah, 7 April 1949, file: Military invasions of Arab homes.

62 Following a complaint of a present Arab about the expropriation of his property, Moshe Yatah, the Ministry of Minorities representative in Haifa, wrote: 'We
frequently receive these types of complaints in our office, and most of the cases are
similar to Mr Samaan's case. Petitions made in this area to the trustee of Arab property
do not result in positive outcomes.' Moshe Yatah to Gad Machnes, 24 August 1948, file:
Samaan Anis, Gimmel-299/92, ISA.

apartments . . . Haifa's Arabs are disappointed and bitter. Many of them are asking whether this is a hint for them to sell their property, pack their bags, and emigrate from Israel.[63]

When Sheetrit left Haifa, he was told that the home invasions had been halted and that order had been re-established. However, this report was inexact: immediately after the soldiers' invasion was stopped, civilians broke into the Arab-owned apartments. The army asserted that it was not authorized to deal with civilian home invasion and that civilian law enforcement needed to be called in to stop the invaders.[64] Elias Kusa (كوسا), a member of the Temporary Arab Committee, said that the situation in Haifa

> resembled the Ottoman period when people would attack the homes of Christians and Jews. The Arabs do not feel safe in their homes, and they are consumed by worry . . . Today [the Arab] who leaves his home is uncertain that he will find it as he left it when he returns. Locks prove insufficient. There are those who board up their doors to protect themselves from home invasion.[65]

The 3,500 Arabs who remained in the city lived in constant terror.

Shabtai Levy, who had served as mayor of Haifa since 1940, demanded a stop to the numerous home invasions, and, at the insistence of Arab representatives, he organized a discussion. 'What they have taken from the Arabs, they have taken, but what they left them, they need to leave alone.' Levy argued that that every group and organization was asserting 'that somebody else is responsible'. The military police claimed that they could not act against civilians, whereas the army asserted that the invaders were sometimes civilians, and, for this reason, they were not responsible for the matter. The military police commander contended that sometimes the home invaders were civilians who wear uniforms during the break-ins. The Ministry of Defense representative at the meeting

---

63 Bechor-Shalom Sheetrit, 'Report concerning invasion of Arab-owned homes in Haifa by soldiers', file: Military invasions of Arab homes.

64 Moshe Yatah to the Ministry of Minorities in the Kiryah, 10 April 1949, file: Military invasions of Arab homes.

65 Meeting with the mayor, April [latter half] 1949, file: Military invasions of Arab homes.

argued that there was need to find housing for soldiers who had just returned from the Independence War:

> Neither I nor the police are capable of keeping homeless people from taking advantage of the situation. I proposed [to one of the Arab representatives] . . . that the Arabs crowd together and make room, but he showed no interest in the idea. People come to me and tell me about empty apartments that they have found. They ask me if they should occupy them. I tell them, 'Occupy them.' I know that this is illegal.

Hanna Naqara (نقارة), an Arab lawyer and activist who was also a founder of the Palestinian Communist Party, was flabbergasted. 'What form of government do we have here? A democratic government or the law of the jungle?' He stated that he was prepared to demonstrate alongside disabled Haganah veterans for their right to housing, 'but we demand a legal arrangement, not a private one.'[66] It comes as no surprise that the issues remained unsettled in the days that followed the Ministry of Defense representative's declaration that he knew that he was breaking the law when he told soldiers to break into 'present' Arabs' homes. In turn, representatives of the Temporary Arab Committee and the Ministry of Minorities tried to resolve the problem. After a discussion in which all the sides participated, a leader of the Greek Catholic community named George Hakim (حكيم), with support from the Temporary Arab Committee, made a seven-room home available to disabled veterans rent-free.[67]

While the scale of looting and pillaging in Haifa was vast, through mid-August 1948, four months after the city's conquest, no more that forty-four civilians had been tried in the Haifa district (a number that includes civilians tried for plundering villages in the area, a topic that will be addressed below).[68] A journalist who visited the city in November, after many months of occupation, reported on the ongoing looting:

66   Ibid.

67   Ministry of Minorities to the Kiryah, 22 April 1949; Report of the activities of the Public Committee for the Housing of Disabled Veterans, 19 April 1949; additional reports and protocols on the topic can be found in file: Seizure and invasion of Arab homes, Gimmel-1323/10, ISA.

68   'Statistics submitted by the police pertaining to abandoned property trials from 15 May 1948 to 12 August 1948', file: General, Gimmel-307/16, ISA.

It turns out that our brothers, the Children of Israel, have also learned this profession [theft] and have done so in a thorough way, as Jews are wont to do. Now 'Hebrew Labour' dominates the field. Indeed, a robber problem has spread in Haifa. Regardless of their ethnicity or country of origin, people from every group in the Yishuv have participated. New immigrants and those released from Acre Prison, veteran Israelis of both Eastern and Western origin with no discrimination between them . . . And where were the police?[69]

One can cautiously assert that the turning of a blind eye to the pillaging contributed to the fact that Wadi Nisnas 'is like Sodom and Gomorrah today', as the inspector-general of the Israeli police, Yehezkel Sahar, put it. Sahar added, 'Robberies, a black market, prostitution, the place is the centre of the underworld'.[70] Like Tiberias before it, Haifa was pillaged and robbed to the full. For months following the end of the Independence War, the theft and home invasions would continue.

---

69   Aryeh Nesher, 'Haifa, a city undergoing renewal' [Hebrew], *Haaretz*, 28 November 1948.

70   Minutes of a meeting held in the Ministry of Police, 1 November 1948, file: Ministry of Police, Gimmel-304/58, ISA.

Jerusalem

Pillaging in Jerusalem, one of Mandate Palestine's largest and most important cities, continued for months after the occupation of the city. The Haganah's and the Israel Defense Forces' gradual conquests of areas of the city, Arab residents' flight, and Jewish residents' departure from neighbourhoods where fighting was taking place all constituted demographic and political upheavals that would configure the events to come. Perhaps due to the importance Jews assigned to Jerusalem, or the fact that Jews always talked and wrote more about it, the literature and memoirs of the people of the time provide much more detail about Jewish pillaging of Arab property there than they do for other important plundered cities like Tiberias, Haifa, and Jaffa. On the eve of the Independence War, 165,000 people resided in Jerusalem. Approximately 99,000 were Jews, approximately 34,000 were Muslims, and approximately 31,000 were Christians. In the years prior to the war and after a gradual movement out of the Old City, Arabs lived in a number of new neighbourhoods. North of the Old City, Arabs lived in the Sheikh Jarrah (الشيخ جراح) and Musrara (مصرارة) neighbourhoods; in the South, Katamon (القطمون), Talbiya (الطالبية), and Bak'a (بقعة) were built as modern neighbourhoods with private homes.[1]

---

1 Menachem Klein, *Connected: The story of the land's inhabitants* [Hebrew] (Tel Aviv: ha-Kibbutz ha-me'uhad, 2015), 91. For photos of Arab homes in Jerusalem during this period, see Walid Khalidi, *Before Their Diaspora: A Photographic History of the Palestinians, 1876–1948* (Washington, DC: Institute for Palestine Studies, 1984), 267–9.

My discussion here of the conquest of northern Jerusalem's Arab neighbourhoods as part of Operation Jebusite will address neither the military operations themselves nor the reason behind the Arabs' flight from the city. The 25 April attack launched by Palmach forces on the Sheikh Jarrah neighbourhood catalysed mass flight from the Arab neighbourhoods. The Bak'a, Talbiya, Katamon, German Colony, and Greek Colony neighbourhoods were quickly emptied of their inhabitants, and in the next few days Haganah forces conquered them.[2] By mid-1948, conquest of the Arab neighbourhoods in the west, outside the Old City walls, and the flight of residents from these neighbourhoods created a situation where, out of a total of 35,000 Arab residents who had previously resided in those neighbourhoods, only 750 non-Jewish residents remained. Most who stayed were Greeks who lived in the Greek and German colonies. On 1 May, Haganah forces entered Katamon.[3]

An interesting and oft-quoted source that offers a glimpse into the lives of Arabs at this time is the diary of Khalil al-Sakakini (السكاكيني), an educator and a Palestinian public figure (indeed, it should be noted that it is also one of the few sources written in real time offering a Palestinian point of view).[4] When the war was already knocking on his door, Sakakini, a Katamon resident, fled the city with his family. 'We left the house, the clothes, the furniture, the library, the food, the giant piano that knew no equal, and the electric refrigerator,' Sakakini sadly mourned in his diary. His home was well stocked, and it also contained financial pledges worth thousands of Palestinian pounds that he had left behind.[5] The Arab educator regretted that he had not brought along the books in his extensive library:

---

2 Yoav Gelber, *Independence versus Nakba* [Hebrew] (Or Yehudah: Dvir, 2004), 172.

3 On the population of Katamon and the fall of the neighbourhood, see Itamar Radai, *Palestinians in Jerusalem and Jaffa, 1948: A Tale of Two Cities*, trans. Haim Watzman (New York: Routledge, 2016), 65–82.

4 On this issue, see Adel Manna, *Nakba and survival: The story of Palestinians who remained in Haifa and the Galilee 1948–1956* [Hebrew] (Tel Aviv: ha-Kibbutz ha-me'uhad, 2017), 39.

5 Khalil al-Sakakini, *'Such am I, O world!': [Excerpts] from the diary of Khalil al-Sakakini* [Hebrew], trans. Gid'on Shilo (Jerusalem: Tziv'onim, 2007), 238.

I do not know what became of them after we left: Were they plundered? Were they burned? Were they respectfully and ceremoniously
moved to a public or private library? Did they make their way to
market counters so their pages could wrap onions?

Sakakini was also concerned about his liquor cabinet:

Farewell, liquor cabinet. We only opened you on happy occasions . . .
there is no doubt that when those who fell upon our houses got to this
cabinet, opened it, and tasted its drinks . . . [they said,] 'for this alone,
it was worth fighting.'[6]

A lack of reliable documentation renders the historian unable to
address the fate of Sakakini's liquor cabinet. Thus, it is likely better to
leave the matter to writers like the Palmach fighter Yoram Kaniuk. What
Kaniuk wrote about Katamon's conquest and hard liquor consumption
was consistent with the Arab educator's fears:

We went down toward Katamon and took it after a short battle. On
the way back, as we walked through the city singing, we saw the
Jerusalemites running to loot, and the residents who weren't looting
applauded us. The residents of Katamon, with its splendid buildings,
had fled, leaving food behind on the tables and beds unmade. In one
home there was a huge radio yelling in Arabic. One of [the soldiers]
shot and killed it [sic]. The homes were wealthy people's homes. We
had never seen such splendour. Gold. Giant Mirrors. Gleaming kitchens, crystal chandeliers, and tons of food. Silver cutlery. Bottles of
liquor stood like soldiers in formation . . . We left, and an armoured
vehicle was brought in and loaded with bottles, especially the big ones
that we later realized were champagne bottles, and we made it somewhere, perhaps it was Kiryat Anavim or perhaps it was someplace
else. We got undressed, every one of us who had not been killed, stood
naked, and sprayed champagne on each other one after another . . .
We were, I now know, the first soldiers in history who washed themselves with sparkling champagne rather than drinking it.[7]

6   Ibid., 240.
7   Yoram Kaniuk, *1948* [Hebrew] (Tel Aviv: Yediʿot Ahronot, 2010), 147–8.

What Kaniuk writes is consistent with other testimonies. For example, one of the Palmach fighters offers the following information about the time his unit spent in a Katamon home:

> We made a chicken coop from a mahogany cabinet, and we swept up the garbage onto a silver platter. There was gold rimmed china, and we would spread a sheet out on the table . . . covered with porcelain and gold. When we finished eating, we picked it up and took it to the basement. At a different location, we found a storeroom with ten thousand tins of caviar, at least that was what the guys said. We did not have bread, but we had caviar. Since then, the guys have not been able to touch caviar. On the one hand we were embarrassed about [our] behaviour, but on the other hand there was a feeling that anything goes. We stayed there for twelve days. Jerusalem was groaning from hunger, and we were gaining weight. There were times that those stationed in the [headquarters in] Notre Dame shaved with champagne. My friend shaved with champagne because there was no water. French champagne. It was a pretty embarrassing feeling of abandon.[8]

A journalist, who sat with his friends in the Ben-Yehuda Café after the neighbourhood was taken, told how an armoured vehicle came to a halt in front of the car and 'a tall wild-haired Palmachnik with a beard' emerged and made the following proposal to the gathered journalists: 'Gang! Who will give me a cup of coffee for a refrigerator . . . our Katamon.'[9] This was the mood.

The neighbourhood was one of Jerusalem's richest ones, and, as in other cities, the pillaging began even before the conquest had concluded. In his book, the city commander, Yitzhak Levi, wrote about soldiers and civilians who broke into empty homes that only a few hours earlier had been occupied by their Arab inhabitants and emerged carrying furniture and clothing, electrical appliances, and food. 'It was a shameful sight,' he declared. According to Levi, many people were disgusted by

---

8   Dov Doron, interview, Collection of the Galili Centre for Defence Studies, 5 February 1984, file: 12-3/41/45, YTA.

9   Avi'ezer Goldsteyn, *Flames in the skies of Jerusalem (Diary of the 1948 siege)* [Hebrew] (Tel Aviv: Ofakim 1949), 120.

what was going on, but 'they were unable to rein in their friends' raging desires'. Levi notes that it took days before they successfully assumed control over the neighbourhood's remaining property.[10] Yet it was clear that the tone was set by unrestrained pillagers, not by those who were disgusted by the depredation. Moshe Salamon, a Haganah company commander who saw combat in the city, wrote in his diary that Katamon's wealth created openings for plunder, and that 'everybody, both enlisted men and officers, got caught up' in it.

The desire for material things enveloped everybody. People went through every home. People searched; one found foodstuffs, while another found precious objects. This ravenousness took hold of me, and I nearly failed to break free. In this area, there were no limitations on human action.

The pillagers pounced on the homes, and the radios and expensive utensils were stolen. 'It is hard to imagine how much wealth people found in all those many homes.'
Salamon noted frankly in his diary:

A desire to hoard nearly drove me mad . . . Before it was too late, I took control of the situation and restrained my passions. It is good that I knew how to do this. Many healthy and virtuous people got caught up in a [similar situation] and found it difficult to extricate themselves. The battalion commander, his deputy, everybody got tripped up. I faltered, but I knew how to save myself before it was too late. Indeed, here is where the slippery slope starts. Therefore, it is easy to understand why people say that during wartime moral and human values get blurred.[11]

---

10   Yitzhak Levi, *Nine Measures* [Tish'ah Kabin]: *Jerusalem during the battles of the Independence War* [Hebrew] (Tel Aviv: Ma'arkhot / Defense Ministry Press, 1986), 219.

11   Mordehai Bar-On, ed., 'From the diary of a company commander during the Independence War: Excepts from the diary of Moshe Salamon, December 1947–May 1948', in Osnat Shiran, ed., *Jews and Arabs in the struggle for the Land of Israel – Studies and documents: Issues in the history of the Jewish Yishuv and the State of Israel's defense*, vol. 6, *Olive branch and sword* [Hebrew] (Ramat Efal: Galili Association for Defense Force Research, 2006), 151–89, 179.

Katamon's wealth blinded Jerusalem's Jewish population. City resident Yair Goren reported that 'an unadulterated pursuit of plunder' took hold in the city's streets. Civilians plundered methodically, set down piles of booty, and continued to steal. 'Men, women and children ran to and fro like blind mice.' The pillagers had taken so much plunder from Arab-owned homes that they needed to protect it from other Jewish civilians who had also come to loot. 'Blood began to flow, because there were so many people arguing over one item or another in a pile, or over multiples items.' Several looters came up with a solution: have one of your children stand guard over the piles that you had accumulated while you continued to rob. Ambitious people who operated on a large scale discovered another way to protect their spoils: they

> took what they took, bought it to an [Arab] apartment they had previously claimed, and left an old man or an old woman there to ensure their occupation of the apartment and their possession of the treasure being assembled therein.[12]

The plunder, one of the neighbourhood residents explained, went on for days.

> I would look out our apartment window and see tens of people walking along carrying spoils . . . I saw them walking like that for days. It was not just soldiers. It was civilians too. They plundered like madmen. They even dragged dining room tables out. This took place in the daylight for all to see.[13]

One of the soldiers described 'a debauched atmosphere'.[14]

Yitzhak Ben-Zvi, a Yishuv leader and the State of Israel's second president, wrote a report about his visit to Katamon 'and other conquered

---

12   Yair Goren, *A Khazar in Jerusalem: From the memoirs of one of the resident-defenders of Jerusalem and other stories whose subject is the Independence War* [Hebrew] (Jerusalem: Ilan, 1997), 250.

13   For Hagit Shlonsky's story, see Nathan Krystall, 'The Fall of the New City', in Salim Tamari, ed., *Jerusalem 1948: The Arab Neighbourhoods and Their Fate in the War* (Jerusalem: Institute for Jerusalem Studies, 2002), 102. Also see Larry Collins and Dominique Lapierre, *O Jerusalem!* (New York: Simon & Schuster, 1972), 309.

14   Doron, interview.

neighbourhoods' on 25 May 1948. His description makes it seem that '"respectable" Jews who see plunder as a natural and permissible thing' participated in the looting and pillaging.[15] In a letter he wrote to Ben-Gurion, he stated that what was happening in Jerusalem was damaging the honour of the Jewish people and the combat forces 'in a terrible way'. Ben-Zvi made clear that he was not referring to military expropriation, something required due to wartime shortages of fuel, food, and other products. Instead, he was talking about pillaging that abounded *everywhere*:

> I cannot remain silent about the theft, both that organized by groups and that committed randomly by individuals. This plunder has become a widespread phenomenon. It is not just happening in Arab-owned homes, but also in the Jewish neighbourhood of Talpiot that has also been targeted by these irresponsible elements. Everyone agrees that our pillagers pounce on abandoned neighbourhoods like locust onto a field or an orchard. These days, when you pass through Rehavia's streets, you see old people, youths, and children returning from Katamon or other neighbourhoods with sacks filled [with] stolen goods every step of the way. The booty is multifaceted: Refrigerators and beds, clocks and books, sheets and clothing. They have already set up a market for the sale of these things.[16]

A plundering and thieving mindset took hold in the city, and Arabs and Jews alike were victimized. A newspaper reporter visited the Talpiot neighbourhood and the homes of a number of Jewish intellectuals living there, and he gave an account of it in the right-wing daily *Herut* [Freedom]. The noted historian Yosef Klauzner's home – on which the journalist Ariel Elitzedek noted a plaque engraved with the phrase 'Judaism and Humanity' – was damaged by shell fragments. Yet for him, it was not a shell that truly damaged the home 'but rather the acts of flesh and blood'. Klausner successfully removed his extensive library in time, so that 'our soldiers only shamefully stole a small number of books'.

---

15   Yitzhak Ben-Zvi, 'The topic of discussion: Acts of robbery in Katamon and in the other conquered neighbourhoods', 27 May 1948, BGA.

16   Yitzhak Ben-Zvi to David Ben-Gurion, 2 June 1948, BGA.

One of the locals told Elitzedek that 'our people', rather that enemy shells, brought about the vast destruction, reporting:

> One of the local residents told me that the destruction caused by our people was greater than the destruction that the shelling caused . . . everything was stolen, and sometimes door and window frames were stolen as well. In Arnona, for example, the robbers could not take a large piano they found in one of the homes with them. What did they do? They stayed there and broke it . . . All of this was either done by Jewish soldiers or civilians! One officer groaned and told me: 'First, they stole from the Arabs, and, afterwards, they moved on to the Jews.'

What happened to Klausner's home is paradigmatic of the experience of many Arab and Jewish intellectuals robbed at that time. Author Shmuel Yosef Agnon's home also sustained damage, as did that of the poet and translator Leib Yaffe, who had died weeks earlier in a car bomb explosion on the grounds of Jerusalem's National Institutions Building.[17]

The *Herut* reporter noted that there was even greater destruction in the Arnona neighbourhood than in Talpiot. Artillery fire damaged many homes, and 'acts of theft were much more extensive [there]'. Due to the security situation, Professor Moshe Zvi Segal had not been able to move his library to a safer location, and now his home was completely breached. Although Segal had moved his library to a room in his home where the roof and walls were still intact and the books were safe from the rain,

> books were now scattered on the wet floor with nobody to care for them. Many books, as well as all the possessions in the home, including the Hebrew typewriter that Professor Segal employed to write his books, had been stolen . . . The destruction caused by enemy shelling pains one's heart and makes it cry, but the destruction and damage caused by those who long exhorted for 'Hebrew Purity of Arms' hurts much more.[18]

---

17   Ariel Elitzedek, 'Residents of Talpiot and Arnona – Victims of shelling and Arab and Jewish robbery' [Hebrew], *Herut*, 24 January 1949.

18   Ibid.

A handwritten document lists the 'inventory' found in a multiroom Katamon home after its contents had been organized. In one room, there were many pieces of furniture for 'decorating the base and the like'. A second room was also filled with furniture, but these had been roughly handled: 'two broken bedside tables, seven broken chairs, two broken armoires'. A third room was 'empty'.[19] A similar list could have been made for the burgled Katamon home of Efrayim Fichman, who was Jewish. While Fichman commanded a Combat Engineering Corps training base, 'people decided to break into his apartment, plunder and rob everything of value, and break and destroy what they could not steal'.[20]

While Jews' libraries were treated disparagingly, the libraries of Arabs were treated even worse, as the following report demonstrates. Military Governor Dov Yosef sent its author, Moshe Morali, to locate a multivolume library of Arab village property-tax records. When Morali arrived at the designated location, he found soldiers living in the building. When he asked whether this was the place where the books were kept, one of the soldiers came over to him and responded:

'Yes, buddy. This is the place you are looking for. Follow me.' I was happy that I had finally found the place. He led me to a field behind the building, showed me a pile of ash, and said: 'Here are the books you are looking for' . . . I was shocked by what I saw, and I asked him: 'You burned everything?' He said: 'Yes, everything. It was hard work for us to get rid of it all. Six bookcases filled with books that were all in Arabic.' I said: 'How could you do such a thing?' He laughed and said: 'They were in Arabic. Both the military governor and one of the engineers who did not want to give me his name approved our book burning.' I said: 'It is not possible that the military governor approved that. He sent me to find them.' . . . [He said:] 'We took the bookshelves and the tables too.'[21]

19   Handwritten document, file: Military governor Jerusalem, Inventory, JS-154, CZA.

20   Efrayim Fichman to the military governor of the Southern District, 10 August 1948, file: Complaints, Gimmel-279/54, ISA.

21   Moshe Morali to the assistant military governor in Jerusalem, 29 September 1948, file: Army complaints, Gimmel-273/51, ISA. This is the proper place to mention the important operation undertaken by the Ministry of Minorities to collect and

Eliyahu Dobkin, a labour movement leader, reported on what was happening in Jerusalem to the Mapai party secretariat:

Things have gotten to the point where people are plundering Jewish property too. In Talpiot, they stole things from Jews. No Arab even set foot there. After the Jews evacuated, it happened in Talpiot. Yet people did not just plunder in Talpiot. They also plundered in poor neighbourhoods, like the 'Pagi' section of the Sanhedria neighbourhood. Jews owned twenty-three apartments in Katamon. Four months ago, when the Arabs seized control of the neighbourhood, they left their apartments. When they expelled the Arabs and the apartment owners returned to their apartments, they found them in perfect condition. Nothing was missing, except in a few rare cases. Yet, four days later, nothing remained. [Martin] Buber found his home exactly as he left

---

preserve the Arabic literature that remained in the country. 'Reality motivated another large, highly fascinating, and important operation in the field of culture – the collection of Arabic books. It came to light as Jaffa was being conquered and homes were being abandoned that tens of thousands of Arabic books were being completely abandoned... This enormous quantity of books, worth hundreds of thousands of Palestinian pounds, was increasingly neglected and people began to maliciously destroy parts of it. Books were stolen, they were thrown in the trash, they were pillaged, they were burned.' Report of the Department for Culture, Education, and Information of the Ministry of Minorities by Yehuda Burla, n.d., file: General – Minorities in Israel, Gimmel, 307/27, ISA. The book collection took place thanks to the initiative of Minister Sheetrit. See: 'I appointed a committee . . . to figure out what to do about all the abandoned Arabic books in all the conquered cities and villages throughout the country, including those in libraries, in stores, and in private homes whose owners left them.' Bechor-Shalom Sheetrit to Yehuda Leib Maimon (minister of religions) and the foreign and justice ministers, 22 August 1948, file: Arab Affairs – Abandoned property, Gimmel-5670/29, ISA. 'Indeed, the government did not touch the books of minorities that remained in the country, but the books that were found in the property of absentees who left the abandoned cities (there were no literary works found in the villages) were collected and organized according to categories. A building was set up where all the literary materials was concentrated: there were about 80,000 books, mostly in Arabic, and a number of ancient manuscripts.' Memorandum on activities of the Ministry of Minorities (May 1948 –January 1949), file: Memorandum on activities of the Ministry of Minorities, Gimmel-304/63, ISA. The Arabic libraries in the country were practically all private. On this topic, see Ammi Ayalon, *Reading Palestine: Printing and Literacy 1900–1948* (Austin: University of Texas Press, 2004); Gish Amit, *Ex libris: A history of theft, preservation, and appropriation at the National Library in Jerusalem* [Hebrew] (Tel Aviv: ha-Kibbutz ha-me'uhad, 2015), 78–126. While there is little doubt that books were plundered and stolen, I find the general tone Amit employs in his discussion of the fate of Arabic books improper.

it. His granddaughter came and said that everything was fine. I do not know what happened after that.[22]

Yitzhak Ben-Zvi also noted there were 'not an insignificant number of cases' where Arab neighbours meticulously protected the property of Jewish neighbours who had been forced by circumstances to leave their

---

22 Minutes of Mapai secretariat meeting, 13 June 1948, file: 2-24-1948-21, LPA. Also see the following comments made by Brit Shalom member David Werner Senator: 'There are a not insignificant number of cases that testify to how Arab neighbours caringly and meticulously watched over the property of Jewish residents after they left Arab neighbourhoods when the fighting broke out. And now, following these neighbourhoods' conquest by our forces, these Jewish residents have been reunited with their things and they have found that nothing is missing.' David Werner Senator to David Shaltiel, 3 June 1948 (with a copy and an accompanying letter to David Ben-Gurion), BGA. Minister of agriculture Aharon Zisling said: 'There are cases where the Arabs passed this trial – Jewish and governmental property remained intact during months of Arab occupation but was plundered and destroyed when it passed over into Jewish hands. It is disgusting!' See Minutes of the Histadrut Executive Committee meeting, 16–17 June 1948, vol. 90 (June–August 1948), Pinchas Lavon Institute for Labour Movement Research Archive (hereafter, LMA). The Jerusalem District military police commander said: 'In the last four weeks, complaints lodged by former residents of the Talpiot and Arnona neighbourhoods, who are currently residing in [other parts of] Jerusalem and Tel Aviv, concerning soldiers breaking into their locked homes in these neighbourhoods and stealing various items from them has skyrocketed . . . there are scores of complaints . . . the aforementioned complaints reflect only a small portion of the cases . . . After Kalman Rozenblit, a member of my unit, visited the locations mentioned in the aforementioned complaints, [he] found that the interiors of these Jewish homes did not appear any different than the sights that we have become used to seeing in [homes in] conquered Arab neighbourhoods like Katamon, the German Colony, etc. . . . Since February, residents have not occupied their homes in the aforementioned neighbourhoods. This large-scale evacuation came to an end in mid-May. During this time, various army units and workers who constructed fortifications in the aforementioned neighbourhoods passed through them. Complaints were being lodged continuously, but their number was not great . . . because former Haganah members, who, for the most part, did not steal Jewish property, were encamped there. In the last few months, when Gahal [Foreign Enlistment – Jews from the displaced person camps in Europe and the internment camps in Cyprus] soldiers arrived in the aforementioned locations, criminal activity increased, as did complaints about it. It is worth noting that in contrast with the Arab neighbourhoods of Jerusalem that were completely emptied of property immediately after their conquest, there are still locked homes in Talpiot and Arnona whose property has gone untouched.' Jerusalem district military police commander to the military governor of Jerusalem, 24 November 1948, file: Complaints, Gimmel-279/54, ISA. After inspecting conditions in Talpiot in March 1949, a security officer in the Jerusalem District wrote that all the homes in the Talpiot neighbourhood had been broken into and 'only a few objects remained in the apartments. Things appeared much like what we had come to expect to see in abandoned Arab neighbourhoods.' District security officer, 'North Talpiot', 30 March 1949, file: 1308/1950-431, IDF.

homes. When those Jews returned after their neighbourhoods' conquest by Jewish forces, the contents of their homes were intact.[23]

The mob stole what there was to steal. 'The confiscators,' reported *Al HaMishmar*, visited Jewish homes in the north of the city too. Residents who were absent from their homes returned to find them emptied.[24] Three months later, *Kol Ha'am* reported that following the shelling of the Mahanayim neighbourhood, residents who evacuated their homes met a similar fate. When they returned, 'they found havoc and destruction everywhere. The robbers went methodically from building to building and took everything that they could get their hands on. Armoires were breached and broken, and mattresses were torn to shreds.' The apartments' appearance made it seem like 'a pogrom has just occurred.' According to the party newspaper, this was not something random: 'The permissiveness that greeted the theft of Arab property in Katamon has borne fruit. After the organized plunder there, people are now extending their hands to take Jewish refugees' property.'[25] Furniture was even taken from the apartment of Meir Laniado, Jaffa's military governor.[26]

---

23 Yitzhak Ben-Zvi to David Ben-Gurion, 2 June 1948, BGA. The Zinati family, a Jewish family that has long resided in the village of Peki'in, tells a similar story. During the war, they were required to leave the village, but they later returned. 'The neighbours gathered up most of the family's possessions and brought them to their homes for safekeeping, and those are the possessions that they are returning now.' Hadassah Avigdori-Avidov, *On the path we took: From the diary of a convoy escort* [Hebrew] (Tel Aviv: Defense Ministry Press, 1988), 188.

24 'The problem of thefts in Jerusalem needs to be eradicated' [Hebrew], *Al HaMishmar*, 11 June 1948.

25 'They started with plunder' [Hebrew], *Kol Ha'am*, 12 September 1948. See Walter Yablonski's letters to the military governor from 21 June 1948 and 24 June 1948. In them, he describes the theft of the property found in his Greek Colony home. Military governor of the Southern District Yehoshu'a Simon's comments of about the case prove interesting: 'All my efforts to look into the robbery of objects from his home have turned up nothing. The police assert that they have never had sufficient manpower to protect private property. Furthermore, the thieves never stopped to consider the notes hanging on the doors through Dr Yablonski's home indicating that the contents were "Jewish property". In connection with this, it will interest you [in the prosecutor's office] to know that Jewish soldiers and civilians stole things from the homes of affluents Jews, who number among Talpiot's founders, without considering for a moment that they were stealing from Jews.' Military governor of the Southern District to the district prosecutor, 14 July 1948, file: Complaints, Gimmel-279/54, ISA.

26 On behalf of Meir Laniado to the military governor of Katamon, 23 August 1948. The things were taken by the Sixty-Third Battalion and arrived at the battalion

In a diary entry for 31 May, the poet and essayist Yeshurun Keshet wrote that a number of individuals whose homes and stores on Ben Yehuda Street had been destroyed in an act of terror came back from the hospital to find that 'the (Jewish!) rabble had pillaged and plundered their furniture and possessions'. Keshet noted that it was not possible to define 'who exactly the "rabble" were in this case'. Many found that things taken from their apartments and stores 'set in place like building materials in bomb shelters that their neighbours built prior to their return'.[27]

In his diary, Moshe Yekutiel Alpert, head of the orthodox Etz Chaim Yeshiva and resident of the ultra-Orthodox Beit Yisrael neighbourhood, wrote about the plunder and destruction carried out by 'Sephardic and Oriental Jews' in homes in his neighbourhood. Members of every Jewish ethnic group plundered, of course, but Alpert chose to emphasize the Sephardic burglars. The neighbourhood mukhtar received numerous complaints about young 'Frenks' who 'stole whatever they could get their hands on, destroyed and broke doors and windows, and took precious objects and expensive things, china services, kitchen utensils, books, etc., from Nahalat Yitzhak and Shmuel HaNavi Street'. During Alpert's visit to some of the plundered homes, he encountered 'havoc and destruction every step of the way'. When the Arabs had not completely destroyed or looted things, 'the Frenks finished [the job]'.[28] Days later, when he went to the police station. Alpert reported

the many robberies that had taken place in the neighbourhood. When they steal, they empty whole homes. They even stole shingles off the roofs. Overall, what occurred is horrible. Our brothers, the children of Israel, particularly Oriental Jews, stole every piece of property from numerous homes.[29]

---

warehouse. See Sixty-Third Battalion adjutant to South Jerusalem military government officer, 23 August 1948, file: Complaints, Gimmel-279/54, ISA.

27   Yeshurun Keshet, *In besieged Jerusalem: Diaries from the home front* [Hebrew] (Jerusalem: Re'uven Mas, 1973), 75.

28   Pinhas Alpert and Dotan Goren, eds, *Diary of a mukhtar in Jerusalem: The history of the Beit Yisrael neighbourhood and its surroundings in the writings of Rabbi Moshe Yekutiel Alpert (1938–1952)* [Hebrew] (Ramat Gan: Bar Ilan University Press, 2014), 137.

29   Ibid., 153.

Alongside the looting, a black market developed for the sale of plundered objects from Arab homes. 'It turns out that many people, many of our municipal residents, are unable – simply unable, it appears – to control their desire *so as to not* take part in the looting,' wrote Keshet in his diary.[30]

Netanel Lorch, an officer of the Etzioni Brigade defending greater Jerusalem, wrote about a machine-gunner under his command in Jerusalem:

> This expert machine-gunner had an additional expertise – the ability to get abandoned property and make his living off of it. We are not talking about rugs, furniture, or jewellery here. This young man was truly proud of his level of professionalism: After [others] had removed an apartment's contents, he would get to work. He would pull up flooring tiles and remove handles and shutters. He would sort the inventory according to what type of material it was made from. Iron would go in one place, and wood in another. He specialized in locks. At the end of the day, he would shamelessly sell the merchandise, because he had earned his daily bread by the sweat of his brow and hard and exhausting physical labour.[31]

Soldiers' plundering demanded different levels of organization. Residents of Jerusalem could plunder and take their booty to their homes (or Arab-owned homes to which they had laid claim), but the soldiers were on duty, and, besides small objects they could hide in their equipment, they needed to bring what they had collected to where their units were stationed. The conquest of the Arab and mixed

---

30 Keshet, *In besieged Jerusalem*, 75. In turn, black markets popped up in each of the mixed cities. The Arab property on the black market enabled stocking up on whatever one needed. The black market sold more than just furniture, merchandise, electric appliances, and other similar items. One could also purchase stolen medical equipment. 'We have learned that lately various people have been approaching dentists in town with stolen medical devices and offering them for sale.' A. Ski (Jerusalem medical service) to the military governor, 16 September 1948. It soon became clear that the Lehi stole medical equipment. See Robert Marcus to the military governor, 27 September 1948. Also see D. Y. Mitshnik to the military governor, 10 October 1948. On the looting of his Jaffa Street optical store, see file: Army complaints.

31 Netanel Lorch, *Late afternoon: My first seventy years (and what preceded them)* [Hebrew] (Tel Aviv: Defense Ministry Press, 1997), 116.

neighbourhoods revealed war's brutality in all of its splendour. Physician E. B. George, who remained in his Katamon apartment after the mandate ended, became the victim of a massive robbery carried out by soldiers. When the military forces entered the neighbourhood, they pounced on "the six furnished rooms" and completely emptied them. The soldiers took 'silver and gold, official documents and bonds, and family jewels'. George's medical equipment, used to care for the city's inhabitants, was plundered too.[32] However, not everybody participated in the plunder. A soldier who had been on watch in the Old City recalled seeing soldiers wandering around Silwan with 'sacks on their backs'. He took his rifle and shot at their feet. 'We yelled and told them to bring everything [over]. They poured out their sacks' contents at the base of the [Old City] wall.'[33] These soldiers acted no differently than the Arabs who had plundered their Jewish neighbours' homes during the 1939 riots.

Looking back, it is impossible to know what merchandise and equipment was legally expropriated and taken out of the city during the Independence War, and what property organized military forces plundered under the guise of 'expropriation'.[34] Of course, there were cases where commanders confiscated property for their units without

32 E. B. George to Bechor-Shalom Sheetrit, 16 February 1949, file: Dr E. B. George, Gimmel-298/95, ISA.

33 Menachem Rosner et al., *Second generation: Between continuity and change on the kibbutz* [Hebrew] (Tel Aviv: Sifriyat ha-po'alim, 1978), 192.

34 The military justice system proved highly flexible on this topic. A legal services staff report from 2 June 1948, entitled 'The plague of plunder and theft', had the following to say about Jerusalem: 'The lack of legal authority over the Palmach which actually spearheaded the plunder issue constitutes an additional problem. Now Palmach commanders have already begun to see that they went too far, and they have occasionally turned to us for help eliminating this problem [that plagues] their ranks. I make a clear distinction between two types of plunder: private plunder – something for which I am prepared to prosecute officers and enlisted men to the full extent of the law; plunder by local commanders who took [the property] to "unofficial" unit warehouses. These commanders assert that the administration frequently proved unable to meet their needs, and, therefore, they went out and got the foodstuffs and fuel that they needed. This is against the regulations, but I am not prepared to pursue them right now while the war is going on.' Quoted in Zvi Inbar, *Scales of justice and the sword: Foundations of military law in Israel* [Hebrew] (Tel Aviv: Ma'arakhot, 2005), 831–2. On the Palmach's plunder of Princess Mary Street (today: Shlomzion Hamalka Street), see Report by Kidron, 28 May 1948, file: 2294/1950-2870, IDF.

requesting district headquarters' permission.[35] Referring to 'robbery by commander', Gideon Hausner, then Jerusalem's military prosecutor, came to the conclusion that 'a *very* high official' and officers were covering for one another.[36]

Many years after the war, commanders in the Palmach's Harel Brigade who participated in Jerusalem's conquest spoke of the city's depredation. Eliyahu Sela, the brigade's deputy assistant chief of staff for operations, told how

> they loaded our trucks with pianos and gold and burgundy armchairs. It was a terrible thing. It was a terrible thing. A soldier would see a radio, and he would say, 'Wow, I need a radio.' Then he would see a china service set. He would throw away the radio and take the china service . . . Soldiers pounced on beddings. They loaded more and more into their coats.

Amos Horev, who participated in the conquest of Katamon and went on to become an IDF general, told of his experiences:

> We went into truly luxurious homes. I was armed with a submachine gun, and I anticipated what was about to happen, so I fired at all the glass display cases and the ancient Chinese vases. I wanted to limit things to vandalism and avoid pillaging.

Brigade commanders knew enough to say that one of the senior commanders, who also went on to become an IDF general, 'decorated his [living room] with the best of what he looted in Katamon.'[37] One scholar asserts that this senior commander was Uzi Narkiss, then a battalion commander in the brigade, and that he stored the plundered

---

35   Levi, *Nine Measures*, 219.

36   Minutes of seminar of military prosecutors, 16 June 1948, file: 2294/1950-2882, IDF.

37   Quoted in Amira Lam, 'Not a platter and not silver' [Hebrew], *Yedi'ot Ahronot*, 18 February 2005. 'Jewish' pianos also disappeared. See the Land of Israel building syndicate to the Jerusalem district commander, 7 July 1948, file: Complaints, Gimmel-279/54, ISA. 'Our piano stood in the apartment of Augusta Bendik . . . the piano can no longer be found in this apartment. Since it is Jewish property and we are assuming that this piano might be found in a Haganah lounge, we are asking if His Honour [Mr] Baum might be able to help us [find] this instrument.'

property in the brigade infirmary.[38] Eventually, Gabriel Rapaport testified that he had 'served as a procurement officer' for his Palmach brigade.[39]

Eliyahu Arbel, the Etzioni Brigade's deputy assistant chief of staff for operations, told of soldiers 'wrapped in [stolen] Persian carpets'. One night, brigade headquarters sent him to Katamon because an armoured vehicle was cruising around the neighbourhood. The armoured vehicle, he explained,

> came to a frenzied halt [in front of me]. I approached it cautiously. Perhaps there were Arabs inside. Then we saw that it was filled with refrigerators, record players, carpets, and whatever you could think to want. The driver said to me: 'Give me your address. I will deliver whatever you want directly to your house.' I did not know what to do. Stop him? Kill him? I said to him, 'Get lost,' and he did. Afterwards, during the truce, we got our salaries. The neighbour tells my wife that there is a really cheap refrigerator for sale at this store. I went to it and the guy from the armoured vehicle was there. He said to me, 'I will give it to you for a hundred liras!' I said to him, 'Are you not ashamed of yourself?!' He answered, 'If you are an idiot, why do I need to be embarrassed?!'[40]

Yosef Ami, an Etzioni Brigade commander, asserted in an IDF History Department interview that 'we faltered [when we participated] in organized pillaging'. According to him, the Palmach and the military police were also involved in theft.[41] Gideon Hausner, then Jerusalem's military prosecutor, made a similar statement at a seminar of military prosecutors held in mid-June 1948. In his opinion, 'The theft wave' was 'the main problem'.

---

38 Quoted in Uri Milstein, *The Rabin file: A myth and its solution* [Hebrew] (Ramat Efal: Sridut, 2005), 118.

39 Gabriel Rapaport, interview, Collection of the Galili Centre for Defence Studies, 17 November 1983, YTA.

40 Quoted in Milstein, *The Rabin file*, 119.

41 Quoted in ibid. See also 'Announcement about cases where our people [Etzioni Brigade] acted in an improper way with the abandoned property in abandoned and conquered Arab settlements', Directive of the Etzioni Brigade staff, 18 May 1948, file: 6127/1949-119, IDF.

Palmach members were the first conquerors [to enter] . . . and they set the tone for the others. After them, the Field Corps arrived. The orders that should have prevented the pillaging were given hurriedly. Sets of conflicting orders were issued . . . the military police were one of the problems. When they organized it, they did not select the best [human] material; it was easy to get them to go along by including them in the pillaging etc.[42]

At the time, the newspapers wrote about military policeman who 'secretly' moved Arab property to their homes.[43] Yitzhak Ben-Zvi heard about soldiers' clubs decorated with 'silver utensils, pictures, and other luxuries', and soldiers and professional thieves working in the conquered areas were breaking into private homes 'and emptying them'. Military watchmen informed him that those who were mobilized 'divided their time in a "rational" manner: they used half their time to work, and they used the other half of their time to visit homes to rob and plunder.' He believed that officers taking a hard line in opposition to plunder and robbery were needed to prevent similar behaviour by civilians.[44] Pillagers frequently acted violently towards guards who did not participate in the despoliation. One night, seven armed men dressed in military uniforms entered a building in the city and stole three United Nations jeeps. Military Governor Dov Yosef told Ben-Gurion that they 'silenced' the guards by telling them 'that they were soldiers carrying out a military operation.'[45] After the thieves were caught, the decision was made to acquit them.[46] On another occasion, eight soldiers stole property from a neighbourhood contiguous with the German Colony right in front of neighbourhood residents (the homes they broke into had been designated for new immigrants from Cyprus).[47]

---

42   Minutes of seminar of military prosecutors, 16 June 1948.

43   Yakhin, 'Arab property and Israel's money in Jerusalem' [Hebrew], ha-Tzofeh, 16 June 1948. Indeed, policemen plundered. See the long list of property that was removed from the home of a policeman who plundered in Jerusalem and the correspondence pertaining to the matter in file: Property from the conquered territories, Gimmel-278-56, ISA.

44   Ben-Zvi, 'The topic of discussion'.

45   Dov Yosef to David Ben-Gurion, 16 December 1948, BGA.

46   Inbar, Scales of justice, 869.

47   Martial law officer, 'Thefts in the conquered territory', 16 October 1948, file: Complaints, Gimmel-274/54, ISA.

Gabriel Rapaport, a Palmach commander who participated in Jerusalem's conquest, explained that he took 'two trucks with boxes and pianos' from the city. Eventually, he would say that he had been told they were for the wounded. Rapaport said that part of what was pillaged went to training camps and Kibbutz Ein Harod in northern Israel. Yet there were also those who took booty for themselves.[48] According to Ya'akov Zahavi, who served in the Palmach's Fourth Battalion, people plundered money from banks and home safes in Katamon. Zehavi added that he was told that the money – at least what was not plundered individually – was meant for 'widows and orphans'. The money, he explained, did not reach its intended destination.[49] Zvi Zamir, a battalion commander who was later head of the Military Intelligence Directorate, explained how those assigned to the movement training camps 'pounced on equipment' in the quarries and 'took it to their agricultural settlements'. There were those who claimed that furniture from Katamon decorated kibbutz recreation rooms for years after the war.[50]

Eliyahu Dobkin, a Mapai party leader, wondered why an army would need 'to confiscate carpets or china'. He told of an officer who took a refrigerator:

> He had a girl lie down on top of a refrigerator, he placed the refrigerator on the truck, went through the roadblock, and shouted, 'a wounded

---

48 Rapaport, interview. In July 1948, Palmach commander Yigal Allon said: 'It is customary that appliances and essential daily necessities are taken for the conquering brigade's use, and a clearance [form] is submitted to the board overseeing abandoned property. That is how I acted when Safed was under my command. I took refrigerators, medical supplies, and cars. [Minister of the Interior Yitzhak Gruenbaum asks: "and Pianos?"] And Pianos. I took the refrigerators for the battalions that fought, refrigerators for the kitchens, radios for the common rooms. Pianos for the common rooms too. I saw it as a legal act. When I heard various rumours, I checked things out and people returned various things. These matters were conducted in an organized manner, and, in Jerusalem, things were done in coordination with the Jerusalem staff . . . 250 vehicles from the last convoy before Passover remained in Jerusalem. An order was given to return them immediately. I gave an order to take advantage of the empty vehicles headed down from Jerusalem and to load them with things that needed to be taken to the hospitals, the kitchens, and so forth'. Minutes of Committee of Five (evening), 4 July 1948, 6, BGA.

49 Quoted in Milstein, *The Rabin file*, 119.

50 Quoted in Lam, 'Not a platter and not silver'.

woman, a wounded woman'. He got through with the refrigerator. It is hard for me to understand [why] you need to destroy a piano [for firewood] to stoke the oven. I do not accept this, and I do not really understand it. [Similarly,] they entered the home of an old non-Jew, who was a friend of the Jews and had lived in Jerusalem for fifty years, and took the watch off his wrist, demanded money from him, and got forty liras from him. The old man cried, and not because they took his watch or his money.[51]

For months upon months, the pillaging continued unfettered. 'Police officials and city leaders have finally gone to war against robbery and plunder,' an *Al HaMishmar* correspondent reported almost a month and a half after soldiers and civilians had begun to gather up spoils. Police Commissioner Reuven Shraibman published an announcement calling on city residents not to participate in acts of plunder and theft, and to make an effort to protect their property and civilian lives.[52] And depredation did indeed claim lives. Netanel Lorch tells of a time when he was stationed at a command post in Notre Dame that a seriously wounded young man entered the building and told them that his friend was lying wounded near the monastery (a no man's land that was surrounded by Jordanian Arab Legion territory). Following a search, the friend was found lying dead, having suffered a direct hit from a shell. Lorch learned that during a briefing they had participated in the previous day, the two young men had found out about a 'treasure' near the monastery: a small carpet and sacks of food. 'The two of them had not even turned seventeen. They certainly deserved a punishment for such pillaging . . . yet

---

51   Minutes of the Mapai secretariat meeting, 13 June 1948. For more on the matter of carpets pillaged from Katamon, see file: IDF Platoon Commander Y. Danzig accused of thefts and plunder, Pei-15/13, ISA. Concerning the pillaging of pianos, in addition to the descriptions found throughout the book, it is worth noting the following affair: combat forces seized a piano from 'a man who was working with others to smuggle it into his home'. Since 'it was impossible to clarify which house this object was taken from, it was decided to give it to the platoon commander [Avraham] Nissenbum as a gift from the platoon for exemplary service'. About this, see the Letter of the commander of the Fifth Battalion's Third Platoon to the military governor of Jerusalem, 27 June 1948. The Military Governor's Office found this acceptable. See Military government district commander to Third Platoon commander, 2 July 1948, file: Property from the conquered territories.

52   Aryeh Tzimoki, 'Jerusalem diary' [Hebrew], *Al HaMishmar*, 1 July 1948.

was not the punishment God gave them a bit too extreme?' wondered Lorch.[53]

Jerusalem's police chief, Shlomo Sofer, announced that 'great efforts' were being made to locate looters in the city.[54] In fact, searches had been conducted in dozens of suspects' homes.[55] The journalist Aryeh Tzimoki reported that 'the efforts' had already achieved 'initial results': a number of people had been tried and received sentences of up to a month's imprisonment. Judge Günter Stoltz announced that in the future, he would sentence people much more harshly.[56] The district commander issued a proclamation stating that 'every act of confiscation that is not approved by the confiscation officer will be considered robbery'.[57] The district commander and the Etzioni Brigade issued an order to combat looting and theft:

> Acts of theft and robbery in Jerusalem's urban neighbourhoods ... are liable to dishonour our campaign and to debase the army's and the civilian population's moral standards ... Every soldier or civilian caught plundering or transporting stolen property in the conquered territories is liable to be shot on sight.[58]

'We are very worried' by the many acts of looting and theft, said the Jewish Agency spokesman, 'and we will do everything in our power to put an end to this situation.' The despoliation contributed to an increase in criminal behaviour, as *Al HaMishmar* reported:

---

53   Lorch, *Late afternoon*, 94. On the pillaging of property found in no man's land in Jerusalem and the dangers involved, see 'Removal of property from no man's land', 27 June 1948, file: Property from the conquered territories.

54   Tzimoki, 'Jerusalem diary'.

55   Ze'ev Lakvir [Walter Lacquer], 'Food ration to residents of Jerusalem increased' [Hebrew], *Al HaMishmar*, 25 June 1948.

56   Tzimoki, 'Jerusalem diary'. According to Laqueur's report mentioned in the previous footnote, sentences of up to six months' imprisonment were handed out.

57   'For the prevention of theft in Jerusalem' [Hebrew], *Al HaMishmar*, 24 June 1948. See 'Standing order to the military police in the conquered territories of Southern Jerusalem issued by the military governor', 8 June 1948, file: Jerusalem military governor, Inventory, J3-154, CZA.

58   'The topic of discussion – Discipline – Acts of robbery and looting', Military governor – the conquered territory in southern Jerusalem, n.d., June 1948, file: Jerusalem military governor, Inventory, J3-154, CZA.

Groups of Irgun and Lehi members, as well as 'private gangs', have gotten used to breaking into stores, hotels, and private homes 'to confiscate' all the property and transporting it to 'warehouses'. In most of these cases, the military police commanders have refused to respond or intervene. When they do intervene, they do so when it is too late.[59]

Circles within the Haganah believed that immediately after Katamon's conquest, a firm hand should have used with looters, 'but, due to the neglectful way that this matter was handled, nothing was achieved'.[60] It is noteworthy that the Jerusalem police chief agreed:

We are arriving late to the war against theft in combat zones. I witnessed a number of incidents and I have become convinced that regular police activity could prevent robbery and extortion... I witnessed how Irgun members broke into a store and how judicious intervention on site averted a robbery.[61]

A member of the Legal Services Staff wrote the following in a report from 2 June 1948, entitled 'The plague of plunder and theft':

This affliction has spread through all the units and has affected soldiers of every rank. It started in Katamon, and it has dispersed to all the conquered territories. The military police's hands are not unbesmirched, it appears, and this has made it impossible to wage an effective war against this evil. We have already tried dozens of people and we are asking the courts to sentence people more stringently. An especially painful aspect of this problem is the issue of officers. Pursuit of the war effort makes it so it is nearly impossible to throw them in

59   'The problem of thefts in Jerusalem'.
60   Ibid.
61   Quoted in Shlomo Niger, 'The Jerusalem police force during the transition from the British Mandate to the State of Israel, 1947–1948' [Hebrew] (master's thesis, University of Haifa, April 2013), 107. When they wanted to stop the pillaging, they did so successfully. See the 29 June 1948 letter sent by the Russian Compound base commander to the military governor, file: Property from the conquered territories. In it, he states: 'I am writing to inform you that by setting up roadblocks . . . and barbed [wire] we have greatly reduced the number of incidents of looting and theft in the conquered portions of northern Jerusalem during the last few days.'

jail. Yet enlisted men have come forward in the spirit of justice to say what they saw their commanders do . . . I certainly do not want to damage the war effort, but thefts and despoliation have taken on frightening proportions and our soldiers are so caught up in this activity that it endangers their combat readiness and their dedication to their jobs. I have personally visited the conquered areas, and I have seen that there is almost no store that has not been breached and almost no house that has not been robbed. I even saw groups actively pillaging. This is the situation in the area around Mamilla Street, in the German Colony and in Abu Tor (أبو ثور).[62]

A journalist who participated in a group tour of Jerusalem in July 1948 and reported on the looting concluded his article with the following sentence: 'Bring judges and policemen to Hebrew Jerusalem, because we have become like all the nations.'[63] Yet there were no judges. That is what can be concluded from a document written by the lawyer Asher Levitsky, a member of the Jewish Agency's Legal Committee. He asserted that 'horrific rumours about pillaging are making their way through Jerusalem's population', but 'there are no rumours about cases where people were tried, or robbers were given harsh sentences'. He also recommended some measures that could be taken in a 'forceful and visible' way to prevent further looting.[64]

David Werner Senator, one of the leaders of the Zionist intellectual group Brit Shalom and a Hebrew University administrator, wrote a letter to Ben-Gurion and the Haganah's Jerusalem District commander, David Shaltiel. In it, he noted that he

could [not] remain silent about the pillaging, both that carried out by groups in an organized manner and that carried out haphazardly by lone individuals. This theft has become a widespread phenomenon. It is not just taking place in Arab homes. They are also [looting] in the Jewish neighbourhood of Talpiot.

---

62 Quoted in Inbar, Scales of justice, 831. On the depredation of Mamilla Street, see 'Mamilla Street', 21 May 1948, file: Property from the conquered territories.

63 'Earthly Jerusalem' [Hebrew], Ma'ariv, 29 July 1948.

64 Asher Levitsky, 'The internal damage caused by plunder and food distribution snafus', 17 June 1948, file: S25\5634, CZA.

Like Yitzhak Ben-Zvi, Senator also distinguished between the expropriation of property and equipment needed for military purposes and the plunderers who descended onto property 'like locusts onto a field'. Senator described the streets of Jerusalem:

These days, when you pass through the streets of Rehavia, every step of the way you see old people, youths, and children returning from Katamon or other neighbourhoods with sacks filled [with] stolen goods. The booty is multifaceted: Refrigerators and beds, clocks and books, sheets and clothing ... The Jewish robbers have brought disgrace and dishonour upon us, and they have done serious damage to our moral standards! A terrible wantonness is spreading, both among youths and adults, because robbery is a contagious disease. They say that measures are being taken to prevent these acts. I am sorry to say that people do not perceive this ... I brought this matter to Interior Minister Gruenbaum's attention. He agreed with me, but he told me that the matter is in Mr Ben-Gurion's hands. He needs to determine how perpetrators will be punished. I was a soldier for three and a half years during the First World War ... I know that it is impossible to avoid a certain degree of licentiousness ... but I am convinced that if [the authorities] do not take up effective measures immediately and wait around for orders that have yet to come and will [likely] never come, because the man who needs to sign them is up to his ears in much more important matters, a cure for this disease will not be found.[65]

The necessities of war set priorities. Zipporah Porath, who was in charge of a first aid station in the city, wrote in her diary in mid-May that she was so absorbed in her job that she 'did the most terrible things without torturing [herself] about them. For example, out of necessity rather than malice, [she] rummaged through the ruins of an Arab hut.' Porath wrote that 'you stop thinking about the dead Arabs whose homes and possessions we use and think instead about the dead Jews, the friends and the parents'.[66] There were others who were more forgiving. In late May 1948,

---

65 David Werner Senator to David Shaltiel, 3 June 1948 (with a copy and an accompanying letter to David Ben-Gurion), BGA.

66 Tzipporah Porath, *Letters from Jerusalem 1947–1948: The War of Independence and the establishment of the State of Israel through the eyes of an American girl* [Hebrew] (Tel Aviv: Tcherikover, 1998), 172. It is important to note that some of the Katamon

Yoram Bar-Gal, who later served as a Hebrew University professor, wrote in his diary that Katamon's conquest 'offered salvation to the city. They brought back endless spoils from there.'[67] When the looting began, he testified to experiencing 'an unpleasant feeling' when he saw 'Katamon's spoils decorating our boys' bodies and their and their friends' rooms'. Bar-Gal wrote that they 'pinched' only small things, not furniture, but that is not accurate. That is the way that memory functions: over the years, the past takes on a rosier hue. In any event, he excused the behaviour of 'our boys' by asserting that they did not 'steal' and merely took 'permissible spoils of war'.[68]

There were others who saw things differently. In his memoirs, John Rose, an Armenian living in Jerusalem, wrote that during this period, Arabs' movement was restricted while Jewish residents were allowed to move around freely, and that this made looting possible. From the balcony of his home in Jerusalem's Bak'a neighbourhood, he observed pillaging 'on a fantastic scale, accompanied by wholesale vindictive destruction of property'. Rose explained:

First it was the army who broke into the houses, searching for people and for equipment that they could use. Next came those in search of food, after which valuables and personal effects were taken. From our veranda we saw horse-drawn carts as well as pick-up trucks laden with pianos, refrigerators, radios, paintings, ornaments, and furniture, some wrapped in valuable Persian carpets . . . Safes with money and jewellery were pried open and emptied. The loot was transported for private use or for sale in West Jerusalem. To us this was most upsetting. Our friends' houses were being ransacked and we were powerless to intervene . . . This state of affairs continued for months. Latecomers made do with what remained to be pillaged. They pried off ceramic tiles from bathroom walls and removed all electric switches and wiring, kitchen gadgets, waterpipes, and fittings. Nothing escaped: lofts and cellars were broken into, doors and

---

break-ins were carried out for defensive purposes or to care for the wounded. See *Jerusalem national guard corps collection* [Hebrew] (Jerusalem: Former National Guard Activists' and Haganah Member's Organization, 1964), 96.

67   Yoram Bar-Gal, *He who dreamed: Natan Shalem and his diaries* [Hebrew] (Tel Aviv: Defense Ministry Press, 2003), 236.

68   Ibid., 216.

windows hacked down, floor tiles removed in search of hidden treasures. Rooms were littered with piles of rubbish and as winter set in
rain poured into these derelict houses . . . It was unbearable to pass
these houses, so familiar, but now within six months become so
strange . . . We lived in the middle of a sea of destruction.[69]

Just as in Haifa, the looters did not limit themselves to 'abandoned'
property; they also undertook enterprising and violent break-ins to
Arab-owned homes whose residents were 'present' and living in their
homes. On 1 July 1948, one Saliba Zacharis wrote,

After it got dark, nine well-armed men arrived at the entrance to my
home and demanded that I open the door. I refused to let them inside,
and they burst down one of the doors, entered the building, took
whatever [property] they wanted, and put the spoils into a car that
was waiting for them . . . They were led by a policeman who had
entered the building on an earlier date, 29 June 1948, to examine the
rooms. Today, 3 July 1948, at two o'clock at night, eight men, a driver
and a truck filled with furniture came to my home, because they
wanted to take our piano. When I refused to open [the door], they
burst into the building and to my apartment. Afterwards, they took
the piano.[70]

The looters and the destroyers did not and could not differentiate
between the property of 'absentee' Arabs and 'present' Arabs. Hanna
Abdul Ahmad Kattan, a resident of Abu Tor, returned home to

---

69   John Rose, *Armenians of Jerusalem: Memories of a Life in Palestine* (London:
Radcliffe Press, 1993), 200, quoted in Nathan Krystall, 'The Fall of the New City', in
Salim Tamari, ed., *Jerusalem 1948: The Arab Neighbourhoods and Their Fate in the War*
(Jerusalem: Institute for Jerusalem Studies, 2002), 111. For the neighbourhood resi-
dents' report on the pillaging of their property, see Letter of representatives of the
Jerusalem [neighbourhood of] Bak'a to the Jerusalem district governor, 1 March 1949,
file: Ministry of Minorities representative in Jerusalem, Gimmel-297/62, ISA.
70   Saliba Zacharis to the military commander, 3 July 1948. This was not the only
time that men in uniform burst into the home and threatened the residents. Also see
'Robbery incidents', Martial law officer of the Southern District of Jerusalem, 7
September 1948, file: Complaints, Gimmel-279/54, ISA. Another time, armed soldiers
entered a Jewish-owned liquor store and stole its contents; Hayyim Yosef Raz to the
commander of District Three, 14 September 1948, file: Army complaints.

discover that everything in his home and his two stores had been taken, and that the buildings had been seriously damaged. The army, it seems, took the property. The Custodian's Office wrote to the Ministry of Minorities because the complainant was a 'present' Arab, meaning it was not authorized to provide compensation.[71] The looting and destruction in the homes of 'present' Arabs influenced their futures and their ability to return to their routines. Aziz Saleh Saba, a German Colony resident, wrote that his home 'was completely looted and destroyed, and all that was left was filth and torn paper scattered through the rooms . . . this fact fated us to remain [in the Red Cross centre] and that is where we are now'.[72] He wrote the letter in January 1949, seven months after the break-in to his home. The homes of foreign residents who were neither Jewish nor Arab were completely plundered too.[73]

The lawyer Netanel Lorch represented Greek and Armenian homeowners in Katamon. During a late May visit to the neighbourhood made in connection with his work, he recorded his general impression: 'A ghost town. All the breached homes have been completely looted'.[74] As previously noted, the situation there was similar to the ones in other Jerusalem neighbourhoods. Minister of Minorities Bechor-Shalom Sheetrit informed Dov Yosef, the city's military governor, that 'all of the belongings and furniture [in the] beautifully decorated' home of a mandatory government official in Bak'a 'had [been] stolen'.[75] The political organ of Palestinian Arabs in Mandatory Palestine, the Arab Higher Committee in Jerusalem lodged a protest to the armistice commission

71   See Hanna Abdul Ahad Kattan to the minister of minorities, 21 December 1948; Gad Machnes to the Custodian's Office, 13 February 1949; H. Bentel (legal counsel to the Custodian's Office) to the Ministry of Minorities, 27 February 1949; and additional documents in file: Hanna Abdul Ahmad Kattan, Gimmel-300/41, ISA.

72   Aziz Saleh Saba to the minister of minorities, 18 January 1949, file: Aziz S. Saba, Gimmel-299/102, ISA. Also see the long history found in file: Naim and Jamil Halbi, Gimmel-299/32, ISA.

73   There are numerous examples of this. See, for example, Letter of Herbert Ruben (apparently to the military governor), 30 June 1948, file: Army complaints. The Czech consulate was also pillaged. According to Moshe Sharett, the Irgun was responsible. Meeting of the provisional government, 11 August 1948. See David Ben-Gurion, *The renewed State of Israel* [Hebrew] (Tel Aviv: Am Oved, 1969), 282.

74   Lorch, *Late afternoon*, 108.

75   Bechor-Shalom Sheetrit to Dov Yosef, 16 November 1948, file: Z. Y. Albinah, Gimmel-298/26, ISA.

about the looting that had taken place in stores near Jaffa Gate and in Arab homes in Talbiyeh.[76]

Many homes in Jerusalem were vacated following Arab flight, and new immigrants and Jerusalem residents who were no longer able to dwell in their own homes, primarily due to their wartime destruction, were quickly sent to occupy them. Journalist Dov Genachowski wrote a short memoir about 'how people got housing in Talbiyeh' in 1948–49. The first way to lay claim to an apartment in Talbiyeh, Katamon, the German Colony, Bak'a, or the Greek Colony, he explained, was 'to go and move in, and sometimes that worked'. The second way to get such housing 'was through the bureaucracy, something that was much more complicated, but it offered a greater chance of success'. Genachowski describes the bureaucratic obstacles that somebody who 'wanted to get a place to live in these neighbourhoods' had to overcome. In the end, 'it was not the names that you knew that were important. They were not what really mattered. What really mattered were the bills given by hand.' Like in Haifa, corruption spread, and it was part of how things were conducted. To succeed, one needed the help of somebody 'in the upper echelons [of the government or the military]'.[77]

Rubin Mass, a Talbiyeh resident and the neighbourhood's Jewish mukhtar, explained his role in the settlement of Jewish refugees in the neighbourhood. 'The Arab residents' apartments were so big that two families were usually placed in each one and there are families who are still living in those apartments today.' Yet, as he described in his memoirs of the period, he also worked to protect the property of expelled residents. The Arab property remaining in each apartment was placed in a designated room that was closed off and affixed with a wax seal, and Jewish families were warned not to touch it.

> For three years, Arab property was protected in those sealed rooms. I think that it was the only place in the country where Arab property was protected in this way. Three years passed and the government sensed an urgent need for rooms for new immigrants and other

76   'The Arabs accuse the Jews of looting their property in Jerusalem and Jaffa' [Hebrew], *Haaretz*, 21 June 1948.

77   Dov Genachowski, *High society parties: And one hundred Jerusalem stories* [Hebrew] (Jerusalem: Karta, 1993), 98–102.

refugees. It [looked to make use of these rooms] and sent government workers to transfer all the property to warehouses. I do not know what the ultimate fate of this property was.[78]

The Talbiyeh Jewish Residents Committee asserted that the neighbourhood 'was the only place in Jerusalem where the enemy's property was not pillaged'.[79] This was not completely accurate. Yet it is clear that people pillaged less in this neighbourhood that they did in other Jerusalem neighbourhoods, perhaps because of the neighbourly relations existing between Jews and Arabs there.[80]

There were new Jewish inhabitants who tried to act justly towards the Arab residents who fled and in whose homes they now resided. Deborah Patinkin, wife of prominent economist Don Patinkin, who laid the foundation for economic studies in Israel and subsequently served as both provost and president of the Hebrew University, later spoke about her and her husband's efforts to connect with their Talbiyeh home's Arab owners: 'We looked for the owners, so that we could buy it . . . We thought that it was their right, that they were the owners. Therefore, we reached out to them.'[81] In contrast, the army took control of apartments of Arabs who remained in the city and did not pay them rent.[82]

---

78   Avraham Even-Shoshan et al., eds, *Ve'Im Bigvuroth: Fourscore years; A tribute to Rubin and Hannah on their eightieth birthdays* [Hebrew] (Jerusalem: Friends Press, 1974), 358–9.

79   The Jewish Residents Committee of the Talbiyeh neighbourhood to Bechor-Shalom Sheetrit, 26 August 1948, Container 1525, Jerusalem Municipal Archives (hereafter, JMA). I am grateful to Lee Rotbert for supplying me with this document, as well as the one cited in the subsequent footnote.

80   Rubin Mass to M. Cohen-Pirani, 3 August 1948, Container 1525, JMA. See the following report from February 1948 for information about relations between Jews and Arabs in the neighbourhood: 'The Christians complain about the poor way that they are treated by the Arabs, who are stealing everything found in homes on the border. The Arabs [meaning the Arab fighters from Hebron] bluntly announced to the people of Talbiyeh that if they continued to maintain good relations with the Haganah and to serve its members tea, they would act vengefully towards them.' See 'On the mindset and the actions of Arab Christians', file: 500/1948-60, IDF.

81   PECLAB, 'Interview with Deborah Patinkin, who lived on 5 Hovevei Zion Street for forty years' [Hebrew], by Tovi Fenster and Hagit Keysar, January 2018, video, 6 November 2018, youtube.com.

82   Vartan G. Matossian to Monsieur le ministre, 15 March 1949, file: Vartan Matossian, Gimmel-299/68, ISA.

Even six months after the city's conquest, the robbery and plunder had not been put to a stop.[83] A licentious atmosphere reigned, and it reached the point where soldiers were shooting at electric wires for the fun of it, causing blackouts in the city.[84] Military Governor of Jerusalem Dov Yosef wrote Ben-Gurion that since the truce, 'another wave of pillaging in homes in areas under military occupation has begun, and, this time, it is mostly Jewish homes in Talpiot [that are getting plundered]'. Yitzhak Levi, the city's military commander, had promised Yosef that he would act to stop the plunder, but it was still ongoing. Yosef wrote to Ben-Gurion, 'It would be useful if you told me that it is necessary to take control of the situation and to punish the criminals.'[85] This odd wording testifies to the central government's half-hearted effort to stop the looting. In another letter written that day, Yosef informed Ben-Gurion that his office was continuing to receive complaints about 'the renewed spread of looting in both predominately Jewish and non-Jewish areas'. He asserted that 'eradication of the problem' was dependent upon the commanders' actions. Yet he emphasized that the military could not be used as a means for achievement of this goal, because he had gotten the impression that 'the commanders do not really want to deal' with the matter. Furthermore, 'these acts are taking place in one of the army's primary strongholds'. He also concluded his second letter to Ben-Gurion with a request: 'I am powerless. Perhaps you can find a way to put an end to this plague.'[86] As in

83   See the numerous orders of the day issued by Military Governor Dov Yosef in file: The military government in the conquered areas of North Jerusalem, Gimmel-287/40, ISA.

84   Teva Company to the Sixth Brigade executive, 11 October 1948; Electric Company to the Jerusalem district commander, 23 November 1948; file: Army complaints.

85   Dov Yosef to the Ministry of Defense, 9 December 1948. BGA. See Letter of Dov Yosef to the Jerusalem district commander, 7 December 1948, file: Army complaints. On Dov Yosef's connection to the pillaging of Jerusalem, see Dov Joseph, *The Faithful City: The Siege of Jerusalem, 1948* (New York: Simon & Schuster, 1960), 144, 326–7.

86   Dov Yosef (military governor) in Jerusalem to David Ben-Gurion, 9 December 1948, BGA. See also Tz. Rekhes (military secretary) to Jerusalem district commander, 25 November 1948, file: Army complaints: 'There was a great deal of resentment among the city residents who were forced to abandon their property for reasons that had nothing to do with them . . . meanwhile, the situation has become so drastic that it requires a large-scale investigation and the taking of immediate action against the commanders who turned a blind eye to the robbery and theft that was carried out in the Talpiot, Arnona, and Ramat Rachel areas.'

Haifa, attempts by the (new) district commander, Moshe Dayan, to put an end to the pillaging proved unsuccessful. On the basis of the available historical evidence, it seems likely that Dayan only made a half-hearted effort to stop the looting.[87] After a few more months passed, the pillaging ended. There were no more spoils to reap.

87 Moshe Dayan, 'Thefts in the conquered territory', 16 December 1948, file: 1308/1950-441, IDF.

Jaffa

In November 1947, more than 70,000 Arabs resided in Jaffa. It was the largest and richest Arab city in Mandatory Palestine, and about 25 percent of the urban Palestinian population dwelled there.[1] An additional 10,000 Jews lived in the Jewish neighbourhoods in the north and centre of the city.[2] 'Only a few weeks ago, the Tel Aviv Municipality could have declared that that there is no reason for a quiet peace-seeking Arab to be afraid to walk around in the city,' wrote the pamphlet of 'Unity', a small binationalist Zionist political party, at the beginning of 1948. 'Today the Jew who dares to walk in the Arab quarter puts his life in danger, as does the Arab who enters a Jewish area.'[3] The proximity of the 'Jewish' city of Tel Aviv and the temptations that each city presented to its neighbour had an effect, for better and for worse, on the connections between the two nations. Until the Independence War, the two cities were not wholly distinct. Yet, during the Second World War, areas of HaYarkon and

---

1 Ya'akov Peleg, 'The battle of Jaffa and its surroundings', in Alon Kadish, ed., *Israel's War of Independence, 1948–1949*, vol. 1 [Hebrew] (Galili Centre for Defence Studies, 2004), 389–421. Statistics about Jaffa can be found on page 389.

2 Menachem Klein, *Connected: The story of the land's inhabitants* [Hebrew] (Tel Aviv: ha-Kibbutz ha-me'uhad, 2015), 82.

3 Unity Organization, 'Do not allow the mob to take control over us [1948]' [Hebrew], in Avraham Yassour, ed., *Jews and Arabs in the Land of Israel: Selected remarks of M. Buber, A. D. Gordon, and documents of Unity* (Givat Haviva: Institute for Arab Studies, 1981), 182.

Allenby Streets in Tel Aviv replaced Jaffa as the central recreational areas for Jews.[4]

When the United Nations voted in favour of the partition of Palestine, violence erupted in Jaffa.[5] In December 1947, the right-wing paramilitary Irgun blew up a barrel of explosives in the middle of the city, and a month later, another Zionist paramilitary group, the Lehi, set off a car bomb near the clock tower in Jaffa's town square. While many residents fled amid the tumult, along with local leaders, at least two-thirds of Jaffa's Arab residents remained there until the city's surrender in mid-April 1948.[6] From the Haganah's perspective, Jaffa was designated to be part of the Arab state; it was surrounded by Jewish territory, and, from a strategic perspective, it did not constitute a meaningful threat. The Irgun nevertheless decided to take the initiative in conquering the city. On 25 April, without consulting Haganah command, Irgun fighters launched an attack on Manshiya, Jaffa's northernmost neighbourhood. Irgun forces shelled the city ceaselessly, causing extensive damage. Later, it became known that the force fighting in the city had desecrated Arab corpses.[7]

In the days immediately after the Irgun offensive began, the British, who for reasons of their own wanted to prevent Jaffa from meeting a similar fate to the one that befell Haifa only days earlier, initiated an international diplomatic effort to avoid this.[8] Yet on 1 May, following a British ultimatum and subsequent agreement that led to the Irgun forces' departure from Manshiya, British soldiers who had been sent in to maintain order began to pillage. A Haganah synopsis of events stated that 'the soldiers were very happy to be sent to a property-filled city

4   For intermittent discussion of the relations between the two cities, see Klein, *Connected*, 78–148. See also Adam Lebor, *City of oranges: Jews and Arabs in Jaffa* [Hebrew] (Jerusalem: Carmel, 2010), 93–112.

5   Mikha'el Ben-Gal, 'Self-defence and attack', in Yosef Aricha, ed., *Jaffa: A historical-literary reader* [Hebrew] (Tel Aviv-Yafo Municipality Press, 1957), 239–41; Itamar Radai, *Palestinians in Jerusalem and Jaffa, 1948: A Tale of Two Cities*, trans. Haim Watzman (New York: Routledge, 2016), 136–67.

6   'A summary of "Hametz" operations in the Jaffa–Tel Aviv area', 2 May 1948, file: 922/1975-949, IDF; Benny Morris, *1948* (Tel Aviv: 'Am 'Oved, 2010), 170.

7   Daily summary, 2 May 1948, file: 105/94, Haganah Historical Archives (hereafter, HHA).

8   Arnon Golan et al., *The battle for Jaffa in 1948* [Hebrew] (Sde Boker: Ben-Gurion Institute for the Study of Israel and Zionism – Ben-Gurion University, 2017).

without people; they decided to "live it up in the dead city"'. Like the soldiers of the Egyptian and Iraqi expeditionary forces, the British proceeded to loot shops and stores for days on end.[9]

On 13 May, the eve of the mandate's conclusion, the Jaffa Emergency Committee, representing the Palestinian residents of the city, signed a capitulation agreement with the Haganah.[10] At this stage, the number of residents left in Jaffa had dwindled from tens of thousands to only 4,000. The absolute majority of the Arabs who evacuated the city had done so quickly, leaving extensive property behind. Following their expulsion, its proximity to Tel Aviv and additional Jewish settlements in the centre of the country enabled lots of people to participate in looting there.

Armed with knowledge about what had taken place in Tiberias and Haifa, the Haganah and the Tel Aviv Municipality acted to prevent looting in Jaffa immediately after it was conquered.[11] Soldiers were stationed at roadblocks, and announcements cautioning against plunder in the city were posted. In practice, however, little more than formal actions were undertaken. For instance, Tel Aviv mayor Israel Rokach issued a proclamation warning about the dangers inherent in 'any attempt to plunder', yet he lacked the power to actually prevent looting. In a letter, he cautioned Prime Minister Ben-Gurion about the situation that developed immediately after the city's surrender:

> Unfortunately, the merchandise in the warehouses and the utensils and furniture in private homes have been subject to shameful looting. We know that soldiers of every rank and from every brigade, military policemen, and even service heads participated in the plunder; they took merchandise without registering what they took or providing a confiscation order.

---

9   Kiryati [Brigade] to the fronts, 'What is going on in Jaffa', Survey 3–4 May 1948, 4 May 1948, file: 8275/1949-136, IDF; Avner to Tene, 'What is happening in Jaffa since the attack upon it', 6 May 1948, file: Aleph`/105/92, HHA; Avner to Tene, 'Events in Jaffa' on 7–8 May 1948, file: 8275/1949-162, IDF; Economic Defense Board, 11 May 1948, file: 105/146, HHA.

10   A copy of the Capitulation Agreement is in file: Agreement between the Haganah commander of the Tel Aviv area and the representatives of Jaffa's Arab population, Kaf 12/8-4, Jabotinsky Institute Archive (hereafter, JIA).

11   See, for example, Proclamation of the Haganah commander of the Tel Aviv district, 14 May 1948, Proclamation no. 630, IDF.

Rokach demanded that the prime minister take 'every possible step to halt the robbery and theft', to condemn what was going on, to return the property that was taken, and to take 'unbiased' steps against the looters. The mayor saw the extensive despoliation as something that 'was seriously overshadowing our heroic action'.[12]

Minister of Minorities Bechor-Shalom Sheetrit and Gad Machnes, ministry director, visited Jaffa immediately after it had been conquered, and they met with the commander of the city and his senior staff. At the ministry's request, stringent guidelines for the entrance of soldiers and civilians into the area were put in place. It was also decided that only the area commander and his representatives would be able to approve the removal of 'abandoned' equipment and materials useful to the army for conduct of the war (also, a list was to be provided to the military governor accordingly – a procedure that does not seem to have been subsequently followed). Finally, 'removal of anything else would not be permitted' unless directly approved by the governor.[13] These guidelines were only selectively applied – something that deeply saddened the Ministry of Minorities staff.

The British Jewish journalist Jon Kimche wrote that the first people 'to loot in a wholesale fashion' were members of the Irgun. While in the beginning they looted dresses and 'ornaments for their girlfriends . . . this discrimination was soon abandoned' and they began to snatch anything they could transport out of the city: everything from furniture and carpets to pictures and housewares. The venting of pent-up emotions through destruction and spoliation which had revealed themselves in all their hideousness in Tiberias, Haifa, and Jerusalem recurred in the resistance-less city. 'What could not be taken away was smashed. Windows, pianos, fittings, and lamps went in an orgy of destruction.'[14]

---

12   Israel Rokach to David Ben-Gurion, 28 May 1948, file: Emergency – Negotiations with the government, Brigade 4, file: 19 aleph`, no. 2, Container 592, Tel Aviv-Yafo Municipal Archives (hereafter, TYA).

13   Military Governor's Office in Jaffa, 'Summary', 15 May 1948, file: 321/1948-97, IDF.

14   Jon Kimche, *Seven Fallen Pillars: The Middle East, 1915–1950* (London: Secker & Warburg, 1950), 224. From the start of the war, the Irgun and Lehi plundered wherever they went. There was a report in January 1948 about the looting of Arab property in the Abu-Laban Orchard (today, the Geha Interchange area); Tene, 26 January 1948, file 105/62, HHA. When discussing the military efforts to conquer Jerusalem, Minister Moshe Shapiro said: 'Members of the Irgun held Sheikh Jarrah, a key location in

Subsequently, Haganah and Palmach soldiers 'join[ed] in the orgy of looting and wanton destruction'. According to Kimche, the looting could have been prevented, 'but it soon became a practice for which there was always a material incentive, a sophisticated justification, and an excuse'.[15]

'Indeed, for a time, it seemed that what had occurred in Haifa would not repeat itself', explained Communist Party member Ruth Lubitz days after Jaffa's surrender. 'In the beginning, rumours flew' about objects being removed from Jaffa and stolen. 'First, people whispered, and, afterwards, they screamed. At present, there is no need to discuss [the matter]'. Hundreds of people roamed through Jaffa and took what they could get. Shabazi Street, in particular, was the epicentre of non-stop traffic. 'Throughout the day you can observe all types of things being brought from Jaffa . . . an endless stream of children and adults carrying various types of furniture on their heads'.

Lubitz wrote about her visit to the city. It was difficult to make one's way through the destroyed city, and none of the roadblocks were functional. 'There is nobody protecting the city', she reported, and she immediately explained what she meant: therefore, 'one can steal here'.

> We run across women on our route; they are sweating from heavy exertion – they are lugging huge bundles of bedding and houseware, couches and other pieces of furniture! Panic and desperation fill their eyes – who knows if they will find what they left behind when they return, or more nimble burglars will get there first and take it.

Children of various ages, 'who knew how to move the goods', participated in the looting. As she put it, one does not need to watch out for soldiers on guard, because 'they do not really get in the way much'. While the women and children took part in light pillaging, the men worked together in organized groups and were able to carry out larger,

---

Jerusalem, for three days . . . they say that they spent those three days plundering.' Minutes of Committee of Five, 3 July 1948, 27, BGA. For a photo of an Arab living room in Jaffa with a large piano in it, see Walid Khalidi, *Before Their Diaspora: A Photographic History of The Palestinians, 1876–1948* (Washington, DC: Institute for Palestine Studies, 1984), 140.

15   Kimche, *Seven Fallen Pillars*, 224.

'more profitable' thefts. Lubitz describes the large-scale organized plunder:

All along the way, there is not a home, a store or a workshop that has not had everything taken from it. Valuable things and worthless things – everything, plain and simple! Papers, torn books, glass shards, and big piles of refuse were all that remained. The sight of ruins and piles of waste, with men roaming around between them, picking amidst the rags trying to get something for nothing, makes a shocking and lasting impression. Why not take things? Why be merciful? The heart is not given over to such thoughts, even though it is clear that the stolen property is the property of working people and the poor, who put in lots of sweat and hard work to get where they were. My heart aches most for these young people, men and women who never stop to consider the sordid nature of their deeds, and these children who, rather than studying or earning a livelihood, spend endless days pillaging, participating in this easy and unscrupulous 'work'.[16]

Ministry of Minorities official Y. Gefen wrote to Minister Sheetrit about his visit to the city a few days after its conquest, 'Throughout the day, I went around the city monitoring how things were being safeguarded. I saw soldiers, civilians, military policemen and sentries breaking through doors and walls to rob and plunder.' Gefen reported on a joint looting operation undertaken by members of the security forces that descended into a quarrel 'with yelling and language befitting a band of thieves'. 'Those on duty,' he asserted, did not deal with thieves who were caught as orders required; 'if one of the commanders knew them,' suspected looters were released without questioning. Gefen suspected that the military police were transferring goods from Jaffa to Tel Aviv. He said that an officer responded to a story about an Arab who tried to call the military police when his store was being robbed by saying, 'You should have shot the Arab.'[17]

---

16   Ruth Lubitz, 'On the purity of our war', *Kol Ha'am*, 30 May 1948. See also Ruth Lubitz, *I chose a life of struggle* [Hebrew] (Tel Aviv: Shahar, 1985), 436. For a completely different description that depicts order in the city, see Efraim Talmi, 'In conquered Jaffa', in Aricha, *Jaffa: A historical-literary reader*, 256–8.

17   Y. Gefen to Bechor-Shalom Sheetrit, 25 May 1948, file: Reports, decisions, and protocols in Jaffa from 23 May 1948 to 20 February 1949, Gimmel-306/77, ISA. See also Yosef Yizr'a'eli, *On a security mission* [Hebrew] (Tel Aviv: 'Am 'Oved, 1972), 98.

One soldier said that the looting's spread was 'a sight that was hard to forget'.[18]

Indeed, there were bands of thieves among the looters. In one apartment, a group of people 'gathered to divvy up the spoils: carpets, merchandise, crystal, clothing, and cameras'. This was 'an organized group of thieves' that included both soldiers and civilians.[19] Irgun soldiers would ride around in cars at night breaking into stores undisturbed.[20] There were people who hired children to loot for them.[21] In practice, nobody was keeping Jaffa safe. 'The population senses how weak the military police are, and this will lead to problems in the future,' wrote the assistant governor for security affairs.[22]

A report on efforts to prevent looting in Manshiya, in northern Jaffa, offers information about what was done to prevent looting (in cooperation with the Department for Arab Affairs). On 18 May, the report's author wrote:

> We found a large group of women, children, and men who stole whatever they could get their hands on: chairs, armoires and other furniture, housewares and kitchenware, sheets, pillows, other bedding and more . . . I divided my men into four squads: one for the beach [area], one for the Yarkon [area], one for the Mea She'arim [neighbourhood] and a squad for the Kerem HaTeimanim [neighbourhood] up until HaCarmel Street. We closed down the main thoroughfares, we patrolled the alleys, and we prevented new people from getting into the area. We captured those who were in the area . . . in many cases, we needed to employ force, and, in many cases, we needed to fire warning shots in the air . . . and we were forced to throw deterrent grenades . . . my men's strenuous effort and the use of force and weaponry enabled us to clear the area of thieves within a few hours . . .

18   Yehudah Tamir, interview, September 1990, file: 16-12/52/54, YTA.

19   'The topic of discussion: Division of the spoils from Jaffa', 25 June 1948, file: 105/26, HHA.

20   For documents about this, see file: The Irgun commander in Jaffa, Kaf 7/8-4, JIA.

21   'Send children to steal abandoned property' [Hebrew], Herut, 14 November 1948.

22   Assistant governor for security affairs to the military government staff commander, 7 June 1948, file: 1255/1953-316, IDF.

We were forced to release . . . the people, . . . because we did not receive orders about what we were supposed to do with them.[23]

Word of the looting and theft spread throughout the country and the world. A month after the surrender, Radio Cairo reported that Jaffa mayor Yousef Haikal (هيكل), who had left the city before it capitulated, was accusing Jews of acts of looting in Jaffa.[24] Jaffa Emergency Committee members admonished the authorities for the looting 'officers, enlisted men, and Jewish civilians, young and old' were carrying out in the city. According to committee members, the plunder 'was being carried out savagely'.[25] They also protested that despite their many appeals to have it stopped, it was ongoing.[26] In a letter to the Red Cross representatives, the Jaffa Emergency Committee noted that the Jewish authorities had caught armed soldiers looting Arab property, but that they had freed them immediately thereafter, and that they continued their work 'in the same exact areas where they had been caught only a few hours earlier'. In a few cases, 'we admit, the property was returned to its [rightful] owners'. The committee noted that merchandise and goods were loaded onto trucks in broad daylight. It was pointed out that 'this was done under Jewish officials' noses'.[27] Jaffa military governor Yitzhak Chisik was of one mind with the Jaffa committee on this point. He remarked that individuals and groups 'had not been given orders' to conduct searches. Instead, their 'goal was to rob and loot'. When they wanted to discover whether Jaffa's remaining Arabs were concealing weapons, 'their strategy was to beat them almost to death, so that they would reveal the hiding places'. Chisik opposed this approach with every ounce of his being.[28]

---

23   'Report on an operation to prevent thefts in Manshiya', 20 May 1948, file: 8275/1949-136, IDF.

24   'The Arabs accuse the Jews of looting their property in Jerusalem and Jaffa' [Hebrew], *Haaretz*, 21 June 1948.

25   '"The Emergency Committee" in Jaffa demands that the Arab residents be returned to the city' [Hebrew], *Kol Ha'am*, 2 July 1948.

26   Emergency Committee of Jaffa to the Representative of the Commander of the Haganah [in English], Tel-Aviv District, 3 July 1948, file: 1255/1953-316, IDF.

27   Emergency Committee of Jaffa to the Red Cross representatives in Jaffa and Tel Aviv, 21 May 1948, file: Conquered Israeli territories, Het Tzadi-2564/9, ISA.

28   'Summary of my comments [Yitzhak Chisik] presented to Mr Eliezer Kaplan and Mr David Horowitz on Saturday, 5 June 1948, at 11 o'clock in the morning, on the situation in Jaffa', file: Various reports, Gimmel-306/62, ISA.

Chisik, the governor responsible for normalizing relations in the city (the military was under his command), ceaselessly protested the treatment of Jaffa's remaining Arabs and the general attitude towards Arab property.[29] He wrote Minister Sheetrit, 'I must say, as you are quite aware, that most of the complaints Arabs have lodged are accurate.' Chisik noted that the steps that he had taken had improved the situation, and that the military was taking additional steps 'to get their men in line, to provide public safety', and to put an end to civilian looting. He sharply criticized the removal of goods and materials from the city at that time. Ostensibly, the army and the state were carrying out this expropriation for military reasons. Yet the military governor 'did not believe that the confiscation orders that were being given … were always justified'.

> Stores were still being broken into [so that goods and materials could be confiscated] and those that had been breached had not been resealed. I dare say that the assault on the property that still remains here – here I am not talking about the materials essential to the military and the war effort – is a serious mistake … you just need to look at the list of items that are being removed daily (30–40 truckloads per day) to see that what I am saying is true.[30]

At the same time that private, partially organized looting was taking place, legally and ethically questionable expropriation and removal of goods by the army and public administration was ongoing. Officially, one needed a confiscation order to remove goods, equipment, or furniture from the city. Yet here, too, lawlessness spread. Governor Chisik reported to the Finance Ministry that furniture was being removed from private homes even 'when the confiscation order indicated a completely different address'. This furniture removal took place before the eyes of controllers on behalf of the military government, and Chisik suspected 'that the controllers knew that this was forbidden and intentionally ignored this fact'. The military governor gave strict orders and demanded

---

29   'The topic of discussion: Summary of meeting between Kiryati [Brigade] and Yitzhak Chisik', 24 May 1948, file: Arab Affairs – Abandoned property, Gimmel-5670/29, ISA.

30   Yitzhak Chisik to Bechor-Shalom Sheetrit, 1 June 1948, file: Conquered Israeli territories, Het Tzadi-2564/9, ISA.

that those who did not follow them be arrested, writing, 'This variety of criminal should be locked up for a long time.'[31] This is not how things actually functioned. Chisik demanded that confiscation of furniture from private homes be stopped 'at least until the government reaches a decision concerning the Arab requests to return to Jaffa'.[32] He did not know that the decision had already been made, principally and informally, not to allow their return.

Red Cross representatives occasionally arranged visits to Jaffa, and Chisik suggested that furnishings not be removed during the ceasefire that went into effect in July. The matter, he remarked, 'usually [makes] a very sombre impression'.[33] Alongside the sombre impression made, the confiscation and looting of property put issues of law and principle to the test.

Arab Committee members protested to the governor about the seizure of not just the property of residents who had left the city, but the property of those who remained. 'His honour certainly remembers that the capitulation agreement promised the residents that after they were identified etc., they would be allowed to resume their lives,' Chisik wrote to Minister Sheetrit. Chisik asserted that Arab residents who were present in Jaffa should not have their property expropriated: 'If property, like a factory, is needed for production of materials needed for the war effort, then it needs to be expropriated and operated in its current location in pursuit of this goal. Its machinery should not be removed.'[34] He protested to the minister who oversaw his work when Ben-Gurion sent him an order that explained that the Ministry of Finance 'could approve the removal of any type of property and that it did not need to receive my prior authorization'. In fact, the governor was only required to arrange 'how the items would be removed from the area'.[35] On 24 May, Ben-Gurion appointed Akiva Persitz, as Ministry

31   Yitzhak Chisik to Akiva Persitz (Ministry of Finance), 20 June 1948, file: Confiscations (Expropriations), Gimmel-306/76, ISA.

32   Yitzhak Chisik to Yosef Ya'akovson (Central Purchasing Commission), 30 June 1948, file: Confiscations (Expropriations).

33   Yitzhak Chisik to Yosef Ya'akovson, 21 June 1948, file: Confiscations (Expropriations).

34   Yitzhak Chisik to Bechor-Shalom Sheetrit, 2 June 1948, file: Confiscations (Expropriations).

35   Chisik to Sheetrit, 1 June 1948. See David Ben-Gurion to Yitzhak Chisik, 22 May 1948; David Ben-Gurion to Yosef Ya'akovson, 22 May 1948; BGA.

of Defense administrator, to supervise the city's abandoned property. One scholar has asserted that this appointment 'took control over the handling of abandoned property in Jaffa out of the hands of the Ministry of Minorities'.[36]

Chisik was convinced that there was little to indicate that a 'very large' portion of the property removed from the city was essential to the war effort. It certainly was not important enough that stores and warehouses needed to be broken into in a disorderly fashion or without preparing lists of what was taken. Among the things that the army took away – and it is impossible to know if they really made it into military hands – Chisik listed 'women's clothing, tricot and men's underwear, candies, furniture and carpets from offices and homes etc. etc. In short, this is a really grave situation.'[37] The military governor's letter conveys a great deal of frustration:

I do not understand why there is a discrepancy between the sentiments of the leaders who oppose everything that is going on and who see it as something negative that we are liable to eventually pay a high price for and [the actions of] the various warehouse and office managers who see Jaffa as an endless font and who are only interested in getting everything they can without consideration of the effects.[38]

What superficially looked like 'a discrepancy' to someone of Chisik's level of authority in fact voiced a political disagreement between high-ranking Israeli officials. Chisik did not publicly express his criticism of how decisions were made and carried out. In a conversation with Red Cross representative Jacques de Reynier, he said that the confiscation of goods did not violate the surrender agreement and that exact lists of goods removed from the city were being kept. Chisik was lying, and he knew it. In any case, the property problem was not a problem, unlike prisoners of war or the wounded, that the Red Cross was charged with addressing.[39]

---

36 Arnon Golan, *Wartime spatial changes: Former Arab territories within the State of Israel* [Hebrew] (Sde Boker: Ben-Gurion University, 2001), 89.

37 'Summary of my comments [Yitzhak Chisik]'.

38 Chisik to Sheetrit, 1 June 1948.

39 Memorandum summary, 'Meeting of Mr Chisik with Mr de Reynier and Mr Guye from the Red Cross', 22 June 1948, file: Conquered Israeli territories. See the

In a conversation with Minister of Finance Eliezer Kaplan and David Horowitz of the Ministry of Finance, Chisik complained that the terms of the surrender the military government had signed with the Arab representatives was not being upheld. The agreement stated that Arab residents would remain free and that it would be forbidden to arrest them, and that property in the city would remain in place and go untouched. 'These two terms are not being upheld', he said, and were being 'systematically violated' by the Israeli side. This found expression in the 'removal of goods and products through theft and expropriation', as well as in the attitude of the army to Jaffa's residents and their property. Chisik protested against the non-stop spoliation and looting being committed by Irgun and Haganah soldiers – and 'all those who have successfully infiltrated the city' – and the 'detentions and illegal searches, the beatings and arrests, thefts, and especially the killings'. Chisik treats as fact the violation of the terms of the surrender agreement by the command-ers of the forces in Jaffa – though he was not certain if these viola-tions were being committed 'intentionally or unintentionally'. In any case, he noted that the soldiers' 'discipline is so poor that there is no way of controlling them'.

Chisik remarked 'in anguish' that as military governor, he had issued explicit orders not to break into homes and stores, which were not being followed. 'Not only do they do not take [these orders] into consideration, but, when speaking with Arabs, they also make demean-ing remarks about me, something that dishonours me and the state that I represent as military governor.' Despite what was written in paragraph 6 of the surrender agreement (it stated that Jaffa's Arab residents would not be detained), dozens of Arab residents were arrested. Chisik not only saw this as 'extremely base' but found it troubling that he, the mili-tary governor, had not been told the names of the detainees and where they were being held. According to him, many of the arrests were completely unjustified. Chisik drew a connection between this fact and 'the discovery of the corpses of five to ten dead Arabs. His honour [Kaplan] has certainly heard about the sexual assaults.' He explained that one could describe what the army was doing in Jaffa in great detail,

protocol of the conversation and additional correspondence in file: The Red Cross and the UN, Gimmel-306/82, ISA.

'but the main thing is that the army does not recognize the [capitulation] agreement or any need to honour it, and it allows itself to do whatever it wants – something that makes it very difficult for me'. In his criticism of the military's behaviour in Jaffa, Chisik was not alone. The chief military prosecutor, Avraham Gorali, addressed the handling of fifteen Arabs' murder:

> An abominable act like the one that took place in Jaffa – if Arabs had committed [it]! Yet they never committed an act like [it]! That they allowed such soldiers to continue serving and that they covered for them when tens of officers knew about it – it is frightful. That the army would not act to punish such a soldier and would let him continue to bear arms – this is the whole battalion's crime.[40]

As previously mentioned, alongside the private looting (whose scope Chisik succeeded in substantially reducing following the lawless days immediately after the city's conquest), Jaffa-office-approved expropriations – in violation of the terms of surrender – continued unabated. Yet Chisik remarked, 'there is no substantive difference or boundary between private property, public property, and the property of residents who have remained in place. The city is ransacked and pillaged, and anybody passing through will be embarrassed when he beholds the ignominious destruction.' Chisik demanded that a decision be made concerning how the terms of the surrender agreement would be honoured. He also looked for allies supportive of his view that 'clear orders concerning how Arabs should be treated' needed to be issued. 'He wanted an end to detentions, beatings, home demolitions, murders', an end to the expropriation of present Arabs' property and a 'temporary' delay in the removal of property from unbreached warehouses.[41]

---

40   Minutes of seminar of military prosecutors, 16 June 1948, file: 2294/1950-2882, IDF.

41   'Summary of my comments [Yitzhak Chisik]'. In the next few months and throughout 1949, many Arabs who had remained asked the authorities to return property that had been expropriated from them. Many times, as we have seen and we will see, the expropriation was illegal. Sometimes, the state did not pay the price that had been agreed upon.

A few days after the city's surrender, Minister Sheetrit arrived in Jaffa for a meeting with the members of the local Arab Committee who represented the remaining Arab residents. Sheetrit, who spoke fluent Arabic and was well versed in Arabic culture, had long been a welcome guest among Palestinian Arabs. Committee member Ahmad Abd al-Rahim (عبد الرحيم) opened the meeting by saying 'that we feel lucky that a long-time friend of the Arab population, who knows our language, our customs and our manners, heads the department that will be dealing with issues related to us'. Committee members praised Governor Chisik who 'understands our feelings and has shown himself to be extremely honest and devoted to his job'. Yet, he asserted, the committee understood that 'Chisik lacks the means necessary to uphold the terms of the capitulation agreement'. The committee members spoke at length about the theft of their property. 'We observe our city in the final stages of its destruction and the wholesale theft being carried out in it daily to the detriment of its [current] residents and those who departed it without doing any harm to your army or your government. Right now, we are sorry that we stayed. We do not know what we will tell those who return.'

Committee member Ahmad Abu-Laban (أبو لبن) conveyed his understanding that the governor wanted to prevent looting but had proved unsuccessful. The committee protested the wholesale removal of goods from the city, and 'that no store or home has remained unviolated. All the goods in the port belonging to Jaffa residents have been taken or are being taken.' Even though the governor had promised to place food in special warehouses to meet residents' needs, Abu-Laban noted that they had begun to remove food too. The committee demanded that a 'decisive order' be issued to prevent food 'and things unconnected to the war effort' from being removed from the city. Abu-Laban, who owned a factory (together with a Jewish partner), was himself one of the victims of the confiscation policy. 'They removed all the machinery from my factory and stole [it],' he complained. However, what bothered Abu-Laban most was not the confiscation of the machinery in his factory but the destruction wrought there:

We do not know what to tell residents whose homes have been destroyed and whose property has been stolen without justification. What fate awaits the store owner, shopkeeper, or barber who finds his business destroyed or looted? How can such behaviour be justified?[42]

Minister Sheetrit, who oversaw Governor Chisik, remarked in a letter to other cabinet members that the governor felt so 'helpless that he was considering quitting his job, especially after organized and haphazard plunder and looting spread like a plague'. Sheetrit, Chisik, and Gad Machnes, the director of the Ministry of Minorities, had met with various military forces and made arrangements for a 'standard procedure' for handling Arab property, but these arrangements, the minister explained, had been cancelled or violated immediately after they had been made. Minister Sheetrit and Governor Chisik saw eye to eye on this matter, and they opposed the continued expropriation of the property of Arabs who had remained in the city. 'Please order the expropriation department,' Sheetrit wrote Ben-Gurion, 'not to confiscate the property of remaining residents until the government establishes a clear and detailed policy concerning this matter . . . that I have ceaselessly raised'.[43] No order was ever given.

On 21 May 1948, days after the city's conquest, Sheetrit met with Prime Minister Ben-Gurion and presented him with a plan that would give the Ministry of Minorities centralized authority over the handling of the Arab population and its property. The prime minister never responded. Sheetrit wrote to the other ministers:

Today I visited Jaffa. I learned that people are breaking into stores and homes and stealing things. [Afterwards,] they leave them wide open and other thieves continue the work. [Meanwhile,] those who have permits to remove certain goods remove other goods for personal use and leave the places where they searched for what they needed wide open for anybody that follows . . . there are lots of military policemen in the streets, but they are no better than anybody else.[44]

---

42   Minutes of a meeting in the Military Governor's Office in Jaffa, 3 June 1948, file: Various reports. For more on Abu-Laban, see Yoav Gelber, *Independence versus Nakba* [Hebrew] (Or Yehudah: Dvir, 2004), 405–6.

43   Bechor-Shalom Sheetrit to David Ben-Gurion, 5 July 1948, file: Conquered Israeli territories.

44   Bechor-Shalom Sheetrit to members of the government, 26 May 1948, file: Various reports.

The lawlessness on the streets continued, as demonstrated by another letter Chisik sent to Sheetrit, which complains of the lack of answers to a number of burning questions that came up in a meeting with Kaplan. 'Since our meeting, things have not gotten better. On the contrary, they have only gotten worse,' he remarked. Even though the soldiers stationed in Jaffa were formally under the military governor's authority, this fact 'did not reflect reality'. The people who were out in the field came up with a way to handle things: representatives of the various branches wandered the city, entering into abandoned or occupied private homes to search for 'all types and kinds of property. Then, when they returned to [Tel Aviv], they would go to the expropriations office to submit a request that asserted that these items were essential to their work.' On 11 June, the date the letter was written, Chisik noted that ninety truckloads of furnishings were removed from Jaffa.[45]

A report documenting the outpouring of goods from Jaffa during a three-week period in May–June 1948 provides the following data: On 9 June, sixty-five 'truckloads left Jaffa'; on 10 June, 106 truckloads left Jaffa; on 16 June, 137 truckloads left Jaffa; on 18 June, 155 truckloads left Jaffa. At the bottom of the table, the author noted that 'the average weight of each truckload was approximately four tons'. For 6 June to 18 June, 1,291 trucks carrying 5,164 tons of goods left Jaffa.[46] In the report, composed in mid-July, Chisik wrote that from the day the office had been established (26 May) until the day the report was written, more than 5,000 trucks with 20,000 tons of goods, valued at 1.5 million liras, had departed the city. He estimated the value of looted property at 'no less that an additional half million liras'.[47]

As in Jerusalem, after the moveable property had been pillaged and nothing more of value was left in the homes, people began to dismantle the homes themselves. They removed floor tiles, doors, shingles, and more (a behaviour that recurred in conquered villages and cities).

---

45 Yitzhak Chisik to Bechor-Shalom Sheetrit, 11 June 1948, file: Various reports.

46 Report of the Jaffa office's activities from 24 May 1949 to 18 June 1948, file: Reports, decisions, and protocols.

47 Yitzhak Chisik, 'Monthly report of the Jaffa government', July 1948, file: 6127/1949-161, IDF. Also see the memorandum of Moshe Erem about 'expropriation' and looting in Jaffa that Minister Sheetrit sent to the prime minister. Bechor-Shalom Sheetrit to David Ben-Gurion, 30 June 1948, file: Destruction, plunder, and looting, 307/27, ISA.

'Lately large trucks have been bringing old shingles from Jaffa and the surrounding villages,' protested the Communist Party newspaper *Kol Ha'am*. Shingles taken off the roofs of Arab homes in Jaffa and sold in Jerusalem sold for seventy mils, while a Jerusalem-made shingle cost 150 mil. 'Up until now the municipal and governmental institutions have not gotten involved in the matter. Does the pillaging of shingles and the damage it is causing in Jerusalem not concern them?' wondered the newspaper.[48]

It was not just the Communists who were bothered by the impact of pillaging and looting on commerce. In a letter to Cabinet Secretary Ze'ev Sherf, the General Merchants Association complained about the plan of the Office of the Custodian of Abandoned Property's to auction off carpets belonging to displaced Arabs; it noted that its members were frightened by the government's and its officials' plan to acquire 'abandoned carpets'. These carpets' origins 'were not in doubt', the association pointed out, and their sale would flood the market and 'undermine the livelihoods of every carpet merchant'. The association's opposition to the government's plan was not just economically motivated. 'One fine day, when peace is achieved and their owners visit [governmental offices], they might find carpets that once belonged to them. Such potential strife far outweighs the perceived benefits.' By buying the carpets and selling them outside the country, the association saw a way to 'prevent such a damaging effect'. As the association stressed, this suggestion was not proffered for 'business' reasons.[49]

On 25 July, two months after his appointment, Governor Chisik decided enough was enough and quit his job.[50] There was no doubt about why: the government did not support his efforts to prevent Jaffa's sacking. Despite numerous entreaties, meetings, and discussions, the looting, the pillaging, and the expropriations continued. A month before Chisik resigned from his position, he wrote the commander of forces in

---

48   'Stolen shingles in Jerusalem's markets' [Hebrew], *Kol Ha'am*, 17 December 1948.

49   Sector secretary and the sector chairman, General Merchants' Association of Tel Aviv, and Jaffa to Ze'ev Sherf, cabinet secretary, 10 October 1948, file: Complaints and demands (in the carpet sector), Gimmel-306/78, ISA; Cabinet secretary to the Jaffa office, 'Carpets for the prime minister's home', 23 August 1948, file: Furniture and office equipment from abandoned property, Gimmel-9040/7, ISA.

50   Dan Yahav, *Jaffa, bride of the sea: From her chief city to poor neighbourhoods – a model of spatial inequality* [Hebrew] (Tel Aviv: Tammuz, 2004), 307.

Jaffa to express his incredulity that the military courts had not acted: 'Despite numerous incidents where soldiers were caught stealing, arrested, and sent to the security officer, I have not received even one report indicating that a criminal had been sentenced.'[51] Subsequently, there were just a few trials. One of the prosecutors stated that 'the thefts in Jaffa had become an infectious disease that had spread to our soldiers there.'[52] 'During my visits to Jaffa,' wrote the Israeli police's inspector-general, 'I always ran into people picking through the city's breached stores. Unfortunately, staffing shortages render us unable to take charge of the situation.'[53]

In July, a month and a half after the city's conquest, the editorial board of *Al HaMishmar* received an anonymous letter. Its author complained about a report describing a tour of Jaffa that had appeared in the newspaper a few days earlier:

Anybody who knows even a bit about what is going on in Jaffa cannot see this article as anything more than an attempt, perhaps an unintentional one, to cover up things that there is no reason to cover up. You are certainly aware of the scandal of wholesale pillaging and expropriation in the city that are completely divorced from the war effort. The 'failures' your reporter discusses in his article are not actually failures. On the contrary, they are regular activities tolerated by those in positions of authority. They are not only, or even principally, 'a legacy of the initial period', as the article stated. A progressive worker's newspaper should not paint an overly rosy portrait of what is going on in Jaffa, especially today's situation.[54]

---

51   Yitzhak Chisik to the commander of forces in Jaffa, 21 June 1948, file: 6127/1949-61, IDF. A month later, Sheetrit wrote: 'Please provide me with a detailed list of criminal trials carried out by the military against soldiers found in possession of abandoned property and what the verdicts were in those cases.' Bechor-Shalom Sheetrit to the IDF chief prosecutor, 18 July 1948 (and additional documents in the file), file: General, 307/16, ISA.

52   Quoted in Zvi Inbar, *Scales of justice and the sword: Foundations of military law in Israel* [Hebrew] (Tel Aviv: Ma'arakhot, 2005), 762.

53   Yehezkel Sahar to Bechor-Shalom Sheetrit, 29 August 1948, file: Military governor of Jaffa, 1255/1953-133, IDF.

54   A. B., 'Impressions from Jaffa' [Hebrew], Letters to the editor, *Al HaMishmar*, 5 July 1948.

Chisik certainly would have agreed with the anonymous author.

The lawyer Meir Laniado was appointed Jaffa's new military governor. In a meeting of representatives from the Ministry of Minorities, the Ministry of Finance, and the Jaffa Arab Committee, it was determined that expropriations and confiscations of furniture, household necessities, and personal property from private homes would not be allowed.[55] In the beginning of July, Sheetrit continued to work to put a stop to the expropriations. Despite being the minister responsible for overseeing the condition of the country's minorities, his opposition to the many acts of expropriation failed to slow the ceaseless movement of goods out of the city.

Pillaging also took place around Jaffa.[56] The residents of the village of Salama (سلمة), just to the east of the city, abandoned it at the end of April; in July, the military removed barriers that were preventing residents from entering it. Tel Aviv's chief municipal inspector turned to the city manager and demanded that he oversee the village's protection, because 'all kinds of suspicious people are beginning to wander around in the area, and they will invade the village, empty it, destroy its homes, etc.'[57] In fact, the plunder had started two months earlier, 'when criminals from the Hatikva neighbourhood' dismantled homes in the village. The supervisor informed the police about this too.[58]

Four months after Jaffa's conquest, pandemonium still reigned, pillaging was going on everywhere, and violence had not abated.[59] In one case, soldiers entered a home, beat the couple living there with a rifle butt, and stole a great deal of property: ten carpets, clothing, a radio, a clock, and more. In another, soldiers broke in 'and, after tying up [the residents] and gagging their mouths', they stole money, carpets,

---

55   Minutes of the meeting on the Jaffa situation, 4 July 1948, file: Confiscation (Expropriations).

56   'They are reporting from Salama that [members of the Haganah] found various civilians wandering in its fields . . . and they are taking stuff to the Hatikva neighbourhood. A grenade or a bomb in one of [the looters'] bags seems to have exploded and killed a child.' See News, 9 May 1948, file: 105/94, HHA. Also see News from 2 May 1948, HHA. The same thing was going on in the village of Yazur: 'Stealing abandoned property' [Hebrew], Al HaMishmar, 1 September 1948.

57   H. Alperin to the city manager, 25 July 1948, file: Emergency – Refugees from outlying neighbourhoods, Gimmel' 04-20, Container 598, TYA.

58   H. Alperin to the police chief, 24 May 1948, file: Emergency – Refugees.

59   Dov Shafrir to Meir Laniado, 17 October 1940, file: Military governor of Jaffa.

blankets, and more. There are numerous appalling examples. Laniado turned to the Forty-First Regiment commander and asked that he look into the events.[60] In a letter to Sheetrit, Laniado wrote, 'I would like to respectfully inform you that I have made no headway.'[61] In another case, two soldiers entered a home, threw the mother and father out of the house, and raped a twelve-year-old girl.[62]

Israeli sailors stationed in Jaffa pillaged property, destroyed homes, and beat Arab residents ceaselessly for days. The unit commander in Jaffa wrote that copious appeals and the submission of numerous reports concerning the sailors' behaviour had not resolved the issue. 'Quite the contrary, there had been no improvement in the situation.' He provided details 'about only two frenzied nights'. The list of what the sailors did is long and detailed: They robbed stores, they broke into homes, and they beat women and men. The sailors also had no problem threatening an Arab policeman when he demanded that they stop stealing. 'It is clear that this list is not complete,' wrote the Jaffa commander.[63] Governor Laniado wrote Prime Minister Ben-Gurion that when he took up his position, he arranged meetings with the military commanders, the police, and the Attorney General's Office to address the depredation. Now, civilians who had committed acts of theft were being brought before magistrates, and soldiers were being arrested. The sentences were ridiculously lenient. After great effort, eighteen sailors had been arrested.[64]

According to an investigation, even staff members of the Ministry of Minorities' Jaffa office, who had pledged to protect property and to restore order, were involved in despoliation. In August 1948, while transferring 'abandoned' property from the Jaffa police warehouse to the custodian's central warehouse, 'two policeman and a controller accompanying the goods stole a sack full of carpets'. There were other

60   Meir Laniado to the commander of the Forty-First Regiment, 10 September 1948, file: Plunder in Jaffa, Gimmel-306/79, ISA.

61   Meir Laniado to the Bechor-Shalom Sheetrit, 20 September 1948, file: Plunder in Jaffa.

62   Office of the military governor of Jaffa, 'Summary', 15 May 1948, file: 321/1948-97, IDF.

63   Commander of the military unit in Jaffa to the Kiryati [Brigade], 28 July 1948, file: 6127/1949-161, IDF.

64   Meir Laniado, 'Weekly report of the activities of the military governor in Jaffa', 4 August 1948, file: 580/1956-252, IDF.

reported cases, and because efforts were made 'to cover things up', one can assume there were many other cases that did not leave a paper trail. As one police inspector explained, 'he tried to cover things up when policemen and controllers were involved.'[65]

The Jewish soldiers and civilians who entered Jaffa brought widespread destruction, treating the city like it was theirs to do with as they pleased. The various Christian communities complained about vandalism in their cemeteries; following these complaints, Governor Laniado visited one of the sites and reported to Minister Sheetrit:

It pains me to tell you that horrible deeds have been carried out. People shattered numerous gravestones, intentionally shot off crosses crowning the tops of headstones and vandalized expensive statutes of Italian marble in horrifying ways. The damages come to hundreds of liras and perhaps more . . . I estimate that the total cost for repairs will come to at least fifteen hundred to two thousand liras.[66]

It turned out that members of the Eighty-Ninth Battalion who vandalized things defiled the cemetery out of boredom.[67] In a different case, soldiers broke into a church and stole what was inside: chalices as well as silver and gold crucifixes.[68] Sheetrit demanded that the Eighth Brigade's prosecutor investigate the cemetery's desecration. It appears that the investigation went nowhere.[69] The vandals did not discriminate, and they did serious damage to the city's Muslim cemetery too:

---

65   Tel Aviv district headquarters, Complaints of the custodian of enemy property lodged against the Jaffa police, 23 September 1948, file: Department of Criminal Investigation, Lamed-95-39, ISA. Also see Report of the inspector general in charge of Jaffa checkpoints, September 1948, file: 1860/1950-1, IDF.

66   Meir Laniado to Shalom-Bechor Sheetrit, September 1948, file: Conquered Israeli territories.

67   'All of the signs point to only one possible option – that that unit [the Eighty-Ninth Battalion] is the one that damaged the cemetery,' wrote the commander of the Forty-First Battalion to Meir Laniado, 14 September 1948. On this affair, see the documents in file: Conquered Israeli territories.

68   Y. Eli (security officer) to the head of the military unit in Jaffa, n.d., beginning of August 1948, file: 6127/1949-161, IDF.

69   Inbar, *Scales of justice*, 1000.

All of the headstones were desecrated and destroyed. Most marble exteriors were not stolen. Instead, they were shattered into tiny pieces and scattered around. The iron and wooden bars that were around a few of the graves were pulled out and some of them were stolen . . . We kicked out a bunch of young punks who were vandalizing and stealing things there yesterday too.[70]

The magnificent Hassan Bek Mosque (حسن بك), built by Jaffa's Ottoman military governor in 1916, was the target of vandalism. 'People are continuing to damage the mosque near Jaffa,' Chisik informed the police. 'On a daily basis, floor tiles and stones are being removed.'[71] One of the reports noted that 'floor tiles and the stones used to build the stairs are disappearing' and 'the place is beginning to look like a ruin'.

The situation was similar in Jaffa's Siksik Mosque (سكسك). 'All that remains of the mosque are its roof beams, and they will soon be gone too,' reported an official from the Israeli government's Muslim Department.[72]

I passed by the Siksik Mosque, and I saw a Jewish youth removing the last of the floor tiles that covered the stairs . . . [the mosque] has been desecrated in a shameful manner. The doors and the window shutters have been torn off their hinges, the tiles have been removed from the floors and wood beams in the ceiling have been removed.

The mosque recalls 'a ruin, and, in a number of ways, it resembles the Hassan Bek Mosque'.[73]

70   Shmuel Yeivin (director of the Antiquities Department) to director of the Department for Muslim Religious Affairs, Ministry of Religions, 14 March 1949, file: Muslim holy sites, Gimmel Lamed-44864/16, ISA.

71   Yitzhak Chisik to the Ministry of Police, 17 March 1949, file: Oversight of Muslim holy sites, Gimmel-308/140, ISA. Also see Yaakov Yehoshua (chief assistant of the Muslim Department) to the Minister of Religions, 3 December 1948, file: Arab holy sites, Gimmel-307/42, ISA.

72   Report of Yaakov Yehoshua, chief assistant in the Muslim Department, ca. March 1949, file: Oversight of Muslim holy sites. See also Report from the Ministry of Religions on Israeli mosques (Jaffa addendum), 10 February 1949, file: Muslim holy sites.

73   Yaakov Yehoshua, 'A visit to the mosques of Jaffa', 14 January 1949, file: Visits in the South, Gimmel-46524/10, ISA.

Just as in Haifa, a decision was made to remove the remaining Arabs from their homes and to group them in an assigned neighbourhood. Soon after, Governor Laniado told the city's Arab Committee, 'It would be best if there were special areas for Jews and areas for Arabs.'[74] Arriving in Jaffa to talk with the committee members, Sheetrit tried to convince them to comply with the forced transfer. 'We cannot oppose the military authorities' wishes,' he said to them. He promised them that notables and the elderly would be allowed to remain in their homes – a proposition to which the Israeli army objected.[75]

Moshe Erem, director of the Ministry of Minorities' Department for Rehabilitation and Cultivation of Arab Relations, expressed to the minister his objection to the Arabs' segregation. Erem asserted that the decision to place all the Arabs in the Ajami neighbourhood (العجمي), which was surrounded by Jewish neighbourhoods on all four sides, did not make military sense, as those responsible for security said it did.

> One should assume that everybody agrees that there is no longer any reason to fear that we will be unable to maintain security in and around the city. Yet that is not enough for them. They are about to set up a barbed wire fence around the Ajami neighbourhood that will meticulously separate the Arab neighbourhood from the Jewish settlement. The arrangement will give Ajami the appearance of a hermetically sealed ghetto. This idea arouses way too many horrible associations, and it is hard to reconcile oneself to it.

Erem wrote about one of the original explanations given to justify the fence: it was intended to protect the Arabs, not the Jews – 'lest the Jews

---

74   Meir Laniado to David Ben-Gurion (and others), 27 July 1948. The committee members expressed their opposition to this decision. See Meir Laniado to David Ben-Gurion (and others), 28 July 1948, file: 580/1956-252, IDF. On how the transfer was conducted, see 'The execution of the transfer of Jaffa's residents to the security zone', 16 August 1948, file: 1860/1950-1, IDF.
75   Bechor-Shalom Sheetrit to David Ben-Gurion, 13 August 1948, file: Conquered Israeli territories. Commander of Tel Aviv district headquarters to Meir Laniado, 28 August 1948; Bechor-Shalom Sheetrit to General Elimelech Avner, 9 September 1948; file: Conquered Israeli territories. See also the documents in file: Transfer of the Arabs to the security zone (to the ghetto), Gimmel-96/306, ISA.

burst into Ajami'. This argument shocked him. 'Do all of us really have a history of rampaging and running amok?' Of course not, he argued, and he demanded that the military and the police take decisive action, and thereby 'restrain [the Jews'] base desires'.

Just as the Mapam Arab Department's Yosef Waschitz pondered the young state's future direction following the concentration of Haifa's Arabs (as cited in the earlier discussion of Haifa's despoilation), Erem mulled over the segregation of Jaffa's Arabs: 'Once again we unnecessarily, and without reason or purpose, do something that plants poisonous seeds in the hearts of Jaffa's residents. A barbed wire ghetto, a ghetto, lacking access to the sea. Is this going to be our governmental policy?'[76] Based on the military governor's report from 13 August 1948, historian Yoav Gelber wrote that Erem's objection bore fruit and the fence was not erected.[77] Yet in the cited report, there is no discussion of this. In the report, the military governor wrote: 'I am considering the possibility of using less barbed wire and allowing greater freedom of movement to the Arabs, so they will not feel like they are in a detention camp.'[78] Isma'il Abu Shehadeh (شحادة), a city resident, explained that 'they fenced us in and there were three gates. You could only leave the area to go to work in one of the orchards on the city's outskirts, and to do this you needed a corroborating [document] from your employer.'[79] A report from February 1949 records that the Ministry of Minorities worked to obtain permits for Arabs, 'so that they could go outside the barbed wire fence'.[80]

Apart from bureaucratic struggles and the disorder caused by settling new immigrants in the city, soldiers and civilians were carrying out

---

76 Moshe Erem to Bechor-Shalom Sheetrit, August 1948, file: General relations, Gimmel-302/56, ISA.

77 Gelber, *Independence versus Nakba*, 406.

78 Meir Laniado, 'Weekly report of the activities of the military governor in Jaffa', 13 August 1948, file: 580/1956-252, IDF.

79 Quoted in Lebor, *City of oranges*, 140. See also Muhammad Abu-Sarari, *The Story of Muhammad Abu-Sarari* (Ra'anana: Docostory, 2000), 41: 'Until 1951, we lived in a ghetto. You could not leave without a permit . . . Jaffa was surrounded by a fence. A fence stretched from Yefet Street to the hospital on Kedem Street and guard stations ran alongside it.'

80 Memorandum on activities of the Ministry of Minorities (May 1948 –January 1949), file: Memorandum on activities of the Ministry of Minorities, Gimmel-304/63, ISA.

organized 'invasions' of homes and buildings.[81] Sailors stationed in Jaffa and a battalion of the Alexandroni Brigade invaded the area assigned to Jaffa's Arabs 'with force and the threat [that they would deploy] an armoured vehicle'.[82] Arab property was plundered and moved out of the city using another armoured vehicle.[83] The Alexandroni Brigade's military prosecutor explained:

> The wholesale pillaging has lasted years and people almost all the way to the top of the government bureaucracy [are involved.] I have been contacted by serious people from the subdistricts and they are ready to work with us, but the first thing we need to do is get rid of the gangs, otherwise we will not get anything accomplished. I could confront them immediately, but we would need to arrange that with those higher up. People have already come to see me to tell me 'not to get involved in such things' and that 'somebody is going to shoot me'. Somebody needs to do something.[84]

Prime Minister Ben-Gurion wrote to Israel Defense Forces chief of staff Yaakov Dori that he saw the act of invasion as 'an unmatched example of undisciplined behaviour and [an example of] improper use of weapons and the command authority granted to an officer'; he asked that this message be disseminated in the press.[85] New immigrants, civilians, and soldiers invaded homes that did not belong to them. The decision was made to remove all residents from their apartments and to group them in 'predetermined locations, with each resident placed together with others from his/her group, and to then settle each group

---

81   Dov Shafrir to the cabinet secretary, 2 September 1948, file: 121/1950-204, IDF; Dov Shafrir to Giora Youseftal 1 September 1948, file: 121/1950-204, IDF; Memorandum written by Tzvi Simon on the subject of unpermitted entrance to Jaffa, 22 September 1948, file: 121/1950-183, IDF. See also the correspondence in file: Olim invasions, Gimmel-306/94, ISA.

82   Elimelech Avner (commander of the military government in the Occupied Territories) to Yaakov Dori, 13 September 1948, file: 121/1950-183, IDF.

83   Commander of the Irgun unit in Jaffa to the commander of the forces in Jaffa, 18 May 1948, file: Commander of the Irgun unit in Jaffa, Kaf 7/8-4, JIA.

84   Minutes of seminar of military prosecutors, 16 June 1948.

85   David Ben-Gurion to Yaakov Dori, 13 September 1948, file: 120/1950-183, IDF; Yaakov Dori to the Eighth Brigade Commander, 23 September 1948, file:121/1950-183, IDF.

– soldiers' families, new immigrants, victims of war, and government officials' families – in an area designated for it'.[86] As in Haifa, seven months after Jaffa's conquest, the home invasions continued with almost no effort made to stop them. 'The welfare officers and the unit commanders need to be told to put an immediate stop to the invasions of homes and apartments in the deserted territories by solders' families,' the minister of defence's adjutant ordered the IDF chief of staff.[87] In December 1948, soldiers from the Oded Brigade's Ninety-Second Battalion appeared at a Jaffa home armed with machine guns and rifles, and seized control of it. When military personnel looked into why they did this, they learned that the soldiers had received instructions from 'the Nation Welfare Officer for Housing to occupy vacant homes in the Jaffa area and lay claim to them, so [their possession of them] would be a fait accompli'. At the area commander's request, they left the home and informed the welfare officer who sent them to Jaffa that 'he should provide them with housing without resort to illegal home invasions'.[88] Not all the home invasions were necessarily carried out with the intention of harming Arabs. For instance, in May 1949, soldiers broke locks placed by the Israeli Ministry of Health on a building designated for use by the Dajani hospital (now the Tzahalon Medical Center) and entered it. Being experienced, they placed guards at the gate lest others enter the building.[89]

In Sheetrit's opinion, the problems stemmed not just from the army but also from Dov Shafrir, the custodian of abandoned property; senior officials at the Ministry of Minorities agreed with him. Following disagreements between Governor Laniado and Shafrir, the minister of

86   Cabinet secretary, 13 September 1948, file: 121/1950-183, IDF. See the detailed report of Aharon Hoter-Yishai from 9 September 1948 on this topic. IDF chief of staff Dori had asked him to look into the invasion, file: 121/1950-204, IDF. See also Report on actions undertaken to organize housing for soldiers' families in Jaffa, 11 October 1948, file: 121/1950-183, IDF. On the anarchy that reigned, see D. Giladi, 'Three [different] authorities fight over Jaffa' [Hebrew], Ma'ariv, 29 September 1948.

87   Nehemiah Argov (the minister of defence's adjutant) to the IDF chief of staff, 8 December 1948, file: 121/1950-223, IDF.

88   Moshe Nakdimon (commander of Battalion 141), 'Invasion attempt of a unit from the Ninety-Second Battalion' , 13 December 1948, file: 121/1950-223, IDF. In the coming months, the invasions continued. See 'The Jaffa governor's weekly report for January and earlier February', 7 February 1949, file: 580/1956-252, IDF.

89   Haim-Moshe Shapiro (minister of health) to David Ben-Gurion, 22 May 1949, file: Apartment invasions, Gimmel-340/41, ISA.

minorities wrote that he, like the military governor, was dissatisfied with the custodian:

> It is clear to me now that the time has arrived for me to appoint a controller to supervise everything going on in Jaffa. I received complaints every day. They are always giving the residents the runaround, and they treat Arab property like it is theirs, whether it belongs to a present Arab or an absentee one. The lawlessness in Jaffa as manifested in the emptying of furniture from homes is on the rise.[90]

Following the expulsion of Arabs from their homes, the matter of furnishing 'the new' homes that had been allocated to them became a topic of discussion: 'To the best of our knowledge, there was no furniture in the homes that the Arabs were offered, because every home that did not have an owner or a guard was completely emptied.' Five months after the city's conquest of the city, Jaffa had been picked clean.[91] As in other cities conquered by the State of Israel, almost nobody was tried in Jaffa. Up until August, no more than sixty-two civilians had faced trial for possession of stolen property in the whole Tel Aviv district.[92] Soldiers who plundered the city almost never saw trial. In the Eighth Brigade, for example, a number of cases were opened, but all were closed.[93] Indeed, the idea of bringing widespread charges was farcical, given that everybody had been involved in the depredation – soldiers and civilians alike. Just like Governor Chisik, Governor Laniado turned to Ben-Gurion demanding that he act to prevent the spoliation. 'The process of liquidating Arab property is drawing to a close . . . if there are goods that have been sold or taken without permission – those who have taken them or purchased them cannot hide them in plain sight.'[94] He demanded enforcement to prevent private looting.

---

90   Bechor-Shalom Sheetrit to Eliezer Kaplan (minister of finance), 3 September 1948, file: Olim invasions.

91   Meir Laniado to Bechor-Shalom Sheetrit, 17 October 1948, file: Reports, decisions, and protocols.

92   'Statistics submitted by the police pertaining to abandoned property trials from 15 May 1948 to 12 August 1948', file: General, Gimmel-307/16, ISA.

93   Inbar, *Scales of justice*, 1000–1.

94   Meir Laniado to David Ben-Gurion, 3 September 1948, file: Destruction, plunder, and looting, 307/27, ISA.

In August, soldiers receiving orders from 'on high' had deviously removed thirty-five truckloads of furniture from Jaffa – in other words, the property had been pillaged by army official mandate.[95] Yitzhak Gevirtz, manager of the Arab Assets Department in Israel's Office of the Custodian, wrote that the military authorities were transferring responsibility from brigade to brigade to 'cover up the fact that a local commander stole abandoned Arab property and his direct commanders were not interested in punishing him for it'.[96] In mid-June, Ezra Reichert, the military prosecutor for the Tel Aviv area, said that it was hard to know where the goods leaving Jaffa had ended up:

> When was this plunder and when was this confiscation? This is just semantics. In cases where the commanders [pillage], there is nothing that you can really do. The phenomenon of pillaging is so widespread. If we start examining things closely, we would need to dismantle the brigade and we would not have an army . . . 'The new chapter' question is a serious one. There will always be a new page. When will the pages run out? When there is nothing left to steal? Then they will steal from Jews.[97]

Prosecutor Reichert was correct. Around the time he made his remarks, Jewish stores and businesses were being emptied out in Jerusalem after Arab homes had been left in ruin by Jewish pillagers. Sheetrit was concerned about what might happen next. In October 1948, he asserted that the degree of lawlessness in Jaffa was so great that people should be worried about the creation of 'permanent criminal organizations that will endure for generations and spread throughout Tel Aviv too'. He painted 'a dark portrait of the absence of

---

95   Y. S. Chelouche (assistant director of the Ministry of Finance's Jaffa office) to Dov Shafrir, 13 September 1948, file: 121/1950-83, IDF. For a similar incident, see Inbar, *Scales of justice*, 753–4. There were also legal expropriations. For example: Olim (recent immigrants) soldiers asked to take furnishings from the available Arab property. Second Platoon commander to the commander of the Naftali Battalion, file: 4663/1949-125, IDF.

96   Yitzhak Gevirtz to the military prosecutor, 17 June 1948. See also Response of the commander of the Kiryati Brigade to the IDF chief of staff, 24 June 1948, file: 2506/1949-91, IDF. See also Inbar, *Scales of justice*, 762–3.

97   Minutes of seminar of military prosecutors, 16 June 1948.

authority, wantonness, acts of looting and pillaging, [home] invasions, and total anarchy' in the city. The ministers continued to
demand that Prime Minister Ben-Gurion intervene.[98] In Jaffa's case,
as in others, it was already too late.[99]

---

98   Report of Minister of Agriculture Zisling on the discussion in the Ministerial
Committee for Abandoned Asset Affairs, 19 October 1948, file: Administration –
Abandoned Property Committee, Gimmel-2186/21, ISA.

99   'How long will this anarchic wave of break-ins to Jaffa homes continue?
Yesterday, they again reported on cases of break-ins to Arab residents' apartments in the
Ajami neighbourhood and the theft of things from them . . . How many articles have
been written, how many speeches have been delivered, and how many serious warnings
have come from the lips of ministers and senior commanders? Yet the responsible
authorities have still not put an end to manifestations of lawlessness. To our great sorrow
and shame, thefts, violations of transportation regulations, home break-ins, and infiltration and invasion of abandoned property, which belongs to the government, have
assumed a prominent place in our history . . . How long will this go on?' 'Lawlessness in
Jaffa' [Hebrew], ha-Boker, 16 December 1948.

Acre

The goal of Operation Ben-Ami, launched in the final days of the British Mandate in May 1948, was to add the Western Galilee to the territory allocated to the Jewish state in the 1947 UN Partition Plan. As part of this operation, Haganah forces conquered Acre. The offensive, taking place from 13 to 14 May and overseen by Moshe Carmel, did not encounter significant resistance. Having conquered Haifa the previous month, Carmel's brigade had headed north through Arab villages until it arrived in Acre. Following the shelling of the city, Haganah forces stormed it, quickly seizing the upper hand. Acre's residents, after learning of the fall of Arab Tiberias and Arab Haifa, had already been in low spirits. On 17 May, Carmel told city notables that they were surrounded and that 'if they continued their resistance and did not surrender within a half hour – we will completely and totally annihilate you.'[1] On 18 May, the city waved the white flag and capitulated.[2] Thirteen thousand inhabitants had resided in Acre in 1946, but following Arab Haifa's fall, many refugees had moved there and the city's population had swelled to almost 40,000. After the occupation, only 5,000 Arab residents remained.[3]

1   Moshe Carmel to the urban notables of Acre, 17 May 1948, in Moshe Carmel, *Northern battles* [Hebrew] ('En Harod: ha-Kibbutz ha-me'uhad, 1949), 159.

2   Benny Morris, *1948* (Tel Aviv: 'Am 'Oved, 2010), 187.

3   Arnon Golan, *Wartime spatial changes: Former Arab territories within the State of Israel* [Hebrew] (Sde Boker: Ben-Gurion University, 2001), 177.

Immediately after seizing control, the Carmeli Brigade established martial law in Acre. Unlike Tiberias, Haifa, or Jaffa – cities with mixed populations and/or Jewish settlements in close proximity – there were few Jewish civilians in the immediate area, and their entry into the city, built within the confines of ancient walls, was forbidden. Despite the limited number of primary sources concerning the aftermath of the conquest, especially in comparison with the numbers of sources documenting what occurred in the large cities, one learns that here, too, looting and pillaging took place. A member of Kibbutz Ein HaMifratz, established in 1938, noted that he 'was in Acre at the start of the occupation. The pillaging was still ongoing. Things were stolen in Nahariya too. There was no oversight over people's behaviour, especially what they did with property.'[4] The army confiscated all the radios in the city.[5] Subsequently, soldiers broke into the safe of the al-Jazzar Mosque (الجزار), then the country's largest mosque, which contained a lock of hair said to have belonged to the prophet Muhammad (in Islamic tradition, Muhammad shaved his hair during his final pilgrimage, or Hajj, to Mecca; his escorts, the Sahaba, saved the hair). According to a government report on the incident, the soldiers were looking for money, and they did no harm to the Islamic relic.[6]

In the initial days after the city's conquest, residents living in the new city were ordered to remove the furniture from their homes and change their places of residence. Following issuance of this order, invaders broke into numerous homes and stole the furniture.[7] Tzvi Sapir, the

---

4   Diary entry, 29 May 1948, of A. Vitaly (?), file: Conquered Israeli territories, Het Tzadi-2564/10, ISA. See also the complaint of Doctor Bernik, an Acre resident, about what happened to his property: Dr Bernick, Gimmel-298/86, ISA.

5   'The conquest of Acre and its condition today', 9 June 1948, file: 105/92/ Bet`, HHA.

6   Haim Zeev Hirschberg (director of the Department for Muslim Religious Affairs) to the minister of religions, late August 1948, file: Conquered Israeli territories, Het Tzadi-2564/9, ISA.

7   'Report on the situation in Acre', 26 June 1948, file: 105/260, HHA. Tzvi Sapir of Kibbutz Ein HaMifratz wrote the following to the Ministry of Minorities on 2 September 1948: 'Since the city's conquest, I have been guarding the property of one of its residents, Afu Shukeiri (الشقيري), brother of Ahmad Shukeiri). The aforementioned has been my friend for many years. His lands border the lands of the kibbutz and, as a neighbour, he has done many things to aid my kibbutz . . . Part of his property is safely in my hands, but I am very concerned about his property in the city of Acre itself. *In fact, it is the only house that remains untouched* . . . Nothing has been taken from it . . . In my

Israeli Ministry of Minorities official placed in charge of handling minorities property in Acre and the Upper Galilee, wrote that the military government in Acre and the surrounding villages 'was seriously flawed'. 'Total lawlessness reigns and has led to the victimization of highly vulnerable Arabs,' he wrote. He remarked that people should question the ability of the bodies to which the city commander had granted authority to carry out their mandate:

> If one would like to characterize that period properly, it would be as follows: A period of pillaging and extortion when every Jew had the opportunity to steal Arab property without any repercussion... When we [first] started working, we endeavoured to guarantee the safety of Arab property. In practice, I dealt with a few cases where work animals and tools had been stolen. The investigations that were undertaken with the aid of government officials bore fruit and robbery cases ceased immediately. Law and order gradually became entrenched with the establishment of an Israeli police station in Acre. It has gradually expanded its activities, and today it operates throughout the whole area. Concerning this, one can state with certainty that from the moment that the long arm of the law was felt, lawless acts came to an end.[8]

Plunder and violence went hand in hand in Acre too. 'A group of soldiers who wanted to rape a girl killed her father and wounded her mother, and their commanders wanted to cover it up,' explained Avraham Gorali, the first IDF chief prosecutor.[9] One of the participants in the murder

---

opinion, this is not the only case where we should have protected the property of an individual whose relationship with us is commendable.' A copy of the letter can be found in Yehoshua'a Lurie, *Acre – the walled city: Jews among the Arabs, Arabs among the Jews* [Hebrew] (Tel Aviv: Yaron Golan, 2000), 531–2, emphasis added.

8   Tzvi Sapir, 'Report of my activities working in conjunction with the military government in Acre and the western Galilee', 13 February 1949, file: General report concerning Acre, Gimmel-310/58, ISA.

9   Quote from diary entry for 5 July 1948, David Ben-Gurion, *The War of Independence* [Hebrew], ed. Gershon Rivlin and Elhanan Oren (Tel Aviv: Defense Ministry Press, 1982), 576–7. Zvi Inbar wrote that there were a number of incidents of rape in Acre and that all of the cases were closed. Zvi Inbar, *Scales of justice and the sword: Foundations of military law in Israel* [Hebrew] (Tel Aviv: Ma'arakhot, 2005), 657–8. Yet at least one case was taken to trial. See file: 922/1975-1033, IDF. Carmeli Brigade military prosecutor Moshe Ben-Peretz explained: 'The platoon commander

and attempted rape was tried and given a three-year prison sentence.[10] A year after the city's occupation, the popular committee representing Acre's residents to Ben-Gurion demanded that 'the onslaught on homes and the theft of their property be stopped immediately, and that stolen goods be returned to their owners'.[11]

---

knew about it immediately after it happened. With the assistance of an Acre priest, I was able to see the girl. It was a terrible and despicable act. Every one of the commanders chose a different way to justify their failure [to pass on what they knew] for more than twenty days. In this way, almost every lead was lost. Many of them did not want to remember what had happened at all; they claimed that the names of those involved were never written down and that they did not know who they were.' Minutes of seminar of military prosecutors, 16 June 1948, file: 2294/1950-2882, IDF.

10   On this matter, see the soldier's letter to David Ben-Gurion requesting a pardon on 2 December 1948, and the opinion given to the IDF chief of staff by Eitan Avissar (of the Military Court) on this topic, 20 December 1948, file: 121/1950-165, IDF.

11   Hussein Muhammad Hussein (حسين, Popular Committee secretary) to David Ben-Gurion, 31 May 1949, file: The Acre Popular Committee, Gimmel Lamed-17102/7, ISA.

Safed

In the medium-sized city of Safed, unlike in the other mixed cities whose pillage is described above, relations between members of the two national groups were already tense. Difficult and blood-drenched memories of riots in 1929 and 1936 haunted the city's Jews.[1] At the beginning of 1948, 1,500 Jewish residents and ten to twelve thousand Arab residents lived in the city. As the British deployment of forces for many years made evident, Safed constituted a linchpin for control of the Galilee; as such, the city's conquest was a primary strategic objective of the spring 1948 offensive Operation Yiftach.[2] Sporadic violence had already begun that January, and when the British withdrew in mid-April, the battle for the city got underway. It soon became clear that the assailants – a combination local Jewish forces, Haganah forces commanded by Meir Meivar, and a Palmach platoon under Elad Peled's command – were neither properly equipped nor of sufficient numbers to advance. As such, they awaited the arrival of the Palmach's whole Third Battalion under Moshe Kelman's command.

---

1   Shmaryahu Ben Pazi, *A community at war: The Jews of Safed during 1947 and 1948* [Hebrew] (Jerusalem: Ariel, 2006).

2   On the conquest of Safed, see the following two articles: Mustafa Abbasi, 'The Battle for Safad in the War of 1948: A Revised Study', *International Journal of Middle East Studies* 36, no. 1 (February 2004): 21–47; Alon Kadish, 'A Reexamination of "a Reexamination" – Comments on Mustafa Abbasi's Article', *Katedra* 107 (2003): 149–54. Kadish's article is a response to the publication of the Hebrew original of Abbasi's article.

On 1 May, Third Battalion soldiers took the villages of Biriyya (بيريا) and Ein Zaytun (عين الزيتون), north of Safed, and blew up the homes in the villages – something Safed's residents observed. Soldiers from the Palmach's Third Battalion massacred tens of Arab prisoners in Ein Zaytun – an atrocity that, in contrast with what happened in Deir Yassin, was concealed for years. To this day, few details about the killings have come to light It is clear that many of the soldiers opposed the murder of prisoners, and that the decision to do so did not come from the brigade command.[3] The shelling of Safed and the Palmach soldiers' entrance into the city triggered mass flight, as coordination in the Arab Liberation Army (made up of volunteer fighters from Arab countries) quickly broke down and they fell easily to the Jewish forces. An Israel Defense Forces report reads: 'The city descended into chaos, and flight from the Arab area began with screaming and yelling.'[4] In fact, on 10 and 11 May, all that remained for the soldiers to do, from a military perspective, was to search the abandoned neighbourhoods.[5]

Even though Safed, like Acre, was not an especially large city, its plunder left its mark on contemporary writings and varied historical documents. Consequently, it is easier for historians to follow the twisting paths of Palmach pillaging than it is for them to chart the plundering committed by organizations like the Irgun or the Lehi, or by other Haganah forces. The reason is simple: the Palmach fighters and the

---

3   For the first written mention of the massacre, see Netiva Ben-Yehuda, *Through the binding ropes* [Hebrew] (Jerusalem: Domino Press, 1985), 243–8. In testimonies given by Palmach soldiers, the speakers note that prisoners were taken, but that they were released. See the testimony of Reuven Netzer, commander of the Third Battalion's C Company, Yiftach Brigade, October 2003, PGA. For numerous testimonies about the massacre, see Uri Milstein, *Blood libel in Deir Yassin: The black paper* [Hebrew] (Tel Aviv: ha-Midrashah ha-le'umit, 2007), 124–8. In contrast, Moshe Vizel, who fought as part of the Palmach's Third Battalion and was part of the force that took the village, wrote: 'I remained there until the next day, towards evening, when we withdrew from the village and returned to Safed. I neither saw nor heard anything related to the killing of prisoners.' Moshe Vizel, 'There is no basis to the massacre' [Hebrew], book supplement, *Haaretz*, 3 December 2008.

4   Operation report on the conquest of Safed, 10 May 1948, file: 122/1975-1066, IDF.

5   On the conquest of Safed, see Benny Morris, *1948* (Tel Aviv: 'Am 'Oved, 2010), 179–82; Tamir Goren, 'The war for the mixed cities in the North', in Alon Kadish, ed., *Israel's War of Independence, 1948–1949* [Hebrew] (Galili Centre for Defence Studies, 2004), 191–6.

movement to which they belonged – the labour movement – were seriously engaged with writing and commemoration.[6] Nonetheless, as testimony concerning the looting of the northernmost city to be conquered multiply, the nuances of and contradictions about what happened multiply too.

Even before the attack on the city, the military forces told Jewish-quarter residents that looting would be forbidden. 'We knew that this time we would need to issue [orders],' Peled, the commander of the Palmach force that took part in the conquest, later wrote.[7] The proclamation that the city commander posted reads as follows:

> Citizens of Safed, until further order, I am declaring a total curfew in all occupied Arab areas. Any individual, citizen, or soldier, who passes the line of defense and enters the Arab quarter and takes enemy property or causes damage to it *takes his own soul.*[8]

When Office of the Custodian official Yitzhak Gevirtz visited the city in early August, almost three months after its conquest, he reported his findings to the chief legal officer:

---

6 Of course, this is not just the case with Safed but for wartime pillaging as a whole. Members of the labour movement, no matter to which organization they belonged, documented their wealth of activities for decades. Therefore, the issue of plunder comes up much more in their writing than it does in the writing of other movements, such as the Revisionist movement. Palmach members – more than any other fighting group – wrote a great deal about themselves. The poet Natan Alterman wrote about this in his poem 'Around the campfire': 'They write poems about themselves and even books. Not leaving the work of writing about them to others is part of the Palmach's character.' Obviously, it is a lot easier to find the historical writing of organizations and institutions than it is to find the writing of individuals. Indeed, the overwhelming majority of pillagers were civilians from cities and villages who did not necessarily belong to an institution or organization. On the plundering of the Irgun, see the following detailed list and the accompanying description of the numerous and diverse acts of looting that the organization carried out in March and April 1948. 'Irgun acts of spoliation – From the beginning of March 1948', 22 April 1948, file: Joint operations and contact between the Irgun and the Lehi and the Haganah 15-185/2, YTA.

7 Elad Peled, *Safed in 1948: Battle diary* [Hebrew] (Jerusalem: Ariel, 2006), 158.

8 Proclamation: 'Citizens of Safed – I declare a complete curfew in all occupied Arab areas', 5 May 1948, National Library of Israel. See also Proclamation: 'Serious warning', 17 May 1948, file: DC304000, Beit Hameiri Archive (hereafter, BHA); 'Proclamation' by battalion commander of the brigade, file: DC30399, BHA.

Following the conquest of Safed, [Palmach] Commander Yigal Allon permitted the men to loot the city for four days. The First and Third Battalions loaded up trucks and took them to the units, apparently the thought was that these goods would be useful for groups establishing new Palmach settlements. The picture of what resulted from what has been mentioned above is astonishing.[9]

One female Palmach soldier candidly noted that one of 'the first manifestations of looting occurred in [the] abandoned [part of] Safed'. One of the other members of her training group explained how they gathered up the equipment – radios, refrigerators, and sewing machines – and battalion command divided up the stolen inventory, giving it to the various training groups.[10] According to one historian, 'The Arabs of Safed were renowned for their industry, and, thanks to it, they amassed great wealth and their homes were like estates and fortresses.'[11] The looters had a great deal to plunder.

While there is no doubt that the military forces gathered up the huge quantity of Arab property that had been left behind in the city, there are disagreements about why this happened. Hayyim Limoni, one of the conquerors of the city, later explained:

There was no looting, there was no time for looting, and it was not even on our minds. Why would we be involved in looting? We came, we carried out the operation to the best of our abilities and we returned to base. Furthermore, we did not have time to loot.

Limoni also explained that Third Battalion commander Kelman had set a curfew and that anybody wandering around in the city was to be shot – a measure taken for security reasons (to prevent the city's Jewish residents from wandering around in abandoned sections of the city), as

9   Yitzhak Gevirtz (director of the Department of Villages in the Office of the Custodian) to the chief justice officer, 3 August 1948, file: General [material] on Safed refugees, Gimmel-310/34, ISA.

10   Quoted in Yehezkel Avneri, ed., HaMahanot HaOlim years: The third decade [Hebrew] (Tel Aviv: ha-Kibbutz ha-me'uhad, 1993), 158.

11   Mustafa Abbasi, Safad during the mandate period, 1918–1948: Arabs and Jews in a mixed city [Hebrew] (Jerusalem: Yad Ben Zvi, 2015), 214. See also Yiftach to IDF chief of staff, 11 May 1948, file: General 15-164/4, YTA.

well as to prevent looting. Limoni did note that the battalion expropriated food to meet their needs: 'Provisions did not always arrive, and,
when they did, we did not always have enough. We were hungry. The
truth was that we were always hungry. Consequently, Kelman concluded
that the battalion should take the food there.' According to Limoni,
Kelman ordered that the huge quantities of property found in the stores
and warehouses be brought to the hotel on Mount Canaan, at whose
foot Safed stands, to prevent the Jewish inhabitants from pillaging it.
'They would not have withstood the temptation, and there would have
been terrible pillaging there,' he asserted. He said that the property was
transferred in an orderly manner, and there was a 'huge collection' of
stuff. Limoni said that he did not know if the property was stolen or
looted thereafter.[12]

Yosef Benderli, a Safed resident appointed by the governor to oversee
the 'abandoned' property in the city, told a fundamentally different
story. According to Benderli, his aims were to prevent plundering and to
organize the huge amounts of property found in Arab Safed. For this
reason, he decided to move the contents of the numerous warehouses
that 'were filled with riches in quantities that no man had ever seen
before', gathering them in the Jewish part of town. His biography offers
an additional reason for his decision to gather up the enormous quantities of property:

> He discovered that trucks from kibbutzim from throughout the coun-
> try were arriving and [their crews] were pillaging the Arab city unmo-
> lested. What he saw as particularly problematic was that while the
> soldiers who had been stationed to protect against looters were allow-
> ing the kibbutz trucks to load up without being bothered, they were
> actively using means of force to prevent the [Jewish] residents of Safed
> from approaching and did not even hesitate to shoot in their
> direction.

We should assume it was an exaggeration to say that they went up to
Safed 'from throughout the country' to loot, but it is certain that kibbutz
members broke into the warehouses and packed what they contained
onto their trucks. Benderli got into heated confrontations with the

---

12   Hayyim Limoni, testimony, 1992, PGA.

governor. Yet their conflict did not revolve around the looting of property. Instead, it centred on who would be the beneficiaries of the property that the city's fleeing Arab residents had left behind. Benderli asserted that the Jews of Safed should be the ones to benefit from the remaining Arab property. This claim had historical justification: 'The Jews of Safed, who were victims of looting, pillaging, and destruction during the 1929 riots, were given neither assistance nor compensation from Jewish nationals institutions and the kibbutzim.' Benderli demanded that removal of spoils from the city cease. Yet he proved unsuccessful. The kibbutz members 'continued to empty Arab homes, workshops, and garages, and took everything that they could possibly disassemble and load up'.[13] Rabbis Avraham Zeide Heller and Efraim Weingott authored a pasquil that condemned those

> who failed to spiritually elevate themselves in this great hour to avoid some serious missteps . . . There are tens of people among us who to our great shame did not know how to control their inclinations and went out to pillage and loot even during the holy Sabbath day, as if we too are a nation 'that lives by its sword' and pounces upon booty and plunder.[14]

Elad Peled, who oversaw the battle to take Safed, later explained that he dedicated a great deal of thought to the question of the battalion's role in the looting: 'The Third Battalion concluded its wartime role in Safed. Then it packed up, arranged what to do with its men and equipment, and disappeared.' Usually, soldiers were not the ones who looted places. He asserted that he never saw any pillaging in Safed at all. 'We [the Third Battalion] did not see it, because we were no longer there.'[15] A decision was made, he told elsewhere, to punish soldiers who were caught looting. And yet, 'pillaging for the unit's benefit was totally acceptable'. Peled was able to describe how the Third Battalion 'descended from Safed in convoys, convoys of trucks with equipment. One could rob and steal for

13   Aryeh Benderli, *Yosef Benderli: Safed patriot* [Hebrew] (Kefar Tabor: Shabtai Gal-On, 1998), 95–6.

14   Proclamation [written] by Rabbis Efraim Weingott and A. Z. Heller, Iyyar 1948, file: DC30407, BHA.

15   Elad Peled, testimony, 30 March 2000, Yitzhak Rabin Center Archive (hereafter, YRC).

the collective. They had already done that [when they were stationed] at the kibbutzim.[16] The difference between 'personal' looting and 'collective' looting was a significant one for the soldiers. One can assume that this is one of the reasons that Meir Meivar, one of the officers who oversaw the force that conquered the city, wrote that the Palmach units left the city after its conquest. 'They were called to carry out other assignments', and they did not have time to rest and recharge. In fact, from Meivar's perspective, the Palmach did not loot all.[17]

Unlike most of her comrades in arms, Netiva Ben-Yehuda, a Palmach fighter who participated in the conquest of Safed, wrote candidly about the pillaging that they conducted in the city. When one reads her novel *Through the binding ropes*, one receives a completely different picture of the soldiers' behaviour in Safed.

> People began to break into shops. First, it was just ones that sold food, so that people could get bags full of candies, nuts, and pistachios to pour over the guys' heads. Afterwards, they dragged out whole sacks of these things and placed them at every store entrance, so that everyone passing by could take as much as he wanted. There were cigarettes too! Suddenly we had a bounty of cigarettes, and English ones to boot! And clothes! You could take what you wanted! The medical supplies in the pharmacy – they were all free! Clean towels too! . . . and, when bad stuff started to happen, an order came down from battalion headquarters to start gathering up all the radios, refrigerators, sewing machines – everything of value – and to bring them to the movie theatre in the Sarah Levi Hotel . . . and loaded trucks began to head out, only to return to reload. When you asked what all these piles were, for whom they were being prepared, then you were told that they were for the training groups who would soon be establishing new settlements . . . Somebody made sure to spread all types of stories, including about big heists, especially those carried out by senior commanders. For example, all of the gold rings that were found in Ein Zaytun, on the floor of [a home of] one of the inhabitants who had fled, had been taken by battalion headquarters, the combat staff,

16 Elad Peled, testimony, n.d., PGA.

17 Meir Meivar-Meiberg, *In the shadow of the fortress: The story of a Haganah commander in Safed* [Hebrew] (Tel Aviv: Milo, 1989), 335.

that night – they had all disappeared . . . one needs to be honest: it was true that there were some serious thieves among us. It is a fact that lots of really valuable stuff in Safed disappeared. Even now nobody knows where it went . . . Yet the fact remains that all the property in Safed was methodically taken. You also need to treat all those who were involved in this business fairly and note that there were no laws against looting then.[18]

Another female solider from the Palmach's Third Battalion wrote the following to her parents:

I got some things in Safed. I found some really beautiful embroidered Arab dresses for Sarah and me, and I might be able to get them altered here. Kaffiyehs and scarves, bracelets and beads, a Damascus table and set of wonderful silver demitasses, and, most importantly, Sarah brought back a gigantic Persian carpet that is brand new and beautiful. I have never seen something so beautiful in my life. A living room [with it in it] would be on par with [the living rooms] of Tel Aviv's richest people. By the way, this stationery also belonged to Arabs.[19]

In Safed, 'private' looting could not be carried out on the grand scale that it was undertaken in cities like Haifa or Jaffa, which had Arab populations numbering in the tens of thousands. In addition, Safed was farther away from large Jewish population centres. Therefore, it was more difficult to get to (for haphazard looting). According to Safed military governor Avraham Hanokhi, they only began to keep records of the property that was removed from Safed ten days after the city's occupation. 'That is when they stopped taking out huge quantities of property', he asserted.[20] According to the military prosecutor for the Oded Brigade, which had participated in the siege, in the days immediately after the city's occupation, military forces – primarily those of the Palmach – removed 'everything that they were able to take (hundreds of truckloads) without any oversight or supervision from the senior

---

18   Ben-Yehuda, *Through the binding ropes*, 285–9.
19   Quoted in Ben Pazi, *A community at war*, 57.
20   Minutes of meeting in Safed, 29 July 1948, file: General Safed, Gimmel-310/33, ISA; Report of Minister Sheetrit to David Ben-Gurion, 13 August 1948, file: 105/260, HHA.

command'.[21] Available sources do not indicate what happened to the goods that were loaded onto those trucks, but it is reasonable to assume that part of it was for the use of the soldiers, who were frequently asked to fend for themselves during the war. Still, the question remains: What about the dresses, jewels, and furniture? Were they put to use over the years by the kibbutzim and those who went on to establish new settlements?

Alongside the military governor, a five-member committee was appointed whose role was to oversee the property of expelled Arabs. In practice, the committee sold it, a great deal of it at low, frequently absurd, prices.[22] Moreover, the committee only began to meet after most of the property had already been removed from the city. Someone said at one of its meetings that it was unproductive to sell the remaining property because it would flood 'the market with furniture and produce no real benefit'. One of the committee members voiced a solution that the Jewish people of Safed had been kicking about: if a large wave of new immigrants did not arrive in Safed soon, then Arab homes should be blown up, 'so that the Arabs will not have homes to return to'.[23] There were Jewish residents of Safed who asserted that 'even if a decision will be made to allow Arabs to return to the country, we will not look kindly on their return to our city'. Underlying the hostile attitudes of the city's two national groups, so clearly reflected in this assertion, were earlier pogroms, as well as the events of the Independence War.[24]

Complaints about the local committee for abandoned property mounted, and Gevirtz, an official in the Arab Assets Department of the Office of the Custodian, headed north to see what had happened to the

21   Chief prosecutor, Prosecutor's Office, Oded Brigade, 26 June 1948, file: General [material] on Safed refugees.

22   Abbasi, *Safad during the mandate period*, 214.

23   Minutes of the meeting of the Committee for Arab Assets in Safed, 5 July 1948, file: Various reports, Gimmel-306/62, ISA. Avraham Wrobel, a member of the Safed Workers' Council secretariat, said: 'At that time, the Haganah district commander made a formal promise [to Safed's Jewish residents] that the Arabs would not return to Safed and asked that the government and the IDF honour this promise . . . [Wrobel's?] proposal was to leave the buildings that were suitable for new Jewish settlers intact and to blow up the rest.' Report on a meeting concerning the future of Safed and the Galilee in a letter from Ze'ev Sherf to Shlomo Kaddar, 3 June 1948, file: Israeli borders, Het Tzadi-2395/12, ISA.

24   Mayor Moshe Pedahtzur, ministerial interview in Safed, 29 July 1948, file: General Safed.

property whose Palestinian owners had fled. 'The principal complaints are that no public announcements were made before merchandise was sold and that what was sold was purchased at unbelievably [low] prices.'[25] The committee's deliberations were disorganized, and real minutes were not taken. Thus, decisions that were made and instructions that were given went unrecorded. The committee wanted to get rid of the Arab property as quickly as possible and it did not look into its value before arranging its sale. The property was sold at below market prices, and 'committee members' close associates purchased the large and valuable items and undoubtedly made huge sums of money from them'. For example, two factories, together with all their equipment, were sold at a low price. Then they were resold and resold again, 'each time at a hefty profit'.[26] Most of the property was sold to private citizens, and chaos reigned. Once 'a corner of the big warehouse' was sold, but information was not supplied about what equipment and merchandise 'the corner' included. A different time, 'sewing machines' were sold, and, apparently, it was not indicated that this lot contained seventy-eight machines. The army representative on the committee, Yitzhak Batist, a Palmach member from Kibbutz Nir David, exhibited bold opportunism, selling a large quantity of property without even consulting the other committee members. Gevirtz noted that Batist also allowed Palmach battalions to take carpets, electronic equipment, and merchandise to Palmach warehouses in Sarafand (Tzrifin in Hebrew) – the very same ones to which Palmach soldiers had brought property they had pillaged in Jerusalem.[27]

Jewish National Fund official Yosef Nahmani, whose descriptions of the looting of Tiberias and Haifa have already been cited, pointed out the difference between Safed's despoliation and the other cities' depredation:

In Safed, a stringent policy was put into effect to prevent the residents from looting and pillaging, but the property was not effectively utilized, because the army did not actually take things that satisfied essential needs. What use do things like carpets provide? This is unfortunate. Through conquest of cities like Tiberias and Haifa and

---

25   Yitzhak Gevirtz (director of the Department of Villages in the Office of the Custodian) to the chief legal officer, 3 August 1948, file: General [material] on Safed refugees.

26   Chief prosecutor, Prosecutor's Office, Oded Brigade, 26 June 1948.

27   Gevirtz to the chief legal officer, 3 August 1948.

large villages, it should have been possible to collect property worth millions [of liras] and to channel [money] into the war effort. Yet due to disorganization and organized theft, a tremendous amount has been lost when we actually need every pruta.[28]

As in other cities, the attitude towards Arabs who remained in Safed after its conquest was contemptible, and the military forces did not stand by the promises they made to the tiny Arab population that stayed behind. After the flight of tens of thousands of residents, only thirty elderly Arab members of the Greek Catholic community were still in the city. After the city's conquest, they were ordered to leave, and the Ministry of Minorities was mobilized to aid in their transfer.[29] Before they departed, they were promised that their property would be protected, but even though their property was placed in a single location, it was quickly stolen.[30] What was not looted was given to various institutions and private individuals, or sold.[31] The property of the community priest, Father Nuni, who had had enough time only to move some of his possessions to Shfar'am, was looted too. In addition to the depredation of his home, people looted and vandalized Safed's Greek Catholic church. 'We found broken down doors, shattered vessels, torn pictures, and broken crosses', wrote the director of the city's Ministry of Minorities branch.[32]

Israel's foreign minister, Moshe Sharett, opposed the army's decision to expel Safed's Catholic community and demanded that part of it be permitted to return. A letter from his office to the administration of the IDF Operations Branch explained, 'We need to treat the country's Arabs with extreme moderation'. 'This is what will test our abilities', the letter asserted.[33] It was not the first time that requests and demands made by

---

28   Yosef Nahmani diary, 3 May 1948, HAS.

29   See the extensive correspondence in file: Refugees from Safed, Gimmel-310/37, ISA.

30   Emanuel Friedman (official in charge of minorities matters in Safed) to Bechor-Shalom Sheetrit, 5 August 1948, file: General [material] on Safed refugees.

31   'The topic of discussion: Safed refugees in Haifa', Ministry of Minorites, Safed branch, 28 January 1949, file: General [material] on Safed refugees.

32   Director of the Ministry of Minorities [branch] in Safed to the Ministry of Minorities in the Kiryah, 26 January 1949, file: Noni George, Gimmel-299/80, ISA.

33   Yehoshafat Harkabi (foreign minister's office) to director of the operations branch, 18 August 1948, file: Christian holy sites, Het Tzadi -2397/7, ISA.

Sharett were ignored. 'The light of bitter experience' led the foreign minister to prophesize that the community's expulsion would lead 'to the monastery's pillaging and vandalization – something that would carry over to the church and its sacred objects'.[34] Prime Minister Ben-Gurion opposed Sharett's (and Minister of Minorities Bechor-Shalom Sheetrit's) position on the tiny Christian community's return to Safed, deciding that 'it is currently impossible to return Arabs to Safed'.[35]

Taking the size of Safed's Jewish population into consideration, a substantial number of cases related to 'abandoned' property came to trial. Up until early August, thirty trials had been carried out, and another twenty were still proceeding.[36] As in other cities, the pillage of property served as a justification (and perhaps a motive – with which we will deal in the second part of the book) for preventing Arabs from returning to Safed. This is the sense that one gets from the following statement:

> This is the people of Safed's demand: A. Arabs should be forbidden to return to the city during the ceasefire. The Hebrew community of Safed will be unable to withstand the pressure that returning Arabs will place upon it, especially since most of the Arab property in Safed has been pillaged since the Arabs left the city, and it is hard to describe how they will respond to this.[37]

---

34   A note in Moshe Sharett's handwriting, 14 August 1948, file: Christian holy sites.

35   Cabinet secretary to the minister of minorities, 1 September 1948, file: Refugees from Safed.

36   'Statistics submitted by the police pertaining to abandoned property trials from 15 May 1948 to 12 August 1948', file: General, Gimmel-307/16, ISA.

37   Sherf to Kaddar, 3 June 1948.

Beisan (Beit She'an)

Days after Safed's conquest and utter pillaging, it was Beisan/Beit She'an's turn. The town, called Beit She'an (in Hebrew) and Beisan (in Arabic), had hundreds of years of history behind it, due to its role as a transit point between Transjordan and Mandate Palestine; agriculture and trade were central to its livelihood.[1] As of 1946, the town had a tiny tourism sector: two hotels, a hostel, three cafés, and two vineyards.[2] In spite of its small size, Beisan, which the UN Partition Plan designated the following year to become part of the State of Israel, was to have tremendous significance for the nascent Jewish state: the town and its surroundings separated the Jewish settlements of the Jezreel Valley from the settlements in the area around Tiberias and the Sea of Galilee. This gave it long-term strategic importance because its conquest would enable contiguous Jewish settlement. Yet it also had immediate strategic value: conquest of the town would help repel a military invasion by the Arab Legion, of the Emirate of Transjordan.[3] Since the demonstrations and violence of the events of 1929, the area's Jewish population had been forced to travel on alternative routes, because Beisan overlooked the

---

1 Mustafa Abbasi, 'Beit She'an during the British Mandate Period 1918–1948' [Hebrew], *Iyyunim bi-tekumat Yisrael* 25 (2015): 487–506.

2 Ibid., 501. See also the document 'Arab al-Sager [tribe] in the Beit She'an Valley', n.d., file: Bet`/105/245, HHA.

3 History branch of the [IDF] General Staff, *History of the Independence War* [Hebrew] (Tel Aviv: Ma'arakhot, 1959), 138.

central crossroads. Nevertheless, in January 1949, the British district governor reported that Beisan and the Jewish settlements in the Beit She'an valley were striving to reach 'an unofficial mutual restraint agreement'. The Arab Higher Committee, under Mufti Haj Amin al-Husseini's leadership, put an end to this initiative.[4]

On 11 May, the Haganah conquered two villages near Beisan – Farwana (فروﻧﺔ) and al-Ashrafiya (الأﺷﺮﻓﻴﺔ) – and their residents fled to Transjordan. The same night, they conquered Tel el-Husn (biblical-era Beit She'an), and from there the combat forces began firing on the town of Beisan with mortars. Arab Liberation Army commander Isma'il al-Faruqi (الﻔﺎروﻗﺔ) and most of his troops fled the city. After negotiations, the local population surrendered the city to the Golani Brigade troops under Avraham Yoffe's command.[5] Prior to this, in the period immediately following Tiberias's and Haifa's conquest, residents of the small Arab city had already begun to flee their homes and move their families to Nablus, Transjordan, and elsewhere.[6] Beisan, which had close to 6,000 inhabitants on the eve of the war, had only 1,000 to 1,200 people left in it. Shmuel Zagorski of Kibbutz Kfar Ruppin was appointed military governor. The residents were told that '[those] who want to remain and live peaceful lives in the city will be able to do so.'[7] On the contrary, the vast majority were exiled to Transjordan days later (with the exception of a small group that was expelled to Nazareth), purportedly for military reasons.[8] Minister Sheetrit believed that expelled

---

4　Quoted in Benny Morris, *The Birth of the Palestinian Refugee Problem, 1947–1949* (New York: Cambridge University Press, 1987), 39.

5　'The battle for Beit She'an', 14 May 1948, file: Bet`/105/92, HHA.

6　'A general survey of the months April and May 1948', 3 August 1948, file: 1196/1952-1, IDF.

7　'Things that happened on 12 May 1948', file: 105/94, HHA.

8　Benny Morris, *1948* (Tel Aviv: 'Am 'Oved, 2010), 183–4. See the letter sent by the exiled Christian residents: 'According to the conditions of the city's surrender, the city's residents should have been allowed to remain in it without being demeaned or having any of their rights revoked. After the surrender, those who wanted to flee fled to nearby Arab lands. Yet we, the city's Christians, decided to stay in our city and to continue to perform our regular jobs . . . and that is how things went for 15 days. On 28 May 1948, the military governor Mr Shmu'el and the military commander Mr Mussa invited us to meet with them and they ordered us to leave the city in the next hour and a half. We told them that there was no way that we were going to do that. When they threatened to kill us [if we did not comply], we saw that there was no room for negotiation and that we had to leave the city . . . The army prepared busses to take us to Nazareth and

residents who had remained in Israeli territory should be permitted to return to Beisan.[9]

A bitter fate befell Beisan. Within a month of its conquest, parts of the town were burned and destroyed, and looters had taken its moveable property as spoils. Prime Minister Ben-Gurion, always shrewdly aware of the historian who would later review his papers, sent this concise telegram to the Golani Brigade in Beisan on 1 July 1948: 'Ask [the commander] Avraham Yoffe if it is correct that he burned all or part of the city of Beit She'an. Was it in accordance with my order [?] Who did it [?]'[10] Two weeks earlier, Minister Aharon Zisling had broached the issue in a cabinet meeting. Zisling, the first minister of agriculture and a Mapam representative, wondered who had ordered Beisan's destruction. In a cabinet meeting on 16 June, a month after the city's occupation, Zisling addressed the destruction of Arab villages and Arab property as a whole, and what this destruction would mean for the future of the groups sharing (or who had shared) the land (a topic also dealt with in the second part of this book). Reporting on his visit to the conquered city, Zisling said he had been told that the local commander had been ordered to destroy the city. 'And, in regard to this example of havoc and destruction, Ben-Gurion,' said Zisling, as he prepared to make a broader statement:

> You did not need to destroy Beit She'an, even if the Arabs were not going to return to it . . . If you do such a thing in the middle of a war

---

we were forced to board them. We left all of our property, including lands, cattle, plantings, homes, furniture, and stores, in Beit She'an military governor's hands.' Rafiq al-Sa'd (السعد) (Christian mukhtar of Beit She'an) to Chaim Weizmann, 22 September 1949, file: Return of Arabs to Beit-Shean, Gimmel-308/42, ISA. The file contains additional related documents. Azaria Alon wrote that 'on 12 May, Beit She'an was conquered and the residents left all the [surrounding] villages, even though not even one shot was fired. They were certain that they would return within two weeks, and they left everything behind. There were three thousand residents in Beit She'an . . . Since it was unclear what would happen in the future, *they were* told: You cannot remain in Beit She'an [actually they were told the exact opposite – A. R.] . . . Then I and many others were shocked when we forced Beit She'an's residents to leave the city. Today I am certain that there was no other way. If you want to talk about humanism, that was most humanistic thing to do.' Azaria Alon, 'Who expelled, how and why' [Hebrew], *Davar*, 10 March 1978, emphasis added.

9   Bechor-Shalom Sheetrit to David Ben-Gurion, 16 September 1948, file: Return of Arabs to Beit She'an.

10   David Ben-Gurion to the Golani [Brigade], 1 July 1948, BGA.

to fortify your position, such destruction is understandable. Yet if after a month, political calculations and issues of statecraft lead you to cold-bloodedly and publicly perpetrate such destruction, the world views it as something completely different. Now I am not just talking about moral justifications, but also about political considerations. This is not how one should handle things.[11]

Several days after Ben-Gurion's telegram, the IDF chief of staff also ordered an investigation to see 'if the rumour was true' that Beit She'an had been destroyed.[12] The Golani Brigade commander denied the assertions, saying that 'the fires in the city were lit by enemy units (gangs) that infiltrated the city to plunder, damage, destroy, and burn'.[13] A different letter written to the Gilboa district commander explained that 'hundreds of Arabs continue to infiltrate Beit She'an nightly to rob and set fire to things'.[14] Different things were said at an executive committee meeting of the Histadrut, the largest trade union in Israel. Meir Ya'ari reported the following:

> In Beit She'an, I met with the commander and asked him questions. He told me that all the inhabitants were expelled after Arab fighters were spotted in Beit She'an. After Beit She'an was cleared, an order was issued to destroy it. They are working with bulldozers there. This kind of work means that Arabs are being expelled from the Land of Israel. I looked into the matter, and it turns out that the battalion commander received an order from his superiors; the brigade commander is not at fault, because he got an order from on high. They asked me if they should refuse to carry out the order, and I cannot tell them to do that. I told them to inform us about every incident, so that we can go to the Histadrut and the government to fight

---

11 For a complete version of Zisling's statement from the cabinet meeting on 16 June 1948, which the Israel State Archives recently blacked out, see Yoram Nimrod, 'Creation of the patterns of Israel-Arab relations' [Hebrew] (PhD diss., Hebrew University, 1985), 301. See also Tom Segev, *1949: The First Israelis*, trans. Arlen Weinstein (New York: Free Press, 1986), 84.

12 IDF chief of staff to the Golani [Brigade], 5 July 1948, file: 922/1975-1025, IDF.

13 Golani Brigade commander to the IDF chief of staff, 7 July 1948, file: 922/1975-1025, IDF.

14 Selek to the district commander, 29 July 1948, file: 6127/1949-109, IDF. See also 'Daily summary', 24 June 1948, file: 128/1951-84, IDF.

against it. There is indeed a policy to expel Arabs from the Land of Israel. The people [giving the orders] say they are acting on behalf of all types of people and I will not point them out.[15]

Ya'ari was referring to Ben-Gurion.

When the Ministry of Minorities became aware of the city's destruction and its damaging effects, its officials looked for ways to provide relief. City resident Adham Salam (سلام) turned to Minister Sheetrit and asked for his help. 'I found out that the authorities in Beit She'an stole and burned all my property,' he reported. 'I am in bad shape.'[16] Sheetrit had a way to stop the destruction in the city: the establishment of a police station in the city.[17] Nothing seems to have been done, however, and in a short time most of the Palestinian property was looted.

There is almost no documentary evidence about the pillaging that occurred in Beit She'an, and I have found no mention of the looting in the city in scholarship on the city's conquest. Books about the Golani Brigade and memoirs written over the years do not mention it either. Of the twelve Jewish settlements in the area on the eve of the war, eleven were kibbutzim. There was no nearby Jewish city. Kibbutz members could have shed light on the pillaging that took place in the fallen city. Yet, unsurprisingly, kibbutz members, like Golani Brigade soldiers, were almost completely silent on the topic. Consequently, the following brief source initially published in the Kibbutz Beit Hashita bulletin in real time and later housed in the kibbutz archive proves exceptional. Shalom Karlitz wrote a short report entitled 'A shameful occurrence'. I will quote it at length, because it shows that the fate of the property fleeing Arabs left behind in Beisan was the same as that of similar property in other cities:

We are not really the ones who can decide if the expulsion of Beit She'an's Arabs was really necessary. Yet we can ask if it was really

---

15   Minutes of the Histadrut Executive Committee meeting, 16–17 June 1948, vol. 90, June–August 1948, LMA.

16   Adham Salam to the minister of minorities, September 1948, file: Yudham Salam Farouk al-Shab, Gimmel-298/58, ISA.

17   Report of Bechor-Shalom Sheetrit to David Ben-Gurion, 13 August 1948, file: 105/260, HHA; Bechor-Shalom Sheetrit to David Ben-Gurion, 6 September 1948, file: 121/1950-183, IDF.

necessary to empty their homes and dwelling places. I am not talking about either the spoils of war or other means of production that make us more resilient here. That is not what I mean. I am referring to those meagre personal belongings that now adorn some of our rooms. These personal belongings have nothing to do with strengthening our ability to endure. What they do represent is completely unjustified looting and pillaging, and exploitation of the weak. I hope members will forgive me for making the following painful comparison. Not long ago, in Europe, we were the victims. [We were] too weak to protect our jewellery and personal belongings which were stolen, packed up in suitcases, and sent back to families in the fatherland. [There they] adorned wives and dwelling places. Is it not true that our blood boils seeing a Jewish object in the home of . . . and that black 29 June ['The Black Sabbath' – a nickname for the day when the British authorities carried out a series of operations against the Jewish community of Palestine in 1946], have we forgotten it? A time when we ridiculed those in uniform who pillaged fountain pens and cameras while we were detained. Have we forgotten all this? How can we not be ashamed? We have heard about disgraceful cases where people have proven unable to restrain themselves that have taken place throughout the country. We were astonished. Is it possible that our fellow Jews would act like this? We shook our heads and said, 'there are a lot of fish in the sea'. Yet we, who consider ourselves to be catalysts, a vanguard, and realizers of dreams, should we be like the rotten among them? Should we not be pained when we see this shameful occurrence? No! No! I will not be silent! I will say clearly, shame on you![18]

---

18   Shalom Karlitz, 'A shameful occurrence' [Hebrew], *Kibbutz Beit Hashita Bulletin*, 18 June 1948, Kibbutz Beit Hashita Archive. The kibbutzim Ein Harod, Sde Nahum, Sde Eliyahu, Beit Hashita, and Hamadia might have pillaged and they might have expropriated Arab property from Beit She'an and additional villages in the area. See Zvi Inbar, *Scales of justice and the sword: Foundations of military law in Israel* [Hebrew] (Tel Aviv: Ma'arakhot, 2005), 622. Ya'akov Rotenberg, the military prosecutor of the Golani Brigade, said: 'Supervision over enemy property was a big problem in [our brigade]. Safed, Tiberias, Beit She'an. ([There was] the case of a young man who was found aiming [a rifle] at an old Arab woman: "He has four bullets and [he] wants to fire them" . . . why are you aiming at the old woman? – Self-defence . . .' Minutes of seminar of military prosecutors, 16 June 1948, file: 2294/1950-2882, IDF.

Ramle and Lydda

The wartime conquests of the towns of Ramle and Lydda (as it is known in ancient Greek, or Lod in Hebrew), which lay in the centre of Mandate Palestine's coastal plain, are singularly controversial among historians when it comes to the outcomes for their residents. The medium-sized cities were conquered during Operation Dani, the principal military offensive that took place during 'The Battles of the Ten Days', that took place in the period between the first and second ceasefires of the Independence War (9 July – 18 July 1948). Among other things, the Israeli forces wanted to conquer the area around Ramle and Lydda to push back the forces of the Arab Legion in the area and reduce the threat that they posed. Between 10 July and 12 July, soldiers from the Kiryati Brigade, the Eighth Brigade, and the Yiftach Brigade's Third Battalion conquered both cities.[1] At the very end of the British Mandate, 19,000 people lived in Lydda. The overwhelming majority of the inhabitants were Muslim, but there were 2,000 Greek Orthodox Christians living there too. Sixteen thousand people inhabited Ramle. Both cities were supposed to be part of the Arab state according to the 1947 Partition Plan. After the cities' conquest, there were 30,000 Palestinians in Lydda, the majority refugees from places that had been conquered in

---

1 Alon Kadish, Avraham Sela, and Arnon Golan, *The occupation of Lydda, July 1948* [Hebrew] (Tel Aviv: Arkhiyon le-toldot ha-Haganah; Misrad ha-bitahon, 2000), 26–42; Elhanan Oren, *The way to the city: Operation Dani July 1948* [Hebrew] (Tel Aviv: Ma'arakhot, 1976), 95–116.

the previous months. Some were from area villages, but most were from Jaffa.

Prior to Operation Dani, an explicit order was issued concerning 'abandoned' property (earlier versions of the order had already been issued in May):

1. Expropriation of property from abandoned and conquered Arab settlements for personal use is absolutely prohibited. Spoils of war will be the property of the army, not individual property or unit property. 2. From the moment that combat forces enter abandoned and conquered Arab settlements, all property found in these abandoned and conquered Arab settlements becomes the possession and the responsibility of the army. It is to deliver it into the possession of designated institutions. 3. Anybody who disobeys this order will be punished to the fullest extent of the law and it will be the personal responsibility of the commanders not to yield in any way and to carry this order out properly. 4. Please bring this order to the attention of all ranks.[2]

The rapid departure of tens of thousands of residents who took little time to evacuate and who forsook their property left many homes and stores well stocked. 'We had gotten experience with this during our time in Safed', someone recounted in *The Palmach book* (written by Palmach members and published a few years after the war), and 'we warned people . . . [that there was] an absolute prohibition on plundering and the taking of booty before we entered the city'.[3] In practice, the pillaging of Arab possessions started even before the cities' depredation. 'We were witnesses to the unsympathetic expulsion of the Arabs of Lod; it reminded us of the story "Refugee Convoys in Occupied Europe". Unidentified soldiers attempted to rob the refugees', recalled a member of the HaMahanot HaOlim youth Zionist movement.[4] 'The sight of masses of Arab refugees recalled Israel's Exile', wrote Palmach

2   This document is reproduced in full as an appendix in Kadish, Sela, and Golan, *The occupation of Lydda*, 104.

3   Zerubavel Gilead, ed., *The Palmach book*, vol. 2 [Hebrew] (Tel Aviv: ha-Kibbutz ha-me'uhad, 1955), 885.

4   Yehezkel Avneri, ed., *HaMahanot HaOlim Years: The third decade* [Hebrew] (Tel Aviv: ha-Kibbutz ha-me'uhad, 1993), 152.

commander and archaeologist Shmarya Gutman under a pseudonym in a November 1948 issue of the kibbutz journal *mibi-Fnim* (From Within). 'Indeed, the Arabs were not bound in chains; they were not uprooted by force; they were not led to detention camps . . . but their fate was *a diasporic fate*.'[5] Minister Zisling said the following days later in a cabinet meeting (it is no longer possible to examine his statement in the Israel State Archives, because viewing access has been revoked):

> It's been said that there were cases of rape in Ramle. I can forgive rape, but I cannot forgive other acts which seem to me much worse. When they enter a town and forcefully remove rings from fingers and jewellery from necks, that's a very grave matter . . . many are guilty of this.[6]

When the soldiers entered the two cities, Kiryati Brigade and Yiftach Brigade members started looting for personal gain. The pillaging was so widespread that it raised concerns that the forces assigned to carry out other assignments would be demoralized as well. Soldiers entered apartments whose residents had recently been expelled and emptied them out. In Lydda, an industrial and mercantile centre, there were 4,900 buildings designated as dwelling places and 480 designated as businesses.[7] Besides factories and extensive marketplace commerce, Lydda had a train station and an airport.[8] 'It was mostly Kiryati [Brigade] men who did [the pillaging]', Yiftach Brigade Commander Mulah Cohen later explained. 'That was how it always was.'[9] Cohen echoed what had been said in *The Palmach book*:

---

5   Avi-Yiftach [Shmarya Gutman], 'Lod goes out into exile', *mibi-Fnim* 13, no. 3 (November 1948): 452–61. Quote is from page 461. Mulah Cohen said that this was the most 'authentic' article written about the city's conquest. Mulah Cohen, testimony, 1996, PGA. See also Menachem Talmi, 'In the area of the defeated enemy', in *In the footsteps of soldiers: Selected reportage* [Hebrew] (Merhavyah: Sifriyat ha-po'alim, 1949), 169–74: 'There is no anguish in our hearts at the sight of thousands of dispirited refugees in the streets stooped over their bundles with lowered faces lowered' (170).

6   Quoted in Tom Segev, *1949: The First Israelis*, trans. Arlen Weinstein (New York: Free Press, 1986), 72.

7   Kadish, Sela, and Golan, *The occupation of Lydda*, 15.

8   Orah Vakrat, *Lod: A historical geography* [Hebrew] (Lod: Tcherikover, 1977), 109–20.

9   Mulah Cohen, 23 December 1997, YRC.

It should be noted that until the Guard Corps arrived, we were able to keep our spirits up and we left off-limits stuff alone. Yet when the Guard Corps units arrived and burst forth in unrestrained pillaging, men from our units let loose. They reached out for abandoned property and took it.[10]

On 12 July, Cohen sent a telegram to headquarters requesting that some type of governmental institution be established to deal with the bounty of spoils in the two cities. Operation Dani headquarters demanded that the IDF chief of staff handle the booty. The telegram to him explained that 'the Yiftach Brigade commander reported that he does not have sufficient manpower to organize the spoils and remove them from Lydda, Ramle, and the surrounding areas'. The Palmach, more sensitive to moral issues related to combat and individual looting that the other military forces, had already ordered its forces to leave Lydda on the night of July 13.[11] David Ben-Gurion wrote in his diary that Yitzhak Rabin was the one who issued this order. 'It is unclear if they left, but soldiers from all the battalions robbed and stole,' he noted.[12] On 14 July, Minister Sheetrit, based on past experience, demanded that the prime minister appoint a governor over Ramle and Lydda, so 'that matters can be addressed through civilian channels, just like they were handled in Jaffa'.[13]

Inquiries were made with soldiers from the Third Battalion who were withdrawn from Lydda and brought to nearby Ben Shemen on the thirteenth and fourteenth of the month.[14] Over the years, Brigade Commander Cohen offered a few different accounts of what happened that are both consistent and revealing. 'Then this disgrace befell us too: some of our men had taken part in the pillaging,' he wrote in his memoirs. The men were gathered up in Ben Shemen and told 'to get rid of everything'. Two Palmach battalions were forced to participate in a

---

10   Gilead, *The Palmach book*, vol. 2, 885. See also Eldad Avidar (Rochel), July–August 1998, file:16-12/52/192, YTA.

11   Oren, *The way to the city*, 125.

12   Quote from diary entry for 15 July 1948, David Ben-Gurion, *The War of Independence* [Hebrew], ed. Gershon Rivlin and Elhanan Oren (Tel Aviv: Defense Ministry Press, 1982), 589.

13   Shalom-Bechor Sheetrit to David Ben-Gurion, 14 July 1948, file: Conquered Israeli territories, Gimmel-2564/10, ISA.

14   Oren, *The way to the city*, 125.

discipline workshop: 'Do not besmirch yourselves with booty. The pillagers, those who gather spoils, are contemptible.' The idea was to cultivate 'communal opposition to the looters,' Cohen wrote.[15] Far from home, the soldiers were unable to take heavy things. 'Each person took what he thought was best', Palmach commander Elad Peled later explained when discussing 'the famous formation', adding that 'there was a lot of silver and gold there.'[16] *The Palmach book*, which discusses the conquest of these two cities at length, explained that 'we were facing another test: the soldiers' inclination for spoils'.

> We knew that if this matter was handled firmly from the outset, we would be able to keep people in line ... We gathered the units together immediately and withdrew them from the city. The next day, the battalions met individually, and the soldiers were forced to consider the serious implications of this matter. Those who had taken prohibited things had to take their spoils to the battalion's culture officer with the proceeds from their sale going to benefit those in the brigade who had been wounded. It should be noted that these self-examination assemblies benefited everybody involved tremendously. The turning over of plunder was not coerced. Instead, it was done voluntarily. Following the gatherings, the air was cleared, and the units came together once again.[17]

During the first few days, private looting was quite intense (and it would continue to some degree during the coming months), but organized plunder's time had yet to arrive. Ramle and Lydda's fate was similar to Safed's before them. Photos of the two cities from the days prior to their conquest give a sense of their great bounty. City resident Fouzi El-Asmar (الأسمر) wrote that 'the people of Lydda were known as well-to-do people. They purchased the furniture of the Germans who lived nearby prior to their departure from the country, and they used them to furnish their homes.'[18] Organized labour, the kibbutzim, and the settlement

---

15   Mulah Cohen, *To give and receive: Memoirs* [Hebrew] (Tel Aviv: ha-Kibbutz ha-me'uhad, 2000), 146; Mulah Cohen, testimony, 1996, PGA; Mulah Cohen, 23 December 1997, YRC.

16   Elad Peled, testimony, n.d., PGA.

17   Gilead, *The Palmach book*, vol. 2, 885.

18   Fouzi el-Asmar, *To be an Arab in Israel* [Hebrew] (Jerusalem: Shahak, 1975), 19.

movements were among the first to plunder the cities. In his novel *Last ones on the ridge*, Yitzhak Tischler draws on his wartime experiences and depicts looting-related dilemmas:

> While we were still pondering the intricacies of the moral questions raised by the plunder of Lod, people arrived and gave us a vivacious and heart-warming description of the training groups' foray into its private homes, stores, and workshops. Indeed, nobody had taken from what had been devoted and everything was given over to those who were settling the land. 'What did command say?' said Hayyim grasping at straws. 'The command is burying its head in the sand. Indeed, the training groups have taken things too far. When people from the Ashdot training farm loaded a D2 tractor onto a large truck, the Third Battalion staff came and ruled, "Enough! You are not allowed to take a vehicle. You can only take smaller stuff."' 'Only smaller stuff? The whole thing is immoral!' Hayyim screamed. 'Immoral?' Dov pounced on him. 'You should have seen what they did in Ramle. Every Kiryati Brigade member went out to loot for himself. They came in cars and trucks from Tel Aviv, emptied the city, and took everything back to their homes. [They took everything] from shoelaces to generators, from chandeliers to Persian carpets, and who knows what else.' 'And if the booty falls into the hands of the training groups, are those not private hands?' said Hayyim, firmly maintaining his position. 'It is better in our hands than the hands of those from the Kiryati Brigade who will show up after us. Who said that we have to do the hard and dangerous work and then leave? In any case, the state, as a state, will never enjoy this property.'[19]

The removal of property from Ramle and Lydda was, at least in part, done with 'permission'. Cohen explained that 'our representatives' turned to Yosef Avidar, head of the General Staff's logistics branch, and requested that the training groups that would soon be settling the land be given the opportunity to 'equip themselves'. 'I did not have a problem with this, and conditions were not such that you could organize and prepare a systematic inventory [of goods].' Cohen's comments make it

19   Yitzhak Tischler, *Last ones on the ridge* [Hebrew] (Tel Aviv: 'Am 'Oved, 1970), 128–9.

seem that the property was either going to make it into private or movement hands:

> Why should this equipment float around and end up going who
> knows where? I have to admit that it was fine with me and not just
> with me. If you ask the members of Hashomer Hatzair who served
> alongside us, you will see their approach was the same as ours.[20]

In a deliberation of the Mapai Central Committee, Prime Minister
Ben-Gurion spoke about a visit that he had made to Lod, and how he
had seen 'those pioneers, the youths' who went daily from Ben Shemen
to Lod to 'steal and filch'. Ben-Gurion also talked about how the training
group leaders sent

> their boys to Ramle to steal for the settlement. And these boys, who
> would not steal for themselves, were ready to go steal for their kibbutz!
> This is a very serious matter, because it is a sin that harms us even
> more than it harms the Arabs. This is a grave failing and it is not the
> first time that we have encountered it.[21]

Ben-Gurion pontificated, but he did not act decisively to put a stop to
the city's depredation.

In contrast, Minister Sheetrit, who visited Ramle immediately after
its conquest, tried to prevent spoliation even before the city had fallen
and demanded that concrete steps be taken to prevent it.[22] Both on his
way to the city and during his visit there, Sheetrit saw 'acts of
depredation', which he reported to the area commander, demanding

---

20   Cohen, *To give and receive*, 146.

21   Minutes of Mapai Central Committee [meeting], 24 July 1948, file: Protocols of
the Party Central Committee, 2-23-1948-1949, LPA.

22   Following a warning that Sheetrit sent to Moshe Sharett the day before, Sharett
wrote Sheetrit about what was going to happen in Ramle and Lod: 'I agreed with the
minister of defence about the following policies: . . . E. We must be as careful as possible
to ensure that searches do not lead to acts of vandalism and destruction. F. We should
employ all available means to prevent acts of looting. We all know how hard it is to
control people's inclinations when conquering [a city], but I hope that the policies above
will enable us to avoid serious problems.' Moshe Sharett to Shalom-Bechor Sheetrit, 13
July 1948, file: Conquered Israeli territories.

that he prevent looting.[23] On a visit to Lod a few days later, he had spoken directly with the Ministry of Finance appointee to oversee 'abandoned' property in the city, Efraim Soltz, who had told him about 'friction with the army'. Sheetrit ordered Soltz to allow goods to be removed from the city only by permit. 'It is impossible to know from whom the property has been taken, because everybody left their homes,' Sheetrit later reflected. It turned out that the army was taking whatever it wanted and was even taking things from homes. Sheetrit gave instructions that 'nothing should be taken from the homes of those still present in the city'. At a certain stage, even staple foods were being seized from the remaining residents. The visit made a bad impression on ministry officials: the city of Lydda looked 'abandoned, and its stores and doors lay breached'.[24] According to Custodian Dov Shafrir, there was nobody providing security for the city, and people could enter it without being accosted.[25] As elsewhere, the lack of guards served as an invitation for burglars.

Y. Yohananof, an Office of the Custodian of Abandoned Property official, warned Shafrir directly, describing the modus operandi criminal soldiers employed for organized removal of goods from the cities:

> Members of the Eighty-Ninth Battalion encamped in our Ben Shemen neighbourhood have employed their weapons to terrorize the roadblock guards when they pass by . . . with trucks loaded with various goods collected in the cities of Ramle and Lod. The guards explained that the troops frequently fired into the air when approaching the roadblocks to scare the guards and make them step back.

The battalion members also threatened 'to put a bullet' in the office's controllers 'if they did not leave areas where they were actively collecting their spoils'. The guards got the message, and they gave up trying to stop military vehicles at the roadblocks. Yohananof explained that when he was visiting Lod, he saw a group of soldiers busy 'loading furniture'.

---

23   A report on the minister's journey to Ramle on 12 July 1948, file: Conquered Israeli territories.

24   The minorities minister's visit to Lod, 26 July 1948, file: Lod, The minister of minorities' visit, Gimmel-304/8, ISA.

25   Dov Shafrir, The flowerbed of life [Hebrew] (Tel Aviv: ha-Merkaz ha-Haklai, 1975), 223.

When he demanded that they unload the furniture, they refused. In spite of Yohananof's credentials as a government representative and vocal protestations, the battalion continued with their transport of the loot, bringing it to their camp.[26] The Palmach soldiers acted no differently; in at least one documented case, they burst through a roadblock set up to prevent property removal.[27]

A portion of the looting soldiers carried out was undertaken for personal reasons under a military guise. 'The robbers of the Forty-Second Battalion' brought loaded trucks from Ramle-Lydda to a private home in Herzliya.[28] No less than 1,800 truckloads were taken out of Lydda in late July.[29]

The pillaging of property in Ramle and Lydda continued for many months after the cities' conquests, even as Ministry of Minorities officials attempted, unsuccessfully, to bring it to an end. Ministry officials asserted that 'the Office of the Custodian had been given the responsibility to ensure that ownerless abandoned Arab property would not get lost [in other words, stolen], not get wasted, and would be given over to the state's Ministry of Finance'. Ministry of Minorities official Moshe Erem wrote Custodian Shafrir that 'the Office of the Custodian is quite aware that, after its conquest and surrender, before an inventory had been taken, Ramle was thoroughly emptied, first by the army and then by the property office'. Erem argued that injury had been done to the Arab residents. 'You cannot strike twice' – once when you expropriate all the supply warehouses and granaries, and a second time when 'you also refuse to allow part of [the value] of this [expropriated] property to be used to provide for the inhabitants who have had everything taken away from them'. Erem referred to a meeting that Shafrir had with Ministry of Minorities director Gad Machnes after which 'the

26   Y. B. Yohananof to Dov Shafrir, 27 October 1948, file: Thefts of goods in Lod-Ramla, Gimmel-297/12, ISA. See also Yitzhak Gevirtz, 'Illegal activities in Ramla on the day of occupation – 12 July 1948', 13 July 1948, file: Capture of goods and assets, Gimmel-297/2, ISA.

27   Zvi Inbar, *Scales of justice and the sword: Foundations of military law in Israel* [Hebrew] (Tel Aviv: Ma'arakhot, 2005), 932.

28   Yitzhak Gevirtz to Dov Shafrir, 25 July 1948; Minutes of the Ministerial Committee on Abandoned Asset Affairs meeting, 26 July 1948; file: Administration – Abandoned Property Committee, Gimmel-2186/21, ISA.

29   Minutes of the Ministerial Committee on Abandoned Asset Affairs meeting, 26 July 1948.

nightmare of the starvation of Lod's residents was temporarily done away with. During the many months that the cities were being emptied, the Ministry of Minorities criticized the Office of the Custodian's activities:

> We will permit ourselves to conclude with the following statement: When they undertook commercial transactions with the Office of the Custodian and purchased various goods, supplies, provisions, and tools that came from the abandoned Arab property, more than a few Jews – not just public institutions and bodies, but individuals as well – benefited excessively.[30]

In an internal Ministry of Minorities meeting held a few days after the two cities' conquest, harsh criticism was voiced. Sheetrit explained that on the day of the conquest, before the Arab residents had departed, he and Machnes, the ministry director, had arrived in Ramle and witnessed the start of looting. According to Sheetrit, the commanders 'showed a readiness to cooperate with us' to prevent future pillaging. When he learned that the command was planning to expel the inhabitants, he turned to Moshe Sharett and received

> a written copy of what had been verbally agreed upon concerning how things were going to be handled. That is to say, full supervision and delayed evacuation. Afterwards, I learned that this decision was not implemented. Lod and Ramle were cleared of their residents. Ben-Gurion was unwilling to say why this decision had not been honoured.

A Gordian knot bound the resident's expulsion to the issue of their property's plunder. At that meeting, Erem inveighed:

> They lied to us about supervision of evacuated residents' property. The promises were not kept. What will happen in the villages that will be conquered today or tomorrow? While there is still hope that the

---

30 Moshe Erem to Dov Shafrir, 12 October 1948 (Shafrir's response to Erem, dated 19 October 1948, can be found in the same file), file: Provision for the Arab population, Gimmel-297/7, ISA.

invaders will go away, they are rousing the local Arabs to fight for their lives.

Erem criticized the removal of Palestinian goods. 'We do not have control over these matters,' he asserted.[31] Meir Ya'ari, one of Mapam's leaders, said, in connection with the residents' expulsion, that 'Ben-Gurion stands here before us not just as the minister of defence, but also as the great minister of intrigues'.[32]

Minister Sheetrit was not the only one surprised by the decision to expel the two cities' inhabitants. Minister Zisling wrote Ben-Gurion:

> During two meetings yesterday that supplied information about the handling of the Arab population in the reconquered area of Ramle and Lod, we heard news and rumours about worrisome policies. I request *a timely and official* announcement of the policy the Ministry of Defense is adopting and the military will be following, and

---

31 Minutes of the second meeting of the Ministry of Minorities, 15 July 1948, file: Department head meetings, Gimmel-307/17, ISA. The scholarly debate about the expulsion of the residents of Ramle and Lydda and Ben-Gurion's role in this matter will not be discussed here, but see Minutes of the Ministerial Committee on Abandoned Asset Affairs meeting, 13 July 1948, file: Administration – Abandoned Property Committee: 'Mr B. Sheetrit: He visited occupied Ramle and had the opportunity to see things from up close. The army was preparing to arrest all military-age men (besides those who had signed the surrender agreement), to take them to the Arab territorial border and to release them. Mr Sheetrit called the foreign minister and asked that he clarify the policy. The response of Mr Chertok [Sharett] was that all the inhabitants who wanted to remain in place would be permitted to do so on the condition that the State of Israel will not be required to support them. Those who desired to leave [their] location would be permitted to do so. Despite the fact that an order has been issued prohibiting all looting whatsoever, our soldiers have become involved in it. After his visit, Mr Sheetrit sent designated officials from the Ministry of Minorities to oversee this matter. Mr E. Kaplan: I discussed the problem of the residents of Ramle-Lod with the minister of defence and received a response that to a certain extent contradicted the foreign minister's response. The minister of defence's response was that the young male residents were to be rounded up, and the rest of the residents were to be encouraged to leave the location. Yet Israel would need to provide for those who remained.' Sharett wrote to Sheetrit about the understandings that he had with Ben-Gurion. In the letter no mention is made concerning expulsion of the population. See Moshe Sharett to Shalom-Bechor Sheetrit, 13 July 1948, file: Conquered Israeli territories.

32 Minutes of the twenty-seventh council of ha-Kibbutz ha-'Artzi in Nahariyah, 12 December 1948, file: (3)29.7-95, YYA.

discussion in the Committee on Abandoned [Assets after which] *explicit* decisions will be made.[33]

A few days later, in a cabinet meeting, Zisling said:

I have to say that this formula [regarding how the army would behave in Ramle] is a subtle order to expel the Arabs from Ramle. If I'd received an order stating that the door is open and Arabs can either leave, regardless of age and sex, or they can stay, but the army will not take responsibility for guaranteeing them sustenance, this is how I would have interpreted it. When such things are said during an actual conquest, at the moment of conquest, after all that happened in Jaffa and other places . . . I would interpret it as a warning: save yourselves while you can and escape.[34]

Meanwhile, the ransacking of the two cities continued. Minister of Finance Eliezer Kaplan wrote to Prime Minister Ben-Gurion: 'Unfortunately, the army is ignoring orders issued by civilian authorities.'[35] Kaplan noted that neither the Ministry of Finance nor the custodian of abandoned property, whom he had appointed, was in control of the situation, and that military forces were doing whatever they pleased. He also knew to declare that a military governor had been appointed without the knowledge of the minister of finance or any other minister, 'except, perhaps, the minister of defence'. This act ran counter to a decision made by the government (an issue explored in the second half of this book). At a certain stage, after the first days of pillage, the army even began to physically block the custodian's representatives from entering the city. This promoted the city's depredation.[36] Custodian Shafrir stated it was 'doubtful' that efforts to protect property in the cities had had any effect.[37]

---

33   Aharon Zisling to David Ben-Gurion, 13 July 1948, file: Administration – Abandoned Property Committee.

34   Cabinet meeting minutes, 21 July 1948, ISA.

35   Eliezer Kaplan to David Ben-Gurion, 18 July 1948, file: Administration – Abandoned Property Committee.

36   Minutes of the Ministerial Committee on Abandoned Asset Affairs meeting, 26 July 1948.

37   Minutes of the Ministerial Committee on Abandoned Asset Affairs meeting, 10 September 1948, file: Administration – Abandoned Property Committee.

Fouzi el-Asmar, a Palestinian resident who remained there, provided a graphic description of the city:

> When the people of Lod left the city, they could not, of course, take any of this. The Israeli authorities wanted the homes in the city vacant, and, apparently, wanted to sell the furniture and the merchandise from the shops. Thus, for months, we witnessed large trucks being loaded with furniture and the removal of merchandise from all of the shops which had been lavishly filled with commodities from throughout the area. Most of the Arab residents did not dare to take anything . . . The sight of the large, deserted city, the open homes, the breached commodity-filled shops and neighbourhoods that had already been emptied and the trucks that worked ceaselessly throughout the day struck fear into our hearts. The men who had come with the trucks would go into house after house and take out any article of value including beds, mattresses, cupboards, kitchenware, glassware, couches, draperies, and other such effects. When I returned home, I wanted to ask my mother, Why are they doing this? That property belongs to somebody . . . But I did not dare to ask . . . The sight of the deserted city, the looting of all its residents' property, and the turmoil of my own mind then have haunted me for years.[38]

Alongside the pillage, and apparently as part of it, people were given free rein to do what they wanted to Arab residents, buildings, property, and even religious buildings.[39] Ramle Arabs complained about how the military authorities were treating them. Days after the conquest, 'elders, women, children, and infants were scorned when they were left without food and water and exposed to intense sun for eight straight hours for no other reason than to humiliate them, demean them, and abuse them'. Due to restrictions on movement, 'residents who left the doors to their homes open for searches lost possessions'. We can assume that these possessions were stolen, not lost. 'Such behaviour,' wrote the Ramle residents' representatives, 'goes against religious rules, man-made laws, and

---

38   el-Asmar, *To be an Arab in Israel*, 19–20.
39   On the affair surrounding the rape of an Arab woman by soldiers from the Eighth Brigade's Eighty-Ninth Battalion, see files: 2994/1950-3014, 6221/1949-2008, IDF.

human conscience, and stands in opposition to the declarations repeatedly made in various circles that the State of Israel maintains equality and does not discriminate.'[40]

Six months after Ramle's conquest, the Arab residents continued to complain about the lawlessness that reigned there:

> All the property of the residents who were expelled from their homes and penned into this neighbourhood has either been stolen by individuals or systematically taken by the Office of the Custodian of Abandoned Property without the population that has remained in place being given the time or the opportunity to safeguard it.[41]

The seizure of the property of residents who were present went against government policy – not just in Ramle and Lydda, but in every city and town. Despite clear instructions on this matter, the Ministry of Minorities director needed to remind people more than once

> that clear instruction needs to be given to the workers under your supervision that they should not touch present Arabs' property. In cases where a present Arab's property has been taken, it is to be returned and the individual affected is to be compensated as soon as possible.[42]

In December 1948, the Ministerial Committee on Abandoned Asset Affairs continued to discuss the segregation of Lydda's Arab residents into two assigned neighbourhoods (something that had already been done in the city), so that the rest of the city could be populated with new immigrants.[43] In the committee meeting, Ministry of Minorities director Gad Machnes said that he 'did not believe that the holding of the Arab residents in fenced concentration camps is

40   Letter from the Arabs of Ramle, 24 June 1948, file: Conquered Israeli territories.

41   Report on Ramle by Shlomo Ashrov, Ministry of Minorities, 2 January 1949, file: Arab villages, Gimmel-302/110, ISA.

42   Gad Machnes to the custodian of abandoned property, 31 August 1948, file: 'Instructions concerning the sale of Arab property', Gimmel-307/32, ISA.

43   On the populating of Ramle with new immigrants, see Danna Piroyansky, *Ramle Remade: The Israelisation of an Arab Town, 1948–1967* (Haifa: Pardes Publishing, 2014).

justified any longer'. (Notably, this sentence, found in the Israel State Archives file containing the committee's meeting minutes, was recently censored.) Machnes asserted that 'our experience in Haifa teaches us that Arabs should be given freedom of movement within city limits'.[44] A Ministry of Minorities memorandum from January 1945 stated that 'the present demands . . . include . . . removal of the barbed wire fence'.[45] When military rule in the area was terminated in July 1949, freedom of movement was finally granted, but the barbed wire remained in place.[46]

The two cities' mosques were also gutted – something, as we have seen, that occurred in many conquered cities. Lydda's large Dahmash Mosque (دهمش) was pillaged, as was the Great Mosque (الكبير) of Lydda. People broke in and looted it so thoroughly that even the water faucets, the bathroom doors, and 'the equipment found inside the tomb at the centre of the courtyard were stolen'. The tomb of Abu al-Fadl (الفضل), in the village of Abu al-Fadl (where the moshav of Talmei Menashe can be found today), was also breached.[47] The mosque and tomb of Abu al-Awn (العون) 'were befouled and the whole place was used as a latrine . . . The courtyard was turned into a cemetery'.[48] Muslim Department chief assistant Yaakov Yehoshua, who reported on the mosques' conditions, wrote that 'the visit depressed me. We saw that the great effort we put into protecting the holy sites had gone to waste'.[49] The military authorities confiscated goods one of the priests was keeping in his church, arguing that it was stolen property. It turned out that someone in the army wanted the property for himself. Meanwhile, the military governor wrote, 'there was a burglary at the warehouses of [the Office of the

44   Minutes of the Ministerial Committee on Abandoned Asset Affairs meeting, 17 December 1948, file: Administration – Abandoned Property Committee.

45   Memorandum on activities of the Ministry of Minorities (May 1948–January 1949), file: Memorandum on activities of the Ministry of Minorities, Gimmel-304/63, ISA. See also 'The topic of discussion: Ramle-Lod district 19 June 1949', Ramle-Lod administration, Gimmel-2201/16, ISA.

46   Meeting at Southern District headquarters, Israeli police, 25 July 1949, Document 60807, Conflict document collection – Akevot Institute.

47   Report of Yaakov Yehoshua, chief assistant in the Muslim Department, apparently March 1949, file: Oversight of Muslim holy sites, Gimmel-308/140, ISA.

48   Report from the Ministry of Religions on Israeli mosques (Ramle addendum), 10 February 1949, file: Muslim holy sites, Gimmel Lamed-44864/16, ISA.

49   Report of Yaakov Yehoshua, chief assistant in the Muslim Department.

Custodian], and, surprisingly, the priest's goods were unexpectedly stolen.[50]

Six months after Ramle's conquest, a Ministry of Minorities official summarized the situation as follows:

> The population's abandoned personal belongings are almost completely gone. After nearly five months of work, the Office of the Custodian of Abandoned Property almost completely cleaned the area of every object of value, both furniture and animals . . . the activities of Office of the Custodian were neither overseen by a representative of the Ministry of Minorities nor the military governor.[51]

Almost no civilians or military personnel were put on trial for looting the city. The assistant of the Kiryati Brigade's military prosecutor provided one of the reasons for this:

> After Lod's conquest, all the units in the area began to pillage . . . They [the brigade's soldiers] turned to me and asked for permission. I told them that I did not know if they needed permission for it, because all the brigades were pocketing stuff. I told them that they could go. What I meant was that they could go take some small things as mementos . . . I saw Palmach members and others bringing spoils to Ben Shemen . . . after a seven-month siege, I had no idea what the procedure was for such matters.[52]

A few months after the occupation of the two cities, the property of the thousands of Palestinians who lived in them was taken by the state or by Jewish citizens. This situation served the political line that wanted to prevent the return of Palestinian residents in the future.

---

50   Major Z. Yavetz (military governor of Ramle-Lod) to the commander of the military government, 3 December 1948, file: Office of Minister Shalom-Bechor Sheetrit, Gimmel Lamed-14820/2. On the affair's development, see file: Property claims of priests, Gimmel-297/14, ISA.

51   Shlomo Ashrov, Report on Ramle, 2 January 1949, file: Ways of life of the Arab population, Gimmel-297/5, ISA.

52   Quoted in Inbar, *Scales of justice*, 776.

Beersheba

Apportioned to be part of a future Arab state, Beersheba was conquered on 21 October 1948, as part of Operation Yoav. It was the last Arab city conquered during the Independence War, and it was conquered after a three-month-long ceasefire (conquered in July, during the ten days between the first and second ceasefires, Lydda and Ramle were the last two Arab cities to be conquered before it). Following the city's conquest, the State of Israel expanded its control over areas that the partition plan had designated for an Arab state. Now Israel controlled territory that spread across wide expanses in the western Negev, as well as in its eastern sector. The city's conquest cut off the Egyptian forces in the Jerusalem area as well as the Hebron hills and Bethlehem to the south, and thwarted the Egyptian command's efforts to open a front along the Gaza–Beersheba road.[1] Before Beersheba was occupied, approximately 350 people lived there.[2] In a meeting of Mapam's Arab Department, it was noted that 'Ben-Gurion decided that there will be no Arabs in Beersheba.'[3]

1 Ardon Cohen, Michael (Miki) Cohen, and Amos Mendelsson, *The Negev Brigade in the War of Independence* [Hebrew] (Tel Aviv: self-pub., 2011), 244.

2 Michael Hanegbi, 'An overview of the conquest of the city of Beersheba and the conditions in it in the days thereafter', 21 October 1948, file:121/1950-223, IDF.

3 Meeting of the Arab Department, 27 October 1948, file: (6)10.10-95, YYA.

According to the British Mandatorial Government's 1945 census, 5,570 people resided in the small 'city' of Beersheba.[4] In the nearby area, there were only a few Jewish settlements (for example, Kibbutz Hatzerim, Kibbutz Mishmar HaNegev, and Kibbutz Be'eri); therefore, it was mostly military forces who committed its looting and pillaging. Because Beersheba was far from centres of power and examining eyes, relatively little disturbed those emptying the town. For example, immediately following its conquest, Ministry of Minorities officials could not get to the town to attempt to minimize the damage, as they had done in other places.

The town's depredation began 'a few minutes after [the military was] in full control of the city's police' station. While the Egyptian prisoners of war were being place in temporary prison camps and people were caring for the wounded, 'masses of soldiers began to let out their anger and to release the tension long pent up within them' through haphazard break-ins to residential homes and stores. As we learn from Negev Brigade commander Haim Bar-Lev's biography,

> noise and the sounds of breaking mirrors and glass filled the streets, pieces of broken furniture flew through the air, and black smoke billowed into the sky. Pillows, blankets, garments, canned food, and weapons for souvenirs – the looters left nothing untouched. Members of nearby settlements looked for tractors and farm equipment. Soldiers loaded sacks of flour and sugar onto trucks. Chaos reigned there. Commanders lost control over their soldiers.[5]

Solel Cohen, a company commander in the Negev Brigade who participated in the city's conquest, later explained that the brigade 'suffered a great deal in the Negev', and that this translated in a 'desire for vengeance' when the city was conquered. Unlike more northern cities where

---

4   *Village Statistics 1945: A Classification of Land and Area Ownership in Palestine* (Beirut: PLO Research Center, 1970), 42.

5   Carmit Gai, *Bar-Lev: A biography* [Hebrew] (Tel Aviv: 'Am 'Oved; Sifriyat ha-po'alim, 1998), 64. See also Michael Hanegbi, 'An overview of the conquest of the city of Beersheba and the conditions in it in the days thereafter', 21 October 1948, file:121/1950-223, IDF: 'Our units burst into town and began to clear it and to take prisoners and spoils. It should be noted that part of the army, mostly Gahal soldiers in the various units, was already breaking into stores and homes, and began to loot in an uncontrollable frenzy that continued during the first few days [after the conquest].'

there was a great deal to pillage, in Beersheba 'there was just destruction', he noted. The 'soldiers fired at armoires and shattered and broke things for no reason'. Cohen remarked that 'there was not really that much to loot. There were pieces of furniture. So what? Are you going to take a piece of furniture?' Additionally, he talked about one of the searches that he conducted:

I opened a door, and there was a frightened Bedouin standing there. We grabbed him and he had a dagger. I took it as a souvenir, and I still have it today. If that is spoils, I took spoils. Initially, I took the dagger because it was terribly sharp.

Cohen figured that somebody may have left some 'buried treasure' in the city. Members of more distant settlements took mechanical equipment.[6]

In fact, Cohen's memory deceived him: a great deal of looting actually took place in the city. Writing in real time, the Rehovot base commander, who was present during the city's conquest, recorded that

it was a horrible sight to see how hundreds of soldiers from the various battalions stormed in to plunder. If an Egyptian counterattack had come, a disaster would have occurred. It was also the reason that the pursuit of the Egyptians broke off and the paths of retreat were not blocked.[7]

One soldier told how he and other fighters were witness '"to the great attack" on . . . the enemy spoils' while they were laying mines and making preparations to defend the city in case of an Egyptian counterattack. He remarked that they also found 'booty' in the city.[8] According to the city's military governor, 'a large portion' of the property was stolen or destroyed by the soldiers.[9] The commander of the Eighty-Second

---

6   Solel Cohen, testimony, June 2002, PGA.

7   Quoted in Yoav Gelber, *Growing a fleur-de-lis: Israeli intelligence in the War of Independence, 1948–1949*, vol. 2 [Hebrew] (Tel Aviv: Misrad ha-bitahon, 2000), 609.

8   Ya'akov [no last name given], Ein Dor, in Levi Dror and Yisrae'el Rozentzvayg, eds, *ha-Shomer ha-tza'ir book* [Hebrew], vol. 3 (Merhavyah: Sifriyat ha-po'alim, 1964), 64.

9   Hanegbi, 'An overview of the conquest of the city of Beersheba'.

Battalion, for his part, permitted his soldiers to loot. According to him, after an hour, not a store remained that was left untouched.[10]

Tzofen Arazi, who participated in the city's conquest, explained:

> After the conquest, there was extraordinary pillaging . . . a few [Arabs] remained there, and we knew them . . . before the war, we travelled to Beersheba, and we would buy things there. The Jews looted Beersheba! No doubt about it. The city was abandoned . . . There were warehouses with different kinds of merchandise, different kinds of tractors, and anything you could want.[11]

According to Bar-Lev, the soldiers' 'wild behaviour' continued for a few hours. Then Negev brigade commander Nahum Sarig went through the streets 'and furiously tried to stop the plunder. Yet he did not succeed.' Sarig ordered the jeep drivers to drive through the streets and to fire in the air. Apparently, this helped get the soldiers, who exited the homes and stores, to assemble.[12] Uzi Narkiss, commander of the brigade's Seventh Battalion, also said that attempts to stop the soldiers' looting did not go well. 'More than a few soldiers took [looting] for granted.'[13] Narkiss quoted what poet Haim Gouri wrote about the city's plunder in his 1950 book *Until the dawn rose*:

> Booty's gold dazzles. The spoils! The spoils! – the black wolf of hatred burst out. Sergei gnashed his teeth. Through the units, the jeep passed: Stop! We have passed over the narrow and painful bridge of human inclinations to the afternoon hours.[14]

Simcha Shiloni, a Negev Brigade commander, later testified to the enthusiasm with which his soldiers looted:

---

10   Zvi Inbar, *Scales of justice and the sword: Foundations of military law in Israel* [Hebrew] (Tel Aviv: Ma'arakhot, 2005), 594–5.

11   Zalman Arazi in Jessica Nevo and Ami Asher, testimony, 'Report of the Truth Commission on the responsibility of Israeli society for the events of 1948–1960 in the South' [Hebrew], *Zokhrot* (December 2015): 18.

12   Gai, *Bar-Lev: A biography*, 64–5.

13   Uzi Narkiss, *A soldier of Jerusalem* [Hebrew] (Tel Aviv: Misrad ha-bitahon, 1991), 113.

14   Haim Gouri, *Until the dawn rose* [Hebrew] (Tel Aviv: ha-Kibbutz ha-me'uhad, 2000), 72.

It was the first time, perhaps the only time, when I gave an order that they did not listen or pay attention to what I said. I gave an order. I held the man by the arm, and I spoke with him . . . I saw glazed-over eyes that were not taking in [what I was saying]. That was the degree to which the desire for spoils had overpowered them. Now I do not remember what I used to free them [from its bonds] . . . I saw that I did not have control over the men. I really had to use force to get them away from the plunder.[15]

On the twenty-fourth of the month, three days after the city's conquest, the brigade command announced that whoever was caught looting would be arrested and tried.[16] Three days later, to prevent the removal of spoils, vehicles travelling alone were forbidden from exiting the city.[17] Michael Cohen explained years later that Sarig 'closed all of the entrances to the city', and 'they took apart every car [that left the city] to see if [those in the car] were smuggling'. Nevertheless, Custodian Shafrir told how his men had captured four military vehicles that were smuggling goods to merchants in the centre of the country. Those involved were officers. Shafrir added: 'It is no problem to keep watch over the entry-ways to the Negev and the Galilee. All you need are roadblocks set up on the few roads leading to them and help from a few trustworthy individuals.'[18] Like in other places, a serious effort was not made.

Soldiers possessed a wealth of stories about the ravaging of the city. Cohen told the following story:

I have a good friend, my good friend was there . . . he was walking in the street with a box of coins that he had taken from one of the breached stores, so I punched him. He was proud about what he did.

15   Simcha Shiloni, testimony, February 1986, PGA. For a similar description of an ecstatic state, see Avraham Adan (Bren), *About the ink flag* [Hebrew] (Tel Aviv: Ma'arakhot, 1984), 121.

16   Cohen, Cohen, and Mendelsson, *Negev Brigade*, 248.

17   'Cars, military personnel, and citizens besides people or cars possessing a proper travel authorization are forbidden to enter the city of Beersheba.' See 'Entrance and exit inspection for the city of Beersheba', 27 October 1948, file: 6308/1949-40, IDF.

18   Minutes of the Ministerial Committee on Abandoned Asset Affairs meeting, 5 November 1948,. The Negev Brigade called for assignment of military policemen who would oversee the prevention of pillaging in the Negev. 'An addition of military police-men', 25 October 1948, file: 6308/1949-40, IDF.

I smacked the cashbox and the coins scattered. Yet there were more serious cases of plundering. Homes, there were private homes that belonged to people of means. You entered homes where the tablecloth and food were still on the table.[19]

The battalion journals exposed some of the looting-related moral dilemmas faced by soldiers.[20] While an explicit prohibition had been introduced concerning looting, the units dealt with it 'in a forgiving manner that recalled the way that the Palmach dealt with petty thefts' when the pilfered item benefited the training groups.[21] Teddy Eitan, commander of the 'Commando Français' (a company of mostly French-speaking soldiers assigned to the Negev Battalion's Ninth Battalion), was unforgiving. When he saw the huge quantity of spoils that his charges had amassed, 'he arranged them in groups of three, and without a word proceeded to lead them on a long march on the hills surrounding the city.'[22] Eighth Brigade commander Yitzhak Sadeh returned plundered watches.[23] Ben-Gurion commented on the spoliation in his diary: 'The brigades had taken tractors, vehicles, and food. It appears that removal of some of the property from the city had been authorized.'[24] Overall, it is unclear what the nature of these authorizations were.

Years after the city's conquest, Tzofen Arazi pointed to fundamental difficulties and dilemmas faced by the soldiers: 'Looting is an unjust thing, but there was nobody to talk with about it! Even if we had wanted to . . .' He added: 'People who had heard that there was total lawlessness in Beersheba, an empty city whose residents were not present, arrived from all over the place. People came in trucks and loaded up everything

---

19 Michael 'Miki' Cohen, testimony, in Nevo and Asher, 'Report of the Truth Commission', 45. See also the testimony of (name redacted by Israel Defense Forces and Defense Establishment Archive) about the looting of a carpet on 2 November 1948, file: 2294/1950-2391, IDF.

20 Alon Kadish, *To arms and farms: The hachsharot in the Palmach* [Hebrew] (Ramat Efal: Galili Centre for Defence Studies; Yad Tabenkin, 1995), 243–6.

21 Ibid., 246.

22 Gai, *Bar-Lev: A biography*, 65. See also Solel Cohen, testimony, June 2002, PGA.

23 Notes from a discussion of the Political Committee, 11 November 1948, file: (6)10.10-95, YYA.

24 Quote from diary entry for 27 October 1948, David Ben-Gurion, *The War of Independence* [Hebrew], ed. Gershon Rivlin and Elhanan Oren (Tel Aviv: Defense Ministry Press, 1982), 780.

that they could.'[25] Kibbutz members were among the looters, and Kibbutz Hatzerim and Kibbutz Mishmar HaNegev in the South, near Beersheba, were among the kibbutzim whose members looted.[26] Shmu'el Bunim, a member of Mishmar HaNegev, explains that the kibbutz members resented that they were unable to steal crops from Beersheba like the members of Kibbutz Hatzerim had (Hatzerim was a few kilometres away from the city). Of course, not everyone had a hand in the looting. Bunim remembers one of the veteran members standing in the kibbutz yard and expressing his anger about the spoils that had arrived on the kibbutz.[27] Subsequently, the kibbutz had a conversation on the topic.[28] In the end, it was decided that 'everything that [members] had taken [to their rooms] needed to be given back'.[29]

Representatives of the Office of the Custodian of Abandoned Property visited the city two days after its conquest. Shafrir remarked that the city was 'breached, broken, and destroyed'.[30] Nehemyah Ben-Tor, a Lehi member who fought as part of the Eighth Brigade, summarized the condition of Beersheba a few days after its conquest as follows:

25 Zalman Arazi, testimony, in Nevo and Asher, 'Report of the Truth Commission', 18.

26 See, for example, the Office of the Custodian's complaint about the plunder given by the Twelfth Brigade commander to the 'Amalim' training group (which established Kibbutz Tzuba in October 1948). Elimelech Avner to the IDF chief of staff, 11 November 1948, file: 121/1950-223, IDF.

27 Shmuel Bunim, in discussion with the author, 13 May 2020.

28 The minutes of the kibbutz conversation from October 1948 are a fascinating document. Nineteen pages in length, they are written by various hands. Reading them, one gets a sense of the various dilemmas the kibbutz members faced. Pinhas Golan: 'In my opinion, the [pillaging in] Beersheba is the height of degeneracy, even if it just expressed itself through burglary and petty theft . . . I was shocked to see how people suddenly wanted to grab stuff when things arrived [in the kibbutz yard] from Beersheba . . . It was plain robbery . . . I am simply saying that if we, as a young kibbutz, count such negative occurrences among our first steps . . . we will bring about the rapid collapse of our kibbutz.' Jack Burshtayn: 'Anyone who was in Beersheba saw that they took everything . . . The question is why the kibbutz is involved in such things . . . We need to get everything back from every member.' It was decided to hold a meeting about the subject and that all spoils taken by individuals to their rooms be surrendered to the kibbutz. Minutes of the kibbutz gathering, October 1948, Kibbutz Mishmar HaNegev Archive. I am grateful to Margalit Zaltzman, the kibbutz archivist, for her aid in locating this document and identifying the speakers' names.

29 Meeting of the Arab Department, 27 October 1948, file: (6)10.10-95, YYA.

30 Minutes of the Ministerial Committee on Abandoned Asset Affairs meeting, 5 November 1948.

The city looked like a ghost town. Here and there smoke rose from ruined homes. The stores were breached and empty, and, in the homes, you could find neither man nor animal. Everything had been taken by our soldiers. Just a few hens wandered around outside trying not to get captured by the guys chasing after them.[31]

In opposition to what is described above, the commander of the military government in the occupied territories, General Elimelech Avner, still claimed in an early November 1948 meeting of the Ministerial Committee on Abandoned Asset Affairs that 'no property was plundered in Beersheba'.[32] In Beersheba, as elsewhere, pillaging went hand in hand with brutality and violence towards Arabs.[33] Nonetheless, few people were held accountable for their actions there.

---

31   Nehemyah Ben-Tor (Arziyah), *Today I will write in pen: The path of a Lehi member* [Hebrew] (Tel Aviv: Ya'ir in the Name of Avraham Shtern, 1991), 382.

32   Minutes of the Ministerial Committee on Abandoned Asset Affairs meeting, 5 November 1948.

33   See, for example, the verdict handed down by the special military court (6/49/mem) in the trial of a soldier who participated in the conquest of Beersheba and tried to kill a prisoner (27 February 1949), file: 2169/1950-2, IDF.

Mosques and Churches

The plunder and destruction of mosques and churches occurred throughout the Independence War. Only a limited number of associated documents survive, and portions of them have been redacted by the state. Although the plunder and destruction of religious buildings in various cities has been touched upon above, a more extensive discussion will be provided here.

Foreign Minister Moshe Sharett spoke about this topic most bluntly.[1] In mid-1949, when the war concluded, Sharett declared that the Catholic front was 'one of the most difficult fronts' on which the State of Israel fought. He noted that Israel would certainly be asked to compensate Christians for the damage that Jews caused their churches. 'It is wild vandalism, desecration of holy sites worthy of savages, not Jews. Yet it has been carried out and is sometimes still being carried out. This vandalism is not just directed against Christians.'[2] Eliyahu Arbel, a deputy assistant chief of staff for operations in the Etzioni Brigade, explained that their 'soldiers destroyed works of art in

---

1   In addition to what follows, see Foreign minister to minister of religions, 30 April 1950, file: The Department for Christian Communities, Gimmel-5812/14, ISA; H. Z. Hirschberg (director of the Department for Muslim Religious Affairs) to the minister of defence, 10 August 1948, file: 121.1950-183, IDF.

2   Moshe Sharett to a group of Mapai activists, early June 1949, in Moshe Sharett, *Speaking out: Israel foreign minister's speeches* [Hebrew], vol. 2, ed. Yaakov and Rina Sharett (Tel Aviv: Moshe Sharett Heritage Society, 2016), 437.

monasteries and churches.[3] The soldiers also looted antiquities that Jerusalem's Hebrew University had collected for years. For example, they took a collection of Second Temple–period Hebrew coins, 'a precious asset [documenting] the Jewish People's history in the Land of Israel', according to Sharett. Placed in the hands of Franciscan monks for safekeeping in Jerusalem, the collection 'was stolen and disappeared. Now it is lost to the world.'

Sharett explained to a group of Mapai activists that when one of the representatives of a Christian church arrived for a visit, he 'had had to make excuses about a security zone to prevent him from him entering the church, [and discovering that] the soldiers were using its nave for latrines and that the whole floor was covered in human excrement'. He described brutality and plunder in the churches: in one church, an expensive crown was stolen; in another, people broke off the finger of a statue – either Mary or Jesus – to steal a ring. 'Jews did such things cold bloodedly, and they occurred here and there, for months.'[4] One of the vandals justified his actions: the Nazis had annihilated 6 million Jews, and he wanted vengeance. He vandalized a statue by carving a Star of David and the word 'Zion' on it.[5]

Comments that Sharett made in a cabinet meeting on 5 July 1949, concerning how the security forces and Jews as a whole were treating religious sites, remain censored to this day and are not publicly accessible.[6] One can assume, however, that what Sharett had to say in that meeting was similar to the following remarks he made in December 1949:

> I want to mention the shocking and terrible sin that the State of Israel committed, first and foremost against itself, by not preparing from the outset to institute iron discipline among its people to prevent them from desecrating other nations' holy sites. I want to point to this thing as a shameful filth-filled page [in our history]. I am using the word

---

3 Quoted in Uri Milstein, *The Rabin file: A myth and its solution* [Hebrew] (Ramat Efal: Sridut, 2005), 119.

4 Sharett, *Speaking out*, 437.

5 Notes from a Discussion of the Political Committee, 11 November 1948, file: (6)10.10-95, YYA.

6 On this, see Ofer Aderet, 'Moshe Sharett broke the silence too – and he was censored' [Hebrew], *Haaretz*, 22 January 2016.

'filth' in the literal sense, because there were cases where our soldiers turned places of prayer into places of filth, latrines, and covered the floors with their excrement. I want to note this. We have been punished for our loose morals and for the shocking boorishness that prevails in our ranks. Here too, I employ the phrase 'in our ranks' in its literal sense, because [it occurred] in our ranks, amongst our boys – and I cannot favour those born in the country over those born abroad – meanwhile, I cannot favour those who experienced a clash [between religions] since their childhood and were educated to hate the church – such inclinations were not cultivated among our children [in Palestine] – and I cannot favour our [Palestinian] sons even though morally despicable acts were unexpectedly committed by new immigrants. It is impossible to imagine what was done. Desecration, conscious desecration, befoulment, the breaking of symbols, breaking off statues' fingers to steal some ring[s], pilfering of precious stones and pearls from monasteries, litter, the tearing of books, theft, things wherein there is no light, objects, objects for ritual purposes used as heating fuel. I can go on and on! The brain finds it difficult to wrap itself around the wild and shocking things that were done in various places . . . You will not be able to enter Capernaum [the monastery there was destroyed]. We are not allowing any tourists to visit Capernaum, because the situation there is dreadful. In most of the churches in Jerusalem, in various places – in Jaffa, in Haifa, and in all sorts of places – the situation is the same. We did not know how to take charge in advance. We did not know in advance how to instil discipline. We ourselves did not know that we were so uneducated or so shamefully educated.[7]

Just as churches were destroyed in the big cities, they were destroyed throughout the country. There are extensive descriptions. The Christian faithful consider the Dormition Abbey of the Benedictine

---

7 Mapai secretariat and faction in Knesset, 31 December 1949, in Sharett, *Speaking out*, 949–50. See also Memorandum of Marie Syrkin from September 1948 (about the survey she made at the end of August to examine the condition of the holy sites in the cities and towns of the Galilee [and North of Haifa] and the cabinet members' response to it), file: Holy sites, Gimmel-307/43, ISA; 'Report on the hostile behaviour of the Christian clergy', Composed by the Twelfth Battalion's intelligence officer, n.d., file: 2168/1950-286, IDF.

community, located on Mount Zion, northwest of Jerusalem's Old City, to be one of their holiest churches. It was thoroughly looted. When Israeli forces captured Mount Zion in May 1948, they removed the resident monks, with the exception of three, whom they allowed to remain to watch over the church and the many valuables contained within. The objects were placed in the church basement, together with other precious objects from different area churches that had been placed there for safekeeping, and the Jerusalem district commander promised the representatives of the church (which was under the special protection of the pope) that the place was safe from looting and pillaging. After a few days, however, the remaining monks were removed from the church, and Irgun and Haganah soldiers broke into the basement and took diamonds, gold, and other precious objects. The stolen objects' value was estimated at hundreds of thousands of liras. The police only succeeded in finding a small portion of the stolen property.[8] Even months after the war concluded, the church's representatives were not allowed to freely access the site. Saul Colbi of the Ministry of Religions hints at some of the reasons for this in internal government correspondence: 'Just between us, we really do not want [this], because, as long as it remains in the army's hands, we cannot be certain that conditions in the church will be acceptable.'[9]

Conditions in the Dormition Abbey were not unlike conditions in other religious institutions. In Jerusalem's churches and seminaries, 'books, most of which are sacred Christian texts, lie strewn across the floors of rooms. Similarly, shreds of clothing and sacred objects are scattered about', one Jewish resident wrote apprehensively.[10] The many break-ins at institutions led Jerusalem district commander David Shaltiel to issue the following order in July 1948:

---

8   Yaakov Herzog to the director of the Department of Christians, 9 August 1948, file: Christian holy sites, Het Tzadi -2397/7, ISA.

9   P. Colbi (Ministry of Religions) to Walter Eytan (Foreign Ministry director), 30 October 1949, file: Christian holy sites. For a description of the condition of the church, see Protocol of a visit to Mount Zion, 19 April 1949, file: Visits in the South, Gimmel-46524/10, ISA.

10   David Benvenisti to the military governor, 21 December 1948, file: Army complaints, Gimmel-273/51, ISA.

I would like to again bring your attention to the fact that we are repeatedly receiving complaints about break-ins to religious and cultural institutions in the conquered areas and cases where their assets and collections have been either damaged or stolen. Included among these institutions are museums and libraries.

He announced an overarching prohibition on entrance to 'holy sites, churches, mosques, monasteries, etc.'[11]

Antonio Vergani, a Patriarchate of Jerusalem representative who was responsible for the Catholic Church's religious structures in Palestine, wrote a report filled with descriptions of churches and chapels 'that had been desecrated' with 'crosses and holy images broken' and 'sacred objects plundered'. Vergani provided a long list of holy sites that had been desecrated, noting that it was possible to find 'one especially saddening detail in every one of them:

Everywhere one could find crosses that had been broken, and crosses from which the Crucified One had been removed and frequently either broken or covered in filth . . . All these acts point to an especially strong hatred for the symbol of our redemption.

Christian holy sites (not only churches) throughout the country were systematically robbed.[12] This is what happened to Bethlehem's Saint Karl Convent on 17 April 1948; Haifa's Saint Anne Convent on 21 April 1947; Haifa's Saint Joseph's Catholic Association, where 'all the furniture and instruments were stolen' on 16 May 1948; the Benedictines' hospice and farm in Tabgha, north of Tiberias, where even the pipe organ was stolen; the Italian hospital managed by Franciscan nuns in Haifa; the Italian school and the Franciscan convent in Tiberias; the Terra Sancta Monastery in Tiberias; the Benedictines' farm in Karm al-Saheb, near Nazareth; the Franciscan monastery north of the village of Majdal

11   'Break-ins to religious and cultural institutions', 26 July 1948, file: Property from the conquered territories, Gimmel-278-56, ISA.

12   During the war, there were cases of destruction, looting, and violence carried out by Muslims against Christians. See 'Harm to Christians', file: 105/195, HHA. See also the following report on destructive acts committed in holy sites that were carried out by Arabs: 'Who is destroying the holy sites and who is insuring their protection' [Hebrew], ha-Tzofeh, 8 June 1948.

(المجدل) on the west coast of the Sea of Galilee; and other holy sites throughout the country.[13]

Perusal of documentation pertaining to the condition of Christian religious institutions reveals a pattern: the pillage of valuable objects and the destruction of ritual objects. The following report, regarding a church in Jerusalem's Musrara neighbourhood, is typical: 'Soldiers from the nearby bases, as well as workers building fortifications, ceaselessly break into the site, destroy various statues and sacred implements, create a serious mess, and pillage things.'[14]

As we have seen elsewhere, rather than making use of spoils, looters sometimes chose to damage them: soldiers lacking a confiscation order robbed copious supplies from the Beit Jimal (بيت جمال) Monastery in the lower Judaean Hills, but they chose to destroy the contents of its wine cellar that they looked upon covetously.[15] One of those involved in the site's conquest wrote:

> At night, immediately after the conquest, officers, as well as others involved [in the battle], began to visit [the site]. The visits intensified with the arrival of morning. It got to a point where sentries had to be stationed at the gate to keep track of the [site's] assets and those exiting [it]. This was largely done to deter people who might feel like taking spoils . . . Every time something is conquered, people instinctually want to demolish, destroy, take, and steal. People particularly liked [to destroy and plunder] buildings like this school. And [to ensure that this does not happen] you need to be watchful. It would be a shame [if something happened] to the things found here.[16]

The Abbot of the Catholic Deir Rafat (رفات)Monastery, located north of Beit Shemesh and Kibbutz Tzora, was shocked that the Israel Defense Forces destroyed the monasteries under his supervision. After the

13   A Hebrew translation of Antonio Vergani's Italian-language report 'Catholic institutions and people in the Galilee prior to the Israeli army's conquest of the area and during its occupation up until 30 August 1948', file: Christian holy sites.

14   Northern District military governor to chief administrative officer, 30 July 1948, file: Property from the conquered territories.

15   Yeshurun Schiff (Jerusalem police commander) to Bechor-Shalom Sheetrit, 3 November 1948, file: Arab holy sites, Gimmel-307/42, ISA.

16   A Harel Brigade soldier's description of the conquest of Beit Jimal, October 1948, file: 922/1975-1233, IDF.

conquest of the monasteries – and the village – belonging to the Patriarchate of Jerusalem, the abbot had been promised that, despite the village's conquest, 'the homes would not be damaged in any way'. Not even two months had passed since the village's conquest when 'the army blew up the old monastery found at the edge of the village, as well as most of the village'.[17] It turns out that a battalion training exercise was taking place and that, 'as part of the exercise', soldiers from the Sixty-First Battalion 'destroyed a number of homes'. Chief Military Prosecutor Avraham Gorali was told that destruction of abandoned homes was 'a regular and accepted practice that was not prohibited'.[18] The monastery was also looted.[19]

As brief discussions in the subchapters on the cities hinted, available sources show that many mosques were also looted and destroyed. The list is long, and the descriptions are painful. The destruction of Muslim religious buildings started during the first days of the war, more than six months before the invasion of five Arab armies. In Jerusalem, in January 1948, Jews demolished the mosque and cemetery on Chancellor Street (subsequently renamed Strauss Street). Besides destroying the headstones in the mosque courtyard, they vandalized the plumbing, the doors, and the windows.[20] A report on Muslim holy sites provides information about the condition of mosques throughout the country. The walls of the Ness Ziona mosque served as a canvas for malicious graffiti, and campaign propaganda was written on its dome: 'Select the Mapai slate.'[21] In January 1949, an anonymous 'honest Jew' turned to the minister of religions, Yehuda Leib Maimon, one of the Mizrahi movement's founders, and told him about Jewish merchants who were selling 'stones and all types of marble'. The anonymous Jew realized that the merchants 'were taking down Arab and Christian gravestones'. 'This brings great shame on us [Jews] . . . most of the merchandise is from

17 Albino Gorla (abbot) to the Department for Christian Communities, 23 September 1948, file: Christian holy sites.

18 Avraham Gorali to Yaakov Dori, 23 November 1948, file: 121/1950-223, IDF.

19 Hadassah Avigdori-Avidov, *On the path we took: From the diary of a convoy escort* [Hebrew] (Tel Aviv: Defense Ministry Press, 1988), 174.

20 Tene, 'Complaint about desecration of Arab mosque', 21 January 1948, file 105/62, HHA.

21 Report of Yaakov Yehoshua, chief assistant in the Muslim Department, ca. March 1949, file: Oversight of Muslim holy sites, Gimmel-308/140, ISA.

Haifa,' he noted.[22] In a meeting at the Ministry of Religions, it was noted that 'there is lawlessness out there. Many people come equipped with entry permits [to holy sites] and recommendations, and "withdraw" books and documents that they have a personal interest in.' It appears that the looters also plundered Jewish holy sites.[23]

In the village of Aqir (عاقر), for example, north of Rehovot and west of Mazkeret Batya (both just south of Tel Aviv), the mosque was desecrated and completely pillaged. The village was conquered in May. Subsequently, the residents fled and were expelled. 'We found the site breached,' wrote Yaakov Yehoshua, following a visit to the village mosque.

> Scattered Koran pages fluttered around the courtyard. The floor tiles had been uprooted, and even the interior room in the mosque, used as a prayer space by dervishes, had been desecrated. The inscription on the mosque's lintel had been torn out.[24]

In Jaffa, looters broke into and desecrated the *sabil* (fountain) of the Sultan Mahmud II (aka the Mahmudi fountain) and the Tomb of Abu Nabbut (أبو نبوت) (Muhammad Agha al-Shami [الشامي], the city's governor at the beginning of the nineteenth century). The Tomb of Abu al-Awn (العون) was broken into and 'the floor tiles were removed.'[25] In Jerusalem, the Tomb of Ukasha (عكاشة), the burial place of Ukasha ibn Mihsan, a member of Muhammad's entourage, was vandalized. It was asserted that the inscription above the keystone (that was knocked over) was stolen by a British officer, but it was Jewish youth groups who lit bonfires and destroyed the structure's walls.[26] Vandals also used the Ein Kerem mosque's walls as a graffiti canvas.[27]

---

22   An honest Jew (anonymous) to Yehuda Leib Maimon (minister of religions), January 1949, file: Oversight of Muslim holy sites.

23   Minutes of a meeting in the Ministry of Religions, 10 August 1948, file: Muslim holy sites, Gimmel Lamed-44864/16, ISA.

24   Yaakov Yehoshua, Report on the visit to Aqir, 27 January 1949, file: Visits in the South.

25   Yaakov Yehoshua, Report on the Visit to Ramle and the Jaffa Mosques, 30 January 1949, file: Visits in the South.

26   Baruch Kanael, Report on a visit to Nebi Ukasha, 19 April 1949, file: Visits in the South.

27   Ibid.

Sometimes, mosques 'were repurposed' for political activities. This is what happened in the village of Yahudiya (Abbasiya, العباسية) in the Ono valley, north of Lod, which was conquered in July 1948. Shortly thereafter, the state began to settle new immigrants in the village. While the invading army had destroyed most buildings by the time the new immigrants arrived, the town's military administrators decided to keep the mosque, with its tall minaret, intact. In April 1949, the mosque's floor tiles had been removed, and 'Koran scraps were fluttering around'. The mosque's beams were used for chicken coops. The Jewish Agency's Department of Housing fenced off the mosque for safekeeping, but the fence was quickly removed. Apparently, this was done by members of the Israeli Communist Party who 'established a clubhouse there'. In the present case, the destruction was not necessarily an expression of anti-Arab or anti-Muslim sentiment. The Tomb of Judah, Son of Israel (according to Jewish tradition, the burial site of the Biblical figure Judah), found in the western part of the village, was also mistreated and turned into a warehouse by invaders.[28] In the Sheikh Murad (الشيخ مراد) cemetery in the Abu Kabir (أبو كبير) neighbourhood, people stole marble headstones 'that they took to use for construction and building repair'. A gravestone inscription from 1215 was found lying outside the cemetery. Koran pages were found lying on the ground.[29] The chairman of the (Jewish) neighbourhood council supplied the police with the names of those who perpetrated this crime, but the police, apparently, let them go without prosecuting them. In contrast, a member of the military who was caught destroying gravestones in the cemetery was given an eighty-day prison sentence.[30]

The Salama ibn Hisham Mosque (سلمة بن هشام), near Jaffa, was also destroyed. The mosque's floor tiles, it was asserted, were taken by the Jewish village mukhtar (the chairman of the Salama neighbourhood council), Menachem Hadi. On the entry door, which had been taken off its hinges, someone had written 'A Cinema for Demobilized Soldiers Will Soon Be Opening'. People had also gotten to work in the

---

28   Baruch Kanael, Report on a visit to al-Yahudiya, 6 April 1949, file: Visits in the South.

29   Baruch Kanael, Report on a visit to Sheikh Murad cemetery in Abu Kabir, 10 May 1949, file: Visits in the South.

30   Baruch Kanael, Report on protection of holy sites, August 1949, file: Visits in the South.

local sheikh's tomb, where funeral monuments were being dismantled. There was no reason to invest in protecting the mosque, 'because
there is almost nothing left to protect other than the walls', wrote one
of the inspectors. On the building dedicated to Wali Bizur ('Wali' is a
term for a miracle-performing Islamic saint) in the village cemetery,
one of the inspectors explained, 'We were surprised to find the
inscription "Sports Club, Yazur". Inside the building, in the Mihrab,
we saw an image of Stalin and communist slogans, with a red flag
above them.'[31]

Ministry of Minorities director Gad Machnes sharply criticized the
pitifully inadequate governmental oversight of Muslim and Christian
religious structures. After ironically referring to the director of the
Ministry of Religions' Department of Religious Affairs and his colleagues
as 'righteous men, whose work is performed by others', Machnes went
on to assert:

> We [the Ministry of Minorities] have been the only ones who have
> addressed this issue. We safeguarded churches and mosques, because
> others did not protect them ... in a hundred villages, there are
> mosques and cemeteries that are being mistreated ... I need to say
> that you [the Ministry of Religions] have arrived a bit late to the party
> and you need to hurry 'to shore up the breach.'[32]

Machnes and other Ministry of Minorities officials were sensitive to the
damage and looting that the holy sites of other religions were facing.
When he learned about the condition of the Sidna Ali Mosque, (سیدنا
علي) at the foot of Herzliya's northern coast, he said that 'we will not be
forgiven for the mosque's neglect and the damage caused to it. It is a
scandal.'[33] Yisrael Galili was also shocked by 'the shameful act' that
occurred in the mosque. According to him, this act

---

31   Baruch Kanael, Report on visits to Salama, Yahudiyah, Kafr 'Ana, Bayt Dajan,
and Mishmar HaShiv'ah (Yazur), protection of holy sites, 8 May 1949, file: Visits in the
South.

32   Minutes of a meeting in the Ministry of Minorities with the director of the
Ministry of Religions' Department of Religious Affairs, 12 August 1948, file: Arab holy
sites.

33   Gad Machnes to the commander of Asher District, 11 May 1948, file: Arab
holy sites.

causes one to seriously worry about the cultural and human standards of our boys and their cultural ideas . . . appreciation of cultural values and religious holy sites are not just state orders but educational and cultural principles that need to be fundamental components of a Hebrew soldier's education.[34]

34   Yisrael Galili to the committee, 26 March 1948, file: Notebook 15-183/3, YTA.

The Palestinian Villages

During the Independence War, the Israeli military conquered about 550 villages. Some of their residents fled during various stages of the fighting, while others were expelled through use of various means of terror: intimidation, gunfire, murder, and more. The villages were gradually emptied of their inhabitants, the reasons for which varied. As many people know, there is a great deal of scholarly disagreement on this topic; we will not address the reasons for this depopulation nor provide description of the looting that took place in each and every village that fell victim to it here. That would demand a whole other book (and, in any case, it is not essential to this work).

Contemporary descriptions would lead one to believe that the contents, as well as the structures, of the overwhelming majority of villages were meagre and that there was neither plentiful nor valuable property to plunder from them. 'When the Arabs left their villages,' an official asserted in a meeting on Arab assets in the Tel Hai region, 'they took all of their belongings with them and besides immoveable assets almost no property remained in the villages.'[1] Similarly, Prime Minister Ben-Gurion wrote that when the Eighth Brigade conquered the village of Bayt Jibrin(بيت جبرين) at the end of October 1948, they 'found it

---

1 Summary of the meeting with the Committee on Arab Assets in the Tel Hai region, 5 June 1948, file: Various reports, Gimmel-306/62, ISA.

empty'.[2] 'In almost every case,' a May 1948 Department for Arab Assets report stated, 'the Arabs were able to take most of their personal belongings with them and they left their homes empty.'

The Arabs mainly left behind crops and flocks, which were either taken (with the custodian's authorization) or pillaged by the army or the agricultural villages.[3] Grains that could not be harvested were sometimes set ablaze, so that Palestinians who remained could not harvest them. Soldiers, following orders, sometimes killed camels and work animals. As we will see in the second part of the book, the burning of crops and the killing of work animals reflected a policy aimed at preventing Palestinians from returning to their homes at the end of the war.[4]

Evidence shows that villages near Jewish settlements were much more thoroughly plundered by both soldiers and citizens than those farther away, which were looted primarily by soldiers. Moreover, less property remained in villages whose residents fled than in villages whose residents were expelled (or fled a short time before military forces arrived). In most villages, livestock and various agricultural crops were the most valuable moveable property left behind. The villages were not centrally located, and their Jewish neighbours lived on kibbutzim and moshavot. This is one of the primary reasons behind the settlement movements' high level of involvement in the plunder of Arab property from villages. A survey of the conquered villages in the Haifa area presented the following observation: 'It should be noted that repeated acts of theft have occurred in the abandoned villages. Whole groups participate in the theft of abandoned property undisturbed.'[5]

The depredation of villages by combat troops began at the start of the war and continued throughout it. Captured by the Haganah, the village

---

2   Quote from diary entry for 27 October 1948, David Ben-Gurion, *The War of Independence* [Hebrew], ed. Gershon Rivlin and Elhanan Oren (Tel Aviv: Defense Ministry Press, 1982), 780.

3   End of May 1948 report of the Department for Arab Assets, file: Various reports.

4   On the harvest, see Arnon Golan, 'The transfer of abandoned rural Arab lands to Jews during Israel's War of Independence' [Hebrew], *Katedra* 63 (April 1992): 122–54; Benny Morris, 'The Harvest of 1948 and the Creation of the Palestinian Refugee Problem', *Middle East Journal* 40, no. 4 (Autumn 1986): 671–85.

5   A. Kishoni, 'Survey of the condition in abandoned villages in the Bay Area', 30 October 1948, file: Aharon Cohen – personal archive, (6)10.10-95, YYA.

of Qaisariya (قيسارية) was the first settlement conquered during the war. Its remaining residents were the first to suffer expulsion, and its property was the first to be looted. Palmach commander Yigal Allon explained: 'We received an order to destroy the Palestine Jewish Colonization Association homes in the village of Qaisariya ... and apparently one group also entered the remaining Arab homes.' The village mukhtar complained that approximately 300 liras were stolen from him. 'They immediately had the boys stand in formation and they were told to give the money back ... everything was returned to the Arabs.'[6] This was an atypical case. In the overwhelming majority of cases, property was not returned (after all, most owners were now absent), and very few people were tried. Not only did administrators fail to hold accountable those who pillaged, but also those who murdered village residents remaining behind – including the elderly, the sick, and others.

For obvious reasons, little documentary evidence of personal plunder committed by soldiers in the villages exists. Perhaps the best-known 'evidence' is the novel *Khirbet Khizeh* by Yizhar Smilansky (known as S. Yizhar), an esteemed Israeli writer. Published in 1949, it deals with the expulsion of the inhabitants of the eponymous imaginary village as the company makes their way through the village, looting whatever they can get their hands on:

And the roofing tiles from above, and the flooring tiles from below, and the wooden boards (we could always find a use for them in our yard) and send them home, there was such a tickling pleasure in getting such easy benefit, in getting rich quick, in picking up ownerless property and making it your own, and conquering it for yourself, and plans were already being made, right away, and it was already decided what was going to be done with almost all of these things at home, and how it would be done – except that we had been in so many villages already, and picked things up and thrown them away, taken them and destroyed them, and we were too used to it – so we picked up the fine-looking ownerless hoe, or pitchfork, and hurled it down to the ground, if possible aiming it at something that would shatter at once, so as to relieve it of the shame of not being of

---

6   Minutes of Committee of Five (evening), 4 July 1948, p. 6, BGA.

use – with real destruction, once and for all, putting an end to its silence.[7]

Khirbet Khizeh's residents were poor, and their property meagre. There was not a lot to pillage. Yet Yizhar described a mood that commonly overcame the forces that conquered the hundreds of villages. The same year that Yizhar published his story, journalist and activist Uri Avnery published his memoir *In the fields of the Philistines, 1948*, which describes the daily life of a Givati Brigade soldier fighting on the southern front. Avnery explains how soldiers boasted about the spoils they had taken: kaffiyeh and agal, old coins, an Arab sword. Looting did not bother officers in the field.[8] Avnery talks about how he and his fellow soldiers helped to remove 'the huge quantity of spoils amassed by the defenders' of Bayt Daras (بيت دراس) after they conquered the village in Operation Barak.[9]

Avnery's description of the pillage proves similar to other accounts of the Givati Brigade's conquest of al-Maghar (المغار), and reports of its despoliation of Bashshit (بشيت), both conquered in May 1948.[10] 'After a half hour of preparation, these forces began the next stage in the operation – the search stage. It was less organized than its predecessor . . . due to the ravenous hunger for spoils and souvenirs that seized members of the search team', notes a text in a commemorative volume honouring the brigade. There were not a lot of spoils, because the homes were empty.[11] The book does not recall anything else about soldiers' looting in Arab settlements.

---

7   S. Yizhar, *Khirbet Khizeh*, trans. Nicholas de Lange and Yaacob Dweck (New York: Farrar, Straus & Giroux, 2014), 38. Beginning of passage modified for accuracy.

8   Uri Avnery, *bi-Sedot Peleshet 1948* [Hebrew] (Tel Aviv: A. L. Hotza'ah meyuhedet, 1975), 58. It was translated as 'In the Fields of the Philistines' and published together with Avnery's subsequent work *Ha-Tzad ha-sheni shel ha-matbe'a* ('The Other Side of the Coin') as *1948: A Soldier's Tale – The Bloody Road to Jerusalem*, trans. Christopher Costello (Oxford: Oneworld, 2008). When passages cited from these two works are available in English, the English translation is cited in the footnotes. In all other cases, the Hebrew original is cited. For a brief depiction of pillaging on the southern front written by Abba Kovner, see Abba Kovner, *Face to face* [Hebrew] (Merhavyah: Sifriyat ha-po'alim, 1960), 389.

9   Avnery, *bi-Sedot Peleshet 1948*, 139.

10   On Bashshit, see Avraham Elon, *The Givati Brigade during the War of Independence* [Hebrew] (Tel Aviv: Ma'arakhot, 1959), 541.

11   Ibid., 552.

The war descriptions in *In the fields of the Philistines, 1948* pale in comparison with those Avnery offers in his 1950 book *The other side of the coin*, which presents the depredation of property in all of its wretchedness:

'You wouldn't guess what is going on in the village! [' said Zuzik. ']We are the only ones on duty. All the other companies are ransacking the houses. Scheike's company found a doctor's house. I'm telling you – a dream. They confiscated two pianos, beautiful oil paintings, armchairs, fountain pens, everything. This is a really rich village!' . . . After the meal it is my turn to wander through the village . . . Squads and companies are scattered throughout the village. Some are relaxing in armchairs, loaded down with prayer beads, fezzes, and swords. Other comrades are proudly showing off their watches and fountain pens. In front of the doctor's house, Yashke's company is sitting and keeping an eye on their treasures. The men are discussing the value of the looted pianos. They have had to accept surrendering one of them to the battalion's dayroom. They intend to sell the other.[12]

Yizhar's and Avnery's depictions, part true and part fictional, are not substantively different from how those who took part in the looting (and those who criticized it) described the events when they occurred. Alex Shafir, commander of the force that conquered Deir Muheisin (دير محيسن) told that after the village was captured in April 1948 the soldiers worked really quickly and 'they accumulated a great deal of booty . . . they looked like Purim clowns, not combat troops. I had no control over them.'[13] What Avnery wrote was quite similar:

In front of the headquarters stands a convoy looking like something out of *The Thousand and One Nights*. The company which was in Sukreir (سويرة) during the night has returned in their armoured vehicles. They look like figures from a fairy tale: fezzes and kaffiyehs on

---

12   Avnery, *1948: A Soldier's Tale*, 280. Translation modified for accuracy.

13   Quoted in Uri Milstein, *History of the Independence War*, vol. 4, *Out of Crisis Came Decision*, trans. and ed. Alan Sacks (Lanham, MD: University Press of America, 1998), 292.

their heads, sparkling daggers in their belts. The armoured vehicles are filled with sparkling booty: long swords, water pipes, masbahas.[14]

Deir Yassin was looted too. Prior to the war, the village – whose conquest and looting were among the most infamous of the war – had good relations with the nearby Jewish settlement of Givat Shaul. In January 1948, the two settlements signed an agreement to maintain good neighbourly relations, and the residents of Deir Yassin promised to announce 'every time' that Arab fighters were present in their village.[15] A month later, the Haganah command noted that when it came to the village's future relations with the Jewish settlement, its leaders were not seeing eye to eye with the Arab forces in Jerusalem, led by Abd al-Qader al-Husseini (الحسيني), whose soldiers were interested in attacking the nearby Jewish settlement.[16] In her diary, Hadassah Avigdori-Avidov, a Palmach convoy escort, wrote that after the conquest of Dei Yassin, someone named L. (she did not give a full name) 'was proud of an embroidered Arab peasant dress' looted from the village. Other women on the military base looked on the male and female looters with equal contempt. Avigdori-Avidov wrote that she 'was overcome by nausea, anger and pain' in the presence of 'the finds' that people brought from the village.[17] Not just foodstuffs and farm animals, but gold, cash, and jewellery were looted as well. The Lehi and the Irgun split the spoils.[18] The Haganah published an announcement harshly condemning 'horrendous behaviour, looting and pillaging, and acts of murder and massacre carried out in the conquered village'.[19]

---

14   Avnery, *1948: A Soldier's Tale*, 247. Translation modified for accuracy.

15   'Conditions of the agreement between Deir Yassin and Givat Shaul', 20 January 1948, file: 105/72, HHA.

16   A bundle of confirmed Arab intelligence from 27 February 1948, file: 500/48-60; Report on the refusal of the village mukhtar to supply volunteers to the Arab military forces, 1 February 1948, file: 105/72; HHA.

17   Hadassah Avigdori-Avidov, *On the path we took: From the diary of a convoy escort* [Hebrew] (Tel Aviv: Defense Ministry Press, 1988), 174.

18   Eliezer Tauber, *Deir Yassin: The end of the myth* (Hevel Modi'in: Kinneret / Zmora-Bitan, 2017), 112–13. It was noted that hundreds of liras were looted. See 'A report on the conquest of Deir Yassin', 10 April 1948, file: General 15-164/2, YTA; Milstein, *History of the Independence War*, 369.

19   'The Haganah in Deir Yassin' [Hebrew], *Haaretz*, 13 April 1948. The telegrams to King Abdullah of Transjordan and the condemnation messages are found in file: Conquest of the village of Deir Yassin, Documents and publications of the Haganah and

One Shmu'el, who wrote from 'somewhere' in the Hashomer Hatzair party journal 'Al ha-homah (On the Ramparts), reported to his fellow movement members about the difficult emotions that he felt upon finding himself in a large village with tens of homes 'and tended fields, chicken coops and cowsheds, and everything, everything, is deserted'. These feelings were foreign to him. 'Relishingly, without any remorse, I began to destroy the village, as ordered. The village was completely decimated. It is also a village of farmers'.[20] Writer and Palmach fighter Netiva Ben-Yehudah said similar things in Through the binding ropes:

> Naami let himself go crazy, which was something terrible . . . in every house that we went into, the first thing he did was make a circuit of destruction. [He did it] before we could even orient ourselves. The more splendid the home, the stronger his inclination to destroy got. When we entered an Arab mayor's home and discovered riches straight out of The Thousand and One Nights . . . Naami tore into everything, and I mean everything. He did not even leave one little stool intact! It took him hours, and we did not really have a lot of time – whatever! For this, he had time. He broke, he shattered.[21]

Someone referred to as P., who also did not give his name, used harsh words to criticize the looters:

> I object to what comrades who permitted themselves to take spoils from the abandoned village did with all my heart. Are we so upset that we do not have the ability to control our emotions? Comrades, remember our children! . . . Let us not be responsible for leaving a distasteful residue in the children's souls. The plate, the bracelet, the ring, etc. – will these remind our children of the heroic war that our comrades fought to free our homeland? Are we less socially

the Jewish Agency, Kaf 5/10/4. JIA. Cf. Yehuda Lapidot, Flames of revolt: The Irgun in Jerusalem [Hebrew] (Tel Aviv: Misrad ha-bitahon, 1996), 317. Lapidot criticizes the condemnation message of David Shaltiel, who, according to Lapidot, asserted that the village was conquered so that it could be looted.

20   Shmu'el, 'A letter from a mobilized member', 'al ha-Homah: Tenu'at ha-shomer ha-Tza'ir be-Eretz Yisra'el, June 1948, 6.

21   Netiva Ben-Yehuda, Through the binding ropes [Hebrew] (Jerusalem: Domino Press, 1985), 292.

responsible than the conquerors of Canaan in the time of Joshua ben Nun? . . . Spoils lead people astray. Behold! Have we not worked ceaselessly to internalize the idea of the brotherhood of nations and the international worker's spirit, so that we will be able to live together with these brothers in peace? The bracelet, the implement, the plate, these are not things that the [Iraqi military forces] brought with them. These belong to the residents of the neighbouring village. There is an institution that deals with enemy property. We need to make sure that the abandoned Arab property is collected, both for its exploitation and its return following a post-war settlement. Let us stand before our children in the future with clean hands and a pure spirit, so that we can tell them about our holy war for freedom.[22]

The people who wrote in favour of pillaging also employed pseudonyms. For example, 'Reporter 'Over 'Orakh' [Roving Reporter] wrote defensively that 'those who talk about "plunder" should shut their mouths. This is not plunder. Rather it is the spoils of war whose acquisition blood made possible. A blood price has been paid for it. Therefore, we take possession legally.'[23]

An additional difficulty faced by those trying to research pillaging in villages relates to how official military documents reported it. While in urban areas there were civilians – journalists and writers, among others – who wrote about what was happening around them, soldiers were usually the only ones who wrote about what happened in the villages, far from densely populated areas. Yet it is clear that the reports commanders wrote from the field to various headquarters and their superiors about what took place in villages during their conquest (and the days after) played down the spoliation undertaken by the soldiers (and their commanders). A report on the conquest of Majd al-Krum (مجد الكروم), written in October 1948 during the final stages of the fighting, illustrates this point.

In early January 1949, more than two months after its conquest, IDF forces searched the village looking to locate 'infiltrators and criminals in

---

22   P., 'Spoils lead people astray', in Levi Dror and Yisrae'el Rozentzvayg, eds, *ha-Shomer ha-tza'ir book* [Hebrew], vol. 3 (Merhavyah: Sifriyat ha-po'alim, 1964), 67–8.

23   Reporter 'Over 'Orakh, 'On the streets and in the villages these days' [Hebrew], *ha-Maskif*, 24 May 1948.

the city [*sic*]'. In a report on the operation, operation commander Tzvi Rabinovitz wrote, 'Two soldiers from the 123rd Battalion company took a few objects from a store. After a short investigation, the objects were returned to their owner. The aforementioned will be tried.'[24] Yet a hand-written document composed by a deputy company commander named Shlomo supplies extensive detail concerning the soldiers' brutal behaviour: 'the soldiers cursed, swore, and rained down blows throughout the operation.' Commander Rabinovitz took part in this behaviour. Deputy Shlomo wrote that the soldiers tortured the village mukhtar, who was sick and lying in bed. 'They hit him hard with the butts of their rifles and they kicked him in the stomach.' Subsequently, the mukhtar was hospitalized in Nazareth, where he was in 'critical condition'. Deputy Shlomo's report also describes the looting, but it brings to mind a very different picture than the one described in the official report:

> During the operation, the company from the 123rd Battalion broke into two stores. [Things] were also stolen from private homes'. Deputy Company Commander Shlomo was the one who told the soldiers not to pillage and he ordered that they be searched.[25]

I leave it to readers to decide which report they find more reliable.

Others who supported the looting in real time hid their role in it. In his memoirs, Kibbutz HaZore'a member Asher Benari tells about the battles near Kibbutz Mishmar HaEmek, the conquest of the neighbouring village Abu Zurayq (أبو زريق), and the conquest of the village of Abu Shusa (ابو شوشة), located between the two aforementioned kibbutzim. The inhabitants of the two villages abandoned their homes and their property and fled eastward. 'Members of Kibbutz HaZore'a who visited the abandoned villages witnessed' soldiers and 'people who came from afar looking for spoils pillaging abandoned property', Benari stated

---

24 For a complete copy of 'Operational report for search in Majd al-Krum', 10 January 1949, IDF, see Adel Manna, *Nakba and survival: The story of Palestinians who remained in Haifa and the Galilee 1948–1956* [Hebrew] (Tel Aviv: ha-Kibbutz ha-me'uhad, 2017), 345.

25 'Report on the search operation in the village Majd al-Krum', 12 January 1949, file: 922/1952-820, IDF. Adel Manna writes that the author of this report was Shlomo Fulman, a representative of the military governor. This is not obvious, because the author of the report presents himself as the deputy company commander. Manna, *Nakba and survival*, 182.

succinctly, but he did not provide further information. He remembers a kibbutz meeting about the subject of 'abandoned' property, writing that a decision was made 'that members of Kibbutz HaZore'a would not search village homes for things of value, but the kibbutz would take in abandoned animals'.[26] In the written history of the kibbutz, the kibbutz's relations with the villages of Abu Zurayq and Qira (قيرة, located between the kibbutz and Yokne'am) are briefly mentioned, but the pillaging that members of the kibbutz conducted in the neighbouring villages is not discussed.[27] Yet, kibbutz member Arnon Tamir later noted that the property of the villages had been cleared out, as can be seen in his testimony that appears elsewhere in the kibbutz history: 'I cannot say that the matter did not bother me. I cannot forget the conversation that the kibbutz had about the property that everyone in the area came to loot'.[28] Thus, in practice, the kibbutz members actively participated in the looting.

Levi Granot, who as a representative of the kibbutz was very involved in the development of relations with the Arabs in the surrounding area, eventually had the following to say:

> I remember that we went [to the village]. [I] remember that we brought property back to the kibbutz ... Walter [Steyn] was in charge of procurement then and I remember him talking excitedly in the [kibbutz] conversation. Forcefully ... There is one sentence that I remember him saying: 'I do not want that our neighbours, as neighbours, will find their property on our kibbutz when they return! ... The ideological [justification for pillaging] was immediately heard. It drove me crazy, and I was among those who fought to keep the kibbutz from getting involved with abandoned property ... There were members who said, 'We are idiots! Everybody in the area is taking stuff and only we dumb Yekkes [are not plundering]'.[29]

---

26 Asher Benari, *Memoirs of a pioneer from Germany* [Hebrew] (Hazore'a: Kibbutz Hazore'a, 1986), 187–8.

27 Roni Kokhavi, ed., *Kibbutz Hazore'a 1936–1996* [Hebrew] (Hazore'a: Kibbutz Hazore'a, 1996), 78–80.

28 Ibid., 80. The book attributes this statement to Levi Granot, but perusal of the protocol of the 1976 conversation between Arnon Tamir and Eliezer Beeri shows that this assertion is incorrect.

29 Levi Granot, interview, 4 March 1976, file: Arabs of the area and the villages Qira and Abu Zurayq, File no. 073, Kibbutz HaZorea Archive (hereafter, KHZ).

At a general meeting held on 18 April 1948, the topic of pillaging was discussed. Eliezer Bauer, a prominent figure in the Mapam party who specialized in Arab–Jewish relations, read a letter to the kibbutz members about 'the crimes committed in conquered villages'. People on the kibbutz, as well as within the movement as a whole, held divergent and opposing opinions concerning the future of the Arabs and their property.[30] Mikha'el Hermoni said, 'Everything we have said up until now [about how to interact with the Arabs] has not been put into practice.' He was addressing 'the "private" petty thefts in Abu Zurayq'. Yosef Shtilman asserted that

> from the beginning, one could sense that we lacked a clear policy [on the matter] . . . [I] oppose this use of plunder [as a means]. It has a negative impact on young people. The kibbutz needs to decide if it wants to take part [in plunder] or not.[31]

In another general meeting, Hermoni seemed to convey that the looters felt misgivings about what they were doing: 'Those members who

---

30   There are two versions of the letter that Eliezer Bauer read – one from the Israel Defense Forces and Defense Establishment Archive and the other from the Yad Yaari Research and Documentation Centre Archives. While the first one has redacted sections, the other can be examined without impediment. The letter was written to part of the Mapam leadership on 14 April 1948. Here is an example of a sentence that the Israel Defense Forces and Defense Establishment Archive's declassification team believes that the public should be forbidden to see: 'Two days after the conquest of the village [Abu Zurayq], the corpses of ten dead people lay unburied.' The letter also deals with the pillaging carried out in the villages. For the original in the Israel Defense Forces and Defense Establishment Archive, see file: 481/1949/14. For the original in the Yad Yaari Research and Documentation Center Archives, see Eliezer Beeri, personal archive, (3-2)7.21-95.

31   General meeting minutes, 18 April 1948, KHZ. In a meeting of Mapam's Political Committee, Eliezer Bauer (Beeri) provided examples of the wartime policy being applied towards Arabs in the area: 'The village of Umm al-Zinat was conquered and the residents who had not left town were expelled. People in the village did not even fire one shot. It needed to be conquered, but [the inhabitants] did not need to be expelled. A systematic effort to destroy the Arabs' economic foundations was under way. The Arabs in the conquered villages of Abu Zurayq and Abu Shusa were either expelled or taken prisoner. It is clear that as long as the war continues, it is not necessary to let them reside in the village. Yet they are levelling the villages. A command was given to destroy everything. There are now those who opine that we should let kibbutzim settle [in them] and not let the [residents] return.' Political Committee meeting notes, 26 May 1948, file: Political Committee meetings, (4)66.90, YYA.

were involved in the emptying of the villages did not want to continue.'
Meanwhile, Menachem Gerson, later director of the Oranim Teachers'
College, saw the removal of property from the villages as highly beneficial: I 'think we need to conduct a thorough search, because there
certainly are a lot of valuable things there'. In complete opposition to
Benari's aforementioned statement that the kibbutz members did not
loot homes, individuals, and the kibbutz as a collective institution,
pillaged. Eliyahu Ma'oz asserted,

> We do not need to lose our minds [because of the war] . . . We should
> not allow mementos or similar such things to find their way [into the
> hands] of members. We also need to get rid of the things we brought
> to the garage, to the farm, and to the children's [house].

Whatever the case, he noted, we should not hand over 'the money to the
Haganah'. It was proposed that another visit be made to the village the
next day 'to see what there is there, and that after that an additional
meeting [be held] to see what we are interested in doing and not doing'.
Arnon Tamir proposed that everything be sold 'because it was the
correct thing to do from an educational standpoint'. This idea did not
receive the necessary votes: fourteen members voted against selling the
property, and eleven voted for the kibbutz to keep possession. It kept
possession.[32] Many years later, rumours still circulate that members of
the kibbutz killed elderly village residents who remained behind.[33]
Kibbutz Kabri plundered the contents of the neighbouring village,
al-Kabri (الكابري), immediately after the village buildings were blown
up.[34]

Meir Ya'ari, leader of HaKibbutz HaArtzi and Hashomer Hatzair, had
this to say in June 1948:

---

32 General meeting minutes, 29 April 1948, KHZ.

33 This is what one veteran kibbutz member who asked to remain anonymous
said to me in a conversation. It is not surprising that the kibbutz members are not excited
to talk about the matter. In any case, I would like to stress that there is no written
evidence of this.

34 Ziama Rappaport, *Kabri – first years* [Hebrew] (Kabri: Kibbutz Kabri, 1994),
12–14. On the blowing up of the village, see Carmeli to General Staff Operations Branch,
21 May 1948, file: General 15-46-165/1, YTA.

Presently, not just the army, but every segment of the labour move-ment's settlement enterprise is involved in looting and pillaging. I do not exclude any part of it, because they are all involved: Kibbutz Beit Alfa, Tantura [Kibbbutz Nahsholim], Qaqun [Kibbutz HaMa'apil]. Robbery, as well as organized pillaging. I am not afraid for the soul of the movement. Nonetheless, I do have a problem with organized pillaging and a bone to pick with those who organized it, and this is what I want to talk about. I have not investigated every-thing, certainly not carefully. That means that I am not certain about everything, and, if I learn that some of what I have learned is inac-curate, it will make me happy. Tantura: I met with Kibbutz [Nahsholim], and they told me that they found odds and ends [in the village] after the looting; I found destruction there, no less than we see on a daily basis. [They] have shown themselves no less immoral than others. The first to arrive in Tantura were farmers from Zikhron [Ya'akov] with big wagons.[35]

One of the soldiers who participated in the battles near Kibbutz Mishmar HaEmek explained:

After [the battle in] Mishmar HaEmek, the Arabs hid everything, but they hid it close by . . . Today – it is not nice to say it – [residents and soldiers] took good sewing machines. In Megiddo, in the archaeo-logical site, there were a lot of valuable things. The cameras and the beds of the American excavators. We took it . . . There, there was terrible looting . . . My senior commanders took [stuff]. The people from [Kibbutz] Mishmar HaEmek took the good mattresses for them-selves. I went to the commander in charge, and I told him that there was a great deal of property there. He said that they would laugh at us if we did not take it, [so we] took [it] and sold [it].[36]

Clearly, not all Kibbutzim looted their neighbours' property. The rela-tions between Kibbutz Na'an and the village of Na'ani (النعاني), in central

---

35 Minutes of the Histadrut Executive Committee meeting, 16–17 June 1948, vol. 90, June–August 1948, LMA.

36 Efrayim Ben Natan, interview, Collection of the Galili Centre for Defence Studies, 8 March 1983, file: 12-3/45/3, YTA.

Israel, were sound, and even when the war broke out, there were no confrontations between them. On 13 May, the Golani Brigade conquered the villages of Abu Shusa, al-Qubab (القباب), and Na'ani. The residents surrendered without a fight, and they continued to work their lands.[37] The mukhtar of Kibbutz Na'an advised the residents to leave the village before fighting between Arab and Jewish forces began nearby; on 10 June 1948, they made a hasty departure. The kibbutz members did not know that their Arab neighbours would not return, and they took time to gather up their meagre property.

> They put the furniture belonging to the family of Abu Shawish (أبو شويش), the village mukhtar, into one house and they sealed it up, so that it would not get damaged ... Yehezkel Livovitz, an Arab Assets Department controller, arrived on site ... Avraham Na'an was appointed to guard the village.[38]

The Arabs of Na'ani joined the large stream of refugees making its way out of the Ramle–Lydda area at that time. They would never return home: in the 1950s, the village was destroyed.[39]

There were other ways to prevent kibbutz members from plundering property. Kibbutz Sha'ar HaGolan member Nahum Boneh recounted what happened when a member brought an 'abandoned' car to the grounds of the kibbutz in July 1948:

> Without a lot of talking or arguments, a group of members made preparations and lit the car on fire that very night. It worked like a

37   Amos Shifris, *Kibbutz Naan – Biography of a place* [Hebrew] (Na'an: Kibbutz Na'an, 2010), 65–6.

38   Memorandum of Yitzhak Gevirtz about the village of Na'ani near [Kibbutz] Na'an, 14 June 1948, file: Report – Arab settlements that were abandoned or destroyed, Gimmel-307/34, ISA.

39   See also the letter written by members of Kibbutz Sha'ar HaAmakim that reports on their relations with the village of Khawaled (الخوالد) and how they 'had assumed clear moral obligations for this village when they had assumed control over it following its residents' removal from it on 15 April. The kibbutz members noted the good neighbourly relations between the settlements and the contributions that the village residents had made to their security. [Kibbutz] Sha'ar HaAmakim to Golani headquarters, 8 August 1948, file: (5)10.95-10, YYA. See also Yosi Amitay, *The United Workers' Party (Mapam) 1948–1954: Attitudes on Palestinian-Arab issues* [Hebrew] (Tel Aviv: Tcherikover, 1988), 97.

magic wand. Ever since then, no member has dared to bring stuff pillaged from the abandoned property [back to the kibbutz].[40]

In mid-May, a short time after Haifa's conquest, the village of Umm al-Zinat (أم الزينات) on the southern slopes of the Carmel Range was conquered by a force from the Golani Brigade. The village mukhtars turned to Minister Sheetrit 'in the name of integrity and compassion', asking to return to their village and requesting that it not be destroyed. A short time earlier, they had written, 'The army seized our flocks and our yield, and it destroyed some of our homes.' The mukhtars noted that they had not attacked soldiers and had not harassed passing vehicles. 'Everybody knows this.'[41] The brigade commander didn't deny it and wrote that booty had been taken from villages in the area.[42] The hurried exodus of residents from many villages in the Haifa, Hefer Valley, Zikhron Ya'akov, and Mount Ephraim areas led Hadera District institutions to establish a special committee to oversee Arab property and assets.[43]

With the departure of village residents in the Petah Tikvah area and the Shomron region, the State of Israel's Department for Arab Affairs appointed controllers to keep an eye on property in the area villages.[44] The reason for this was clear: they quickly recognized that Jewish residents living in the area would utterly pillage any village in the area left unguarded.[45] Residents of Ein Ya'akov plundered Bayyarat Hannun (بيارة حنون), just south of Netanya.[46] The same thing happened to the village of Khayriyya (الخيرية).[47] Property was pillaged in the Zikhron

40   Quoted in Ofra Bril, 'Abandoned property' [Hebrew], *ha-Zeman ha-yarok*, 17 November 2016.

41   The mukhtars to Bechor-Shalom Sheetrit, 1 September 1948, file: Village of Umm al-Zinat, Gimmel-302/108, ISA.

42   Carmel Brigade commander, 'The topic of discussion: Booty', 7 June 1948, file: 6680/1949-6, IDF.

43   'The Arabs are leaving their villages in the Hadera District' [Hebrew], *Davar*, 28 April 1948.

44   Gad Machnes to [the] Alexandroni [Brigade], 29 April 1948; 'Appointment of a watch supervisor over the villages of Hiriya and Saqiya and their lands'; and additional documents in file: 2506/1949-91, IDF.

45   'News summary for the Alexandroni Brigade (11 May 1948)', file: 2506/1949-80, IDF.

46   'Plunder of the property of Hannun', 20 April 1948, file: 2506/1949-91, IDF.

47   'Alexandroni Brigade bulletin', 15 May 1948, file: 6127/1949-117, IDF.

Ya'akov area and sold by civilians in Tel Aviv.[48] Soldiers took grain from the villages of Tira (الطـيـرة) and Dayr Tarif (ديـر طـريـف), transporting it in military vehicles for sale in Petah Tikvah.[49] Department for Arab Assets official Yitzhak Gevirtz wrote to the Alexandroni Brigade to tell them that they were not operating in accordance with established understandings and that the army was continuing to sell 'abandoned' property 'in violation of all the orders that had been issued'. Gevirtz was told that people were dismantling the irrigation pipes in Arab orchards and selling them.[50] As we will see in the next chapter, the dismantling and removal of irrigation pipes (with or without authorization) and the drying up of orchards functioned as part of a policy for prevention of Arab refugees' return.

In mid-1949, a short time after the first ceasefire agreement was signed, approximately 200 residents of the village of Wa'rat al-Saris (وعرة السريس), near the village of Ata (today Kiryat Ata), requested Minister Sheetrit's assistance. For several months, they had asked for permission to return to their homes and the authorities had not granted their request. 'We have learned that Jewish people have been settled in our village and it is forbidden for us to live there.'[51] Kfar Ata Council president Erich Böhm joined the residents' protest. 'Even in the most difficult times, [the residents of the village] remained loyal to us,' he wrote. 'They never participated in hostilities and, so they would not even come into conflict with us indirectly, they evacuated their place of residence.'[52] They did not return.

People from every social stratum took part in despoliation of the villages. After Zarnuqa (زرنوقة), Qubeiba (القبيبة), and Aqir (عاقر) were conquered in Operation Barak in May 1948, 'ceaseless mass looting occurred [in them]', wrote the Rehovot region commander in early June.

---

48   Handwritten report to the regional commander, 27 July 1948, file: 4663/1949-46, IDF.

49   Yitzhak Gevirtz to the general prosecutor, 22 July 1948, file: 6127/1949-109, IDF.

50   Yitzhak Gevirtz to the Alexandroni [Brigade], 6 July 1948, file: 2506/1949-91, IDF. See also Protocol of consultation on the motors [machinery] in the orchards, 14 September 1948, file: Orchards and citrus growers, Gimmel-307/35, ISA.

51   Letter of the residents of the village Wa'rat al-Saris to the minister of minorities, 6 May 1949, file: Village al-Saris, Gimmel-302/103, ISA.

52   Erich Böhm (Kfar Ata Local Council president) to Bechor-Shalom Sheetrit, 10 May 1949, file: Village al-Saris.

He added that it appeared that neither the soldiers of the Givati Brigade's Fifty-Fifth Battalion forces nor the Guard Corps men were doing anything to stop the depredation (soldiers in the battalion had even stolen money from prisoners on various occasions).[53] Residents of the nearby moshavah pillaged non-stop – even though the moshavah was being bombed by Egypt at that time – and their influence, opined the regional commander, was 'destructive'. The spoliation had a dual outcome: on the one hand, it brought about 'the throwing off of all moral inhibition', but, on the other, it led to complaints that the army was not acting to prevent the pillaging.[54] When moral inhibitions were removed, it was not only the depredation that spread but also vast destruction. Destruction perpetrated in Zarnuqa and Qubeiba led the Department for Arab Assets to comment that this was

> destruction that has no other reason or purpose than expression of the urge to purposelessly destroy. Machines, work animals, homes, and granaries that could have been of use to the army itself and the state treasury were destroyed, killed, and burned. This happened despite the fact that the department's representative begged the soldiers not to do such things.

It was not the Arabs that the soldiers were harming, 'but state property'. The department added that the state was not rich enough to allow 'us' to destroy things 'for fun'.[55]

---

53   'Prisoner complaints', 6 July 1948, file: 105/260, HHA. See also Twelfth Brigade commander to the battalions, 14 January 1949, file: 6809/1949-14, IDF: 'I have received confirmed reports that in a number of cases our soldiers have stolen money and clothing from enemy prisoners who fell into our hands.'

54   Rehovot Regional Commander, 'The topic of discussion: The plunder of Arab villages, 8 June 1948', file: 410/1954-144, IDF.

55   'Property of Qubeiba and Zarnuqa', 2 June 1948 (?), file: 410/1954-144, IDF. Ben-Gurion received other information about what was going on in the village: 'After an on-site investigation, it became clear that the rumour that you heard about the destruction of Zarnuqa and Qubeiba is baseless. No destruction occurred there.' Operations branch to David Ben-Gurion, 8 July 1948, file: 2315/1950-15, IDF. A. Kaplan wrote in a letter to the editor of Al HaMishmar (n.d., 1948; Aharon Cohen Archive, file: (4)10.95-10, YYA): 'What I have to say concerns the way that our boys [Mapam affiliates] are behaving in the Arab villages without concern for whether [their inhabitants] did us wrong or not. [It seems like] the very fact that the village is Arab and its residents are Arab is enough that one can act like a barbarian in them.' Kaplan offers a description of

The newspaper *Kol Ha'am* provided a more detailed description of the looting of villages. A couple of days after the villages were conquered and the residents were expelled, the villages were left at the mercy of looters. The paper described a reality that seemed drawn from gangster stories:

---

the conquest of Zarnuqa provided to him by one of the soldiers: 'The soldier told me how another soldier opened a door and shot an old Arab man, an elderly woman, and a child with one wave of his Sten [rifle]; how they removed Arab men, women, and children from the homes and made them stand outside in the sun without food or water until they turned over the forty rifles they had been asked to provide. The Arabs said that they did not have any [guns]. Finally, they expelled them from the village and sent them off in the direction of the village of Yibna (يبنى). The Arabs argued: "You are sending us to our enemies, to those who we fought against and did not allow to enter our village. Are we not your friends?" Yet this did not help, and, screaming and wailing, [they] left the village . . . The soldier explained that the Arabs witnessed the soldiers breaking into the small markets and stealing cigarettes and biscuits and stealing everything of value from the homes as well. One squad commander stole pieces of furniture for his home. After the village's conquest, it remained wide open to satisfy the lust for plunder that seized hold of many of the village's Jewish neighbours. For two days, a continuous stream of women and children from the Yemenite neighbourhood [nearby] stole stuff . . . It was an abominable sight and a mark of shame for the Hebrew settlement.' Yitzhak Gevirtz, director of the Department of Villages in the Office of the Custodian, wrote to Givati Brigade Command on 21 July 1948 that the soldiers in the village of al-Khaima (الخيمة), near Kfar Menachem, which had been captured days earlier, were burning homes and the granary. 'This destruction is of no use to anybody, and it is impossible to see it as a militarily necessity. Is it not possible to dissuade the soldiers from performing purposeless and aimless acts of destruction?' The same day, Gevirtz sent an additional letter to Givati Brigade Command. In this letter, he gave instruction that following the conquest of the village of Tell al-Safi (تل الصافي) the property of an Arab family that had 'strong [ties] with Jews' was to be protected. Indeed, the family's property was gathered up, but, subsequently, 'soldiers went in, destroyed all the furniture, and left their property in ruins'. Gevirtz noted that the soldiers' behaviour was not just destroying property. 'It was also [destroying] any possibility of maintaining ties with the Arabs.' Yitzhak Gevirtz to Givati [Brigade] Command, 21 July 1948, file: 6127/1949-109, IDF. The two letters were also brought in the Minutes of the Ministerial Committee on Abandoned Asset Affairs meeting, 26 July 1948, as examples of failures to enforce the law; file: Administration – Abandoned Property Committee, Gimmel-2186/21, ISA. Subsequently, in October 1948, an effort was made to fight pillaging in the Rehovot region. See Meeting summary Front D headquarters / Abandoned Asset Affairs districts, 1 October 1948, file:2294/1950-2931, IDF. See also 'Operation Tihur' Order, 26 November 1948, file: 2294/1950-2931, IDF. Destruction of property in the villages was widespread and people needed to fight it. See Galilee district commander, 'Protection of abandoned property', 14 November 1948, file: 1137/1949-84, IDF: 'Before the command discusses the matter with the controller of abandoned property, this order forbids the blowing up of homes in abandoned villages that have any property whatsoever in them.'

Every day people steal all kinds of things from the village. They do not just take isolated objects. They come in trucks and empty the grana- ries, take furniture from homes, and tear out windows, doors, and floor tiles. There is a rumour circulating that an Irgun company that was bivouacked in the village charged every person that wanted to enter the village a half lira . . . The police conducted a search in the She'arim [neighbourhood], but that was all for show: a couple of things were confiscated. If the police really wanted to stop the despo- liation, it could have acted like it did in Aqir and Qatra. Then the Haganah commander issued an order that anybody who entered those villages would be shot. Nobody entered those villages.[56]

At the same time, in the north of the country, soldiers from the Alexandroni Brigade waged a hard-fought battle against Iraqi forces near the village of Qaqun (قاقون) in the Hefer valley. IDF forces conquered the village on 5 June. At a conference of Mapam-affiliated military personnel held at the end of July, a participant explained that the conquered village looked like it had been through a 'pogrom'. Peri Paz was surprised not just by the destruction, sadism, and 'purposeless destruction of dishes and furniture' but by 'the unrestrained pillaging' as well. In his view, this type of pillaging could create a 'type of soldier' similar to the one Erich Maria Remarque describes in his 1931 novel *The Road Back*. The book was translated into Hebrew immediately after its publication, and it is reasonable to assume that the participants were familiar with it and its author, whose famous anti-war tale *All Quiet on the Western Front* had been published two years prior. In *The Road Back*, Remarque intricately describes the return home of a soldier who fought in the trenches during the First World War and proves unable to success- fully reintegrate into German society. Instead, he develops disdain and revulsion for his surroundings and becomes deeply pessimistic. This type of person, who murders and plunders, stood in stark opposition to that which the labour movement educated its members to become. Paz explained how soldiers in Qaqun attacked a guard that had been put in place to safeguard property. 'This looting in the Arab village damages the soul', asserted Paz, arguing that 'there was no guiding or directing hand. [Therefore,] property worth hundreds of liras that probably

---

56   'The depredation in Zarnuqa' [Hebrew], *Kol Ha'am*, 15 June 1948.

should have been confiscated was lost.'[57] The Department for Arab Assets determined that "the soldiers had robbed the village".[58]

The village of Abu Ghosh (أبو غوش) which remained neutral throughout the war and whose residents were expelled (though subsequently they were allowed to return), was also systematically plundered. A report written in early June 1948 describing a visit to the village notes that 'the lawlessness was beyond description'. Palmach soldiers burst into the French monastery in the village, 'took whatever they could get their hands on, broke statues and crosses, broke open the wine barrels, and many of them put beaded necklaces with crosses from the "booty" around their necks'. Homes and stores were breached, and soldiers took control of homes through 'confiscations'. The report observes, 'The anarchy in the field is so extensive that every company commander in the Palmach is choosing the house he likes most.' When, in the end, an effort was made to reduce the number of 'expropriations' and it was agreed that only one home would be expropriated, the soldiers complained when the Arab owner was permitted to remove some of his possessions from the home. 'One of the commanders said that what was left in the home could not compare with what he took [plundered] in Katamon. Meanwhile, every man set his eyes on a specific object and things began to be divided up.' The author of the report concluded that it made sense that the residents of the village 'were continually surprised and did not know what to think' about Israeli rule.[59] It bears emphasis, once again, that expropriations from 'present' Arabs were illegal. In a short vignette written by Menachem Talmi, a Palmach soldier boastfully tells his friend about his future conquests: 'A few more villages, and then I will move on. I already selected a villa there, up in the mountains.'[60]

On 31 May 1948, the Negev Brigade conquered the village of Huj (هوج), in the northwest Negev. The Jewish mukhtars of the three

57   Minutes of conference of military personnel, 25–26 July 1948, file: (2)206.90, YYA.

58   Zvi Inbar, *Scales of justice and the sword: Foundations of military law in Israel* [Hebrew] (Tel Aviv: Ma'arakhot, 2005), 708.

59   Yitzhar (Ya'akov Bashmi), 'Our relations with Abu-Ghosh', 5 June 1948, file: 105/92, HHA.

60   Menachem Talmi, 'In the area of the defeated enemy', in *In the footsteps of soldiers: Selected reportage* [Hebrew] (Merhavyah: Sifriyat ha-po'alim, 1949), 173.

kibbutzim in the area – Dorot, Nir Am, and Ruhama – turned to Prime Minister Ben-Gurion three months later, following the expulsion of the inhabitants, to protest the treatment of village residents and their property. The village, the representatives of the kibbutzim wrote, provided assistance to the Jewish settlements throughout the years and even hid Jews when the British were conducting searches. The army promised the village 'that we would protect their property . . . [Yet] despite headquarters' promise, the homes in the village had been subject to frequent break-ins. Everything had been either stolen or broken. What remained in the homes had been blown up and a number of homes had been burned. The flocks were also stolen.' The village of Kawfakha (كوفخة) met with a similar fate. The territories of local Bedouin, indigenous people of the desert in southern Israel, who had also aided Jewish forces, received contemptuous treatment too: homes were destroyed, property was stolen, and fields were burned. The Jewish mukhtars demanded that a system be put in place to protect Arab property.[61] Ben-Gurion provided them with a laconic response:

> I thank you for informing me about how the army illegally mistreated Arab friends. I see that a copy of your statement has been sent to Negev headquarters. I hope that headquarters will take heed of what you have said, will act to prevent such unfair and unjustified acts in the future, and, to the extent possible, will try to set right what has taken place.[62]

The residents of Huj were exiled. Minister Bechor-Shalom Sheetrit worked unsuccessfully to allow their return.[63]

There is a great deal that we do not know about matters related to Bedouin property. For example, the Thirteenth Battalion killed a number

---

61   The mukhtars of [Kibbutz] Dorot, [Kibbutz] Nir Am, and [Kibbutz] Ruhama [Aryeh Parda (Dorot), Ya'akov Gavri (Nir Am), Eli'ezer Frish (Ruhama) to David Ben-Gurion, 4 August 1948, file: Conquered Israeli territories, Het Tzadi-2564/9, ISA. It is interesting to note that only a few years ago, the Israeli State Archives felt it appropriate to make this document privileged and to limit public access to it. See the notice about this in file: Report – Arab settlements that were abandoned or destroyed.

62   Ben-Gurion to the mukhtars of [Kibbutz] Dorot, [Kibbutz] Nir Am, and [Kibbutz] Ruhama, 29 August 1948, BGA.

63   Bechor-Shalom Sheetrit to the Middle East Department (Foreign Ministry), 26 September 1948, file: The return of the Arabs of Huj, Gimmel-302/97, ISA.

of Bedouin, and the Ministry of Minorities tried to figure out what really happened.[64] Moshe Yatah, branch director of the Ministry of Minorities office in Haifa, wrote that they told office officials 'that it would be best not to send telegrams about cases involving complaints about the army. And [I] suggest that in the future we send secret letters by special messenger in such cases'.[65] Such letters were not found in the relevant files. Nonetheless, a short note about looting was found. Army brigades had stolen the cattle of the al-Hujeirat tribe, which resided in the area east of Shfar'am near Bir al-Maksur (بير المكسور) and had members serving in the IDF. 'If the objective was to bring about their departure, the way they were treated facilitated this goal's accomplishment.'[66]

In a short period of time, the Israeli forces emptied many villages of their inhabitants, and, just like in the cities, it was impossible to differentiate between personal and collective looting, expropriation for military purposes, and 'expropriation' to fulfil individual desires disguised as 'military necessity'. For example, the army gathered all the cattle, sheep, and goats in the village of Deir Hanna (دير حنا), whose residents had neither fled nor been expelled, and led them out of the village. 'Our current condition is dire', the mukhtars wrote to Ben-Gurion. The residents had not put up a fight when their village was captured.[67] They protested their livestock's removal from the village, and they did not

---

64 Moshe Yatah of the Ministry of Minorities wrote: 'The army, according to what the Hujeirat said, entered with three names, asked for the men, and shot them dead on the spot. The army asserts that when it asked for the men by name, they began to flee and the army fired at them.' Report of Moshe Yatah to Gad Machnes, 19 September 1948, file: Hujeirat Arab[s], Gimmel-310/69, ISA.

65 Moshe Yatah to the Ministry of Minorities in the Kiryah, 16 August 1948, file: Hujeirat Arab[s].

66 'Giora Vayd report', written out by A. Chelouche, file: Hujeirat Arab[s]. Soldiers also stole a flock of sheep from the residents of Kurnub (كرنب), southeast of Beersheba. The commander of the Twelfth Brigade wrote: 'We have yet to receive orders concerning how the army should treat the Bedouins in the area . . . As long as this matter is being debated and no decision has been reached, the army should not act in opposition to a potential political policy. Therefore, the battalion commanders need to make sure that their men do not harm the inhabitants that they come into contact with who do not resist and whose behaviour and current location do not conflict with military needs. In addition, no harm should come to the inhabitants' property.' Twelfth Brigade Command, 'The army's attitude to the Bedouin residents of the area', 25 November 1948, file: 834/1953-380, IDF.

67 The mukhtars to David Ben-Gurion, 13 November 1948, file: Village of Deir Hanna, Gimmel-302/72, ISA.

know if it was legal. The district military governor reported to the minister of minorities that 'it is correct that the army took flocks from Dir Hanna illegally', and charges were brought against those responsible.[68]

The army also took all of the livestock from the villages of Bueine (بعينة) and Arraba (عرابة), in the Beit Netofa valley. The number of livestock taken from the village was high: 2,000 sheep, 500 goats, and 100 head of cattle. 'Our village is very poor, and it subsists on its livestock alone', wrote a resident named Ali Talal Abd al-Mu'ti (المعطي).[69] After Bueine was captured during the conquest of Nazareth, Sheetrit demanded that the livestock be returned to their owners in the two villages. 'Their residents did not abandon them, and they are considered present Arabs.'[70] Thus the 'expropriation' was illegal in this case as well. Again, the military governor reported to Sheetrit that 'the matter was under investigation', indicating that he was handling the matter of compensation for the flock owners.[71] Additional documents on this matter were not found.

Archival documents tell the story of another robbery that occurred in the village of Reineh (الرينة), near Nazareth. Aharon Cohen, a member of Mapam's Arab Department, spoke about information he received from an A. H. C. (probably Aharon Hayyim Cohen, an Arab Department representative in the Histadrut). Cohen sought to clarify matters:

> Why were fourteen Arabs, including a Bedouin woman and a member of the Brit Po'alei Eretz Yisra'el labour union, Yousef al-Turki, murdered in the village of Reineh in the beginning of September? They accused them of smuggling and arrested them near the village (?), took them to the village, and murdered them. The whole village was in an uproar. If you believe that someone is smuggling, [the residents] said, you take them to court and you punish them in accordance with the law. How could they be

68   The military governor of the Galilee and [Jezreel] Valley to the minister of minorities, 31 December 1948, file: Village of Deir Hanna.

69   Ali Talal Abd al-Mu'ti to the government of Israel, November 1948, file: Ali Talal Abd al-Mu'ti, Gimmel-298/59, ISA.

70   Bechor-Shalom Sheetrit to Dov Shafrir (Custodian of Abandoned Property), 16 November 1948, file: Arab villages, Gimmel-302/110, ISA.

71   The military governor of the Galilee and [Jezreel] Valley to the secretary of the minister of minorities, 9 December 1948, file: Ali Talal Abd al-Mu'ti, Gimmel-298/59, ISA. For more on this matter, see Village of Bueine, Gimmel-302/75, ISA.

murdered like this this without a trial?! . . . [People need to figure out] what they did with the cash that the murdered people had on them. The Sheikh Taher al-Tabari (الطبري) . . . believes that this type of murder – this case from Reineh is not unique – is committed in order to rob [the victims].[72]

Al-Tabari was right: this was not the only case. Knesset member Tawfik Toubi conveyed the following to the Knesset plenum:

On 30 October 1948, two days after the conquest of Jish (Gush Halav) in the Safed region, the army surrounded the village and searched it. During the search, soldiers robbed a number of homes and took 605 liras, jewellery, and precious objects. When the robbed forcefully demanded receipts for their property, they were taken away and shot to death. The villagers went to the local commander Mano Friedman and protested against what had happened. He ordered that the corpses of the dead be returned. One of those killed had a finger missing (it had been amputated so that a ring could be stolen). These are the names of the dead: Yousef Salim Hashoul – twenty-four years old; Raful Yousef Hashoul – forty-eight years old; Elias Andrus Haddad – twenty-four years old; Fares Andrus Haddad – thirty-four years old. The murdered men are survived by their wives and children.[73]

Although there is only meagre evidence, small and extremely poor villages were robbed too. No more than 300 people lived in the village of Biriyya (بيريا), near Safed, which Israeli forces conquered in the lead-up to their successful assault on Safed. Village resident Mustafa ibn Muhammad Salam (سلام) wrote Minister Sheetrit that his home had been robbed and destroyed. 'They even removed the roofing tiles and

---

72   Letter of Aharon Cohen, 29 September 1949, file: Aharon Cohen – personal archive, (2)9.10-95, YYA.

73   Minutes of the Knesset plenum, 14 November 1949, Knesset Archives (hereafter, KAJ). Atrocities Israelis and Palestinians committed against one another are outside the scope of this discussion. Yet based on documents available to the public (later we will discuss how a portion of the documents dealing with war crimes, such as the Shapira Report on Operation Hiram, is not available for examination), it is clear that such cases were not so rare. Sometimes, after many years, soldiers and civilians speak publicly about war crimes that they had kept hush about for a long time.

the doors and took them.' One should assume that the combat forces did not need roofing tiles and doors, and that it was civilian residents of the area who pillaged these things. 'I have nothing to live on,' wrote Salam, noting that his petitions to the responsible authorities in Safed had not accomplished anything.[74]

The village of Rama (الرامة), a few kilometres from Karmiel, surrendered after planes scattered leaflets stating that the State of Israel would protect the villagers and their property. The residents did not resist and surrendered immediately. Yet the next day a wholesale and retail merchant who lived in the village reported that 'the Israeli army ordered the residents to clear out of the village in the next fifteen minutes. Consequently, none of the inhabitants were able to leave with the clothing and food they needed.' The merchant explained that the army entered 'his store and his home and took everything he had, [including] the goods in his haberdashery and his home appliances'.[75] Village resident Jamil Abdullah Nakhla (نخلة) stated that the inhabitants tried to convince the soldiers not to expel them:

> We based [our argument] on the leaflets that had been thrown down to us . . . before the occupation . . . that stated that all of the residents would be treated well if they surrendered and did not resist the Israeli forces.

When the residents returned to their village after a temporary, week-long expulsion, they learned that the army had taken 'all of [their] food and all of [the] furniture and mattresses' from their homes. Nakhla noted that at the same time he was trying to convince village residents that nothing bad would happen to them, 'the army robbed our homes'. Furthermore, the property of Priest Yakub al-Hanna (الحنا), who collaborated with the Arab Salvation Army and 'encouraged the village residents to flee prior to the military conquest', was left untouched, because 'somebody stepped in on his behalf'.[76] As one of

---

74   Mustafa ibn Muhammad Salam to the minister of minorities, 17 January 1949, file: Mustafa al-Salasi, Gimmel-298/31, ISA.

75   Abdullah al-Khuri Ibrahim to the minister of welfare (via the minister of minorities), 4 March 1949, Abdullah al-Khuri Ibrahim, Gimmel-298/50, ISA.

76   Jamil Abdullah Nakhla to Bechor-Shalom Sheetrit, May 1948, file: Jamil Abdullah Nakhla, Gimmel-299/81, ISA.

the village residents summed things up, in practice, the army 'robbed the homes of the rich'.[77]

The Oded Brigade captured the central Upper Galilean village of Suhmata (سحماتا), located on land where Moshav Hosen and Moshav Tzuriel are found today, on 30 October 1948, and it was pillaged too. UN observers who visited the site reported 'extensive looting of villages in Galilee', and the UN report noted that 'this looting . . . appeared to have been systematic as army trucks were used for transportation'.[78] Similarly, as Tawfik Toubi's earlier comments hinted, the village of Jish (الجش), northwest of Safed and home to 1,200 residents, was also looted. Aharon Hayyim Cohen, a Mapam Arab Department representative in the Histadrut, reported to the Ministry of Minorities on a visit he made to the village. In contrast with previous visits when the residents greeted him warmly, this time he was received 'coldly'. The village residents protested how the authorities had treated them brutally. 'Most of the homes were robbed' by Irgun men and others. Cohen added that 'Mahmoud Rashid (راشید) himself – who did such a remarkable job on behalf of our interests during the Arab Revolt of 1936 – was taken from his home blindfolded. The way he was led to the police station was insulting and it demeaned his honour'.[79]

Earlier scholarship has addressed the massacre in Eilabun (عيلبون), but it is worth reviewing here in brief. The Golani Brigade conquered the village late at night on 29 October. Subsequently, the brigade members murdered twelve residents in an organized act of vengeance, undertaken in response to the public parading of the decapitated heads of two Israeli soldiers killed fighting against the Arab Salvation Army a month earlier. The village notables asserted that the parade had not gone through their village but had had taken place far away, and that the villagers had not participated. Nonetheless, the brigade expelled the village's residents; some remained in the area, while others fled to Lebanon. In the days following the conquest, all the village's moveable property was gradually filched. 'The army robbed the village homes and

77   Summary report of a visit of the minister of minorities and the ministry director to the village of Rama, 7 November 1948, file: Village of Rama, Gimmel-302/80, ISA.

78   United Nations Department of Public Information, 'Report on Northern Palestine Fighting', press release PAL/370, 6 November 1948, UN Archive, un.org.

79   Aharon Hayyim Cohen to Gad Machnes, 18 September 1948, file: Rashid Mahmoud and Husseini, Gimmel-300/58, ISA.

took everything valuable that was easy to move', wrote the notables, the mukhtars, and the priests to various government ministers. After the easily transportable moveable property was removed, the animals and fruit were snatched. Days later, furniture and clothing were taken, and eventually there was nothing left.[80] In the months after their expulsion from Eilabun, the villagers worked hard to get the State of Israel to permit them to return home. Sheetrit recommended that Prime Minister Ben-Gurion accede to their request.[81] When they were finally allowed to return in the summer of 1949, they found their village pillaged and destroyed. A United Nations Truce Supervision Organization report notes that the homes in the village had been burglarized and that pictures featuring religious icons had been destroyed.[82]

The army also took a huge amount of property from the village of Tantura (طنطورة) following its conquest in May 1948.[83] A few days after the conquest, journalist Shlomo Shehori surveyed the village and reported to readers of the newspaper *Davar* [Word] that 'wealth and

80   Priests, mukhtars, and notables of the village of Eilabun to the Ministry of Religions, 21 January 1949, file: Christian holy sites, Het Tzadi -2397/7, ISA. For a slightly different (translated) version, see Priests, mukhtars, and village notables of Eilabun to the minister of minorities, 21 January 1949, file: Conquered Israeli territories, Het Tzadi-2564/10, ISA. See also Heads of the Roman Catholic Community to Bechor-Shalom Sheetrit, 10 November 1948. The military governor, Elisha Soltz, wrote that 'according to the information that I have at my disposal, when our army conquered the city, the decapitated bodies of our two soldiers were found.' Elisha Soltz (military governor of the Galilee and [Jizra'el] Valley) to Bechor-Shalom Sheetrit, 12 December 1948, file: Village of Eilabun, Gimmel-302/81, ISA. Soltz received incorrect information.

81   Bechor-Shalom Sheetrit to David Ben-Gurion, 8 February 1949. See also additional correspondence in files: Village of Eilabun, Gimmel-302/81; Village of Eilabun, Gimmel Lamed-17037/20, ISA.

82   Quoted in Nahla Abdo and Nur Masalha, eds, *An Oral History of the Palestinian Nakba* (London: ZED, 2018), 242.

83   Many villages in the Haifa area were seriously looted. 'Immediately after the conquest of the villages of Ayn Ghazal (عين غزال), Jaba (جبع), and Izjim (إجزم), officials [overseeing Arab property] went to these villages to supervise property removal. On site, they spoke with the commanding officers present and requested that they aid them through prevention of looting and pillaging. They were promised such assistance, but the promise was not kept. Various things of value were taken away. The Alexandroni Brigade took a new tractor. People made off with sewing machines and radios. Obviously, my men did not authorize such activities. These acts were committed without their knowledge and without any authorization whatsoever.' Assistant Supervisor of Arab Property in the Northern District to the Northern Quartermaster's Branch, 29 July 1948, 200716/1949-142, IDF.

affluence burst forth from every corner . . . when you enter rooms, you find all kinds of fine things: rugs, carpets, modern armoires, and all kinds of utensils, delicate china services, and expensive crystal.'[84] In early May, prior to the village's fall, the Palestinian mukhtar told the residents of nearby Zikhron Ya'akov that 'he was assuming' responsibility for the Jewish property within the village boundaries.[85] The village residents were considered 'present'; therefore, their property could not be expropriated without compensation (and prior authorization). Nevertheless, one resident, Hassan al-Hajj Suleiman, tried unsuccessfully for months to get his land and property back. 'Behold the Jews ploughed my land and my wife's land . . . What crime did we commit, Mr Minister?' he wrote to the minister of minorities. They had also been told that 'they had the same rights as Jews' when the village had been conquered. In practice, the reality was different. 'Is the Israeli government really planning to discriminate against its Arab citizens?' wondered Suleiman.[86] A Ministry of Minorities representative in the Haifa District, Moshe Yatah, tried to find out which governmental institution had taken possession of Suleiman's lands and was preventing him from accessing them. It was not the custodian of abandoned property, inasmuch as the Arab residents were 'present'. Therefore, what was going on was likely illegal.[87]

The spoliation took on a different form in every location. Numerous incidents of plunder and robbery had occurred in practically every Galilean village. 'Every battalion performs searches and expulsions,' noted one intelligence report, remarking that there were also 'cases where Arabs were identified and executed by military personnel'. One of the reasons that there are numerous descriptions of plundered Galilean villages is the fact that their residents did not flee and many of them remained in the territory now claimed by the State of Israel. Clearly, the decision makers viewed the population's decision to remain in place as undesirable. In an internal army study by Yitzhak Moda'i in the 1950s

---

84   Shlomo Shehori, 'In Conquered Tantura', Davar, 11 June 1948.

85   'News summary for the Alexandroni Brigade (11 May 1948)', file: 2506/1949-80, IDF.

86   Hassan al-Hajj Suleiman to Bechor-Shalom Sheetrit, 4 November 1948, file: Hajj Suleiman al-Hindi, Gimmel-298/33, ISA.

87   Moshe Yatah to the Haifa District headquarters, 30 November 1948, file: Hajj Suleiman al-Hindi, Gimmel-298/33, ISA.

about Operation Hiram, which sought to capture the Upper Galilee region from the Arab Liberation Army in October 1948, he wrote the following about expulsion of the population:

> Based on officers' and enlisted men's testimony and official reports . . . it is clear that our forces in the Galilee were not passive and that their attitude toward the inhabitants cannot be seen as having contributed in any way to their decision to remain in their villages . . . On the contrary, even though our forces tried to get them to leave and frequently employed means that were neither legal nor delicate, most of the Galilean Arab population nonetheless decided to remain in its villages.[88]

Jewish settlements harassed Arabs that chose to remain in the villages. Kibbutz Misgav Am, established by members of the youth movement HaNoar HaOved VeHaLomed (NOAL) and located in the Galilee panhandle, threatened its Arab neighbours, telling them that if they did not sell the cattle raised in their villages to the kibbutz, 'they would open fire on them'. Meanwhile, 'the soldiers who were involved in security in the area continued to participate in robberies and confiscations during the occupation'.[89] Some soldiers established a commercial network between Israel and Lebanon, buying and selling everything from food to gold. One official reported, 'They have almost free rein to conduct their activities despite our many requests to get it stopped.' The military police did little to prevent 'the lawlessness out in the field'.[90]

Shepherds from the village of Jish had their flocks stolen from them by members of nearby kibbutz Ayelet HaShahar. The Ministry of Minorities got involved, writing the kibbutz mukhtar that 'we understand that your people most certainly took the sheep in error. [Therefore,] we ask you to please return them to their owners.'[91] Gad Machnes,

---

88   IDF History Department study of Operation Hiram, file: 922/1975-189, IDF.

89   Abraham Kidron to commander of Front Aleph, 2 December 1948, file: 2560/1951-2, IDF.

90   Abraham Kidron to the military government, 17 December 1948, file: 1860/1950-60, IDF.

91   Ministry of Minorities (Safed Branch) to the mukhtar and community of Kibbutz [Ayelet Ha]Shahar, 28 March 1949, file: Minorities-General Safed, Gimmel-306/109, ISA.

director of the Ministry of Minorities, protested about another error that occurred at the time, and in his petition to the Office of the Custodian he tried to be polite:

> Mr Yosef Nahmani of Tiberias has informed us that your Galilean controllers have been given an order to take all livestock, as well as every type of food, found in the villages, and that they are supposed to only leave a week's worth of food in these villages.

Machnes noted in his letter that this order had almost certainly been given in error.[92] In his diary, Nahmani made note of the impressions his visits to captured Galilean villages made on him. 'We were in Tur'an (طرعان), Rummana (رمانة), Kafr Manda (كفر مندا), Eilabun, Kafr Anan (كفر عنان), and Fureidis (الفريديس) dropping off grains and housewares. It was hard to witness.'[93] Confiscations, expropriations, and the pillage of work implements, stock, and cereals sealed the fate of villagers whose lives were dependent on agriculture. The inhabitants of Kafr Manda, on the edge of the Beit Netofa valley, turned to Sheetrit hoping that he could help prevent the confiscation of their property, explaining that they were doing this 'so that we can sow our fields and not miss out on [planting] season.'[94]

It was not just Arab villages that were robbed. The German colony of Waldheim (today the semi-cooperative village Alonei Abba) was seriously plundered after its Templer residents abandoned it, and the village was captured by the Fourteenth Battalion of the Golani Brigade on 17 April. One of the brigade's soldiers had this to say about the events:

---

92   Gad Machnes to Shmuel Zagorski ([Office of the] Custodian of Abandoned Property) 29 November 1948, file: Abandoned Arab Assets, Gimmel-310/28, ISA. See also the comments made by the mediator Ralph Bunche in a report that he submitted a short time before the murder of his predecessor, Folke Bernadotte: 'Report by the United Nations Mediator on the Observation of the Truce in Palestine during the Period from 11 June to 9 July 1948', S/1025, 5 October 1948, UN Archive, un.org.

93   Yosef Nahmani diary, 13 November 1948, HAS.

94   Muhammad Ona Allah and Ahmad Kaml al-Zahr to Bechor-Shalom Sheetrit, 19 December 1948, file: Manda, Gimmel-302/76. See also the letter of Muhammad Jaber Muhammad (محمد) to Bechor-Shalom Sheetrit, 24 September 1948, file: Muhammad Jaber Muhammad, Gimmel-300/89; ISA.

I was lucky that I was not with those who stormed and captured that day, and I was not put to the test. Consequently, my conscience is clean, and my hands were not defiled by the property of Amalek. When you saw the figures walking around in the courtyards, and, especially, when you saw the apartments and the storerooms, you were unconsciously reminded of the famous verse [from Ecclesiastes] that quickly transformed itself in your mind: 'riches kept by the conqueror thereof *to his detriment*.'[95]

Mapai and its leaders addressed the pillaging of the colony. 'All the Jews stole and robbed,' asserted Prime Minister Ben-Gurion. 'It began at Waldheim, at Waldheim it was done for all to see,' he emphasized.[96] Ya'akov Rotenberg, the military prosecutor of the Golani Brigade, spoke critically about the 'organized robbery' that the Kibbutzim carried out in the colony. They 'come to places like Waldheim and Bethlehem with a couple of trucks, pilfer machines, etc.'[97]

Zvi Yehuda, a Moshavim Movement leader and a Mapai member of the first Knesset, recounted his visit to the colony and to Bethlehem (of Galilee) (بيت لحم) two days after the conquest:

My world went dark. An order had not been given to conquer them. Instead, local people, members of Hashomer Hatzair, HaKibbutz HaMeuhad, Hever HaKevutzot, and the Moshavim Movement, initiated it. There was no mixing – it was a pure group [all of them were members of labour movements]. When I got there with the commanders, . . . I said to them: 'Why are you not embarrassed[?] How could you allow such things to happen?!' They answered me: 'You can say whatever you want, but we are proud of our boys.' They brought me 2,000 liras that they found – no army functions like that. I told them that I did not know how many thousands [of liras] they chose not to

95   Quoted in Binyamin Etzioni, ed., *Tree and dagger: The battle path of the Golani Brigade* [Hebrew] (Tel Aviv: Ma'arakhot, 1951), 104.

96   Minutes of Mapai Central Committee [meeting], 24 July 1948, file: Protocols of the Party Central Committee, 2-23-1948-1949, LPA. Golda Meyerson (Meir) also addressed the looting. See Party Central Committee meeting, 11 May 1948, file: 2-23-1948-1949, LPA. See also the discussion of Mapam: Political Committee meeting notes, 26 May 1948, file: Political Committee meetings, (4)66.90, YYA.

97   Minutes of seminar of military prosecutors, 16 June 1948, file: 2294/1950-2882, IDF.

bring to me . . . yet what army [am I talking about]? I saw how they came from the agricultural settlements in automobiles, not just big trucks. They put stuff in sacks and purses, and they carried off what they could. They broke and trampled the rest. What vandalism! After I had spoken, they called to the man [who] accompanied me and they said to him: 'Why did you bring Zvi Yehuda? He will go to the [Histadrut] Executive Committee [of which he is a member] and tell them what happened here. Who gave you permission to bring him here?' I asked to visit the [training] camps, and I still have not received permission. And I am the executive committee member who is in charge of the Mobilization Department[!] I was denied access because I told our dear friends from the Palmach and every other group that you can imagine that they needed to stop looting. There, [they could not have received] an order from on high. Superiors could not [have issued an order like that]. It appears that our education, our spiritual cultivation, was insufficient, no matter what we might try to tell ourselves. This has nothing to do with military headquarters. Pillaging has no headquarters. An evil spirit took hold of our boys and our people. They are pilfering, stealing, and destroying.[98]

Both agricultural settlements and private individuals derived benefit from the property and the animals that the Arabs left behind.[99]

---

98   Minutes of the Histadrut Executive Committee meeting, 16–17 June 1948, vol. 90, June–August 1948, LMA.

99   There are many different examples. I will provide just two of them. Members of Kibbutz Yehiam pillaged a workshop in the village of Tarshiha (ترشيحا) that was conquered on 30 October 1948. A village resident went to the kibbutz to demand that his property be returned, but 'the people of [Kibbutz] Yehiam drove him off with insults and threats'. Mapam's Arab Department wanted to know what happened. It petitioned the kibbutz twice and demanded a response. Initially, the kibbutz ignored the petitions. See Letters from Aharon Cohen to Kibbutz Yehiam from the dates 5 November 1949, 25 December 1949, file: Aharon Cohen – personal archive, Arab Department, Correspondence January–December 1949, (2)9.10-95, YYA. After movement institutions got involved, the kibbutz admitted that it had 'procured' things in the village. On this, see Kibbutz Yehiam to Aharon Cohen, 14 February 1950. It turns out that besides the workshop equipment, the kibbutz members also stole a radio from the village. Following a decision of the Executive Committee Secretariat, the kibbutz announced that it would return the looted property. Yehiam Secretariat to the Executive Committee Secretariat, 11 July 1950 (and additional documents in the file), file: Aharon Cohen – personal archive, Arab Department, Correspondence 1950–1951, (3)9.10-95, YYA. See also documentation of Minister Sheetrit's involvement in efforts to return the Tarshiha

Custodian of Abandoned Property Dov Shafrir declared that 'after inquiries were made' with a number of agricultural settlements, they 'admitted' that they had 'abandoned' Arab property in their possession. Nonetheless, most of the agricultural settlements claimed that the animals 'fled or were slaughtered'. An extremely high number of sheep were acquired illegally. Yet the only live sheep located were a flock of 500 sheep found on Moshav Ein Zeitim (which was abandoned a few years later). It turns out that the Second Brigade commander made it possible for the agricultural settlements to seize property from the villages.[100] Ben-Gurion tasked Zalman Mishary, the national metalworks' human resource manager, with compiling a detailed list of all the Upper and Lower Galilean agricultural settlements possessing property 'that they "took" from Arab villages at the time of their conquest and thereafter – cereals, furniture, and all kinds of things' and flocks. This was a 'special mission' undertaken on behalf of the minister of defence.[101] As in the cases of Ramle, Lydda, and Beersheba, Shafrir believed that the depredation could have been prevented. 'In the first week after the Galilee's conquest', he wrote, 'the army controlled all the villages. Despite the numerous petitions that I made to the military police, we were unable to set up roadblocks and to organize effective security.'[102]

In the files of the Israeli Ministry of Minorities, one can find numerous Arab complaints about the treatment that they and their property

---

resident's property in file: Yunus Muhammad Khurshid, Gimmel-299/54, ISA. Residents of the village of Ma'lul (معلول) complained to the prime minister that the residents of Nahalal stole their flocks and were only willing to return them if financial compensation was provided. See Ma'lul village residents to David Ben-Gurion, 23 March 1949, file: Arab complaints about military treatment, Gimmel Lamed-17118/40, ISA.

100   Dov Shafrir to Shmuel Zagorski, director of the Villages Department, 10 December 1948, file: Abandoned Arab property held by Jews on agricultural settlements, Gimmel-310/43, ISA. Several agricultural settlements gathered abandoned equipment from Beisan and its environs. See Inbar, *Scales of justice*, 622.

101   David Ben-Gurion to Zalman Mishary, 11 November 1948, BGA. In the Ben Gurion Archive, I was not able to locate any additional documentation related to the just mentioned mission/list. After he learned about the removal of property from the village of Hittin (حطين), Eliyahu Zusman from the Tiberian prosecutor's office wanted to check the warehouses on the kibbutzim. Inbar, *Scales of justice*, 622.

102   Dov Shafrir to Shmuel Zagorski, director of the Villages Department, 10 December 1948; Dov Shafrir to Eliezer Kaplan, 19 December 1948; file: Abandoned Arab property held by Jews.

received. This is invaluable documentation, particularly because the complaints are written in the first person – something relatively rare in available historical sources addressing the relations between the two nations in this period. Of course, the Arab complainants are 'present' Arabs, not Arabs who fled or were expelled from the country. There are many examples, but they are not very diverse: universally, the Arab inhabitants protest the looting of their property. The mukhtar of the village of Jisr al-Zarqa (جسر الزرقاء), Dib al-Ali (العلي), requested the ministry's aid to assist '[him] in rebuilding [his] robbed and destroyed home'. Not only were his farm animals, clothes, and kitchen tools stolen from him, but so was his fishing boat.[103] The Ministry of Minorities investigated many of the complaints that it received, though its officials were not always convinced of the veracity of the complaints. In any event, they were frequently dependent upon information received from representatives of the military government. For example, Hassan Arafat (عرفات), mukhtar of the village of Qatra (قطرة), near Gedera, protested the damages that both Jews and Arabs had caused to his property, complaining that the army had taken mechanical equipment he owned.[104] In the Ministry of Minorities' opinion, 'his complaint proves unrealistic and should be shelved'.[105] It is clear that there was not a lot that the Ministry of Minorities could not do in most of these cases. When addressing the case of the village mukhtar of Jisr al-Zarqa, an office secretary wrote,

His case is not unique. There are hundreds and perhaps thousands like it. The cabinet has yet to discuss the idea of compensating war victims. Consequently, it would be best to advise him to make only modest financial claims.[106]

---

103 Dib al-Ali to Bechor-Shalom Sheetrit, February 1949, file: The mukhtar Dib al-Ali, Gimmel-298/61, ISA.

104 Hassan Arafat to Bechor-Shalom Sheetrit, 26 November 1948, file: Hassan Arafat, Gimmel-300/2, ISA.

105 This is what is written by hand on the letter from Tzvi Shnayder (secretary-general of the military government in Jaffa) to the Ministry of Minorities, 25 November 1948, file: Hassan Arafat, Gimmel-300/24, ISA.

106 T. Eshbal to the Binyaminah Village Council (to Whom the Mukhtar Delivered His Complaint), 28 February 1949, file: The Mukhtar Dib al-Ali, Gimmel-298/61, ISA.

The months passed, and the overwhelming majority of Palestinians that remained in the country had their property appropriated without compensation.

In this way, over the course of a few months, soldiers and civilians alike plundered countless villages across the country.[107] The tools and the daily bread of both 'present' and 'absent' Palestinian peasants were stolen and destroyed. They could no longer return to their destroyed homes.

---

107   As I noted at the beginning of this section, it is impossible within the frame-work of this study to describe the plunder of each and every village. See Inbar, *Scales of justice*, on the pillaging of Shajara (الشجرة), where, according to the Twelfth Brigade, 'the commanders did not maintain control over their men, many of whom strayed into village homes for wholly unmilitary purposes', 609; on the plunder of Iksal (إكسال), 614; on the pillaging of Saqiya (ساقية), 715. See Benny Morris, *1948* (Tel Aviv: 'Am 'Oved, 2010), on the looting of Dawayima (الدوايمة), 362; on the depredation of Majdal (المجدل), 363; on the despoliation of Beit Jan (بيت جن), 303. Among others, the Irgun plundered the villages of Sindiyana (السنديانة), Sabirin (صبارين), Ijzim (إجزم), and Yahudiya (يهودية); the Department of Arab Affairs to David Ben-Gurion, 19 May 1948, file: Destruction, plunder, and looting, 307/27, ISA.

Collective Looting

In mid-April 1949, two months before the war concluded with the signing of an armistice agreement with Syria, Custodian of Abandoned Property Dov Shafrir summarized the activities of his office since its establishment in July 1948.[1] A month after that, someone would declare in a discussion of the Knesset's Finance Committee that 'the robbery of abandoned property has still not been put to an end'.[2] In August 1950, when he left his position, Shafrir published two long articles in *Davar* based on the report.[3] The property issue, he wrote in the first article, was 'one of the biggest and most complex issues connected to the War of Independence'. The feeling of victory seemingly permitted 'the pleasure of enemy spoils, and the urge for vengeance and physical temptation caused many people to stumble'.

> Only resolute action employing the full powers vested in the military and the administrative, civil, and legal authorities could have possibly saved souls, as well as property, from moral failure. Such resolute

---

1 'The Custodian of Absentee Property, report on activities up until 31 March 1949', 18 April 1949, file: Office of the Custodian of Absentee Property, Gimmel-5434/3, ISA.

2 Minutes of Finance Committee meeting, 15 May 1949, KAJ.

3 Dov Shafrir, 'Absentee assets' [Hebrew], *Davar*, 27–28 August 1950. See also Dov Shafrir, *The flowerbed of life* [Hebrew] (Tel Aviv: ha-Merkaz ha-Haklai, 1975), 220–44.

action was never undertaken. Perhaps, under the conditions, it could not be undertaken. Things quickly got out of hand. 'The recognition' of a large part of the population that the property was abandoned dogged the work of the custodian's offices and caused regretful misunderstandings. The tempestuous period of the war, the arrival of thousands and tens of thousands of new immigrants, a new government's establishment, the pressure created by material needs and the demand for their satisfaction with apartments and other materials that were available as 'abandoned property' caused great bedlam with home, store, and warehouse invasions carried out both in a private manner and in an organized manner by institutions and responsible bodies. Those were shadows that darkened the historic act of national liberation. When you travel the country, through cities and villages . . . sorrow dilutes your happiness – the sorrow of the shadow – the shadow of Achan who took devoted things.[4]

Shafrir's report, which is thirteen pages long, includes an additional fourteen pages of tables and data. The data and numbers are a statistical representation of the events described throughout this part of the book. Shafrir wrote that there is no way of knowing what befell a large portion of this property – the furniture that was in Arab homes, for example. He further noted:

This was a complex and difficult affair that went on for a long time. When controllers arrived at the vast majority of homes [his office was responsible for close to 50,000 homes], they were breached, and their furniture broken. It should be noted that no clothing, housewares, kitchenware, jewellery, and bedding, with the exception of mattresses and similar things, made it to [our] warehouses. Only a small number of rugs were collected – 509 total carpets. Most furniture was found damaged or destroyed.[5]

Behind the tables, a bitter truth was hidden: the Jewish population pillaged thousands of stores, and tens of thousands of homes and

---

4 Shafrir, 'Absentee assets'.
5 'The Custodian of Absentee Property, Report on activities up until 31 March 1949'.

buildings.[6] In some of the cities and villages, this was the property of neighbours who lived across the way. The vast majority of Arab inhabitants did not take part in the fighting at all.[7] 'They will not conquer the Land of Israel, they will steal it,' said Chief Military Prosecutor Avraham

6   To date, an exact calculation of the value of looted, stolen, and expropriated moveable property has not been made. The custodian's 1949 report presents various estimates and costs. The value of property sold and donated by the Office of the Custodian up until March 1949 stood at 3,975,740 Palestinian pounds (P£). Rental income for buildings, apartments, etc., is not included in this sum. The value of buildings and lands left behind by Palestinians is not included in this sum either. The value of the property looted and stolen during the war would need to be added to this sum, but this is, of course, impossible to do. According to the calculations of the United Nations Palestine Conciliation Commission (PCC), the value of the property Arab inhabitants left behind was slightly more than P£19 million. The commission noted that this is only a very rough estimate based on the following calculation. In 1945, the national income for Arab Palestine was P£62 million. The estimate that was adopted set the value of Arab moveable property at 40 percent of this number – that is, P£18.6 million. The PCC's Refugee Office estimated the value of different types of property as follows: industrial equipment – P£3.4 million; commercial shares – P£4.3 million; motor vehicles – P£1.3 million; agricultural equipment and livestock – P£13.1 million; total – P£22.1 million. The final number represents the value of Palestinian Arab property as a whole in 1945. Therefore, one needs to take away approximately a quarter of this number (not all Palestinian Arabs became refugees). Yet one needs to add at least P£2.5 million, a number equalling the value of the damage done to 'present' Arabs' homes. This gives a sum total of P£19.1 million. For comparison purposes, if we employ available historical currency converters to convert 1948 Palestinian pounds into 2020 new Israel shekels, the value of Arab moveable property in 1948 is today equal to about 3 billion Israeli shekels (820 million US dollars). Progress Report of the United Nations Mediator on Palestine Submitted to the Secretary-General for Transmission to the Members of the United Nations, 16 September 1948, UN Archive, un.org. See also Don Peretz, *Israel and the Palestine Arabs* (Washington, DC: Middle East Institute, 1958), 146–8; Henry Cattan, *Palestine, the Arabs and Israel: The Search for Justice* (London: Longmans, 1969), 78–80.

7   In March 1948, David Ben-Gurion wrote that indigenous Arabs were not interested in fighting against the Jews. See David Ben-Gurion to Moshe Sharett and Golda Meir, 14 March 1948, BGA. Minister Aharon Zisling said: 'Palestinian Arabs did not fight. Foreigners fought.' See Cabinet Meeting Minutes, 16 June 1948, ISA. It is possible to find echoes of this fact in the press of the time. See: 'Your deeds will bring you closer and your deeds will make you more distant – this proverb should be remembered when considering victors and *the thousands of Arabs who remained in the country, most of whom, as everybody knows, did not want this war* . . . without a doubt, these people need to be helped and everything possible needs to be done during this state of emergency to get their lives back to normal.' Menahem Kapeliuk, 'On our war's side effects' [Hebrew], *Davar*, 19 September 1948, emphasis added. It is surprising how much this fact, well known to decision makers in real time, has become blurred over the course time. There are, of course, political reasons for this.

Gorali.[8] He knew what he was talking about: there were those who complained that his private library contained books that had been looted from Jaffa lawyers' abandoned homes.[9] Gorali described the pillaging of property as a 'breaker'.[10] Unchecked thievery also prevented the fair and efficient handling of apartment and building distribution. Minister of Finance Kaplan reported to the Knesset that most of the assets that made it into the custodian's hands were already illegally occupied by various invaders.[11] In his book *Connected*, Menachem Klein reflected:

> The waves of violence between Jews and Arabs that took place at the end of the mandatory period that frequently involved acts of murder and incidents of violence for its own sake raise two questions: How can neighbours who share their daily lives act so brutally towards one another? How do people lead a peaceful and polite daily life alongside those who will soon fall victim to their violent behaviour?[12]

Indeed, these are difficult questions to answer. Nonetheless, the issue of plunder proves even more difficult to unravel. The depredation occurred after the Arabs were expelled from the cities and the towns, and the public could not know for certain whether the Arab residents would return later (we have seen, for example, that Nahmani believed Arabs' property needed to be protected until they returned). Furthermore, a few Israeli murdered, but many pillaged. At the beginning of the war,

---

8   Mina Shamir quotes Avraham Gorali in Zvi Inbar, *Scales of justice and the sword: Foundations of military law in Israel* [Hebrew] (Tel Aviv: Ma'arakhot, 2005), 401n898.

9   'I know that important law books (written in English) that were abandoned by Arab lawyers in Jaffa have miraculously made their way to attorney A[vraham] Gorali's private office in Tel Aviv . . . I do not know if the chief military prosecutor has the right "to confiscate" abandoned property for his private use and pleasure . . . all of these books are elegantly bound and contain the seal of an Arab lawyer. Is this not a criminal offense for somebody who does not hold such an esteemed office, and all the more so for a man responsible for upholding law in the defense force?!' Reuben Nohimovsky to David Ben-Gurion, 10 October 1948, BGA.

10   Avraham Gorali to David Ben-Gurion, 8 June 1948, file: The legal service 15-178/2, YTA.

11   Minutes of the Knesset plenum, 22 November 1949, KAJ.

12   Menachem Klein, *Connected: The story of the land's inhabitants* [Hebrew] (Tel Aviv: ha-Kibbutz ha-me'uhad, 2015), 144–5.

philosopher Martin Buber and the 'Unity' Association had published the following statement:

> Savagery has rapidly infected the struggle taking place throughout the country, and [it has infected] the elderly, women, and children [as well] . . . a war psychosis, a psychosis of fear that leads us to see every passer-by as a stranger – at least one who resembles a stranger – a raider and a murderer, an attacker and an enemy, spreads among us [too]. This is the mental state that motivates the masses to act, killing and murdering passing strangers.[13]

Buber and his associates' calls for people 'not to loot' fell on deaf ears.[14]

In his report, Shafrir referred to the biblical figure Achan, son of Carmi, whose deeds had once caused the Children of Israel to lose in battle. Joshua turned to God and wondered why he was routed in the battle of Ai. God responded:

> Israel hath sinned; yea, they have even transgressed My covenant which I commanded them; yea, they have even taken of the devoted thing; and have also stolen, and dissembled also, and they have even put it among their own stuff. (Joshua 7:11)

This verse asserts that it was not just Achan who committed the sin of plunder; the punishment was collective because the sin was collective.[15] It was not just a single Achan who took of the devoted thing during the Independence War; the Jewish Israeli people, in their multitudes, participated in the despoliation. Then, they strove to wash their hands clean with water flowing from stolen faucets they had removed from Arab neighbours' apartments.

---

13   Unity Organization, 'Do not allow the mob to take control over us [1948]' [Hebrew], in Avraham Yassour, ed., *Jews and Arabs in the land of Israel: Selected remarks of M. Buber, A. D. Gordon, and documents of Unity* (Givat Haviva: Institute for Arab Studies 1981), 182–3.

14   See the epigraph that opens the second part of the book.

15   On this, see Micah Goodman, *Moses' final oration* [Hebrew](Or Yehudah: Devir, 2014), 207–10.

The Plunder of Palestinian Property – Politics and Society

You . . . speak about thousands who you say are waiting for me to call them 'to battle against this danger', namely the internal danger of 'the spirit of violence, the spirit of nationalism, the spirit of militarism'. Yet where were those thousands . . . [when] we . . . published . . . what it was possible to publish 'against robbery and plunder, against the anti-Arab discrimination, and against the destruction of their villages?' How few were the voices of encouragement! . . . 'Redemption' of an external kind can be paid for with the blood of our sons. Internal redemption can only be created by gazing directly at the brutal face of truth.

Martin Buber[1]

---

1   Martin Buber, 'Facts and Demands: A Reply to Gideon Freudenberg', in Paul Mendes-Flohr, ed., *A Land of Two Peoples: Martin Buber on Jews and Arabs* (New York: Oxford University Press, 1983), 238–9. Translation modified for accuracy.

A Poison Spreading through the Veins of Society

At the end of May 1948, Yosef Weitz, a top Jewish National Fund official, wrote that 'the plunder of Arab assets serves as a topic of conversation in various [social] circles. Everybody is pointing to the robbery and pretending to challenge it, but, in practice, everybody is robbing and looting.'[1] Weitz does not indicate which 'circles' he was talking about, but in May – after the plunder of Tiberias, Haifa, Jerusalem, Acre, Safed, and Beisan (Beit She'an) – the robbery of Palestinian property was so widespread that the Israeli public knew all about it. Nonetheless, perusal of contemporary newspapers shows that plunder as a broader trend was seriously downplayed.[2] This is an interesting sociological phenomenon: plundering and keeping quiet about it. It is what Moshe Erem, a Ministry of Minorities official and a member of the first Knesset, was referring to when at a June 1948 Mapam Council he asserted that it was necessary to break the Israeli public's 'bond of

---

1   Yosef Weitz, *My diary and my letters to my sons* [Hebrew], vol. 3, *A guard of walls* (Tel Aviv: Masada, 1965), 291.

2   In his book, Gish Amit asserts that 'engagement with the plunder of Palestinian property assumed an important place in Israeli public discourse in 1948 and 1949 . . . The daily press also dedicated a great deal of attention [to plunder].' Yet Amit does not provide sufficient evidence for these claims. He only relates four brief references to it from 1948 issues of *Al HaMishmar* and an additional article from a 1949 issue of *Haaretz*. Gish Amit, *Ex libris: A history of theft, preservation, and appropriation at the National Library in Jerusalem* [Hebrew] (Tel Aviv: ha-Kibbutz ha-me'uhad, 2015), 82–3.

silence' related to every facet of robbery and plunder.[3] *Davar* reporter
Menahem Kapeliuk wrote:

> To put it very delicately, it would have been better if the sights and
> facts that one runs across when touring most of the occupied loca-
> tions had never arisen. Emphasizing its negative aspect, our press
> alludes to this matter, but not enough is said. Enlisted men and offic-
> ers who are extremely uncomfortable with these negative phenomena
> have not infrequently said to the author of these lines that the press
> has not fulfilled its duty and has not unequivocally condemned
> specific acts that the War had not at all necessitated. Not only are
> these acts unproductive, but one should expect that they will prove
> damaging sooner or later.[4]

Indeed, there were those like author and publicist Moshe Smilansky who
were unsparing in their criticism. Yet he also wrote months after the war,
when most of the property had already been looted. In his opinion,

> the inheritance bequeathed to our state by the 440 abandoned villages
> turns out to be quite large . . . how has *the public* treated this inherit-
> ance? 'A ravenous hunger "to grab stuff" has seized all the inhabitants.

---

3   'In Support of Standing Firm on the Political Front', *Al HaMishmar*, 27 June 1948.
What Erem referred to as 'the bond of silence' I refer to as 'propagandic concealment'.
'The silence' was not the natural result of 'the relationship' between the regime and the
Jewish public but, rather, a calculated policy. Everybody knew about mass plunder, but
they did not report it in the media (some of which were affiliated with various political
movements or political institutions). The fact that there were scattered articles addressing the topic does not make plunder into something that goes through appropriate
channels – namely, print journalism – to assert its presence in the public sphere. What
is the political reason for a taboo on public mention of the well-known fact that people
were pillaging? The secrecy teaches and confirms that what was happening was a crime.
In this sense, depredation was not a secret, but it was simply something that it was best
to keep quiet about in a general societal sense.
4   Menahem Kapeliuk, 'On our war's side effects' [Hebrew], *Davar*, 17 September
1948. Kapeliuk also addressed a claim that certainly helped strengthen the motivation to
plunder, or, at the very least, neutralized its anti-social sting: 'It is surprising and regretful that the military and civil courts did not employ all of their authority and influence
to prevent, or, at the very least, minimize the acts that are, as they say, inevitable with a
conquering army. Many times, soldiers and civilians have responded that one should not
be too critical of this [behaviour], because if those defeated today had been the victors,
they would have left nothing and would have destroyed as much as they could have.'

Individuals, kvutzot and kibbutzim, men, women, and children, everybody pounced on the booty, [including] doors, windows, door-frames, bricks, roof tiles, flooring tiles, scrap-iron, and machine parts' – that is what the custodian of abandoned property says. There are those that say that the hands of some of its 'custodians' are not clean either. How did the state treat the inheritance? Not only did it not know how to restrain the public and to protect the huge quantity of moveable property from plunder and robbery, but it also did not know how to protect immoveable property.[5]

Clearly, the whole Jewish population did not plunder and rob. Retrospectively, however, one cannot determine, in each and every location, how many people actually participated in despoliation. Yet, this book's central claim does not require such an estimate. It is enough that many people robbed; enough that the overwhelming majority of the *Palestinian* property that remained behind was pillaged. Thereby, as will be subsequently explained, there was enough to implicate the population as a whole (or as a collective) in a crime, even though not every member of it participated in the depredation. One can assume, based on the sources supplied in the first part of the book, that people of the time saw a substantive difference between collecting 'souvenirs' that were kicking around in the streets and breaking into the apartment of an Arab living in the adjacent neighbourhood (as happened in many cities) to empty his house. Yet – and there is no doubt of this – one who pillaged and robbed their neighbours knew that was what they were doing. In an imagined dialogue with an imaginary Arab (and one can ponder whether he really is imaginary) to whose village home he enters with the intention of looting, journalist and politician Uri Avnery, himself a veteran of the war, sheds light on the types of excuses that helped the looters perform their task:

I swear to you! I am not guilty. I didn't want this war. Really, I did not. Of course, I know that it is forbidden to steal. It says so in the Bible, and I am sure it says so in the Qur'an too. As a matter of fact, I do not need your prayer beads and headband. I have more than enough. I have robbed enough in other villages . . . It is a psychological law,

5   Moshe Smilansky, 'From our lives' [Hebrew], *Haaretz*, 1 September 1949.

Ataullah. It is a unique pleasure to take a stranger's property. Property for which you neither need to pay nor work. It is a temptation that it is impossible to resist. *Before every battle, people dream about plunder, and, perhaps, about girls that they will be able to rape.*[6]

Netiva Ben-Yehuda, mentioned during the discussion of Tiberias's and Safed's depredation in the first part of the book, wrote in a more explicit manner. She pointed out that soldiers knew that the looting of Arab property constituted a social crime. It was clear to us, she explained, that we were violating a serious prohibition: *Thou shalt not steal*. In her book *Through the binding of ropes*, she writes:

It was not that laws no longer existed, but rather the opposite. All those laws that you would obey with all your strength, the strictest ones embedded within you even when you were fast asleep – precisely those were now permitted. Even more than that: inasmuch as you violated more such prohibitions, your reputation improved. You would get a medal for it.[7]

Elsewhere in the book, Ben-Yehuda wrote at length about the significance of the ancient prohibition's annulment:

Another thing should be acknowledged: Deep inside our brains, each one of us has a sort of policeman who does not let us just take whatever we want from others; if you violate this policeman's rules and steal something, your heart quakes, right? That policeman's actual strength only becomes clear when you are with a plundering army. You take something, and you violate this serious no-no, you are not 'a

---

6   Uri Avnery, The other side of the coin [Hebrew] (Tel Aviv: Zmora-Bitan, 1990 [1950]), 101–2. Avnery added: 'The desk [in my house] is covered with all sorts of things I brought back on previous "Leaves" – small items of booty . . . pictures that I lifted from Arab homes. This is one of my quirks. I collect pictures of Fellaheen, especially those of women and children. I want to remind myself later who our "enemies" were.' Uri Avnery, *1948: A Soldier's Tale – The Bloody Road to Jerusalem*, trans. Christopher Costello (Oxford: Oneworld, 2008), 313.

7   Netiva Ben-Yehuda, *Through the binding ropes* [Hebrew] (Jerusalem: Domino Press, 1985), 163. See also 'On the plunder', *BaMivtza* ('Carmeli') 5, file:1147/2002-43, IDF: 'Do not try to convince me that you do not need to plunder and destroy stranger's property. I know that quite well.'

thief', and you are not afraid of anybody, you are not afraid to get caught. Yet your heart pounds, it skips a beat, and you turn beet red, because you did it in front of everybody, in the light of day, and your hands tremble, you cannot get enough air, you are bathed in sweat and you begin to argue with yourself exactly like you argue with yourself before you kill an enemy, particularly your first enemies. This is because what you are doing is violating an awesome prohibition that is deeply rooted in your brain. It will affect you throughout your life and in that moment as well. How did it influence us? We immediately began to make light of the property, the bounty, and to break and throw things. We also started to get unruly, punches started to get thrown, and, worst of all, we started stealing from one another. In the Palmach – where there were never thefts – people began to steal from each other! . . . Property and human life were becoming the same – worthless! Why was all this happening? It was happening, because no matter how tough you are and how many terrible things that you have experienced – it did not make a difference: You enter into somebody's private space, to a home whose privacy is evident for all to see, and your heart begins to pound at the moment that you first begin to think: I can take whatever I want! This thought in and of itself is a crime. You see the most private and intimate place in the world – exposed, revealed, trampled, visible to your foreign and out of place eyes – and this alone corrupts you. This alone is a transgression, a crime. You know this quite well. Oof, how you know this.[8]

The looting is occasionally mentioned in military journals and bulletins published during the war.[9] 'Oy, what happened to our Zionism' is the title of an article from *BaMivtza* (On Campaign), the Carmel Brigade bulletin. It asserts that the soldier who loots, steals, or kills severs themself from inner discipline and morality and 'ceases to be a soldier'.[10] The

---

8   Ben-Yehuda, *Through the binding ropes*, 285–6.

9   While the contemporary press was methodically examined for this book, military journals were not. In any case, based on the limited research written about these journals and the author's unsystematic study of some of them, it appears that looting was not one of their central concerns. This subject is worthy of separate study.

10   Quoted in Israel Rozenson, *Soldiers' writings in BaMivtza, BaMishlat, and BaMivtzar, journals of IDF units, from 1947–1949* [Hebrew] (Jerusalem: Carmel, 2016), 96. See also the short articles from *BaMivtza* 5: 'On the plunder' and 'A bit of truth about the plunder', file: 1147/2002-43, IDF.

article 'Do Not Reach Out for the Plunder!' in the Fifty-Fourth Battalion's journal, not only opposed the commercial and 'acquisitional urges' that had seized hold of the soldiers, but also the dangers that came along with them: soldiers got wounded because they were robbing things rather than fortifying their positions. In this sense, the pillager 'pays with his blood'.[11]

The settlement movements – both the soldiers who belonged to them and their political leadership – were the most critical of despoliation. Even in the journals of their youth movements, whose members participated in the fighting, one finds articles opposing looting. 'The affliction has spread to our camp!' wrote David Vinograd in ba-Ma'alah (On the Rise), the newspaper of the Zionist HaNoar HaOved VeHaLomed (NOAL) youth movement. The forces assuming control over huge quantities of property, dealing with prisoners of war and destroying settlements require 'purity of arms and soldierly humanity'. Vinograd demanded that precautions be taken, and warning constantly given, to combat 'the unpleasant trends that have been found in the ranks of all of our brigades'.[12] Hashomer Hatzair member Levi Dror wrote in a similar vein in a collection of writings about the socialist Zionist youth movement, the Hashomer Hatzair book. He warned about how 'moral corruption in Yishuv society' was manifesting itself in plunder and accumulation of wealth,

under the frequent guise of 'national responsibility' . . . and how this was being done in broad daylight, without any public censure. It is no surprise that these temptations also knocked at the door of

---

11   Quoted in Rozenson, Soldiers' writings in BaMivtza, BaMishlat, and BaMivtzar, 97. See also the following statement made in issue 6 of the Eighth Brigade's journal (31 October 1948): 'Yesterday we blessed the conquerors of the villages, but today we will speak to them harshly, because they bring danger to our door. You enter a village and there are chickens running around and cows bellowing. People also find food pantries. Before the shooting has stopped, robbery is in full swing out in the open . . . Yet be careful, robbery develops in stages. You smile with understanding and forgiveness for just a moment and a happy kumzitz turns into petty theft, grand theft, and plunder. Command needs to be much more careful . . . we know that the struggle with the enemy is difficult, but man's struggle with himself is many times more difficult.' Quoted in Oz Almog, The Sabar: A portrait [Hebrew] (Tel Aviv: 'Am 'Oved, 1997), 311.

12   David Vinograd, 'The vicissitudes of our military organization' [Hebrew], ba-Ma'alah: 'Iton ha-no'ar ha-'oved, 3 September 1948.

our precious and devoted soldiers, simple people devoted to the cause. The voices of our nation's conscientious and morally brave members have been drowned out by the tumult caused by the IDF's brilliant victories, and who really pays attention to 'minor details'?[13]

A long article published in *'Alon ha-Palmach* (Palmach Bulletin) pointed to depredation's dangers. Its pseudonymous author, 'Niv', was less bothered by the pillagers' disregard for military discipline (and the dangers that it posed to soldiers) than he was by plunder's societal effects. 'The question is how it affects *us*, the objective of our war, the character of our army, and what it is liable to do to *us*.' In his opinion, acts of murder and robbery would worsen the relations between the two nations and become a permanent factor fanning the flames of hatred between Jewish Israelis and Arab Palestinians:

At the moment in the middle of battle when one individual or another stops participating in the joint effort on behalf of the common good and begins looking out for himself, he removes a brick from the building's foundation. He pulls out one of our unique army's cornerstones . . . Think about it [this is a letter to a friend]. Rather than feeling the full weight of the yoke of limitless devotion and personal responsibility for the [collective] good, that individual's thoughts are elsewhere. As everybody knows, sin begets sin. You begin 'to accumulate' during wartime and you 'feel like' doing this a lot. Does it have an end? . . . We are all currently in the military. Yet common sense teaches that we all await the day that we will start 'looking out for ourselves' again.[14]

Like 'Niv' before him, Uri Avnery found the long-term effects of despoliation disturbing. 'If it is permissible to rob Arabs, why just Arabs?' he

---

13   Levi Dror, 'When thou goest forth to battle' [Hebrew], in Levi Dror and Yisrae'el Rozentzvayg, eds, *Hashomer Hatzair book*, vol. 3 (Merhavyah: Sifriyat ha-po'alim, 1964), 30.

14   Niv [pseud.], 'Letter to a friend' [Hebrew], *'Alon ha-Palmach* 68 (3 July 1948): 29–31. Republished as 'Spoils of war – and discipline' [Hebrew], *ha-Medinah*, 5 August 1948. See also 'Social problems in a battle situation' [Hebrew], *'Alon ha-Palmach* 62 (18 May 1948).

wondered in *The other side of the coin*. Avnery criticized both those who pillaged and those who remained silent when the cities were emptied. In his opinion, the looting could not have been kept within Jaffa's and Arab Haifa's boundaries:

> Do they not understand that limits were not possible here[?] If you can steal the property of an Arab whose personal wishes made no difference in this war and probably never did anything to harm the Yishuv, why is it forbidden to 'confiscate' the property of a bourgeois Jew who has amassed capital[?] Moral principles are either absolute or, in the end, they will completely disappear.'[15]

Examination of the limited amount written about looting during the war shows that the authors who addressed it did not just fear how it would affect the relations between the two nations; they were perhaps most concerned with how it would affect the plundering Jewish society. In a party pamphlet published during the war, Aharon Cohen, a Mapam Arab department member, talked about 'a labour movement leader' who said:

> I am afraid of the loss of innocence, the loss of the idea that man needs to live by his labour rather than by plunder and robbery, because there is something here that smacks of great moral failure. Instead of combat activity, theft-related behaviour.[16]

Vinograd, in his article in *ba-Ma'alah*, pointed to social phenomena that he expected to see develop due to the failure to address plunder:

> We should not pretend that there have never been cases in the short history of our conquests where important operations have failed, and

---

15   Avnery, *The other side of the coin*, 86–7. Avnery also writers about the theft of Jewish property in his book. 'Our tent is an oasis in this desert of a camp. Jamus and I have assembled all our booty from the last year here – the deep armchair that we "borrowed" from the Irgun after Altalena Day, the nargileh I got in Chudad, two chairs from the Jewish café which charged an extortionate price for two cups of ice cream, a folding chair from an Egyptian battalion's headquarters, and a bookcase we found in an abandoned British barracks.' Avnery, *1948*, 362. Translation modified for accuracy.

16   Aharon Cohen, *Let's clarify things for ourselves (Conversations with comrades in uniform)* [Hebrew] (Tel Aviv: Mifleget ha-po'alim ha-me'uhedet be-Eretz Yisra'el, 1948).

we have incurred losses and damages because people have been obsessed with robbing and pillaging. There is nothing preventing this problem from spreading. Just as people *intentionally* want to teach the nation devotion and support for its army, every aspect, both internal and external, of an army's behaviour can *inadvertently* teach the nation. A civilian adopts a mindset that says: since they expect me to sacrifice in the same way that a soldier is expected to sacrifice, I can act like one. And this is how the problem, like an infectious disease, can pass from soldiers to civilians. Many decent and honourable people come to see enemy property's 'acquisition' and 'confiscation' as something permissible and natural. Then [people are] suspicious [of one another], [and] skirmishes and disputes [proliferate] – the home front's 'moral' decline. This description is not overblown. The clear-sighted among us can see the general outlines [of this scenario] taking place in a number of the territories we currently occupy. There is one way to put an end to this problem. A resolute war against depredation! It needs to be conducted in two stages. First, explanation and education; second, forceful uprooting of this weed. We need to remember that no price is too high for purification of the ranks and cleansing of the environment. What seems trivial in the field today, can come back to bite us tomorrow. It is better to take action before it is too late.[17]

Eliezer 'Livneh' Liebenstein, a Mapai Knesset member and one of his party's few members who publicly protested the looting in real time, saw the robbing of Arab property, in all the myriad forms that it assumed, as a dangerous abomination. As far as he was concerned, the whole population knew about the despoliation, but not everybody 'felt the shame' and 'the tragedy of it'. Livneh did not distinguish between 'collective robbery' and 'individual robbery'. In practice, he maintained, the former form was perhaps even more loathsome because it demanded preparation and judgement. 'As the amount of thought being put into pillaging increased, its immorality multiplied', he wrote. Livneh, like the others just discussed, saw the looting of property endangering 'the morality of the nation and its inner life':

---

17 Vinograd, 'Vicissitudes of our military organization'.

The one who denies Arab property rights will eventually have little respect for Jewish property; one who is hostile to members of the neighbouring people will also ridicule members of his own people. The moral and social effects of property effortlessly and dishonestly attained are greater than its material and financial value: it alienates people from work and seduces them into behaving dishonestly; the honest man begins to look like a policeman and the prankster like a hero. Booty does more than just destroy the victim. It damages the perpetrator's soul; if its influence rears its head even slightly during wartime, much of its poison spreads through society's arteries during subsequent times of peace. A fighting army has commanders, and a fighting nation has a government. If Israel has leaders, they must come now and man the breach. While such action might make people unpopular, it is a touchstone for true *leadership*.[18]

The writer Haim Gouri gave poetic expression to a similar idea in his book *Until the dawn rose* when he spoke about the 'people [who] picked at the spoils' after the conquest of Abu-Ageila. Gouri quotes Issachar Shadmi, the brigade commander whose soldiers committed the infamous 1956 Kafr Qasim massacre, who declared: 'You begin with this, and you end up with Satan.'[19] This is the same idea that poet and essayist Yeshurun Keshet intended to express in his diary after he witnessed the ravaging of Jerusalem up close:

My nation's way is hidden from my eyes; I fear those murky forces that have suddenly arisen from its bottommost layers like a type of mould rising from the bottom of a vessel to pollute all of the beverage contained within it.[20]

Two years, more or less, after most of the articles just discussed were published, Tuvyah Cohen publish a long article in *Ner* [Candle], a 'Unity' group journal that was unparalleled in its criticism of the

18   Eliezer Liebenstein [Livneh], 'Abominable robbery' [Hebrew], *Ma'ariv*, 30 July 1948.

19   Haim Gouri, *Until the dawn rose* [Hebrew] (Tel Aviv: ha-Kibbutz ha-me'uhad, 2000), 108–9.

20   Yeshurun Keshet, *In besieged Jerusalem: Diaries from the home front* [Hebrew] (Jerusalem: Re'uven Mas, 1973), 31.

dominant policy towards the Arab population. The article addressed the influence that actions undertaken against Palestinians during the war had on Israeli (Jewish) society. Cohen wondered: 'Have we waited generations for a state, for a state like this? Does this society we live in here in our state accord with our dreams for it in our vision of national renewal?' The answer to these questions was no. Tuvyah, who fought in the war, wrote that after the invading Arab forces had been repelled in the north, an evil spirit began to blow; 'many soldiers in the battalion, drunk with victory and achievements, pounced to gather spoils in the conquered villages, and officers and commanders were among those most active in these efforts.'

Alongside acts of plunder, Israeli forces did horrible things to the Arab inhabitants, Cohen explained. One soldier proudly told how he had 'taken care of' an elderly Arab woman who had remained in the village of Lubya after it had been evacuated:

This became something fashionable [to do]. I complained to the battalion commander about what was going on and I requested that he put a stop to this wild behaviour that had absolutely no military justification. He shrugged his shoulders and said that 'there was no order from up high' to prevent it . . . after that the battalion descended down [a slippery] slope. Its military accomplishments mounted, but, alongside them, atrocities multiplied too.

Tuvyah writes that there were many people who secretly found these things painful and were certain that they were being orchestrated from 'the top':

The only reason that I discussed this specific affair that I witnessed in detail is that I believe that it gives expression to many of the negative phenomena that subsequently took hold in our lives. It is natural that when you relax the leash and cultivate aggressiveness and unruly behaviour that they become difficult to direct. The aggressive spirit becomes second nature and there is no way to restrict it to just one specific area. This chronicle of crime that began to expand in the Jewish community following the conclusion of the war with robberies and acts of rape that frequently paired up with murder proves this. It seems to me that the immorality and corruption of the black market are, to a certain extent, nothing more than the aftergrowth that developed, directly or indirectly, against the shameful background of 'the abandoned property', a matter that did quite a bit to taint our social lives. I am surprised at those who raise a fuss when people learn that fourteen kibbutzim were involved with the black market. Why are we only condemning them now when it affects us? Tens of kibbutzim and moshavs reached out for the filthy lucre that people referred to as 'abandoned property'. What would stop someone who uninhibitedly plundered from profiting through the black market? Why was it permitted then and now it is forbidden? . . . Everything is connected; that is how things unfolded and brought us to the troubling development that everybody is currently writing and talking about so much – because it is affecting us now – the moral and social crisis in our state.[21]

Cohen was not the only one who thought that even though plunder had been forbidden de jure, the authorities had permitted it de facto. Ruth Lubitz, whose impressions of her tour through plundered Jaffa were presented in part I, wrote of the self-destructive dangers that accompany acts of violence and pillaging: 'The masses suffered from a psychosis that allowed them to loot property without being able to understand that there was something unjust about what they were doing.' Lubitz believed that plunder would not stop at Arab city limits and would continue into the Jewish cities. Around her she saw 'people so involved in robbery' that they talked about it uninhibitedly. She looked for who was responsible, and she determined:

Guilt lies with the leaders who did not employ the means at their disposal to punish those who looted. Failure to punish them teaches the community that it is actually fine to steal. Let us not forget what Haifa taught us. If the leadership had not 'forgotten' the lesson of Haifa, what happened in Jaffa and other places would not have occurred. The masses were not the first to plunder. The Irgun was the first to do so. For whole days, vehicles loaded down with goods flowed in from Jaffa. There were trucks that transferred merchandise

---

21   Tuvyah Cohen, 'On the character and the causes of the State of Israel's moral and social crisis' [Hebrew], *Ner* 9-12 (9 March 1951): 10–11.

'confiscated' by the Haganah – 'things necessary for out war effort'
[they claimed]. Individual initiative and the masses only came later. If
you do not put an immediate stop to this phenomenon, public service
messages and requests are not going to have any effect . . . it is true
that you cannot prevent every case, but, if there had been a guiding
and punishing hand that had instructed the public on how to act,
such [cases] could have been instances [demonstrating] what was out
of bounds for the general public. Since nothing like that took place,
the only possible conclusion that can be drawn is that leading institutions knowingly gave free rein to things. It is definitely possible to
stop various acts of robbery immediately and without great
difficulty.[22]

Cohen and Lubitz were not the only ones who maintained that important government officials were behind the plunder; as we shall see, some
of the ministers and leaders of the various movements thought so too.

---

22   Ruth Lubitz, 'On the purity of our war' [Hebrew], *Kol Ha'am*, 30 May 1948.

Personal Plunder and Collective Pillaging

Those who have read the first part of this book are aware that the military forces played a decisive role in the despoliation – both its individual and collective manifestations. Nonetheless, it is important to stress again that such behaviour was prohibited, at least de jure. In his expansive (and censored) study of the military legal system in its initial years, the chief military prosecutor Zvi Inbar wrote that 'plunder in conquered territories was one of the gravest phenomena of the War of Independence'.[1] He quotes Avraham Gorali, the Israel Defense Forces' chief prosecutor, who asserted in mid-1948 that despite 'the many trials, the investigations, and the actions that we take . . . we have yet to successfully put the criminals in their place'. The primary reason for this, Gorali argued, was the tendency to cover up for criminals.[2] The statistics, however, do not reflect Gorali's assertion that there were 'many trials'. Through 18 November 1948, after Israeli forces had conquered all of the Arab and mixed cities, only 175 soldiers were tried for possession of abandoned property.[3]

---

1 Zvi Inbar, *Scales of justice and the sword: Foundations of military law in Israel* [Hebrew] (Tel Aviv: Ma'arakhot, 2005), 400.

2 Ibid., 401.

3 Ibid., 404. The military prosecutor of the Kiryati Brigade stated: 'We have seventy cases and that is not even ten percent of what there would have been if the chief prosecutor's office had done its job. My conscience is not clear, because only a few of the seventy [cases] have been taken to court. They [the enlisted men] are scapegoats. [Their]

Netanel Lorch, a founder of the IDF History Department (and secretary-general of the Knesset in the 1970s), served in the Etzioni Brigade during the Independence War. In his autobiography, he writes that only after a long delay did they begin trying to stamp out depredation. The order, according to him, was that a soldier caught in possession of 'abandoned' property would receive a twenty-eight-day sentence. However, he errs: there was no such order. Nonetheless, he effectively describes the atmosphere of the time:

> Catching criminals was not easy to do. If there were not caught red-handed, it was hard to prove that they had not brought it with them from home or they had not inherited it, even if it was a piano.

Yet it is clear that even when they caught a looter in the act, they did not act with sufficient resoluteness to deter subsequent looters. Lorch decided to put a solider who was caught pillaging on trial, and he describes what subsequently happened:

> The next day I got a call from the deputy battalion commander, Aryeh Langer, to whom I reported and who was also a good friend of mine. The matter of H had come to his attention. Even though he knew that justice and the law demanded that he be put on trial, he wondered if it would be possible to take other things into consideration and to act mercifully. Was H not an exemplary soldier[?] Would it not be a pity to lose a soldier like him? Was he not a soldier who does no harm to others and does his job quietly and efficiently? I was forced to admit that he was that kind of soldier . . . [Lorch reduced the charges to a more minor offence.] The matter went to trial in battalion headquarters; in this case, the deputy battalion commander adjudicated. The accused was sentenced to seven days

---

constant refrain: "Why me? What about the officers?" . . . The resolution [to punish those who have stolen property] dissipated when it became clear that the "robber" was only one in a thousand. The question is why should the good enlisted man be put on trial and not the good officer?' Minutes of seminar of military prosecutors, 16 June 1948, file: 2294/1950-2882, IDF. See also Report no. 6 of the Legal Services, 23 June 1948; Report no. 7, June 1948; file: The Legal Service 15-178/2, YTA. For a detailed discussion of soldiers' trials in its fifth chapter, entitled 'Crimes of theft and plunder in the files of the Legal Services', see Anat Stern, 'Legal system of the I.D.F. during the 1948 War: Creation and implementation' [Hebrew], PhD diss., Hebrew University, 2010.

confinement on base – and that is how judgement and mercy found simultaneous expression.[4]

Even before the IDF was established (that is to say, before the State of Israel came into existence), the brigades and battalions of the Haganah published announcements stating that looting was forbidden. The senior command repeatedly warned that removal of property from Arab settlements was prohibited, and that the property in them belonged not to the combat units but to the Haganah that represented the institutions authorized to deal with this property. On 3 May 1948, the senior command made the following announcement to the combat units:

---

4   Netanel Lorch, *Late afternoon: My first seventy years (and what preceded them)* [Hebrew] (Tel Aviv: Defense Ministry Press, 1997), 117. The reports of various brigades make clear that they treated property crimes with great leniency. Some of the government ministers thought that the sentences being handed down were ridiculous, and they believed that there should be much stricter sentencing. See the letters of the minister of justice Pinchas Rosenblüth (Rosen) to Eliezer Kaplan, 17 October 1948: 'As an engineer, [Menahem Harash] was put in charge of dismantling an Arab factory in Beit Dagan, and, apparently, he took several machines worth 1,500 liras to his personal warehouse . . . prior to questioning before an investigative judge began, the accused returned all these machines, as well as additional [stolen] property that neither the army nor the police knew anything about. In light of this, the police agreed to alter the charge to theft according to clause 270. This made it a misdemeanour, rather than a crime, and the accused was fined twenty-five liras. I appealed this to the district court arguing that this punishment was too lenient . . . the charge in this case, as well as those in hundreds of cases just like it, [leads me to believe that the problem] is not the judge who sentences leniently, but the police's problematic habit, a habit that had already taken firm root during the administration of the previous government, of making deals with defendants and then telling the judges that the matters had been resolved.' Minister Sheetrit felt that the punishment was too lenient, but he did not want to interfere in legal proceedings. File: Menahem Harash, Gimmel-299/42, ISA. See Minister Rosen's position: 'In my opinion, there is a pressing need to meet to discuss . . . all the trials where abandoned assets are not enumerated and trials concerning robbery and theft as a whole. Mr Bentov also discussed this matter with me, and he suggested that we completely do away with the use of fines to punish this offence and replace it with a minimum one-month prison sentence. I completely agree. How this matter is currently playing out is an embarrassment to the State of Israel. The government response has been inappropriate.' Bechor-Shalom Sheetrit to Mr H. Cohen, 5 September 1948. Minister of Agriculture Zisling joined the critics and wrote: 'On the meagre list of cases provided, the [perpetrator of the] most serious robbery received the most lenient sentence. Do you plan to supply judges with sentencing guidelines and to investigate complex cases?' Aharon Zisling to Pinchas Rosenblüth (Rosen), 10 September 1948. File: Arab Affairs – Abandoned property, Gimmel-5670/29, ISA.

Hebrew soldier! When you enter a conquered or an abandoned Arab settlement and see assets and property, do not get seduced into taking them. You need to meet the challenge posed by harmful and indecent temptation. Plunder corrupts [both] the individual and the [whole] camp, and you must distance yourself from it. Remember, you are a Hebrew fighter and defender. You must maintain your honour both during and after the battle. Remember that the distance separating the honour of a warrior from the disgrace of the looter is short. To prevent their unit's corruption, commanders have been assigned the role of strictly overseeing their behaviour. An order is hereby given to all members. Anyone who violates this order will be punished.[5]

Throughout the war, the brigades reissued these orders in different formulations.[6] Here is an excerpt from a different order issued by the Carmeli Brigade: 'Officers of every rank and all enlisted men need to know that the taking of spoils for personal benefit or use without documented approval is a serious criminal offense.' The order also emphasizes that possession of 'souvenirs' would be considered a criminal offense and an act of insubordination.[7] Yet, out in the field, the commanders – including those who did not participate in the looting – did not enforce the orders. When he composed an operation report, the Givati Brigade commander who oversaw the May 1948 conquest of the village of Aqir in the Judean foothills wrote that 'when entering a village, one needs to give detailed orders about proper behaviour', and he added that there is also a need to provide 'clear orders concerning robbery and plunder by combat forces'. He then asserted that, 'it is undoubtedly not a commander's responsibility to confiscate plunder from his subordinates. *Military policemen need to be assigned to deal with this matter.*'[8] It should be noted that at that time military policemen were an organic

---

5   Zerubavel Gilead, ed., *The Palmach book*, vol. 1 [Hebrew] (Tel Aviv: ha-Kibbutz ha-me'uhad, 1955), lxii. For the original document, see file: 6127/1949-109, IDF.

6   IDF chief of staff to the brigades, 31 March 1948, file: 922/1975-1219, IDF. 'Behaviour in conquered locations', 27 October 1948, file: 1046/1970-434, IDF. 'The topic of discussion: Robbery and plunder', 11 May 1948, file: 2644/1949-417, IDF. IDF chief of staff to the brigades, 14 June 1948, file: 661/1969-44, IDF. Order of the Harel Brigade commander, 29 October 1948, file: 922/1975-1233, IDF.

7   'Enemy spoils', 9 April 1948, file: 6680/1949-4, IDF.

8   'Halam' operations, 6 May 1948, file: Aleph`/105/92, HHA.

part of the brigades – which made enforcement of looting prohibitions very difficult.[9]

We do not know how the commander quoted above acted in the conquered village. Yet, if other commanders serving in the various brigades shared his view that commanders were not responsible for the prevention of looting, verbal orders given and oral comments made almost certainly did not set the norms followed by soldiers during conquests. The authors of a book on Golani Brigade commander Shimon Avidan wrote succinctly that in the brigade, 'a serious ongoing effort was made to prevent abuse of village refugees and prisoners of war, to put a stop to looting and to teach soldiers that enemy combatants were people too'. Furthermore, the authors argue that the soldiers were informed that they were shaming and endangering themselves and that arrangements were made to prevent pillaging.[10] Indeed, sources support these assertions. For example, the brigade commander's orders (which also contained reports on events of the preceding days) noted that there were cases where soldiers' 'behaviour towards the abandoned property in the conquered and abandoned Arab settlements was offensive', and the orders were copied and reprinted numerous times.[11] Yet to what extent did these orders actually influence what happened? Did orders that were printed in black and white and distributed to commanders express a sincere effort to the stop pillaging? In my opinion, the descriptions

---

9   Minutes of seminar of military prosecutors, 16 June 1948. See also Michael Hanegbi, 'An overview of the conquest of the city of Beersheba and the conditions in it in the days thereafter', 21 October 1948, file:121/1950-223, IDF: 'Preparations should be made to have a special company or battalions of military policemen that will assume responsibility for order in cities immediately after their conquest and will prevent robbery and looting. The principal thing here is that robbery is more than a damaging human phenomenon. It is also something that distracts soldiers and commanders working to prevent it.'

10   Shaul Dagan and Eliyahu Jackier, *Shimon Avidan-Givati: The man who became a brigade* [Hebrew] (Giv'at Haviva: Yad Ya'ari, 1995), 128–9. The conquest of Majdal (المجدل, Ashkelon today) is brought as an example by the authors who note that a company of older men was allocated to serve as military policemen. Subsequently, they quote Jehuda Wallach, who explains that the depredation only began after Givati forces handed over the city to the Guard Corps (131). In a closed meeting of Mapam, Majdal is brought as an example of how proper preparation can stop despoliation. As someone at the meeting put it, 'If you want to do it, you can'. Political Committee meeting notes, 11 November 1948, file: (6)10.10-95, YYA.

11   Brigade commander's orders, 11 May 1948, file: 6127/1949-118, IDF.

found in the first part of this book require us to answer no to the latter question.

In June 1948, after the conquest of most of the Arab and mixed cities, it appeared that a decision had been made to adopt a more decisive policy concerning the trials.[12] The first truce's implementation contributed to this. At the end of June, for example, Avidan reported that a citizen accused of seizing plunder from an Arab village was sentenced to either a twenty-day prison term or a fifty-lira fine.[13] Yet as a rule, the sentences were always lenient, if not absurd.[14] This is one of the reasons that Minister Mordechai Bentov proposed the adoption of an automatic month-long minimum sentence for those caught taking spoils and the discontinuation of fines punishing looters.[15] Perhaps in this way it would be possible to neutralize commanders' and judges' discretion and frighten the pillagers.

In his effort to combat pillaging, Brigade Commander Avidan had the help of famous poet and Vilna Ghetto partisan Abba Kovner, who served as the Givati Brigade's education officer.[16] Writing battle missives that always bore the title 'Death to the Invaders!' Kovner provided an important part of the soldiers' spiritual sustenance. Yet, in a missive entitled 'The Great Turning Point', issued on 21 October 1948, following the conquest of Beersheba (after which the city was completely looted, as described in the first part of the book), Kovner wrote: 'The spoils

---

12   Givati Brigade commander, 'Military courts for the trying of citizens who are not defence force personnel', 11 June 1948, file: 922/1975-899, IDF.

13   Brigade commander's orders, 27 July 1948, file: 6127/1949-118, IDF.

14   For a list providing the names and sentences of people tried for possession of abandoned property from 5 May to 12 August 1948 (a total of 231 tried people), see file: General, Gimmel-307/16, ISA.

15   Pinchas Rosenblüth (Rosen) to Mr H. Cohen, 5 September 1948, file: Arab Affairs – Abandoned property, Gimmel-5670/29, ISA. 'Both civilian and military courts are taking it easy on those on trial for crimes related to abandoned property said D. Shafrir in a press conference that took place today in Jaffa . . . apathy exists in the Yishuv concerning this type of crime . . . Things have gotten to the point where a man that stole abandoned property worth 1,500 liras is fined . . . twenty-five liras by a civilian court.' 'Leniency in cases against those committing abandoned property crimes' [Hebrew], Al HaMishmar, 6 January 1949. It is interesting to compare this article with the less substantial report in the newspaper Davar. See 'Oversight of abandoned property' [Hebrew], Davar, 7 January 1949.

16   Dagan and Jackier, Shimon Avidan-Givati, 129.

taken from the enemy will carry the memory of our heroes into battle.'[17] Even people within Mapam, Kovner's own political party, were critical of the battle missives. For instance, a central figure in the party referred to Kovner as 'a fascist propagandist'.[18] Criticism of Kovner was based on texts such as the following battle missive from July 1948. He wrote:

> Suddenly, the earth grew soft – bodies! Tens of bodies beneath the wheels. The driver recoiled: people under the wheels of his [vehicle]. Just a second. Remember [Kibbutz] Negba. [Remember] Bayt Daras. Run them over! Boys, do not hesitate. The sentence of murderous dogs is death. By excelling at trampling these bloodthirsty dogs, you will deepen your love for Beauty, Virtue, and Freedom, and that is not all. Boys, gird your loins: behold our jeeps will be amphibious tomorrow! We will proceed through a stream, a stream of the invaders' blood . . . until they will be immersed up to their necks! – Until the dogs will not return to the confines of their lair. Run them over! Be ready.[19]

It is highly doubtful that Kovner's nationalist propaganda helped prevent looting, rather than encourage it (or at least justify it).[20]

---

17   Abba Kovner, Battle missive, 21 October 1948, file: 922/1975-900, IDF.

18   Abba Kovner to the party secretariat, n.d. [late November], file: Aharon Cohen – personal archive, (6)10.10-95, YYA. It is interesting to note that the director of security of the defence establishment felt it best to keep the public from seeing Kovner's complaint about an active member of his party. Like additional documents that were previously open to the public and are cited in this book, this document was made unavailable to the public several years ago and was only made accessible to the public again after I filed a request. The 'secret' things that Kovner wrote to the party leadership and that the defence establishment wanted to hide from the eyes of the public have previously been mentioned in published scholarship.

19   Abba Kovner, Battle missive, 'Anglo-Farouk dogs beneath our wheels', 14 July 1948, file: Gidi Eilat collection, Shimon Avidan, Battle missives, (3)6.97-95, YYA. See also Rafi Mann, 'Why Abba Kovner's battle missives aroused serious deliberation in the IDF' [Hebrew], Haaretz, 25 September, 2015, haaretz.co.il.

20   This is not the place to deal seriously with the problematic enthusiasm with which virtuous people in the labour movement, especially those affiliated with HaKibbutz HaArtzi, have greeted Kovner's vulgar nationalism for decades. I do not consider myself an expert on Kovner. Yet, after reading more than thirty battle missives he wrote between June 1948 and May 1949, I find it difficult not to be horrified by this movement icon's intellectual world. Indeed, this aversion does not have a 'scholarly' basis. To put it bluntly, Kovner texts aimed to dehumanize Egyptian soldiers, and they

Among the fighting forces, the Palmach acted most decisively to combat plunder and robbery. After the conquest of Ramle and Lydda, its commander, Yigal Allon, spoke in opposition to despoliation at a gathering of officers. Allon noted that there were not 'a lot of instances of robbery and looting where [Palmach members] took [things] for

---

are chock full of the most vulgar militaristic and racist jargon – something evocative of the most ignorant anti-Semitic literature. Even in their time, these elements were unusual in the Hebrew 'literary' landscape. For example, the term *kalgas* (trooper), frequently employed by the poet to raise the morale of the soldiers, was usually used in Israel to describe Nazis. In general, the excessive rhetoric about how the Jews need to take vengeance on the Egyptian soldiers for . . . the murder of millions by Hitler and the Nazis should, at least today, arouse astonishment (and, in practice, even then it did). 'Great is the night of retribution! There is justice for Israel and justice says: Israel's blood is avenged!' asserts Kovner (21 October 1948). In a different battle missive (17 July 1948), he writes to the Givati soldiers that 'around you glisten the stupid eyes of the dogs of the Nile – to the Nile dogs! To the Nile! [Send them] not with a curse, with a prayer or with love, [but with] pressure on the trigger: Slaughter. Slaughter. Slaughter.' The brave Jewish nationalist, who takes vengeance on the Egyptian soldiers for the destruction of European Jewry in his missives, promises 'that the bodies of the invaders will yet fertilize our fields and cause them to flourish!' (12 July 1948). Above we saw his entreaties to run over the Egyptian soldiers, to which he adds: 'Please, great-grandsons of Pharoah, please: Only in a puddle of blood! . . . May the wadi rise and wax with blood' (16 July 1948). He sees the Egyptian soldiers not as people, but as animals: 'It is hard for the defenders of [Kibbutz] Negba to man their positions, because they are facing off against stinking Egyptians' (17 July 1948). Frequently, [the Egyptian soldiers] are dogs: 'Massive waves of dogs attack and smash their heads' (14 July 1948) or, 'To the Nile, dogs! To the Nile!' (17 July 1948). Subsequently, they are snakes: 'Cobras, come back!' ('Light of the hour of forced truce'). When the Egyptian soldiers lie dying on the ground, Kovner calls: 'Invite the birds of the sky' (21 October 1948). Porat justifiably notes that the Palmach did not love this style. The vulgar and primitive jargon found in Kovner's missives was not found, for example, in Natan Shaham's missives. He just reported about what was going on and supplied his soldiers with the information they needed. Some may find Kovner's 'Soviet' style (the battle missive from 13 July 1948 possesses the bombastic title Negevgrad, an allusion to the Battle of Leningrad) and scholarly analyses of the battle missives' poetics exciting, and can perhaps even give Kovner a pass due to his partisan past, but Arnan (Sini) Azaryahu was not the only one who thought that the Kovnerian style was grounded in an effort to read the Independence War through the lens of World War II. Azaryahu justifiably asked if Kovner understood that the Egyptian soldiers were not Nazis. Similarly, Yitzhak Ben-Aharon believed, as Porat tells us, 'that the general consensus was that there was no place for the cultivation of hatred even in an existential war'. While we can neither fully address the Palmach's critique of Kovner's bloody lyricism nor Yigal Allon's critique of it here, Kovner's battles missives have continuing relevance today in relationship to the question of how soldiers perceive their enemies. It seems that the 'Kovnerian' approach has achieved primacy today. It is important to remember that at the time the Zionist socialist left did not see the Arab soldiers

themselves' and not for their units – something that the law permitted. Then just twenty-nine years old, Allon nonetheless recognized the potential impacts of looting on his command:

There is no doubt that when these phenomena become regularized and accepted, they are liable to create a situation where the units not only cease to function like human societies, but where they will also cease to operate like combat units. The dangers that lie in wait for the image of man are more powerful than any other that previously lay in wait for it.

Allon felt that the wielding of authority and the use of imprisonment were not enough to resolve the problem. It would be necessary for commanders to set a personal example and undertake 'thorough reflective labour'. In his opinion, how the commanding officer chose to behave in the first home in a village [that he entered] and 'his attitude towards that refrigerator [belonging to an Arab]' set the tone. 'Up until now', he asserted, 'we have usually gotten through this experience unscathed'. As he saw things, (the only) advantage of the truce that went into effect was that it allowed us 'to take account of things and to stop our descent down the slope endangering our human image'.[21]

---

as 'Nazis' or 'animals'. It saw them as the victims of imperialism, Arab militarism, etc. On Kovner and the battle missives, see Dina Porat, *The Fall of a Sparrow: The Life and Times of Abba Kovner*, trans. and ed. Elizabeth Yuval (Stanford, CA: Stanford University Press, 2009), 244–50. Benny Morris's assertion that Jewish soldiers committed more massacres of civilians and Arab prisoners of war than did Arab soldiers does seems more comprehensible when considered against the background of Kovner's writing. Benny Morris, *1948* (Tel Aviv: 'Am 'Oved, 2010), 437–8. Indeed, Kovner never called for such action. In fact, in a battle missive written after the annexation of the Triangle to Israel, Kovner wrote: 'Our hands should remain clean! Indeed, this is the order. Acts of abuse against Arab residents are prohibited. Acts of plunder and robbery are forbidden, as is rape.' (Battle missive, 8 May 1949) Nonetheless, one who commands soldiers to trample and slaughter should not be surprised when they act mercilessly towards the dying and the dead. Copies of the battle missives found at the Yad Yaari Research and Documentation Center Archives can be found in the following: file: Gidi Eilat collection; Aharon Cohen, Battle missive, file: (5)8.10-95, YYA.

21 Yigal Allon, 'Excepts from an address to a gathering of brigade officers' [Hebrew], *'Alon ha-Palmach* 69 (11 August 1948). See also 'A strong hand for wiping out robbery and lawlessness' [Hebrew], *Ha-Tzofeh*, 13 August 1948: 'These orders from the chief of staff concerning robbery, theft, and the behaviour of military personnel in general were published In the Palmach newspaper: 1. Lately ceaseless acts of robbery,

Nonetheless, the sources indicate that since the Palmach prioritized labour settlement more than the other fighting forces, most of its commanders saw the collective removal of property ('public looting') as a legitimate act whose legal status was substantively different from that of personal pillaging.[22] "Theft or robbery in support of Zionist revival or Zionism's realization is permitted', said David 'Bibi' Niv, the Negev Brigade's intelligence officer. Indeed, Niv viewed plunder committed by an individual as loathsome, but 'when you take a private automobile, an elegant Buick, and give it to Nahum Sarig [commander of the Negev Brigade], it is perfectly fine with me'.[23] It turns out that when you are

---

plunder and theft by IDF personnel has increased tremendously... I declare and announce: A. The Israeli Defence Force ... will not tolerate in its ranks robbers, thieves, and other criminals who sully Israel's name with their deeds and whose deeds create a state of general lawlessness in the army ... 6. Senior command has decided to cleanse the army and to put a stop once and for all to the lawlessness and criminal acts that have multiplied in the ranks of the army and undermine general morality and soldierly discipline, and, as a result, chip away at their combat readiness. Commanders who prove unable to maintain law and order in their units and fail to punish those guilty of the acts enumerated above will be put on trial and dismissed from their positions'. See the comments of 'Bo'az' in 'An old matter' [Hebrew], 'Alon ha-Palmach [Palmach Bulletin] 68 (3 July 1948): 27–9: '[The plunder] is so significant for the young state that it will be forced to enforce its laws ... Robbery deprives the military unit of its unity, and, in this way, disarms it. One hundred scattered soldiers cannot defeat ten organized and disciplined soldiers who know their roles'. Towards the end of the first truce, IDF chief prosecutor Avraham Gorali wrote: 'When the fighting starts up again and there are further conquests, there will be an urgent need to take the necessary steps to prevent the phenomena that accompany the military's undisciplined behaviour in conquered territories – robbery, property damage, etc. I would like to repeat what the earlier communication said about the need for military prosecutors to accompany the battalions in their brigades. The military prosecutors are responsible for setting up drumhead court-martials that will operate quickly and efficiently'. Quoted in Inbar, Scales of justice, 404. See the letter Ben-Gurion received from Nahum Het, the Ministry of Defense's first legal advisor, who suggests that preparations be made for a renewal of fighting and the depredation that will follow: 'Our military prosecutor's office was unprepared to take preventative measures and was also unable to get robberies under control after they started and just kept going'. Nahum Het to David Ben-Gurion, 29 June 1948, file: 597/1956-15, IDF.

22   The following example comes from Commander, 'The soldiers' problems' [Hebrew], 'Alon ha-Palmach 69 (31 May 1948): 'A battalion officer who has been placed in charge of enemy property gathers up the spoils – our soldiers do not take anything for themselves. The objective is to convert all of the possessions into cash that can be used to either support the families of the fallen or to serve combat units' essential needs'.

23   Testimony of David ('Bibi') Niv, May–July 1989, PGA. On the looting of the aforementioned automobile, see Elimelekh Avner to IDF chief of staff, 'The removal of property and merchandise from Beersheba', 27 October 1948, file: 121/1950-223, IDF.

pillaging, the boundaries between personal and collective pillaging blur. Elad Peled, who commanded the force that conquered Safed, also said that depredation on behalf of the unit was considered acceptable: 'the Third Battalion departed Safed in convoys, convoys of trucks filled with equipment. One can steal or rob on behalf of the collective. They had already been doing that [when we were stationed] on the Kibbutzim.' According to him, personal looting was forbidden in the Palmach for moral reasons.[24] Yiftach Brigade commander Mulah Cohen said that in the Palmach, they responded to personal plunder 'in the most severe way possible . . . we talked about it, and it worried us'.[25] Nonetheless, we have already seen that Palmach soldiers plundered for personal gain.

Training groups would receive the heavy equipment that had been plundered because 'it was for the collective'; such equipment was stored in warehouses in Sarafand (Tzrifin in Hebrew) 'for future kibbutzim'. According to Peled, when they went to the warehouse after the war, 'the warehouses were empty and tidy. Somebody else had "cleaned them out"'.[26] Not everybody in the Palmach agreed with this approach.[27] The author Yitzhak Tischler addressed the matter of collective plunder:

> The debate about booty was not a new one. [The topic] first [began to be discussed] during the battles near [Kibbutz] Mishmar HaEmek, when we combed and cleansed the southern Plain of Manasseh in the approach to Wadi Ara; with the passage of time, it [started to be] more frequently debated . . . Even then there were those who turned up their noses [at such behaviour] and stressed how the pillaging of

24   Testimony of Elad Peled, n.d., PGA.
25   Mulah Cohen, 23 December 1997, YRC.
26   Elad Peled, testimony, 30 March 2000, YRC. Peled acknowledges that this is a rumour. In a quote presented earlier, Allon also noted that the equipment taken from Safed was brought to these warehouses. On equipment supplied to training groups, see Mulah Cohen, 23 December 1997, YRC. Cf. Assaf Agamon, interview, Collection of the Galili Centre for Defence Studies, 6 August 1984, file: 12-3/41/3, YTA.
27   In his book, Mulah Cohen provides a letter written by 'a veteran Palmachnik' who complains to the Ministry of Defense that 'since the end of the first truce, stock-keepers [quartermaster clerks] have been taking things from the kitchens, food storage pantries, spoils and clothing warehouses, and quarters and selling them. The veteran soldier brings a long list of pillaged items that were sold. In the end, it turned out that some of the property was stolen. The stockkeepers were kibbutz members'. Mulah Cohen, *To give and receive: Memoirs* [Hebrew] (Tel Aviv: ha-Kibbutz ha-me'uhad, 2000), 145–6.

the villages constituted a moral decline. In contrast, there were those who justified the act by painting it as a form of retribution or some other nonsensical thing . . . Yet it changed this time. In Safed, a change took place. In that Galilean city, only the Third Battalion took pleasure in the spoils, whereas our battalion could wash up with clean hands. Another excuse was added this time – what we did not plunder, the Field Corps would plunder . . . The debate played itself out, like the previous debates on this topic, without any clear resolution. Those who took spoils felt justified in their actions, and those who opposed it refrained from using bombastic rhetoric. None of them demanded that the property be returned, [and] none of them declared that he would be unable to live on a training group settlement or kibbutz part of whose property was amassed through robbery and not physical labour.[28]

28   Yitzhak Tischler, *Last ones on the ridge* [Hebrew] (Tel Aviv: 'Am 'Oved, 1970), 130.

Opposing the Plunder

At the beginning of the war, in the preliminary stage of the Arab exodus from areas under Jewish control, fear that Arab property would be destroyed and plundered made some Israelis recognize that a mechanism needed to be established to oversee it. In February 1948, prior to the conquests (which occurred after the Haganah switched from a defensive to an offensive posture), Haganah chief of staff Yisrael Galili announced that 'expropriation of enemy property for the personal possession and private use of an individual member or the possession and use of a group of members is absolutely forbidden'. He saw despoliation and the killing of Arabs as activities that damaged the Jewish population and stained its reputation.[1]

In the first months of the war, before Prime Minister David Ben-Gurion dismissed him from his position in the beginning of May, Galili played a central role in creating frameworks for overseeing military operations.[2] Writing by hand in late December 1947 and early

---

1   Yisrael Galili to the brigades, 16 February 1948, file: 922/1975-1207, IDF. Galili learned that an Arab had been kidnapped and murdered. On this, see file: 922/1975-207, IDF.

2   Galili left his position on 3 May 1948. See his letter bearing this date, file: Haganah chief of staff dismissals 15-46-174/1-2, YTA. Galili was very involved in the prevention of robbery and plunder. See, for example: Journal entry, 26 March 1948, file: Journal 15-48/180/9, YTA. See also entries and telegrams from 22 March 1948, 24 March 1948, file: Journal 15-1881/4, YTA; and Galili's handwritten entries, file: General 15-164/3, YTA. Galili appointed a chief expropriation officer days before he was fired.

January 1948, Galili composed general guidelines for how the Haganah should treat Arabs in the new Jewish state: without discrimination and inequity, and with an aspiration for coexistence.[3] This was not euphemism; Galili displayed a sensitivity to the image of the enlisted men and addressed incidents where Arabs were attacked or had their property looted.[4] In the first stages of the war, he acted to prevent depredation and called for the provision of clear orders on this topic.[5] On 22 April, for example, the guideline concerning 'interaction with [residents of] villages that have surrendered' was that 'in any case where Jewish patronage is requested, one should seriously consider if it is possible to allow the Arabs to remain in place or if they should be sent *to the rear*'.[6] The Committee for Arab Affairs, appointed by Haganah headquarters, operated unsuccessfully in this spirit during the first months of the war.[7] Overall, Galili's attitude towards the local Arab population and towards the State of Israel's future relations with other entities in the region was substantially different from that of Ben-Gurion.[8]

The topic of depredation and the struggle against it was a central topic addressed at meetings of the advisers for Arab affairs (who advised the Haganah and operated in the field).[9] Leadership had

---

See A. Ben Yisrael to Yisrael Galili, late April 1948, file: General 15-164/3, YTA. On the last day at his job, Galili succeeded in sending orders to all commanders prohibiting plunder. See 'The topic of discussion: Abandoned property', 3 May 1948, file: Harel Brigade 12-4-53/12, YTA.

3   Handwritten on the document 'Suggested guidelines for the Arab minority' that Galili prepared for a 'discussion on Semitic matters' held on 1–2 January 1948. Participants included Jewish Agency department heads, senior Haganah leaders, and advisers for Arab affairs. The discussion was held to decide how to respond to Arab violence that had started a short time earlier and if there was a possibility to respond to it selectively. File: General 15-163/2. YTA.

4   Political Committee meeting notes, 5 February 1948, Political Committee meetings, File: (1)66.90, YYA.

5   See Hillel (Yisrael Galili) to Oded 16 February 1948, and the order attached to the letter; Oded to Hillel 18 February 1948, file: 481/1949-8, IDF.

6   'Guidelines for interaction with surrendered villages', 22 April 1948, file: 4663/1949-84, IDF, emphasis added.

7   Ben-Tzion Mikhaeëli, *Yitzhak Gevirtz – ish Shefayim* [Hebrew] (n. p.: Kibbutz Shefayim, 1986), 62.

8   For a brief discussion of these differences, see Yoram Nimrod, 'Creation of the patterns of Israel-Arab relations' [Hebrew], PhD diss., Hebrew University, 1985, 273–6.

9   Summary of meeting of advisers for Arab Affairs, 31 March 1948, file: 4663/1949-125, IDF.

vested them with the authority to give orders to the brigade and district commanders, and they were responsible to Galili. In the beginning of April, the decision was made to appoint people to oversee and guard the property. The decision was also made to turn to the Jewish National Council and to demand that the anti-profiteering courts be given the authority to punish looters (recall that until the end of the mandate, the British were the sovereigns).[10] The Jewish National Council approved the advisers' suggestion.[11] After the conquest of the first Arab cities, when Galili was still the Haganah chief of staff, the advisers were 'called upon to make every effort to return stolen Arab property and to file lawsuits against those who refuse to return it'.[12] Initially, they succeeded at their work, but they quickly lost their ability to do their jobs.[13]

In the brigades, they knew, at least formally, that they needed committees to oversee the vast quantities of property.[14] Galili not only foresaw what was going to happen in plunder-related matters but also predicted what was going to happen to the Arab population in general (and prisoners of war in particular). On 3 March, before pillaging had begun in the cities, he instructed Gad Machnes to call a meeting to discuss 'the question of how to interact with [residents of] Arab villages'.[15] In March, the Haganah High Command established a committee that was designated to deal with Arab assets. In the beginning, it needed to deal with villages in enclaves that were designated to become part of the Jewish state's territory according to the partition plan. At the end of the month, Galili announced to the brigade commanders:

---

10 Summary of meeting of advisers for Arab Affairs, 6 April 1948, file: 2506/1949-91, IDF.

11 Summary of meeting of advisers for Arab Affairs, 13 April 1948, file: 4663/1949-125, IDF. See also Jewish National Council Executive Committee to Anti-profiteering Courts Executive Committee, 11 April 1948, file: 2506/1949-91, IDF.

12 Summary of meeting of advisers for Arab Affairs, 9 May 1948, file: 6127/1949-109, IDF.

13 On their successes, see what Yitzhak Gevirtz said in the summary of a meeting of the Committee for Arab Assets in Tiberias, file: Tiberias: Committee for Arab Affairs, Gimmel-29/310, ISA. On the appointment of guards in the various regions that were conquered, see file: 2506/1949-91, IDF.

14 Supervisory Committee, Alexandroni Brigade, 2 March 1948, file: 2506/1949-91, IDF; 'The topic of discussion: Enemy assets', 12 May 1948, file: 410/1954-144, IDF.

15 Yisrael Galili to Gad Machnes, 3 March 1948, file: 481/1949-50, IDF.

The Knesset's [Haganah's] behaviour towards Arabs dwelling in [either] the area that has been designated for the Hebrew state or in Arabs enclaves in continuous Jewish territories is grounded in the Zionist movement's Arab policy: recognition of all the rights, needs and freedoms of the Arabs in the Jewish state without discrimination and with the aspiration for honourable and free coexistence. During the fighting, one may go against this policy only if security conditions and the necessities of war demand it.

Galili appointed a committee to advise the army on how to deal with the Arab settlements. Its members were Gad Machnes, Yehoshua 'Josh' Palmon, and Moshe Dayan.[16] He instructed all the brigade commanders to operate in accordance with Machnes's instructions in all matters related to Arab property. The committee formulated concrete ways to respond to 'the looting of Arab property'.[17] Galili wrote to Yigael Yadin, the chief of staff from the end of 1949, that 'every headquarters needs an officer who will be responsible for operations in enemy villages after the departure of their residents or their conquest'.[18] When Galili was fired from his role as Haganah chief of staff, the support the committee had for their activities dissipated.[19]

In April 1948, a month before the British departed Palestine, the National Administration was established to serve as the future State of Israel's provisional government.[20] The Office for Minority Affairs, alternatively known as the Department for Arab Affairs, operated as part of

---

16   Yisrael Galili to the brigade commanders, 24 March 1948, file: 922/1975-1219, IDF.

17   Yisrael Galili to the brigade commanders, 13 April 1948, personal archive.

18   Yisrael Galili to Yigal Yadin, 22 April 1948. See also the entries and telegrams from 22 March 1948 and 24 March 1948, file: Journal 15-1881/4, YTA.

19   See Gad Machnes to David Ben-Gurion, 10 May 1948, file: General 15-164/4, YTA: 'We cannot fulfil the role of protecting and overseeing abandoned Arab property assigned to us as long as the brigade commanders and the district commanders do not have explicit orders not to allow the removal of any property at all from conquered areas without the permission of the Department for Arab Affairs . . . Therefore, please give strict orders to the brigade commanders.'

20   At the end of March 1948, the Jewish Agency's Executive Committee approved the establishment of the 'People's Council' together with the 'Temporary National Administration'. On the structure of government at the time, see Pinchas Medding, 'Government Institutions during the First Year of Independence', in Mordechai Naor, ed., *The first year of independence* [Hebrew] (Jerusalem: Yad Ben Zvi, 1988), 69–86.

this government, and it was headed by Bechor-Shalom Sheetrit, who would, in a short time, serve as the first (and last) minister of minorities of the State of Israel.[21] Sheetrit submitted a detailed proposal for the handling of 'abandoned' property and suggested that a person be appointed in every conquered Palestinian villages whose role would be, on the one hand, to prevent despoliation and robbery, but, on the other, to oversee expropriations and confiscations for military needs. Sheetrit's proposal strove to provide the Ministry of Minorities with an important role in organizing the interaction between the Jewish government and the Arab minority and its property.[22] It appears that he gained the support of future minister Mordechai Bentov of Mapam.[23]

When the state was established, the Department for Arab Affairs moved to the Ministry of Minorities, where it operated as the Department for Arab Assets. A short time earlier, after the conquest of Tiberias and Haifa in April, local committees for the handling of property had been established in the two cities, and they continued to operate after statehood in conjunction with the Ministry of Minorities. Yosef Nahmani, who was a member of the northern committee established after the conquest of Tiberias's Arab quarter, wrote in his diary that 'if the work is [performed in] an organized manner, one can hope that we will know how to fully protect the remaining Arab property and that when [the Arabs] return, they will be able to receive it'.[24] Since Jerusalem was outside the government's jurisdiction until the beginning of August 1948, a separate Department of Abandoned Asset Affairs operated there, and the security situation drastically minimized its interaction with the Ministry of Minorities.[25] Even though an office for Arab assets of the Ministry of Minorities was established in Jaffa, Ben-Gurion appointed a separate individual to oversee 'abandoned' property there.[26] The

21   For a short English-language biography of Sheetrit, see file: The minister Bechor Sheetrit, Gimmel-300/80, ISA.

22   Bechor-Shalom Sheetrit, 'Memorandum of the Office of Minority Affairs', submitted to the National Administration 10 May 1948, file: Various reports, Gimmel-306/62, ISA. See also 'Summary of meeting with Amitai', 6 May 1948, BGA.

23   Minutes of the National Administration, 3 May 1948, ISA.

24   Yosef Nahmani Diary, 4 May 1948, HAS.

25   End of May 1948 report of the Department for Arab Assets, file: Various reports.

26   Arnon Golan, *Wartime spatial changes: Former Arab territories within the State of Israel* [Hebrew] (Sde Boker: Ben-Gurion University, 2001), 14.

Ministry of Minority's opinion of this appointment was unfavourable, as articulated in part I's discussion of the plunder of Jaffa. Machnes requested that Ben-Gurion, in his role as minister of defence, give 'strict orders to the brigade commanders telling them to have the area commanders strictly enforce the absolute prohibition on removal of Arab property from the conquered areas, even for [the use of] military units, without permission of this department'. He noted that unit commanders and private individuals were currently removing Palestinian property without any type of permit.[27] Mapai politician David Hacohen demanded that 'only one central body have control over the property and that all personal benefit from this property be avoided'.[28] When it came to addressing the matter of abandoned property, Ben-Gurion did not exert his full weight.

During April and May, the large Arab and mixed cities were conquered. A Department for Arab Assets report noted that the evacuation of 170 cities and villages 'created serious challenges for the department', the greatest of which was 'the unrestrained urge to rob'. Many problems could be prevented, the report asserted, if the army acted in cooperation with the department. 'The department takes pains to not only prevent robbery and destruction, but to return stolen property', the report explained.[29] The department worked to prevent looting undertaken by both the defence forces and private citizens. In a conference of area councils held in Tel Aviv, the participants were told that those who seized Arab property 'were stealing from the state'. The department demanded that the area councils work with 'the residents to control the urge to loot that was enveloping the public like a large wave and seriously threatening our future'.[30]

The destruction of Palestinian villages occurred in conjunction with their depredation, and, despite various government ministers' repeated

27   Gad Machnes to David Ben-Gurion, Department for Arab Affairs, 10 May 1948, BGA.

28   'Meeting in the office of the prime minister concerning problems related to Arab refugees and their return', 18 August 1948, file:2444/19, ISA. For more on this meeting, see Ben-Gurion's diary entry for 18 August 1948: David Ben-Gurion, *The War of Independence* [Hebrew], ed. Gershon Rivlin and Elhanan Oren (Tel Aviv: Defense Ministry Press, 1982), 652–4.

29   End of May 1948 report of the Department for Arab Assets.

30   Comments made at a conference of area councils in Tel Aviv, 26 May 1948, file: IV-235-1-2251C, LMA.

petitions, Ben-Gurion did not get involved. At the time, people began to assert that responsibility for the destruction of villages lay with the senior commanders whose actions brought it about, rather than with the minister of defence, the supreme commander – an assertion that scholars and journalists have subsequently repeated. Minister of Agriculture Aharon Zisling said that he 'repeatedly requested a response concerning the destruction of villages that was undertaken without consultation with the Committee [for Abandoned Property] and request for its consent. [He] did not accept the idea that the commanders of the various fronts were responsible for this. Only the minister of defence is responsible to the committee: the front commanders are responsible to him.'[31]

---

31   Minutes of the Ministerial Committee on Abandoned Asset Affairs meeting, 1 October 1948, file: Administration – Abandoned Property Committee, Gimmel-2186/21, ISA. The policy of destroying villages will not be discussed at length here. Despite a wealth of materials about this topic, it has not received serious scholarly treatment recently. In fact, the chapter on this topic in Morris's book remains the most comprehensive on this matter. See Benny Morris, *The Birth of the Palestinian Refugee Problem, 1947–1949* (New York: Cambridge University Press, 1987), 155–69. On the lack of a *military* justification for the destruction of the villages, see the memorandum of Moshe Erem from the Ministry of Minorities: Moshe Erem to Bechor-Shalom Sheetrit, October 1948. On the lack of an *economic* justification, see the letter of Yitzhak Gevirtz: Yitzhak Gevirtz to Bechor-Shalom Sheetrit, 23 June 1948, file: Destruction of homes and villages, Gimmel-307/28, ISA. There is a great deal of material pointing to the fact that the destruction of villages was undertaken without the government's approval. See, for example, what Minister of Finance Eliezer Kaplan said after he received news that a village had been destroyed: 'According to a government decision, all such destruction requires [approval of] a special committee, and headquarters needed to provide the government with a list of the Arab villages that they were considering for destruction.' Eliezer Kaplan to David Ben-Gurion, 4 August 1948, file: 6127/1949-85, IDF.

Sheetrit, 'Professional Mourner'

As the minister responsible for Arabs (minorities), Bechor-Shalom Sheetrit, as mentioned in the previous chapter, proposed that he coordinate Arab-related activities and that his ministry take the lead in these matters. At the time, there were few leaders more committed than him to improving relations between the two national groups. He demanded that people not be appointed to Arab-related positions without his knowledge – something that was already being done.[1] In a memorandum submitted to the National Administration, he wrote that the Jewish people, well versed in suffering, would know how to put the principles of freedom and equality into practice in their relations with the Arab minority in their state. 'Man is judged by the same criteria that he uses to judge others,' he wrote to the members of the administration. 'The time has arrived for us to stop talking the talk and start walking the walk,' he asserted.[2] He based his demand that the handling of the Arab population and its property be concentrated in a single location on the assumption that 'the government needed to think long term'.[3] In his opinion, it had not done that.

1   Bechor-Shalom Sheetrit to members of the government, 26 May 1948, file: Various reports, Gimmel-306/62, ISA.

2   Bechor-Shalom Sheetrit, 'Memorandum of the Ministry of Minority Affairs', presented to the National Administration, 10 May 1948, file: Various reports.

3   Minutes of a meeting that took place at the Haifa Municipal Building, 6 June 1948, file: Various reports.

On 11 June, after a few villages had been conquered, the ministry of finance proposed the establishment of a 'Supervisor of Arab Property', an institution composed of members of the Ministries of Defence, Treasury, and Minorities. Finance Minister Kaplan offered the opportunity to head up this institution to Dov Shafrir, who accepted.[4] On 24 June, the Knesset approved the 'Abandoned Territory Directive, 1948', which gave the government the authority to deal with property in conquered territory. In a government meeting held in mid-June, a decision was made to establish a four-minister committee whose role would be to make decisions concerning oversight of 'abandoned' assets. Sheetrit was the one who pushed for this committee's establishment.[5] After two meetings, the committee decided to give authority over the disposition of agricultural property to Minister of Agriculture Zisling, and authority over the remaining property to Finance Minister Kaplan.[6] On 15 July, Dov Shafrir was appointed the custodian of abandoned property.[7] Sheetrit protested against Shafrir's appointment to Kaplan. While he did not have a personal problem with Shafrir, what bothered him was that, once again, he was not involved in the making of a decision that he had the authority to make. He wanted to know who had appointed Shafrir and what authority gave them the right to do so: 'If you hold firm to your position[, Kaplan], I will have no other choice than to discontinue my involvement with matters pertaining to abandoned Arab property in the country.'[8] Kaplan argued that it was fruitless to publish regulations as long as there was no certainty that the army would act in accordance with the law and the regulations. The minister of finance suggested that they talk with Prime Minister Ben-Gurion to

---

4   Dov Shafrir, *The flowerbed of life* [Hebrew] (Tel Aviv: ha-Merkaz ha-Haklai, 1975), 222.

5   Cabinet meeting minutes, 14 June 1948, file: Activities of the Custodian of Absentee Property, Gimmel-5434/1, ISA. See Sheetrit's memorandum, sent to all the members of the government: 'The problem of minorities and abandoned property', 14 June 1948, file: Arab Affairs – Abandoned property, Gimmel-5670/29, ISA.

6   Aharon Zisling to administrative team, 13 July 1948, file: Administration – Abandoned Property Committee, Gimmel-2186/21, ISA. For minutes of the two meetings on 13 July 1948, and 26 July 1948, see the same file.

7   Eliezer Kaplan to Dov Shafrir, 15 July 1948, file: Activities of the Custodian of Absentee Property.

8   Bechor-Shalom Sheetrit to Eliezer Kaplan, 20 July 1948, file: Activities of the Custodian of Absentee Property.

see whether 'a department director had already been appointed to the general staff to manage the conquered territory'.[9]

In mid-June 1948, the minister of minorities sent a long letter to the cabinet members 'present[ing] the full extent of the minorities problem to them'. He already feared that the other members of the government would look at him as 'a professional mourner'. It is clear that Sheetrit put a lot of thought into this letter, which voiced his disappointment with the current state of things. Due to the importance of this long letter, written during the first truce, it needs to be treated in detail. Sheetrit argued that 'our attitude towards the Arabs that abandoned their property', as well as those who fought against Israel, 'have been faulty and defective'. He demanded 'that a clear policy of equal civil rights be declared' to avoid damaging repercussions. Sheetrit praised the idea that stood behind the establishment of the Ministry of Minorities, but he was critical of the fact that his ministry was not 'one of the important authorities delineating our policy'. As he saw it, he had been making suggestions about how to approach things for days and weeks, and they 'had not been adopted. Even [earlier] suggestions that had been acted upon had been undermined and violated immediately after they had been put into effect'. Sheetrit declared that no government policy concerning what would happen to property found in conquered cities and villages had ever been set, and he described a situation where the military acted without oversight.

Sheetrit noted that his proposal that every brigade be accompanied by a Ministry of Minorities advisor did not receive adequate consideration. One of the results of the lack of consultation with – or, more accurately, disregard for – the responsible ministry (the Ministry of Minorities) was that 'the residents of the cities and villages were uprooted from their homes'. In many cases, he asserted, 'the government and army disregarded the Ministry of Minorities' demands and requests'. Sheetrit's letter paints a picture of lawlessness: the Ministry of Defense and the army operated as they saw fit, without any guidance from government officials, and '[carried out] demolition operations without having been given the authority to do this by the Israeli government'. In addition, Arab residents were arrested without justification and were only released

---

9   Minutes of the Ministerial Committee on Abandoned Asset Affairs meeting, 26 July 1948, file: Administration –Abandoned Property Committee.

after the Ministry of Minorities got involved. Sheetrit and his ministry worked hard to prepare regulations and orders that were not adopted, and those that were adopted were not enforced. 'We have still not succeeded in expelling the spirit of lawlessness from our camp,' he wrote at the end of the section of the letter dedicated to governmental failures.

In the latter half of the letter, Sheetrit went into detail about the effects of the government's poor treatment of the Arab population. The effects that he enumerated included: 'robbery and theft committed by the army and civilians'; 'violation of clauses in capitulation agreements guaranteeing that property would be safeguarded'; 'military personnel driven mad by their desire for plunder'; equipment with military importance neglected, while 'civilian possessions that did not correspond to any military necessity, such as carpets, electric refrigerators, couches, radios, etc., were stolen'; illegal seizures and expropriations; and irrigation equipment and machinery for orchards, garden plots, and agricultural fields 'torn out, stolen, and even destroyed for no reason'. 'We have reason to believe,' he continued, 'that many of the possessions that were expropriated and seized for military purposes did not make it to their intended destination due to purposeful disregard for organization and effective oversight.'

Sheetrit demanded that the government grant him the authority necessary to address the damage caused during months of fighting and to prevent further damage. To put an end to looting and robbery, he again suggested the cessation of direct collection of abandoned property from homes and that a representative of the Ministry of Minorities accompany forces undertaking conquests of Arab territory. An agent of the ministry, the minister opined, could advise the force commander on the ground, and, following conquest of a specific territory, he could serve as a civil governor there. In general, Sheetrit called for a stop to 'destruction or demolition of property' without government knowledge and 'the promulgation of a strict order to army commanders instructing them to delay every operation that the minister of minorities asks to have delayed until they receive clear orders from the minister of defence after the minister of minorities has had an opportunity to confer with him'.

In his long letter, Sheetrit got into the nitty-gritty, and he made recommendations about what should be done in a given territory in the hours and days after its conquest: immediately after the conquest of a given area, a curfew should be declared. It would help prevent looting. Roadblocks should be established at all the entrances and exits from the settlement, and, during the curfew, unauthorized people should be refused 'entrance into the conquered territory, especially people whose goals are spoils, plunder, and vengeance'. Simultaneously, those in charge on the ground should prepare a list of the holy sites in the area, so that they could be 'effectively safeguarded against desecration and destruction'. Following completion of these initial steps, the curfew should be rescinded, and authority could be speedily transferred to a (civilian) military governor recommended by the minister of minorities and appointed by the minister of defence. (In practice, the Ministry of Minorities was successful in appointing military governors in only two conquered cities, Jaffa and Nazareth. Whereas, as you will recall, Ben-Gurion appointed someone to his liking to deal with property expropriation in Jaffa.) The governor should have a police force at his disposal. At the same time, the military force that had conquered the area should evacuate the area and be replaced by another military force 'responsible for the area's defence'.[10]

These recommendations were not adopted by Prime Minister and Minister of Defence David Ben-Gurion.

---

10 'The minorities in the State of Israel', 14 June 1948, file: Minorities – Organizational, religious and policy affairs vis-à-vis minorities; file: Het Tzadi-2402/29, ISA; Long memorandum in Sheetrit's handwriting, 14 June 1948, file: Various reports. Apparently, the latter is the version that Sheetrit employed when composing the final printed document that was sent to the ministers. On a note attached to this draft, 'sent to all cabinet members on 14 June 1948' has been written. On the way that Sheetrit thought that the conquest of villages and cities needed to be carried out to prevent plunder, destruction, and abuse, see the document 'Specification of the procedure for managing Arab cities and villages that will be conquered by military forces', file: Arab property general, Gimmel-307/26, ISA. Sheetrit submitted this proposal to Ben-Gurion and did not receive a response. '[1.] In every case that the conquest of an area of Arab settlement is undertaken, a representative of the Department for Arab Affairs will be embedded at the headquarters of the operational force where he will advise the commander in all Arab-related matters. 2. The Department for Arab Affairs will appoint its representative at the operational headquarters discussed above with the understanding that he will subsequently serve as the military governor or the adviser for Arab affairs in the conquered area.'

Ben-Gurion Ignores Minister Sheetrit and the Ministry of Minorities

The conquest of cities and villages and the ongoing plunder and robbery taking place in them caused despair among Ministry of Minorities officials – not just on account of the depredation, but also the fact that Prime Minister Ben-Gurion did not offer them any support or assistance. In a meeting of senior ministry staff, Nahmani wondered, 'What is our legal status? Brigade commanders are not permitting us to handle abandoned property.' He noted that the army was even selling carpets. Machnes remarked that while the Ministry of Minorities was trying to deal with the despoliation and robbery, 'the ministers were giving conflicting orders about how to handle them'.[1] In a different meeting, Machnes mentioned that Ben-Gurion had given orders conflicting with the ones the Arab Department had issued concerning Haifa, and that this made the pillaging in the city possible. Meanwhile, in Jaffa, where 'we prepared in advance for proper order, the army prevented us from organizing and putting oversight in place. Consequently, robbery and theft started as the city was conquered.' Machnes pointed out that things were being carried out in ways that completely contradicted the agreed-upon arrangements, and that the Ministry of Minorities needed to receive greater authority. Otherwise, 'our work is meaningless, and it would be best if we just made ourselves scarce. Why are they degrading

---

1   Minutes of a meeting in the minister of minorities' office, 6 July 1948, file: Abandoned Arab assets, Gimmel-310/28, ISA.

us like this, and not taking us into consideration, except to blame us for things . . . I proposed that we close [the office] and leave our jobs.'[2] Bechor-Shalom Sheetrit understood how his ministry director felt. As far as he was concerned, the limited order that actually existed was thanks to the Ministry of Minorities. 'Up until today, we have done a great deal. Nonetheless, we can only issue warnings and fight in areas under our jurisdiction. The government, however, can make decisions about these matters,' he said.[3] 'In summary,' Sheetrit declared:

> The situation is quite dismal. I will submit a detailed memorandum and demand that a final settlement be reached on these matters. Four points will serve as the primary basis for [my argument]. 1. From a political point of view: the way things are playing out is proving detrimental and has already proven damaging to us. There is a powerful echo. The consequences are dire. The villagers, knowing what is liable to happen to their property, are capable of fighting for their lives, their property, and their homes . . . 2. From an economic point of view: the actions currently being undertaken seriously damage the national economy. There is no oversight. The individual is benefitting at the state' expense; sometimes nobody benefits when only the urge to destroy is satisfied. 3. From the Ministry of Minorities' point of view: the acts being committed and the way that our efforts to take control of the situation are being subverted erode our authority and place the Ministry of Minorities' very right to exist to perform its designated roles in question.[4]

Machnes was not the first person responsible for the handling of Arab property who protested against the government's unwillingness to

---

2 Minutes of a second meeting in the Ministry of Minorities, 15 July 1948, file: Meetings of department heads, Gimmel-307/17, ISA. Machnes wrote the following to the General Staff: 'Even after clear procedures have been put into place for the expropriation of abandoned Arab property for military needs, soldiers and their commanders continue to plunder and commit lawless acts.' This statement is followed by a list that enumerates 'only a small number of the cases of despoliation and interference with their work that our department's overseers struggle with on a daily basis as they desperately attempt to do their jobs'. Gad Machnes to the General Staff, 24 June 1948, file: 6127/1949-109, IDF.

3 Minutes of a meeting in the minister of minorities' office, 6 July 1948.

4 Minutes of a second meeting in the Ministry of Minorities, 15 July 1948.

address this issue. Several months earlier, before the state's establishment, Galili's and Sharett's confident Ezra Danin had been responsible for the handling of 'abandoned' property. Danin explained:

> When performing this work, I chanced upon many people, even good people, involved in grave instances of avarice and lawlessness. Jewish neighbours of the abandoned Arab villages, including well-known kibbutzim, plundered, robbed, and took whatever they could get their hands on – contents of granaries, machines, and much more. In such matters, I was not prepared to be forgiving or to yield. I very quickly saw that I had no choice but to resign.[5]

In the subsection on the plunder of Haifa, we noted that Danin was unsurprised by Ben-Gurion's orders not to try to convince Haifa's Arab residents to remain. During Ben-Gurion's visit to the city, he saw the reverse of the policy position that Galili advocated and that had previously been in ascendence. As you may recall, this coincided with Ben-Gurion's firing of the Haganah chief of staff. This act reflected more than just an effort to reorganize the structure of government; it was part of Ben-Gurion's effort to radically alter the goals of the war.

Throughout the war, Sheetrit ceaselessly protested the robbery of Arab property, and the treatment of Arabs more generally. 'I am sick and tired of repeating this on a daily basis,' he wrote to Ben-Gurion, who continued to ignore his letters. Sheetrit asserted:

> We make decisions and take pains to establish a government on foundations that will prevent robbery, stealing, thefts, and corruption, and gaping breaches that leave us vulnerable to the faults enumerated above have been produced by the acts that Arab property has caused us to commit. When the mandatory government ruled, we cleansed the bureaucracy through removal of dishonest elements, and we fired clerks for financial transgressions; we are not setting up a government that can restrain people who cannot control their evil inclinations and prevent [them from acting on them].

---

5   Ezra Danin, *Zionist at any price* [Hebrew], vol. 1, ed. Gershon Rivlin (Jerusalem: Kiddum Press, 1987), 234.

At the end of his letter, Sheetrit declared that 'if I do not receive a response [again], I will stop dealing with property-related matters, and the government will assume responsibility for them'.[6] No letter from Ben-Gurion responding to the minister of minorities has been found in either the Ben-Gurion Archives or the files of the Ministry of Minorities.[7]

As we saw in the first half of the book, throughout the war Sheetrit strongly objected to the army's expropriation of the property of Arabs who had remained in the country ('present' Arabs). General Elimelekh Avner, commander of the military government in the occupied territories, did not see eye to eye with Sheetrit on the meaning of 'abandoned property', claiming 'things are not that simple'. In Sheetrit's opinion, the property of an Arab living within state borders was not 'abandoned', and it did not matter where he was when his settlement was conquered by combat forces. Avner, on the other hand, maintained that if an Arab was in Nazareth and his property was in Lod, then his property in Lod was 'abandoned'.[8] Sheetrit disagreed with Avner on a number of other issues as well. For instance, Sheetrit opposed 'the establishment of ghettoes for minorities', arguing that they had the same legal right to freedom of movement that Jews did.[9]. The Ministry of Minorities instituted a rule that the home of an Arab would only be opened in his presence. 'Unfortunately, in most cases, nobody obeys this rule. Yet since the opening of the Ministry of Minorities [branch office in Haifa on 1 July 1948,] we are determined to have it followed,' wrote Moshe Yatah, director of the Ministry of Minorities' Haifa branch.[10]

6   Bechor-Shalom Sheetrit to David Ben-Gurion, 1 July 1948, file: Arab Affairs – Abandoned property, Gimmel, 5670/29, ISA.

7   I would like to thank the Ben-Gurion Archive staff for their assistance and for their efforts to locate Ben-Gurion's letters to Minister Sheetrit from this period.

8   Minutes of the second meeting of the Committee for Governance in the Occupied Territories, 2 September 1948, file: The Military Government, Gimmel- 308/141, ISA. See also Moshe Yatah to Sheltering Services (Haifa), 8 August 1948, file: Invasion and seizure of Arab homes, Gimmel-1323/10, ISA: 'According to the Minister of Minorities' orders, an Arab present within state [boundaries] possesses the same property rights as a Jew.'

9   Minutes of the sixth meeting of the Committee for Transfer of Arabs from One Location to Another, 1 December 1949, file: Committee for Transfer of Arabs, Gimmel-1322/22, ISA.

10   The Ministry of Minorities also opposed limitations on the ability of present Arabs to transfer funds to and from their bank accounts. See Moshe Yatah, 'An overview of the condition of minorities and their demands', 27 October 1948, file: Internal information, Gimmel-302/62, ISA.

Throughout the war Sheetrit wrote a number of letters to Ben-Gurion and submitted a number of proposals and reports to him. Rather than concluding that Ben-Gurion's replies were lost over the years, it is more reasonable to assume that Ben-Gurion never responded. Here is another example of a letter that Sheetrit wrote to Ben-Gurion, to which the latter also seems not to have replied:

On Friday, 19 November 1948, in a meeting held at your office in the Kiryah, I raised the issue of General Avner's failure to follow the government-approved policy to only appoint military governors with the consent of the minister of minorities and the minister of the interior. You responded by saying that you did not remember exactly what the government had decided and that you would look into the matter . . . I checked the matter. I would like to provide you with the decision that the government reached concerning this matter on . . . 21 July 1948 . . . [A quote from the decision:] 'A department for conquered territory's management will be established in the general territory. Approval of the ministers of defence, minorities, and interior is required for appointment of the department's director. The department director will appoint military governors in the conquered territories who have received the approval of the three aforementioned ministers.' . . . It is clear from what was just been stated that the appointments of military governors in Beersheba and Majdal without the knowledge and consent of the Ministries of Minorities and Interior violates the above-mentioned decision. Therefore, I ask that you instruct General Avner to write to the two aforementioned offices concerning the appointments to get their approval of them.[11]

---

11 Minister of minorities to minister of defence, 23 November 1948, file: Office of Minister Bechor-Shalom Sheetrit, Gimmel Lamed-14820/8, ISA. Quotes from diary entry for 19 November 1948, David Ben-Gurion, *The War of Independence* [Hebrew], ed. Gershon Rivlin and Elhanan Oren (Tel Aviv: Defense Ministry Press, 1982), 832. Sheetrit is quoting from the minutes of a cabinet meeting that have been fully redacted and are therefore unavailable for examination. A letter written by Nehemiah Argov, Ben-Gurion's adjutant, to General Avner has been located. In it, Argov writers that 'the minister of defence *would like to remind you* that every appointment of a military governor requires the approval of the minister of defence, the minister of interior, and the minister of minorities'. Nehemiah Argov to Elimelekh Avner, 2 December 1948, file: 121/1950-223, IDF, emphasis added.

In the following months, Ben-Gurion continued to ignore the Ministry of Minorities and its minister.[12] Ben-Gurion went on to appoint military governors in most of the conquered locations, and he did so without the responsible ministers' approval, and without even considering concrete proposals presented to him by the minister of minorities. Sheetrit wrote to Ben-Gurion that 'the condition was unbearable and that real steps needed to be taken to put an end to unrestrained depredation and to implement responsible and effective governmental oversight over [abandoned] property'. He proposed that roadblocks, each manned by army and civilian watchmen and an official of the Department for Arab Assets, be set up on the country's major roads. He believed that this would make it possible to prevent a large portion of the looting.[13] This letter also remained unanswered.

A Haifa district intelligence officer reported that 'every time that the "Ministry of Minorities" was mentioned [in Acre and Haifa] it was like a *monster* that disturbed military personnel, especially the garrison force, in performance of its duties'.[14] The secretary of the Ministry of Minorities recommended 'performing only *practical activities beneficial to minorities* and keeping quiet about all the problems created by senior officials who serve as an obstacle to our ministry and against which [the ministry] struggles'.[15] In mid-1949, with the war's conclusion, after being prevented from doing its job for months, the Ministry of Minorities would be closed.[16] The man who concernedly referred to himself as 'a professional mourner' wrote in a ministry memorandum,

---

12   For example, in one of the cabinet meetings, Sheetrit wondered why the Ministry of Minorities had not been invited to participate in a discussion about the settlement of Bedouins in Beersheba. In the meeting, Sheetrit said, 'I wanted to receive the minister of defence's word that no step would be taken in the matter until the government was informed of it!' Cabinet meeting minutes, 28 November 1948, ISA.

13   Bechor-Shalom Sheetrit to David Ben-Gurion, 4 July 1948, file: Damage, robbery, and theft, Gimmel-307/27, ISA.

14   Intelligence Office (Haifa District) to the district commander, 20 August 1948, file: 244/1951-129, IDF, emphasis added.

15   Y. Danïeli (secretary of the Ministry of Minorities) to Dr N. Bero, 17 March 1949, file: General, Gimmel-307/36, ISA.

16   Moshe Yatah wrote that the fact that 'in most offices of the ruling government there is still opposition, either emotional or mental, to the Arab citizen, a tendency to discriminate against him, and an unwillingness to fulfil his demands' constitute some of the reasons why the ministry should not be closed. Moshe Yatah to the Ministry of Minorities, 26 January 1949, file: The future of the Ministry of Minorities, Gimmel-304/71, ISA.

I do not want to complain or get angry about the fact that they did not consider my opinions and chose not to even invite me or allow me to participate in every meeting or discussion of Arab affairs that took place outside of the framework of National Administration and provisional government meetings.[17]

Sheetrit was an experienced politician. He knew that the Ministry of Minorities also had 'political pathways' that restricted its operation. He remarked that he had 'a relationship with and a strong connection to the office of the foreign minister', Moshe Sharett.[18] In April 1949, Mapam Arab Department official Yosef Waschitz wrote:

> There is reason to fear that the liquidation of the Ministry of Minorities did not take place because there is no longer a need to defend minorities, but because influential people do not want somebody defending the Arabs and having a decisive role in how plans concerning them will be put into effect.[19]

With the passage of time, few Israelis would remember what Sheetrit and his men had worked to accomplish.[20]

---

17   Bechor-Shalom Sheetrit, 'Memorandum of the Office for Minority Affairs', presented to the National Administration 10 May 1948, file: Various reports, Gimmel-306/62, ISA.

18   Minutes of a meeting that took place at the Haifa Municipal Building, 6 June 1948, file: Various reports, Gimmel-306/62, ISA.

19   Yosef Waschitz, 'Is there a need for a Ministry of Minorities?' [Hebrew], *Al HaMishmar*, 6 April 1949.

20   Few research projects have been undertaken on the Ministry of Minorities and Minister Sheetrit; these topics are deserving of further study. To the best of my knowledge, only one academic article has been written about the Ministry of Minorities' activity. See Alina Koren, 'Good intentions: The short history of the Minority Affairs Ministry. 14 May 1948–1 July 1949' [Hebrew], *Katedra* 127 (2008): 113–40.

The Existence of a Policy for Expelling and Robbing the Arabs

In July 1948, several days after the conquest of Ramle and Lydda, when the General Organization of Workers in Israel (the Histadrut) was still a major force and a leader in Israeli society and politics, its executive committee had a long discussion about the topic of plunder. Mapai affiliate Reuven 'Barkat' Borstein said that there had been an opportunity to formulate and establish ways of interacting with the Arab population, and 'we, unfortunately, did not know' how to take advantage of it. The Histadrut, he declared, cannot take pride in many of its accomplishments, and it did not do enough to establish a new existential framework. Barkat proposed that the executive committee 'express its desire that [the future of] Lydda and Ramle not be like the future of all the other cities that we have conquered'.[1] Subsequently, Yosef Sprinzak, a Mapai affiliate, spoke in coded language:

For weeks and months, things have been taking shape in an uncontrolled manner (to put it mildly). Facts are being created that prove spiritually distressing to everybody in this building, and our feelings of upheaval sometimes find voice in our meetings. Yet, at the same time, the facts continue to be created and everything proceeds down the same road as before. This is the way things are with regard to

---

1 Minutes of the Histadrut Executive Committee meeting, 14 July 1948, vol. 90, June–August 1948, LMA, 12.

robbery, plunder, and the behaviour of occupying Jewish forces in the places where we have succeeded in becoming occupiers.

Sprinzak noted that they 'saw what was brewing' and that the intention had been to prevent despoliation in Jaffa. Yet,

> in Jaffa, where on the day that the capitulation agreement was signed they promised us that everything would take place in an orderly fashion, everything proceeded just like it had in Haifa . . . the question can be asked if these results were necessary, rational, and foreseeable.

Sprinzak remarked that there were those who feared the pillaging of Arab property would make it 'impossible for us to repeat our declaration that we want peace with the Arabs and that we promise them good treatment'.[2] His statement, whose nuances one can assume the other meeting attendees were able to parse, hints that the looting aligned with the policy direction some circles within the governmental wanted to take. Sprinzak said that he used the word 'uncontrollable' to 'put it mildly'. Others were less polite about how they phrased things. Eli'ezer Bauer of Mapam asserted that plunder and robbery were neither moral nor military issues, but political ones:

> It is not a coincidence that this type of robbery and expulsion is taking place – there is an undeclared, yet highly effective, plan to make it so no Arabs will remain in the State of Israel. Therefore, robbery is not encouraged, but nothing is done to prevent it. Things are being done in such a way that the Arabs' economic foundation is being destroyed; if we declare that they can return and if they want to return, they will neither have a place to live nor a way to make a living. Currently, it is easy to do things that will not be possible later. Yet there is a need to discuss if it is possible and desirable from a political perspective to have a substantial number of Arabs within the territorial boundaries of the State of Israelis. Only such a discussion will produce practical results in plunder-related matters.[3]

---

2   Ibid., 15.
3   Ibid., 16.

Ya'akov Hazan, another Mapam leader, also saw the pillage of property as an expression of policy, and he remarked that the plunder that was taking place was bringing him to 'the point of despair'. He declared that the civilians, not the soldiers, were the 'the true robbers'. In his opinion, 'the Jewish people in the Land of Israel is involved in robbery and plunder', and this 'resulted from a political strategy' that views Arabs as unworthy of consideration. For scholars looking for historical documentation, the following statement made by Hazan proves extremely significant:

> The acts of robbery and plunder are an anarchic instrument that helps realize an intentional political strategy. In the Land of Israel, a political strategy without letters, [in other words, without documents that keep a record of it,] is developing. Hints are given that they want to see only 15,000 Arabs in Haifa – here you have a political strategy.

Hazan believed that if Ben-Gurion had wanted to stop the robbery and plunder, he could have. Hazan said that the Jewish people, 'a nation of thieves', could be blamed but that he preferred to 'blame the political strategy'. He then addressed the plunder of Jaffa, saying that if Jaffa's Military Governor Yitzhak Chisik had had governmental support, the widespread despoliation that occurred there could have been prevented. 'With each passing day, I am more certain of this. If you look at things differently, it proves impossible to understand what occurred in Lod and what occurred in Ramle.' According to him, such things will continue 'as long as the current political strategy remains in place'.[4]

---

4 Ibid., 21–22. Despite the disagreements they had, Hazan's colleague Meir Ya'ari saw the plunder and the expulsions as two sides of the same coin: 'A policy to remove Arabs from the Land of Israel exists . . . I am certain that the Arabs will write a full account of their dispossession. It will disgrace us forever and the Arabs will be returned to [our country]. The best of our youth perform these activities either in accordance with orders from on high or in accordance with silence from on high. Everybody has sworn that they did not intend [to bring about population] transfer, but all of us know what is going on here . . . We need to stop the acts of vandalism being carried out against enemy property. In the end, they do spiritual harm to our soldiers and distort how the world sees us.' Minutes of the Histadrut Executive Committee meeting, 16–17 June 1948, vol. 90.

In the meeting, Zalman 'Aran' Ahronowitz, a labour movement leader, and Pinhas 'Lavon' Lubianiker, an opponent of Ben-Gurion, rejected the idea that there was 'a hidden political agenda'. Lavon argued that 'the dominant public consciousness stands in opposition to our wishes'.[5] Aran added that the robbers' desire for a 'property transfer' did not necessarily mean they wanted a population transfer. Aran saw the 'the eternally robbed [Jew] becoming the robber'.[6] Yet it is unlikely that Lavon had a substantial disagreement with Hazan. More than a year later, in a meeting at the Mapai office, Lavon explained that the way Mapai was interacting with the Arab population was yielding only negative results. The policy, he explained, was one of 'transfer', which made it 'impossible to conduct outreach when Arab oppression is the policy goal'.[7] Eliyahu Hacarmeli of Mapai offered an additional perspective on the despoliation:

> I have participated in the debate about plunder more than once . . . once they said that pillaging was a unique talent of Oriental Jews. The Ashkenazim have now performed this activity better than we did. As usual, they inhibited our successful performance of it.[8]

Mapam had been formed in January 1948 with the merger of the Hashomer Hatzair Workers Party and the Ahdut ha-Avodah-Po'ale Tzion movement, two socialist parties critical of the ruling party, Mapai. The Hashomer Hatzair element of the new party was highly critical of how the Jewish leadership engaged with the Arab population and its

---

5   Minutes of the Histadrut Executive Committee meeting, 14 July 1948, 25.

6   Ibid., 17. Concerning the depredation of Jerusalem, Aran said: 'Members of the military police, the Haganah, and the Palmach are participating in organized robbery and confiscation. Something that has not taken place elsewhere occurred there – the robbing of abandoned Jewish homes. First, it was the homes of the rich, and, later, it was in poor neighbourhoods like Sanhedria. This is a disgrace, and it proves disastrous to us . . . This spectacle took place throughout the city and non-participants need to prove they were not involved.' Minutes of the Histadrut Executive Committee meeting, 16–17 June 1948.

7   Minutes of Mapai office meeting, 19 January 1950, file: Party office – minutes, 2-25-1950-13, LPA, 8. For more on Lavon and his policy towards the Arabs, see Adam Raz, *The Kafr Qasim massacre: A political biography* [Hebrew] (Jerusalem: Carmel, 2018), 25–34.

8   Minutes of the Histadrut Executive Committee meeting, 14 July 1948, 19.

property during the war.[9] One should recognize that Mapam, Israel's second-largest party, was the one with the most sway in the Palmach. In the party's central committee meetings, they discussed issues of plunder and robbery at length, proposing ways of dealing with them among party members in the army and more generally.[10]

Aharon Zisling, a government minister and a member of Ahdut ha-Avodah, saw the theft of Arab property as a failure. Perhaps the robbery could have been prevented, he asserted, if Mapam were not so weak.[11] It follows that he saw the theft of property as the product of a policy that reflected extant power relations between the state's various leaders. Ya'akov Hazan, a member of HaKibbutz HaArtzi, was no less critical: 'They expelled the Arabs from the Land of Israel, and they vandalistically and almost completely destroyed villages.' Hazan saw the expulsion of Arabs and the looting of their property as actions that would create 'enemies for at least two generations. If there is a [state of] constant war, Zionism will not have a future. Perhaps we will live on into the future, but Zionism will not.'[12] Eli'ezer Bauer described the pillaging that was taking place in Haifa at that time: 'The strategy that is concerned with not leaving anything behind', he declared, 'seems to be political.' He remarked that this political strategy aims 'to create a situation where the Arabs will be unable to return'. Moshe Erem, who worked in the Ministry of Minorities, demanded that the party do everything in its power to influence its members, because 'the enemy's property is gradually disappearing'. There is a need to work directly with commanders and comrades who 'can serve as a brake to destructive activities', he clarified. Barukh Lin, a trade union administrator, proposed a different solution: 'to line up a few Jewish soldiers against the wall'. Lin was not only worried about the fate of Jews in Arab lands, but also about how 'we are sowing the seeds of a fascistic spirit among our youth that will eventually cost us

9   Eyal Kafkafi, 'Ideological development in the Kibbutz Me'uchad during the period of the Cold War, 1944–1954' [Hebrew], PhD diss., Tel Aviv University, 1986, 105–11.

10   See Minutes of Mapam Party Central Committee meetings, 11 May 1948, 15 July 1949, file: Meetings of Mapam Central Committee, (2)67.90, YYA.

11   Minutes of Mapam Party Central Committee meetings, 11 May 1948.

12   Minutes of Mapam Party Central Committee meetings, 15–16 September 1948, file: Meetings of Mapam Central Committee.

dearly'.[13] Moshe Sneh, a leader of the Israeli left, also saw the plunder as an expression of policy. 'It is not by chance, and it is not negligence that there are no clear regulations,' he opined. 'I think that it is not carelessness, but intention. The intention is to get rid of the Arab minority during this war.' Y. Aharoni of Mapam said that 'we helped promote undesirable aims. Ben-Gurion did not say to steal. He just did not forbid robbery, and we carried out the robbery'.[14] Aharon Cohen, a member of the HaKibbutz HaArtzi Arab Department, declared in criticism that 'our members are acting in accordance with the policy Ben-Gurion chose'.[15]

More than the other movements (and political parties), HaKibbutz HaArtzi worked to address the pillaging in which its members had taken part. The movement leadership warned about

> worrisome expressions of a lawless and inhumane attitude that has manifested itself here and there in our kibbutzim. A danger exists that some of our affiliates will adopt the cynical attitude of ruling circles and will become the tools of a policy that is alien to our spirit.

The movement leadership demanded that the kibbutzim train people to assume watchman roles and to develop cordial relations with their neighbours.[16] The Executive Committee Secretariat informed soldiers

---

13   Political Committee meeting notes, 26 May 1948, file: Political Committee meetings, (4)66.90, YYA. See also what Lin had to say in the Political Committee meeting, 15 June 1948, file: Political Committee meetings, (5)66.90, YYA.

14   Minutes of conference of military personnel, 25–26 July 1948, file: (2)206.90, YYA.

15   Political Committee meeting notes, 15 June 1948, file: Political Committee meetings, (5)66.90, YYA.

16   HaKibbutz HaArtzi, Security Department, 22 June 1949, (1) 6.18, YYA. See also the comments of Yitzhak Ben-Aharon: 'I would like to say another thing. All of us, without distinction or exception, are shocked by the fact that our members, especially our members, participated in the despoliation . . . the iniquity has spread in our camp. We demanded and we demand (and this needs to be one of the takeaways from this conference) that an iron fist be employed indiscriminately and without mercy or favouritism against every soldier who is tempted to loot and against every soldier who touches what has been devoted. Every piece of Arab property, large or small, important, or unimportant, is forbidden to Israel's army and every one of its soldiers. We need to suppress and uproot this danger threatening our morality and our image with all the means that we (and the army) have at our disposal.' Minutes of conference of military personnel, 25–26 July 1948.

and new recruits who had been mobilized that incidents of robbery, depredation, and abuse had been exposed. 'The facts of robbery and plunder that have spread throughout the country are much more troubling. The struggle against them has not adopted sufficiently stringent tactics, and, as a result, it has had little success against them.' The Executive Committee noted that 'instances of lawless behaviour, robbery, and abuse of the non-combatant Arab population by irresponsible elements that have occurred again and again seriously harm the character of the State of Israel and its defence forces'.[17] After the second truce, between July and October 1948 declared by the UN Security Council, when robbery and violence again dominated the scene, the secretariat announced:

> Lately rumours have spread on our kibbutzim about how our mobilized members, as well as kibbutzim, have dealt with the non-combatant Arab population and abandoned property in the conquered territories in ways that diverge from our movement's ideological and moral principles. The HaKibbutz HaArtzi Executive Committee dedicated a substantial portion of the discussions in its last two meetings to investigating these issues. Such rumours cannot be left unaddressed. Conclusions must be drawn . . . We have concluded that every deviation from the path and basic principles of the movement must be addressed with a strong hand.[18]

Yisrael 'Idelson' Bar-Yehuda, later a minister of interior and minister of transportation from Ahdut HaAvoda, pointed an accusing finger at his party: 'Did the party tell our kibbutzim to return what they stole? Did they force anybody to stand trial in places where our party has control? It said that this was not nice, and that was about it.' In his opinion, Mapam had turned into a party of good intentions, not one of good deeds.[19] The comments that the director of the Land and Afforestation

---

17   'A letter to the mobilized, Merhavyah, 25 August 1948, HaKibbutz HaArtzi HaShomer HaTza'ir, Executive Committee secretariat', file: (8)18.1, YYA.

18   HaKibuutz HaArtzi secretariat to the kibbutzim and to all of our mobilized members, 12 November 1948, (1)5.18, YYA.

19   Minutes Mapam secretariat meeting, 13 July 1948, file: (4)62.90, YYA. In his diary, Yosef Nahmani wrote: '[Ze'ev] Karp from Ashdot Ya'akov and Ben-Tzion Yisra'el from Kinneret came to visit me. They are members of a committee that the Jordan Valley

Department of the Jewish National Fund Yosef Weitz made in his diary in mid-June 1948 correspond with the assertions made by Idelson: 'Meir Ya'ari angrily expressed his feelings about the evacuation of Arab villages, as if he does not know that all his kibbutz members are carrying this [policy] out with true devotion.'[20] Ya'ari and Hazan had substantially different views about the expulsion of Arabs. In a Political Committee meeting, days after Haifa's and Jaffa's conquest, Ya'ari said:

> If they say, 'Jaffa's presence by Tel Aviv proves disturbing,' then it is good that they fled. If everything that proves disturbing [to us] needs to be uprooted, then we need to uproot the whole country – all the Arabs in the Land of Israel need to be removed . . . If everything that bothers us needs to be uprooted, [then] we do not need to differentiate between righteous people [and Arab combatants] . . . They say that

---

kibbutzim set up to deal with Arab lands. As they have consumed, they have only gotten hungrier. Aggressiveness is a contagious disease, and it destroys moral frameworks.' Yosef Nahmani diary, 26 July 1948, HAS. At a conference, Aharoni had the following to say: 'I call it the collapse of ideological foundations. What I am referring to here is the attitude towards the neighbouring nation, robbery, plunder, and everything connected to them . . . Where do I think blame lies? It lies with us, our members, and our kibbutzim. Our people took part in the pillaging. To a great extent, our people and our commanders are responsible for destruction and robbery. I am convinced that if there had been a party line or if we had intellectually engaged with this issue in advance, we could have prevented it. Our power and our status in the army and the Palmach made it possible for us to stop this. We did not do so . . . I would like to say to Beni Marshak that I do not believe that property stolen from Arab villages needs to serve as the core of the Harel [Brigade]'s available supplies. [Marshak] tries to say that robbery is a bad thing, but, if he says that there are Arab villages that need to be destroyed, he creates a justification for robbery and destruction. Ideological foundations have crumbled.' Minutes of conference of military personnel, 25–26 July 1948. In a meeting of Mapam's Political Committee, Aharon Cohen said: 'The fact is that for five months we did not sort [our relations with the Arabs] out, and now everything has been decided. The property problem is no longer relevant, and the villages have been destroyed . . . a decision made too late is like a decision never made . . . We were a major reason for [the Arabs] departure . . . Their departure delivers a negative political message about us, because we did not do everything in our power to prevent them [from leaving] . . . We [and] our behaviour broke them. These are facts that testify to the Jewish left's political failure. In practice, we have maintained [the same] policy up until today. It is how things were handled in Beit She'an and the other villages. Yet following all the things that happened there, they choose to try an Arab who stole a pair of stockings. This is regretful.' Political Committee meeting notes, 15 June 1948.

    20   Yosef Weitz, *My diary and my letters to my sons*, vol. 3, *A guard of walls* [Hebrew] (Tel Aviv: Masada, 1965), 303.

this is a military operation . . . If there are such villages, do we need to uproot them? Therefore, all the villages need to be uprooted.[21]

Ya'ari had already expressed opposition to the return of Arabs who were expelled or fled from the country in July 1948, offering only a vague explanation for this stance.[22] The compromise between the different positions led the executive committee to assert that 'the party opposes the removal of Arabs from the emergent Jewish state's territory'.[23]

21   Political Committee Meeting Notes, 27 May 1948, file: (4)66.90, YYA.

22   Meir Ya'ari: 'I am not speaking about the return of Arabs that have already been expelled. In my opinion, the expulsion of Arabs from the Land of Israel is a huge disaster, but returning Arabs that we have made into enemies so that they can serve as a fifth column is something else.' Minutes of the Histadrut Executive Committee meeting, 16–17 June 1948, vol. 90, June–August 1948, LMA.

23   Decisions of the Political Committee made on 15 June 1948, published in secretariat journal, no. 4, 23 June 1948, file: (1)10.95.11, YYA.

'Ben-Gurion, This Is Your Fault!'

In May 1948, Yosef Sprinzak, the Knesset's first speaker and a Mapai member, published an article in *Davar* that addressed the depredation whose destructive effects were beginning to be felt in the Yishuv. The war then taking place, he wrote, was testing the Jewish people. The soldiers need to zealously preserve honour in battle,

> lest a desecrating barrier arise between the army of war and the army of redemption, and lest the curse of impurity that is as always accompanied by a storm of self-defence and conquest stick to us. Do not allow actions and urges that are capable of turning an army into a seething and unruly mob cause our war effort to fail.

Sprinzak quoted the Book of Esther: 'but on the spoil they laid not their hand' (9:15) and commanded that 'all couch grass' liable to damage Hebrew independence be uprooted. It was the Jewish people's behaviour towards the Arab minority that would prove the sincerity of its desires. Sprinzak concluded with the call: 'May our camp be pure. May nobody who will make our declarations into empty words be found therein ... Add the phrase "be pure!" to the Haganah's call to stay strong!'[1] Yitzhak Tabenkin, a HaKibbutz HaMeuhad member, expressed a similar sentiment:

---

1 Yosef Sprinzak, 'May the war be pure' [Hebrew], *Davar*, 9 May 1948.

I am frightened when I hear about robbery and rape. Yet I am frightened by it from the perspective of a Jewish man, from the perspective of a socialist man, and from the perspective of a man building a Hebrew nation.[2]

Golda Meir, as one of the leaders of the Zionist labour movement, spoke at length at a meeting of the Mapai Central Committee and was highly critical of the despoliation of Arab property. The State of Israel entered the war unprepared, she noted. If it were prepared for the victories to come, she said, it 'certainly would have sat and made plans . . . how will we act? What will we do? What will happen?' Meir asked that 'the theoretical and abstract' 'brotherhood of nations' be set aside, remarking that in light of the events that had taken place, 'it was impossible that we will not be asked to pay full price'. The party, she noted, needed to announce what it wanted and to provide the public guidance pertaining to the pillaging. As far as she was concerned, this would be 'no less exalted' than the Arab policy. Meir confessed that she hoped that the public 'would not [act] like all the other nations' when it came to Arab property. She demanded that 'something dramatic' be done, and she 'wanted to warn [others] that we could shift to the other extreme . . . Indeed, the thing will never cease.' In her opinion, the party needed to assign serious manpower to perform educational work that would lead people to 'feel nausea if they touched anything that even whiffed of war profiteering'. Meir told about her meeting 'with a wonderful girl, one of our girls . . . and [she] said to me: "You should have seen how trucks full of furniture [from Katamon] passed . . . it was wonderful to see it!"' Meir opposed collective pillaging:

Afterwards, the question remains – can the collective do whatever it wants? The collective as a kibbutz, the collective as a military unit? Can the collective, for the unit, use this merchandise to ensure that it has a radio, a piano, a furnished common room, and a furnished dwelling? In a well-known location, I said to a very serious man who is unmatched in tactical matters and who makes a very favourable

2 Minutes of conference of military personnel, 25–26 July 1948, file: (2)206.90, YYA.

impression: Listen, comrade, I heard that they are carrying a piano seized from Arabs up to the soldiers' quarters. He said to me: What is the problem? There is a military need for a piano. The soldiers needed a piano. It was the spoils of war. Can a kibbutz take [spoils]? If the kibbutz can take [spoils] and the unit can take spoils, there is no way around it – the individual will take spoils too. Comrades, in my opinion, the sin began to spread during World War II when we gave ourselves licence and said that it was permissible [to take things] from non-Jews.

In her remarks, Meir got down to the nitty-gritty of how despoliation could be prevented in conquered areas. Her proposal was nearly the same as Minister Bechor-Shalom Sheetrit's previously described plan, as well as that of Yosef Weitz, the director of the Land and Afforestation Department of the Jewish National Fund:[3] the appointment of a civilian responsible for handling abandoned Arab property in every location immediately after its conquest was one of this plan's key features (additionally, she remarked that in her opinion women could play a decisive role in preventing depredation). Meir explained that she had been talking about this plan for days, and that she demanded that her party take the necessary bureaucratic steps to have a few hundred people appointed. According to her, all the officers that she spoke with thought it was a good idea. 'We need to be saved from the embarrassment too', she said, exposing her feelings on the matter. She called for votes on two concrete proposals – the

---

3   In May 1948, Yosef Weitz wrote the following in his diary: 'Even [Eliezer] Kaplan is quite bitter about [the pillaging], but he sees no way of addressing it. I said that things would get resolved if the army stopped handling the spoils and it had no control over Arab assets.' Weitz, *My diary and my letters to my sons*, vol. 3, *A guard of walls* [Hebrew] (Tel Aviv: Masada, 1965), 291. See also Minutes of the Histadrut Executive Committee meeting, 16–17 June 1948, vol. 90, June–August 1948, LMA: 'We are certainly all implicated in robbery and plunder, because we can protest them and work to prevent them through political and economic organization. If we fail to undertake such measures and whatever happens happens, it will be a very difficult phenomenon for us [to address] from a social, a moral, and an economic perspective. We need to fight this phenomenon right now. First and foremost, [responsibility for Arab property] needs to be taken out of the army's hands. I [Weitz] propose that [in] this meeting of [the Histadrut Executive Committee] [we] direct this demand to the proper addressee [Defense Minister David Ben-Gurion]. The army does not need to touch the property and it does not need to be put in charge of it.'

holding of serious discussion in party institutions about the issue of plunder and the selection of a party official who would be responsible for establishing the infrastructure necessary for combatting despoliation. 'If we do this,' she said at the end of her statement, 'property will be protected, and we will protect something more valuable than property – our boys' sense of self-worth. They will be able to emerge from this war with a greater sense of self-worth than they feel now.' The remainder of the meeting minutes are missing from the Labour Party Archives in Beit Berl, and it is unclear what the party institutions did with Meir's proposal.[4] In any case, nothing like this was undertaken in the field.

Yitzhak Ben-Zvi, a Mapai leader and the second president of Israel (1952–63), also demanded that Prime Minister Ben-Gurion take the acts of robbery more seriously. He argued that they were causing demoralization.[5] Elsewhere he wrote:

The Jewish robbers have brought disgrace and dishonour upon us, and they have done serious damage to our moral standing! A terrible wantonness is spreading, among both youths and adults, because robbery is a contagious disease. They say that things are being done to prevent these acts. I am sorry that people do not sense this and that the chosen means are evidently not all that effective. I brought this matter to the attention of Mr Gruenbaum, the minister of the interior. He agreed with me, but he told me that Mr Ben-Gurion is in charge of this matter and that he needs to determine sentencing for perpetrators . . . A certain degree of licentiousness cannot be avoided, and there is nothing like [*word unclear*] as a means for combatting acts of robbery. Yet I am convinced that if [the authorities] do not take up these measures immediately and wait around for orders that have yet to come and will [likely] never come, because the man who needs to sign these orders is up to his ears in much more important matters, a cure for this disease will not be found. I ask again, is there nobody in Jerusalem possessing a conscience, experience, and requisite legal experience who can be

---

4 Party Central Committee meeting, 11 May 1948, file: 2-23-1948-1949, LPA.

5 Yitzhak Ben-Zvi, 'The topic of discussion: Acts of robbery in Katamon and in the other conquered neighbourhoods', 27 May 1948, BGA.

assigned the role of guarding the Jewish people's and our combat forces' honour?[6]

Yisrael Galili felt the same way, stressing that 'unpleasant things have taken place. There have been cases of theft, desertion, and rape – matters that will determine the Jewish army's human and social character.' He stated that Ben-Gurion was 'working hard' and had little time, expressing his 'doubts that in a matter of a few months [he] could fully consider every military government-related matter.'[7] It highly unlikely Galili actually believed that a heavy workload was the reason the prime minister had not dealt with the issue. Indeed, at that very instant, Ben-Gurion found time to intervene in purely tactical battlefield issues (to the surprise of commanders, who asserted that the prime minister did not understand these matters at all).

A month after Golda Meir spoke up at the party central committee meeting, Mapai leader Eliyahu Dobkin reported on the robbery and plunder taking place in Jerusalem. A large portion of the population, he remarked, 'is supporting itself through robbery and depredation', and he declared that 'Jews had lost God's image'. In his opinion, the army was doing whatever it wanted: 'Everybody is confiscating. Everybody has the right to confiscate, not just headquarters. Every Guard Corps and Field Corps company can take what it wants.' Dobkin remarked that he felt that 'a few people, perhaps just one man, created this reality. Yet, that is the situation.' He did not say who this one man was but of course he meant Ben-Gurion. Dobkin, who was an eyewitness to Arab Jerusalem's despoliation, reflected:

> If the level of [despoliation in other locations] reached only 50 percent of what we saw in Jerusalem, this is a highly worrisome phenomenon we must take into consideration, because it can destroy many of the bases of our existence and leave behind very serious scars.

Like many others, Dobkin also noted that serious action was not being taken to combat the plunder. According to him, only after despoliation had gone on, largely undisturbed, for months did Ben-Gurion finally

---

6   Yitzhak Ben-Zvi to David Ben-Gurion, 2 June 1948, BGA.
7   Minutes of Committee of Five, 3 July 1948, BGA, 5–6.

send a telegram stating that serious measures should be taken against the looters. Yet, Dobkin declared, the punishments handed out were ridiculously lenient. He demanded that the despoliation be combatted through organized administrative action, trials, and serious punishments, and public service messaging. 'The third approach has found only minor expression. The first two approaches have not been employed at all.'[8]

The subject of Arab property and its plunder arose several times in cabinet meetings, but it is difficult to effectively follow the cabinet's decision-making process because the state censor has made it difficult to analyse the historical documentation. For example, on 18 July 1948, according to clause 5 of its agenda, the cabinet addressed the condition 'of the Arab population and its property in abandoned territory'. Yet everything on this topic has been classified as 'privileged' and cannot be examined.[9] (The question immediately comes to mind: Over seventy years after the events, do cabinet discussions from 1948 about Arab property constitute a danger to Israeli state security or its foreign policy?) In a different meeting, only part of whose minutes can be examined today, Prime Minister Ben-Gurion spoke about 'moral failings of the type I did not even imagine existed and that seriously harm our military readiness'. He remarked that he would dedicate himself to addressing such inner failings; he criticized Mapam representatives in the cabinet whose 'incitement of elements within the army against the government did not assist the war effort . . . and aided in the growth of these failings'. This is followed by a redacted passage. Minister of Agriculture Zisling, from Mapam, responded firmly to Ben-Gurion's remarks:

> Ben-Gurion, this is your fault! I want to say that here. You decided to assume sole responsibility (and that is the reality) without shared deliberation, without cooperation, and without equality. Instead, you employed a rhetoric of equality lacking true equality, [and undertook] actions in accordance with a [political] policy about which you did not consult with your colleagues [in the government] and whose intentions perhaps would not have been found

---

8   Minutes party secretariat meeting, 13 June 1948, file: 2-24-1948-21, LPA.
9   Cabinet meeting minutes, 18 July 1948, ISA.

acceptable if [the cabinet] had clarified them. In this way, you are contributing to the collapse of shared responsibility's foundations. Both organizationally and through the frequent claim that it is impossible to sit around this table to deliberate on matters of security and war you have resisted [it] this whole time [and that] is not bolstering the war [effort]. Now you do not need to preach to these people [the cabinet] about equality. It is a topic in which they are well versed. You are not a judge yet. If there will be a judge and an inquiry, then you will be under investigation and you will not be a judge. You can judge yourself, but you cannot judge others . . . You want more power for war, for the army, [and] for equality within the army. You do not need to tell me that somebody will be defended and somebody else will not [be defended]. Concerning the matter of plunder, nobody should be given preferential treatment as long as nobody gets it! We demand cooperation and the sharing of responsibility, work, and essential information.[10]

The same day, either before or after the cabinet meeting, Zisling sent Ben-Gurion a letter. In it, he wrote that the cabinet occasionally addresses 'questions pertaining to the "handling" of property'. The ministers express 'shock, bitterness, and shame, and we never arrive at any conclusions about how to address them'. In the minister of agriculture's opinion, the rampages of civilians and soldiers 'confirm that in terms of their character and their scope these activities could not be carried out except in accordance with *an order*'. Zisling posed a number of questions to the prime minister:

Who gave the order to demolish homes and to annihilate settlements in Beit She'an, the villages surrounding it, and in other areas throughout the country? On what basis was an order given (I heard that its execution was delayed) to dismantle diesel [engines] connected to the irrigation systems in Arab orchards [and thereby dry up the orchards]? Is there any basis to rumours that at various times responsible authorities expressed 'theories' that listeners perceived as orders concerning 'estimates' of the number of Arabs that one should try to leave in settlements that they were evacuating (Haifa and other

---

10   Cabinet meeting minutes, 16 June 1948, ISA.

locations)? If there is any basis to the information that I have received, responsibility derives from a governmental source. How could such trends and activities persist in opposition to what has been agreed upon in government deliberations. Whatever the case, 'private' plunder continues.[11]

In a discussion of the Histadrut Executive Committee, Zisling continued to address the uncertainty about where the orders to destroy Arab property and the Arab economy originated:

Alongside the process of despoliation taking place in Jerusalem and Jaffa, there is another process underway throughout the country – the destruction of the economy, the uprooting of trees, the laying waste of settlements that will need to be completely rebuilt. I do not know who is responsible for this, but I would like to direct the Histadrut Executive Committee's attention to this process. It is not just the moral collapse of officers and enlisted men that we are seeing . . . The boys give it their heart, but they are unwilling to pass up the opportunity for plunder and theft. Yet I am not talking about individuals running amok. I am talking about a much more serious phenomenon. I do not know who ordered the removal of diesel motors from Arab orchards so that they can no longer be irrigated and the demolition of all the homes in a village out of a political consideration that somebody decides to act on independently; I do not know the origin of the sense that statistically precise numbers of inhabitants need to remain in different locations 'after' [the conquest] . . . We need to have control over things . . . We need to look into this matter day and night until we know the source responsible [for issuing these orders]. In my opinion, both the civil government and the army are to blame. Responsibility for what has

---

11   Aharon Zisling to David Ben-Gurion, 16 June 1948, file: Arab Affairs – Abandoned Property, Gimmel-5670/29, ISA. It is interesting to note that in a different file in the Israel State Archives where a copy of the quoted letter was found, they decided to remove the letter from the file and prohibit public examination of it. See file: Administration– Abandoned Property, Gimmel-2185/31, ISA. The destruction, plunder and/or expropriation of agricultural machinery was a very serious matter for the Arab agriculturist. There are numerous examples of this and statements on this topic made by Sheetrit and others have already been provided.

occurred reaches all the way to the top, to the cabinet and its military government.[12]

At a Mapai party conference, Yosef Sprinzak – who, as we saw above, politely employed the word 'uncontrollable' to describe the actions undertaken towards Arabs – felt free to speak more openly. Demanding an open discussion of Arab policy, he remarked that 'the transfer question' could be discussed if people wanted to employ this 'strategy'. As he put it, the matter of Arab relations was one of the greatest political questions of their lives and future. 'Everybody is talking about' the expulsion of Arabs and the plunder of their property, he declared, adding:

> Then there is the question of who is creating the facts [on the ground]. Behold, nobody can tell you . . . I want to know who is creating them. Orders are creating the facts. There is no need to debate whether facts are being created. They are being created . . . We are hearing stories, and I would like to be careful about what I say. We are receiving information about a strategy, advanced by either the government or a different authority, that involves creation of facts [on the ground], expulsion, and the forcible removal of the Arabs from the country.[13]

---

12 Minutes of the Histadrut Executive Committee Meeting, 16–17 June 1948, vol. 90, June–August 1948, LMA. For a detailed description of the theft of motors employed in the orchards, see Report on the investigation of Karl Kottman, 22 February 1948. See also Report on the investigation of Asher Hatchuel, 22 February 1948, file: The Legal Service 15-46-178/1, YTA.

13 Minutes of Mapai Central Committee [meeting], 24 July 1948, file: Protocols of the Party Central Committee, 2-23-1948-1949, LPA. See also the following comment made by Sprinzak: 'There are still many complex matters whose unusual features remained jumbled. I do not accept that this was actually a matter of robbery – it was committed in an overarching and harmonious way. Everybody kept quiet about it, and this building [the Histadrut] kept quiet too . . . I would like to point out that there is one thing that I just cannot believe: that not even a hint of democratic ideas exists [in this country]. There are things that I hear about, and I do not know who made these decisions; I know that they were not approved by the [Histadrut] Executive Committee, by the non-existent Jewish National Council, by Jewish Agency officials who sit around like superfluous [parts], by the State Council, and not even by members of the government. If so, who is making the decisions? When the bullets are flying, one cannot ask such questions. Yet during a truce, this question needs to be raised . . . I get tangled up in two words: decision and order. I hear that there is a need to destroy Beit She'an, but I do not know who decided that. I heard people saying that the commander thinks that there was an order . . . a terrible disorder still prevails in the state, but I am not ready to

Zisling and Hazan were not the only ones who saw Ben-Gurion as the policy's architect; Minister Sheetrit did too. 'The destruction of Arab villages continues,' wrote Sheetrit to Ben-Gurion. 'I do not know who authorized it and on what basis.'[14] A week later, in another letter to Ben-Gurion (to which Ben-Gurion apparently did not reply either), he wrote:

> I ask you to order the army not to uproot whole Arab orchards and not to sell any property belonging to Arabs before the government determines a clear policy concerning these matters, because such activities damage state property . . . I have raised this issue numerous times in cabinet meetings, and the army is still doing as it pleases.[15]

---

criticize [people for] this disorder, because I am willing to take the reasons behind it into consideration.' Minutes of the Histadrut Executive Committee meeting, 16–17 June 1948.

14   Bechor-Shalom Sheetrit to David Ben-Gurion, 1 July 1948, file: Arab Affairs – Abandoned property, Gimmel-5670/29, ISA. In an internal Ministry of Minorities meeting, Sheetrit said: '[Ben-Gurion] favours a policy of destroying Arab villages. There are villages that are endangering security, and they need to be destroyed.' Minutes of a meeting of the minister with the department heads, third meeting, 22 July 1948, file: Meetings of department heads, Gimmel-307/17, ISA.

15   Bechor-Shalom Sheetrit to David Ben-Gurion, 8 July 1948, file: Nabulsi Orchards, Gimmel-307/17. In a cabinet meeting on 27 June 1948, Zisling raised the issue of the destruction of villages. Today, his comments have been redacted from the minutes and one cannot examine them in the Israel State Archives. For the reader's benefit, they are provided here: 'When I walk down the street, I hear rumours about the destruction of property, and I want to know who gave the order to destroy it . . . I was in Beit She'an, and trustworthy people told me that the military commander received an order to destroy it . . . I am supplying facts about the destroyed villages that I saw. In the Hefer Valley, I saw villages that were not destroyed in the fighting. Instead, their residents abandoned them. Now they are destroyed and those who destroyed them need to be summonsed to account for their actions . . . Who destroyed the village of Sarkas (السركس) found in the Hefer Valley? In one of the earlier meetings, I mentioned the name of [Moshe "Mussa"] Goldenberg [of Beit Alpha] who told me about an order to destroy (forty villages) and mentioned your name [Ben-Gurion]. I remarked that I did not believe that the order had really been given in your name. Now I am not talking about the political aspect of this matter, but only about the fact that it seems as if things are taking place on their own.' As previously mentioned, this statement is currently redacted from the minutes in the Israeli State Archives, but I have two alternative sources for it: Tom Segev, *1949: The First Israelis*, trans. Arlen Weinstein (New York: Free Press, 1986), 84; and Yoram Nimrod's notes of what Zisling said (there are only minor differences between the two sources), available from the Oranim Group Archive. When it was accessible to the public at the Yad Tabenkin Archive in Ramat Efal, both Nimrod and

The reality did not change, and Ben-Gurion did nothing to prevent the destruction.

Two months after the war's conclusion, a statesman like Sprinzak, who was not blind to the facts, would continue to assert that 'the present situation proves highly surprising to honest and naive people'. In a discussion of the Foreign Affairs and Defense Committee on 'the status of Arabs in the State of Israel', he would assert that 'there is an everyday practice, and it is not clear why this policy and not some other has been adopted'. Sprinzak, like others, was committed to acting in accordance with the code of high politics; when minutes were being taken, he would not mention the name of a statesman who was responsible for the adopted policy, but he would declare that there was a policy, as if it were a natural phenomenon. In a meeting of the committee, Yosef Sapir, a leader of the centrist General Zionists party, said that the Arabs in Israel live in 'a type of ghetto'. He continued:

> The subconscious premise that the presence of Arabs in the territory of the State of Israel is undesirable constitutes one of the primary factors behind the situation that has recently been created with respect to the Arabs and it underlies my point of view. Based on it, people arrive at a variety of different conclusions. One draws conclusions about defence, the structure of the economy, and every aspect of life. Based on numerous activities that took place and went unpunished, I draw a clear

---

Segev examined the file containing Zisling's statement. When I went to look at it, the archive staff, after repeated effort, proved unable to locate it. See also the following statement Sheetrit made. It helps give a sense of the destruction and how fully the policy of destroying Arab property was applied: 'When the Defense Forces stood ready to conquer Beit Dagon, part of their plan was to blow up the factory ["Golden Spindle"] ... When taking the value of this factory, one of the few important factories in the whole Middle East, into consideration, Mr Gad Machnes believed that this property should not be destroyed. Instead, he felt that efforts should be made to leave it intact and that efforts should be made to protect it from partial or total dismantlement, destruction, or plunder by irresponsible elements, especially military forces personnel, during the conquest and thereafter, similar to what had taken place in many other factories ... I cannot conclude my letter without noting that this is the only instance where two factories were not lost and remained intact and in reliable hands. For this, the Committee for Arab Assets should be congratulated.' Bechor-Shalom Sheetrit to Eliezer Kaplan, 29 July 1948, file: Factory confiscations, Gimmel-307/24, ISA. See also Minutes of the Ministerial Committee on Abandoned Asset Affairs meeting, 26 July 1948, file: Administration – The Abandoned Property Committee, Gimmel-2186/21, ISA.

conclusion. It is a rational conclusion to draw based on these activities that serve as the continuation of activities that took place before the state's establishment. Yet it does not lead us to conclude that the Arabs [living] near the borders will need to make themselves scarce, because the Arab's natural conclusion will be that it would be best for him to leave the State of Israel. Such a policy was expressed at a certain time.

As far as Mapam member Yitzhak Ben-Aharon was concerned, the lawless treatment of Arabs during the war and in the months immediately thereafter could be traced to one address – the Israeli government. Ben-Aharon demanded:

The fundamentals of the policies that are putting things into motion from above [need to be investigated]. I do not think that things happened, because the government was disorganized. When it wanted to take care of things, it did so. One needs courage to act against conscience and in opposition to one's commitments. It is unreasonable to believe that chaos reigned in this specific area and order could not be achieved. Matters in this area can be organized. We need to shine a rational light on this matter and take it out of the darkness in institutions of authority where it [has been dealt with up until now]. We need to clarify how orders and commands are being received and how they are being carried out.[16]

With the passage of time, officials like Avraham Tamir were prepared to name names. As the deputy assistant chief of staff for operations in the

---

16   Foreign Affairs and Defense Committee minutes, 29 August 1948, ISA. See also the letter of Foreign Minister Moshe Sharett to David Ben-Gurion about the military activities that were undertaken in Nazareth. Primary significance here does not rest with the affair itself but in the foreign minister's protest against the wholesale autonomy that Prime Minister and Minister of Defence David Ben-Gurion took for himself in the decision-making process. 'The search took place in Nazareth on June 18, and, two days later, the Arab Knesset member from Nazareth protested against it in a Knesset meeting. He was promised that this matter would be investigated, and an effort would be made to prevent the recurrence of such events. The fact that an incident identical to the initial incident took place three days later forces people to draw one of two conclusions: anarchy reigns or promises the government makes in Knesset are just a bunch of hot air.' Moshe Sharett to David Ben-Gurion, 29 June 1949, file: Conquered Israeli territories, Het Tzadi-2564/10, ISA.

Central Command after the war, Tamir was responsible for the destruction of many villages. In an interview conducted at the Yitzhak Rabin Center (a research library) many years after the war, he would explain that Prime Minister Ben-Gurion asserted the 'policy that [the villages] needed to be destroyed, so that they [the refugees] would not have a place to which to return'. He continued, 'I mobilized all the Central Command's engineering battalions, and I flattened all those villages within forty-eight hours. Period. There was nowhere to which to return.' It is worth noting that this interview, like more than a few of the protocols and documents cited above, was closed to public examination a number of years ago by order of the defence establishment – specifically, the director of security of the defence establishment.[17]

In November 1948, President Chaim Weizmann visited Yosef Nahmani, a head of the National Fund for Israel, and told him that he had heard that people were robbing, raping, and oppressing Arabs. 'This will come back to bite us . . . in our state, the quality, not the quantity, will determine things,' said Weizmann. The president, who had known Nahmani for years, wondered if they were consulting with him about Arab policy. 'I answered: they do not ask [me questions]. As president of the State of Israel, are they consulting with you? "No", he answered me in a despairing and depressed whisper. "No, you are right, they do not ask [me]." Weizmann was very depressed.'[18] The two men's conversation stirred Weizmann up, Nahmani wrote in his diary, and the president asked him to come see him again the next day. Weizmann said:

> '[Thinking about] what our boys did to the Arabs made it so I could not calm down the whole night. What can be done to prevent such indecent and oppressive acts?' Mr President, my friend, I answered,

17   Avraham (Abrasha) Tamir, interview, 10 October 2002, YRC.
18   Yosef Nahmani diary, 13 November 1948, HAS. A few days earlier, Nahmani had returned from a tour of the Galilee with Minister Sheetrit, Gad Machnes, and others. They had visited the village of Safasaf (صفصاف), whose residents IDF soldiers had slaughtered on October 29. Nahmani added the following comment to the brutal description of the massacre he provided: 'Where did such Nazi-like brutality come from? They learned it from them. One officer said to me that those who had been in the camps were best able to excel. Stories about the acts of atrocity that were committed made a very unpleasant impression on Sheetrit, Machnes, and the others. Was there no more humane way to drive off the inhabitants than to employ such methods and then plunder their property?'

there is a state now that has a government to lead it. [Private individuals] can no longer conduct politics. I no longer have any influence. Only the government has the ability to rein in the instincts that some of our boys have allowed themselves to freely express. After pondering things for a while as his eyes expressed their distinctive Weizmannian despair, he answered me, 'Yes, you are correct . . . unfortunately, all I can do is express my personal opinion. I have no influence. They are working to prevent me from having any influence.' What he said was very sad.[19]

---

19 Yosef Nahmani Diary, 14 November 1948, HAS.

The Nazareth Affair – Ben-Gurion Had 'The Strongest Historical Instincts'

In light of the fact that mixed and Arab cities were emptied of their residents and the property that was left behind, the city of Nazareth proves a mystery to the observer. Not only were the residents of this northern Christian city not expelled, but almost no robbery and plunder took place there. The vast majority of scholarship treating the city of Nazareth's conquest during the Independence War points to the Israeli elite's fear (associated primarily with Ben-Gurion) of harsh responses from the Christian world if Nazareth's fate resembled that of other Arab and mixed cities.[1] It is important to remember that Nazareth was the only conquered city whose Arab residents all remained after the war. This should prove surprising to this book's readers.[2] To better understand the manipulative nature of Prime Minister Ben-Gurion's political behaviour, let us consider the reasons why Nazareth's Arab inhabitants neither fled nor were expelled, and why none of their property was plundered.

1   Mustafa Abbasi, 'The conquest of Nazareth: The Arab city that survived the war' [Hebrew[], *Iyyunim be-tekumat Yisrael* 20 (2010): 101–21. See also the comments of Moshe Carmel: Ben-Gurion 'was very conscious of the need not to let something happen in Nazareth that would make the Christian world angry with us . . . The soldiers behaved properly, and there was still concern about the negative effects it would have on world public opinion if they acted improperly.' Moshe Carmel, Oral History Department interview, 8 March 1978, BGA, 27.

2   Conditions of Nazareth's surrender, signed 16 July 1948, file: 2315/1950-15, IDF. Hayyim Laskov signed the surrender agreement on the state's behalf.

Of course, there is documentation that supports the claim that Ben-Gurion wanted to defend the Christian city and prevent its inhabitants' expulsion.[3] First, unlike in other places conquered by the Israeli army, Ben-Gurion took pains to announce to the military command in advance that Nazareth's destiny would not be like that of the other cities. The prime minister wrote Yigael Yadin, the second chief of staff of the Israel Defense Forces:

> Before the conquest of Nazareth begins, you need to prepare a special force, both loyal and disciplined, that will not allow any other Jewish soldiers to enter the old city and will ensure that no monasteries and churches are robbed or desecrated. Any attempt by our soldiers to commit robbery should be mercilessly met by machine gun fire. Inform me about how you plan to carry out this order.[4]

Following issuance of the order, the commander of the northern front informed the soldiers 'who would be attacking Nazareth' that the city was 'the cradle of Christianity, a holy city for many millions of people. Christians throughout the world turned their gaze toward it. It had an abundance of churches, monasteries, and holy sites', and the soldiers were warned not to enter the churches and not to plunder. The directive stated that 'the operation commander has received particularly strict orders to take immediate action against those who violate this directive'.[5] It should be emphasized that the written orders said nothing about the local Arab population. Indeed, in sharp contrast with its behaviour in

---

3   Ben-Gurion also expressed worry about Jerusalem's Old City. See his 4 June 1948 letter to the commander of the Etzioni Brigade about 'serious complaints about despicable acts'. File: 2644/1949-314, IDF. See also his letter from 15 July 1948: 'If you successfully conquer the Old City, our soldiers will create a serious and potentially disastrous problem if they rob and desecrate Christian and Muslim holy sites. If there is a real chance that you will be able to conquer the Old City, you need to prepare a special force, both loyal and disciplined, that will guard all the entrances to the Old City and prevent soldiers from entering it. In pursuit of this objective, you might even want to mine all the entrances [to the Old City] and make this information public. Inform me if you have the means necessary [to accomplish this].' BGA. This letter shows that when Ben-Gurion wanted to prevent depredation, he knew how to do so.

4   David Ben-Gurion to Yigael Yadin, 15 July 1948, BGA.

5   Order of the day, 16 July 1948, file: No. 171, Container 19, BGA.

other cities, the army almost completely forwent acts of intentional vandalism of holy sites.[6]

Alongside protection of holy sites that found various expressions, including notices the army posted on holy sites announcing that soldiers were forbidden from entering them, property confiscation was also forbidden (except for vehicles and weapons), and after the conquest life in the city quickly returned to some semblance of normalcy, albeit under military occupation. Summing up the first three months of Nazareth's occupation, Military Governor and Ministry of Minorities official Elisha Soltz wrote: 'In Nazareth, there was no pillaging, and the Custodian of Abandoned Property's Office did not confiscate the residents' property.'[7] In practice, the (relatively) lenient policy applied to the city's residents was criticized by the Israel Defense Forces. 'A state of terror and intimidation is not being imposed in the city,' wrote the deputy commander of the Golani Brigade critically, 'and quite often I think that our overly gentle behaviour does not suit the conditions of the war that we are currently fighting and that when combat resumes our benevolent rule in Nazareth is liable to blow up in our faces.'[8]

Why were the resident of Nazareth not expelled? In a diary entry from 18 July 1948, Ben-Gurion wrote:

Yesterday morning Moshe Carmel gave the order to uproot all the residents of Nazareth. Brigade Commander [Ben Dunkelman] hesitated. When I was asked about this matter yesterday [in a telegram from Hayyim Laskov, commander of Operation Dekel], I telegrammed him immediately not to expel them.[9]

6   Christian notables to the military governor, 23 July 1948, file: Bet/105/92, HHA. Sheetrit visited Nazareth and wrote: 'Acts of robbery and abuse did not take place . . . the city's mayor expressed his wish that the name of the Israel Defense Force not be stained by mention of acts of robbery and harm to civilians. In general, he noted his satisfaction with our army's behaviour.' See 'Report of the minister of minorities' visit to Nazareth on 19 July 1948', file: Nazareth general – reports, Gimmel-308/44, ISA.

7   Elisha Soltz (military governor of Nazareth), Report of the activities of the military government, 17 July 1948 – 17 October 1948, file: 121/1950-223, IDF.

8   Deputy [Golani] Brigade commander to commander of the Northern Front, 4 September 1948, file: 260/1951-54, IDF.

9   Quote from diary entry for 18 July 1948: David Ben-Gurion, *The War of Independence* [Hebrew], ed. Gershon Rivlin and Elhanan Oren (Tel Aviv: Defense

Obviously, according to the prime minister's diary, he prevented the expulsion of Nazareth's residents. Laskov's telegram states: 'Inform us immediately, by the quickest means possible, whether we should expel Nazareth's residents from the city. In my opinion, except for clergy, they should all be expelled.' Ben-Gurion wrote by hand on the telegram: 'Do not expel people from Nazareth.'[10] This thesis is so entrenched in the scholarship that researchers critical of Ben-Gurion, such as Uri Ben-Eliezer, see the case of Nazareth 'as an exception that proves the rule. When Ben-Gurion wanted to prevent expulsions, he did so easily.'[11] Ben-Eliezer, like many others, relied on this diary entry. Yet there are a number of primary sources that place the entry's accuracy into question.[12] Indeed, it is not surprising that many people disregard them.

A few years after the publication of Ben-Gurion's war diaries in 1982, in a long interview conducted on behalf of the Ben-Gurion Institute for the Study of Israel and Zionism in Sde Boker, Moshe Carmel, who commanded the northern front, addressed what the prime minister wrote in his diary, including how Ben-Gurion attributed a desire to expel the Arabs to him. Closed until recently to public examination, the

Ministry Press, 1982), 599. Undated Telegram: 'According to the order of the minister of defence, residents of Nazareth are not to be expelled.' Yirmiyahu to Golani [Brigade], file: 1281/1951-50, IDF.

10   Battle Command, Seventh Brigade to the General Staff, 17 July 1948, BGA.

11   Uri Ben-Eliezer, *The Making of Israeli Militarism* (Bloomington: Indiana University Press, 1998), 177. See also Yigal Elam, *The executors* [Hebrew] (Jerusalem: Keter, 1991), 45–6; Yossi Goldshtayn views what happened in Nazareth as proof that Ben-Gurion opposed the expulsion of Palestinians during the war: Yossi Goldshtayn, *Ben-Gurion: A biography* [Hebrew] (Ramat-Gan: Bar-Ilan University Press, 2019), 718.

12   Michael Bar-Zohar, *Ben-Gurion: A biography*, vol. 2 [Hebrew] (Tel Aviv: 'Am 'oved, 1977), 775–6. Readers will also find the following letter sent to the *Hadashot* editorial board interesting: 'What a beautiful view! David Ben-Gurion said to his friend while they watched the expulsion of Haifa's Arab population. Dr Michael Bar-Zohar presents this and other discoveries testifying to the gap between Ben-Gurion's declared policy on the Arab question and the policy that he put into effect on [a radio] program . . . On the eve of the invasion of the Old City, Bar-Zohar explains, Ben-Gurion sent a telegram to his soldiers, and, in the telegram, he requested that they not expel Arabs. "All the commanders knew that the telegram was merely pro forma," said Bar-Zohar. "The only one who took the telegram at face value was Hayyim Laskov, who oversaw the conquest of Nazareth. When Ben-Gurion arrived in Nazareth and saw the Arabs, he angrily asked Laskov: 'What are they doing here?'"' Didi Yizra'eli, letter [Hebrew], *Hadashot*, 19 October 1986.

recording, which is more than an hour and a half long, deals at length with the issue of what took place in Nazareth. In the interview, Carmel explained that what Ben-Gurion wrote in his diary was not wholly accurate. Neither his actions in Haifa nor his actions in Acre were motivated by a desire to expel Arabs, Carmel asserted, and Ben-Gurion knew it. Carmel added that people

> more [knowledgeable] than him [had told him] that they found all types of problems, inaccuracies and even mistruths in Ben-Gurion's diary and [they had] the impression that Ben-Gurion was interested in promoting specific views of history on various matters, even when they did not accurately reflect how things unfolded at the time.

It should be emphasized that on the recording, Carmel did not say that Ben-Gurion ordered him to expel the Arabs. On the contrary, according to him, the two men agreed: the Arabs were to be left in Nazareth.[13]

Remarks relevant to this topic later made by Mordechai Maklef, who replaced Carmel as Carmeli Brigade Commander in May 1948, did not accord with what the prime minister recorded in his diary. Maklef, who later became the third chief of staff of the Israel Defense Forces, said that when Ben-Gurion arrived in Nazareth after its conquest, he asked: 'Why are there so many Arabs here? Why did you not expel them [?]'[14] Regarding Ben-Gurion's order that a machine gun be set up to shoot any pillaging soldier, Maklef said that Ben-Gurion distinguished between positions that he held 'in practice' and 'those that would be left to history', and he agreed with what Carmel said in the statement quoted above. He believed that the prime minister had a highly refined historical sense, and he was very careful about how his positions were represented 'in written documents'.[15] In other words, Maklef, who served as IDF chief of staff under Ben-Gurion, suggests that we take this historical

13   Moshe Carmel, interviewed by Shabtai Teveth, 7 August 1988, BGA.

14   Maklef said that Ben-Gurion arrived in the city days after it was conquered; this is incorrect. He only made it to the city in late October, as Ben-Gurion's diary entry for 31 October 1948 explains. See Ben-Gurion, *The War of Independence*, 788.

15   Mordechai Maklef, interview, 16 October 1975, file: No. 171, Container 19, BGA.

documentation with a grain of salt (we will subsequently address Ben-Gurion's dispute with Yigael Yadin, which is relevant to this topic). Hayyim Laskov, to whom Ben-Gurion addressed the telegram, briefly and indirectly referred to the situation on the first day after the city's conquest:

> As long as the Seventh Brigade was in Nazareth, there was no plunder . . . *I do not know what happened in the territory* of the Thirteenth Battalion or after the Seventh Brigade left Nazareth during the afternoon of the following day.[16]

Maklef's comments were made in the mid-1970s, and contemporary sources contain nothing that directly backs them up. Indeed, the only evidence that we have about how Ben-Gurion addressed this matter is what he wrote in his diary and the short telegram. There are subsequent sources, however, that do accord, generally, with what Maklef said. After having taken over command of the Seventh Brigade from Shlomo Shamir in late June, Ben Dunkelman commanded the Seventh Brigade during its conquest of Nazareth in Operation Dekel. In 1976, Dunkelman published his English-language memoir, *Dual Allegiance*.[17] The original manuscript had included a page-long description of the conquest of Nazareth which, though elided in that edition, was translated and published in in 1980 in the magazine *ha-'Olam ha-zeh* [This World]:

> Two days after the second truce came into effect [in other words, on 20 July], the Seventh Brigade was ordered to withdraw from Nazareth. Avraham Yaffe, who had commanded the 13th battalion in the assault on the city, now reported to me with orders from Moshe Carmel to take over from me as its military governor. I complied with the order, but only after Avraham had given me his word of honour that he would do nothing to harm or displace the Arab population. My demand may sound strange, but I had good reason to feel concerned on this subject.

---

16 Quoted in Netanel Lorch, *Late afternoon: My first seventy years (and what preceded them)* [Hebrew] (Tel Aviv: Defense Ministry Press, 1997), 184, emphasis added.
17 Ben Dunkelman, *Dual Allegiance: An Autobiography* (New York: Crown, 1976).

Only a few hours previously, Hayyim Laskov had come to me with astounding orders: Nazareth's civilian population was to be evacuated! I was shocked and horrified. I told him I would do nothing of the sort – in view of our promises to safeguard the city's people, such a move would be both superfluous and harmful. I reminded him that scarcely a day earlier, he and I, as representatives of the Israeli army, had signed the surrender document, in which we had solemnly pledged to do nothing to harm the city or its population. When Haim saw that I refused to obey the order he left.

Barely twelve hours later, Avraham Yaffe came to tell me that his battalion was relieving my brigade; I felt sure that this order had been given because of my defiance of the evacuation order. But although I was withdrawn from Nazareth, it seems that my disobedience did have some effect. It seems to have given the high command time for second thoughts, which led them to the conclusion that it would, indeed, be wrong to expel the inhabitants of Nazareth. To the best of my knowledge, there was never any more talk of the evacuation plan, and the city's Arab citizens have lived there ever since.[18]

In fact, Carmel's last statement is inaccurate: there is a real-time entry in the diary, as well as the short telegram. Perhaps, after many years had passed, Carmel forgot about the telegram, and it could be that the truth is even more ambiguous. In a different interview than the one quoted above, he had this to say: 'Ben-Gurion would never conclude a conversation with an order. He relied on you to understand his intentions and to do what was needed.'[19] It is reasonable to presume that this telegram, which appears to be unique in the explicitness of its inquiry about the expulsion of a conquered city's population, placed Ben-Gurion in a

---

18   'How Nazareth was saved' [Hebrew], *ha-'Olam ha-zeh*, 9 July 1980. Peretz Kidron, who served as the ghostwriter for the book, wrote about his involvement in this project and Dunkelman's self-censorship in a subsequent article. I have quoted Kidron's English-language version of the excised passage that appears in his article rather than the translated version that appeared in *ha-'Olam ha-zeh*. There are no meaningful differences between them. Peretz Kidron, 'Truths Whereby Nations Live', in Edward Said and Christopher Hitchens, eds, *Blaming the Victims: Spurious Scholarship and the Palestinian Question* (London: Verso, 1988), 86–7.

19   Moshe Carmel, Oral History Department interview, 8 March 1978, BGA, 16.

situation that he had never before faced during the course of the war (and Nazareth's conquest was carried out after most of the war's urban conquests had already occurred): he could not give a direct order to expel the inhabitants, because, at this stage of the war, every population transfer required the government's consent.[20] Furthermore, Ben-Gurion did not give expulsion orders in writing.[21]

---

20 The case of Acre's residents demonstrates how application of a policy of displacement through transfer of an Arab population from one place to another was becoming increasingly difficult. On 19 July 1948, at the same time that Nazareth was being conquered, Minister Sheetrit learned that there was a plan to uproot the residents of Acre and move them to Jaffa. Sheetrit wrote: 'To the best of my knowledge, the orders are that residents are not to be uprooted from their places of residence without *written* orders from the minister of defence, and, even then, there is a need to differentiate between the different types of people that will be uprooted . . . therefore, as long as no such order is issued Acre's residents are not to be uprooted from their homes.' Emphasis added. Bechor-Shalom Sheetrit to Yaacov Shimoni (Foreign Ministry's Middle East Department), 19 July 1948. The following day, Minister of Finance Eliezer Kaplan wrote to Sheetrit: 'I read your letter about . . . the evacuation of the Arab residents with great interest. The question of evacuating Acre is new to me too, and the proposal to transfer [the Arab residents] is hard for me to understand.' Eliezer Kaplan to Bechor-Shalom Sheetrit, 20 July 1948. On this matter, see the documents in file: Return of Arabs to Jaffa – general, Gimmel-307/15, ISA. It is reasonable to assume that Acre's Arabs were not transferred due to Sheetrit's intervention. See also the following statement made by Sheetrit: 'I have learned that the army is about to move the villagers of Ijzim again. I informed General Avner that it is prohibited to do this without an order from either the minister of defence or the authorized ministerial committee.' Bechor-Shalom Sheetrit to the director of the Ministry of Minorities Haifa branch, 30 November 1948, file: Office of Minister Bechor-Shalom Sheetrit 14280/9, ISA. Cf. Benny Morris, *The Birth of the Palestinian Refugee Problem, 1947–1949* (New York: Cambridge University Press, 1987), 109–10. It is also worth noting that destruction of villages also required the approval of Minister Sheetrit.

21 A short time after the conquest of Ramle and Lydda, and just before their residents' expulsion, Ben-Gurion gestured at Yigal Allon and Yitzhak Rabin with his hand. Scholars have beaten to death the subject of this hand gesture's relationship to the wartime expulsion of Arabs and the source of the orders to carry it out. We cannot address all the details of the 'hand gesture affair' here. I would just like to note that it was Peretz Kidron, who translated *The Rabin Memoirs* from Hebrew to English, who brought this affair to light. He supplied the *New York Times* with a copy of the uncensored Hebrew manuscript of Rabin's book that contained the passage about the affair, which a ministerial committee headed by Justice Minister Shmuel Tamir refused to allow to be published. David Shipler, 'Israel Bars Rabin from Relating '48 Eviction of Arabs', *New York Times*, 23 October 1979; Peretz Kidron, 'Rabin straightened up to the right' [Hebrew], *Haaretz*, 4 May 1994. Based on an interview that he conducted with Rabin, Ben-Gurion biographer Michael Bar-Zohar wrote that Ben-Gurion 'did not

As a matter of historical record, here, Maklef's and Dunkelman's testimonies (as well as, to a degree, Carmel's) are arguably more credible than Ben-Gurion's. While the question of why Nazareth's residents were not expelled extends beyond the scope of this book, it is worth dwelling briefly on the city's exceptional status as the only conquered city that was not plundered. At first glance, the reason for this appears simple: there was no depredation in Nazareth, it seems, because its residents remained in their homes.

In my opinion, Dunkelman is not the only one who should be credited with preventing the expulsion of Nazareth's residents. The minister of minorities and members of his team – Gad Machnes, Moshe Erem, and Yitzhak Chisik – should be given credit too. Minister Bechor-Shalom Sheetrit, possessed of his experience in Ramle and Lydda – where (as discussed in part I), he visited *hours* before the inhabitants of the two cities were expelled and where he

---

officially order any planned operation intended to expel the Arabs who had not fled, but he hinted at it to his officers and enlisted men. A discussion that took place in the Operation Dani headquarters after the conquest of Ramle and Lydda was etched into Yitzhak Rabin's brain. A flanking manoeuvre was employed in the conquest of the two cities, and the Arabs did not flee. About 60,000 of them remained in place. What should be done with them? Yigal Allon, the operation commander, raised this question in a meeting that Ben-Gurion, Galili, Yadin, and Yitzhak Rabin also participated in. The participants spoke for an hour; some of them believed that the Arabs should be expelled. Ben-Gurion did not open his mouth . . . The discussion ended without any decision being reached . . . When those present began to disperse, Rabin and Allon exited with Ben-Gurion. Allon asked Ben-Gurion: "What should we do with the Arabs?" According to Rabin, Ben-Gurion waved his hand backwards in a vigorous motion and let slip: "Expel them!"' Bar-Zohar, *Ben-Gurion*, 775. See also Morris, *Palestinian Refugee Problem*, 345. Historian Yoav Gelber interprets things in a completely different way, and he asserts that 'this story is not very reliable'. Yet Gelber is relating to the interpretation that Morris gives to the story rather than Rabin's own testimony as related by Bar-Zohar (in fact, Gelber does not mention it at all). Gelber writes: 'It is just as possible that Ben-Gurion waved his hand to get rid of an annoying fly on a hot dry summer day . . . It was not customary for the minister of defence to convey orders through the waving of his hands. Instead, he formulated them lucidly and meticulously and then handed them down orally or in writing.' Yoav Gelber, *Independence versus Nakba* [Hebrew] (Or Yehudah: Dvir, 2004), 242. Yet statements made by Moshe Carmel, whom I consider to have been more familiar with Ben-Gurion's modus operandi than Gelber, have been provided above: Ben-Gurion did not give detailed orders. Instead, he left it to his subordinates to figure out what he intended and to act in accordance with it.

thought he had successfully countered Ben-Gurion by making various moves to prevent the inhabitants' expulsion, including enlisting Moshe Sharett – showed up in Nazareth on 19 July 'to observe the state of affairs in the city'. This was the day *after* Ben-Gurion had written the diary entry where he stated he had prevented the expulsion of Nazareth's inhabitants. At this stage, Sheetrit had already gotten his nominee for military governor in the city officially approved (one of two governors the Ministry of Minorities successfully appointed during the war). Prior to being appointed governor, Elisha Soltz had managed the Ministry of Minorities' Galilee Branch. (Soltz was officially appointed on 18 July, but he had already assumed the position a few hours after Nazareth's surrender.) 'We need to put life in the city back on track', Sheetrit declared during his visit to the city, and he quickly sent letters to the ministers of justice, interior, transportation, and health demanding they act in service of this goal in the areas under their control.[22] He even sent a copy of the report of his visit to the city to every cabinet member.[23] At this stage, expulsion of the city's residents would have been a clear violation of the government's order not to expel inhabitants without its consent and written approval.

In conclusion, conditions aligned to create a unique situation in Nazareth. Present on site were a field commander (Dunkelman) who was unprepared to expel residents without a clear written order (which was never issued during the course of the war), and a minister (Sheetrit) who had tirelessly fought the prime minister's policy for months. Since there are so few sources pertaining to this topic, it is also worth noting what Yiftach Brigade commander Mulah Cohen had to say about it. According to him, it was due to the pressure that Moshe Sharett and others placed on Moshe Carmel that Nazareth's residents were not expelled.[24]

---

22   'Report of the minister of minorities' Visit to Nazareth on 19 July 1948', file: Nazareth general – reports.

23   Bechor-Shalom Sheetrit to all cabinet members, 21 July 1948, file: Nazareth general – reports.

24   When offering testimony about the expulsion of Arabs in northern Israel, Mulah Cohen said that Moshe Sharett opposed it. He then added: 'Moshe Sharett and his friends kept pushing Moshe Carmel not to expel Arabs from Nazareth'. Mulah Cohen, testimony from 1996, PGA.

I have addressed what occurred in Nazareth at length for two reasons: first, because how Prime Minister David Ben-Gurion wielded power teaches us a great deal about how policy becomes reality; and second, because how he acted teaches us about how a leader thinks about historical writing in real time. As our discussion proceeds, it is important to keep both in mind.[25]

---

25 Sociologist Uri Ben-Eliezer wrote: 'Sociologically, one of the most interesting aspects of the conquests and expulsions was that even though the policy was not explicitly articulated, either orally or in writing, everyone knew about it . . . there was more to it, though, than the fact that policy was not explicitly enunciated. Throughout the war, Ben-Gurion and his colleagues employed moderate rhetoric, presenting Israel as a nation seeking not only peace but an alliance with the Arabs . . . The truth is that the gap was integral to the politics practiced by the leadership at the time. The Israeli leaders walked softly and concealed a big stick.' Ben-Eliezer, *The Making of Israeli Militarism*, 174–5. Historian Benny Morris wrote: 'in 1948 Ben-Gurion carefully avoided issuing such written orders [expulsion or the changing of Arab's place of residence].' Morris, *The Birth of the Palestinian Refugee Problem*, 110. In another place in his book, Morris writes: 'Ben-Gurion consistently distanced himself in public from the destruction of the Arab villages as, more generally, from any linkage to expulsion of Arabs. He was probably driven more by concern for his place in history and the image of himself and of the new State he wished to project for posterity . . . In his diary, Ben-Gurion occasionally seems to have deliberately tried to put future historians off the scent' (165). In contrast with Ben-Eliezer and Morris, I do not view the political leadership as monolithic.

Ben-Gurion and the Plunder of Property

Ben-Gurion addressed despoliation a number of times during the Independence War, and most of these public references (i.e., taking place in some type of meeting) were responses to things said by other speakers. In early June, in response to references to the theft of property by Mapai member Beba Idelson, Ben-Gurion said 'on behalf of the government' that he intended 'to employ all means at our disposal to fight against such ugly and degrading acts . . . that have been revealed in our camp in these frenzied days.'[1] Two weeks later, in a cabinet meeting, Ben-Gurion referred to 'Arab flight' and stressed:

> It was not really surprising to me. What constituted a bitter surprise was how it changed my view of Jewish power, particularly Jews' moral strength. I discovered moral defects that I had never even imagined that seriously flaw our military.[2]

---

1 Minutes of the Jewish National Council meeting, 3 June 1948, ISA.

2 Cabinet meeting minutes, 16 June 1948, ISA. In *The War of Independence*, editors Gershon Rivlin and Elhanan Oren, who frequently edited the text to read as they saw fit, quote Ben-Gurion as having said the following in the cabinet meeting that we have just referenced: 'Arab flight. It was not really surprising to me. The only thing that surprised me and surprised me bitterly was the revelation of moral defects amongst us, defects that I did not even suspect existed; *I am speaking here about the widespread plunder that every part of the Yishuv participated in.* I see this flaw not only as a moral problem, but as a serious military problem.' David Ben-Gurion, *The War of Independence* [Hebrew], ed. Gershon Rivlin and Elhanan Oren (Tel Aviv: Defense Ministry Press,

In late June, in a Mapai central committee meeting, Ben-Gurion spoke at length on the topic:

> Something unexpected happened to us too. Since it happened to us, it feels like we have been punched – the matter of robbery and plunder. It turns out that most Jews are thieves . . . I say this simply and intentionally, because, unfortunately, it is true . . . The people of the [Jezreel] Valley stole! The pioneers' pioneers, the parents of the Palmach youth! Everybody participated in this, by God, even the people of Nahalal! . . . I am uncertain, I cannot swear, but the people [of the Jezreel] Valley got involved in this, and this is a blow to everybody. This is truly frightening because it reveals that something is fundamentally wrong . . . Yet how did we start stealing and robbing? Why did people rooted in the soil, builders, creators, and pioneers, decide to act in this way? What happened? This could not have

---

1982), 524, emphasis added. As can easily be noticed through comparison of the two quotations, the sentence in italics does not appear in the cabinet meeting minutes found in the Israel State Archives. It is reasonable to assume that Rivkin and Oren simply copied the sentence from *When Israel fought in battle*, a collection of statements that Ben-Gurion made during the war, initially published in 1950 and republished numerous times thereafter. See David Ben-Gurion, *When Israel fought in battle* [Hebrew] (Tel Aviv: 'Am 'Oved, 1975 [1950]), 128. In the preface to the book, Ben-Gurion wrote that 'the anthologized statements are the simple and unadorned truth' (11). In this way, historians like Tom Segev ended up quoting Ben-Gurion's statement as cited in *The War of Independence* even though the prime minister never uttered the sentence in opposition to widespread plunder in the cabinet meeting. See Tom Segev, *1949: The First Israelis*, trans. Arlen Weinstein (New York: Free Press 1986), 69. For another example, see Yosi Amitay, *The United Workers' Party (Mapam) 1948–1954: Attitudes on Palestinian-Arab issues* [Hebrew] (Tel Aviv: Tcherikover 1988), 38. It should be noted that significant portions of the minutes for this cabinet meeting have been redacted, and perhaps Ben-Gurion said something in this spirit at a different point in the meeting. The tremendous liberty that Ben-Gurion took when describing events of the war led Aharon Zisling to publish a pamphlet entitled *Truth and distortion: On the revival of the state and the Independence War, a response to David Ben-Gurion* [Hebrew] (Tel Aviv: la-Merhav, 1959), in which he sharply criticizes how Ben-Gurion treated sources. 'On the tenth anniversary of the State of Israel's establishment, statements were published [and made available to the general] public and official speeches were delivered that either selectively cited official documents and minutes or that referenced them in a very loose manner. This was done intentionally to give the descriptions that they contained the authority of historic description . . . Consequently, I come before you to suggest and request that you help publish all the meeting minutes and protocols of the provisional government and its various committees' (3).

happened by chance. What exactly happened with the Arabs happened. It was not just one Arab who fled. The Arabs fled everywhere, and they fled here too. Then every Jew stole and robbed . . . Everybody, everybody stole and pilfered. I was naive when they informed me about such things at the beginning of the war. Then Palmach members were the ones involved. I sent a special investigator to look into what happened. I sent [Ya'akov] Riftin to look into things and he did so. I thought it was enough that people knew that somebody was watching who knew about the robbery and thefts and that specially assigned people [to address this issue] were unnecessary.[3] Unfortunately, I erred. Everywhere Jews have an opportunity to rob and steal, they do so. This is a much more serious matter than it seems because it points to something fundamentally wrong with every member of our collective. You can now ask if we possess the means necessary to stamp out this problem. Yet you need to bear in mind

---

3   On 10 February 1948, Ben-Gurion wrote to Ya'akov Riftin, a Mapam affiliate and a member of the Yishuv's security committee. In the letter he instructed him to investigate a series of crimes that the Shai (the Haganah's intelligence arm) had informed him about. Ben-Gurion wrote: 'Complaints and serious accusations about vindictive behaviour and lawless acts undertaken by some of the Haganah's and the Palmach's members have reached me: robbing of Arabs; murder of Poles and Arabs for no reason or without sufficient reason, and certainly without trial; improper behaviour towards Jews; cases of theft; misappropriation of funds; torture of Arabs during questioning; etc. These acts, if they indeed occurred, constitute a political and moral danger to the Haganah and to the Yishuv, and the most powerful methods available should be taken up to tear them out by the root. First and foremost, you need to get to the truth of the [various] matters and put those responsible on trial. To aid you in accomplishment of this [task], I would like you to check a series of facts that were presented to me by Shai directors.' David Shaltiel, the head of the Haganah's intelligence service, was the one who informed Ben-Gurion about the criminal activities. Less than a month later, Riftin submitted an eighteen-page report that addressed the crimes that had been committed and the steps that needed to be taken. Through efforts undertaken by the Akevot Institute, this report was made available for public examination for the first time in 2021. See 'Riftin report' [Hebrew], Akevot Institute, akevot.org.il. On the Riftin report, see Zvi Inbar, 'The military advocate general – historical aspects' [Hebrew], *Mishpat ve-tzava* 15 (2001): 7–15; Zvi Inbar, *Scales of justice and the sword: Foundations of military law in Israel* [Hebrew] (Tel Aviv: Ma'arakhot, 2005), 142–4. A draft of Ben-Gurion's letter can be found in his archive, and it was composed on 5 February 1948. Its phrasing is slightly different from the letter sent to Riftin. On the report's decades-long concealment and efforts to make it available, as well as efforts to prevent this, see 'Archivist report on archival declassification' [Hebrew], Akevot Institute, 15 January 2018, akevot.org.il. See also Ofer Aderet, 'Liquidation companies' [Hebrew], *Haaretz*, 6 July, 2018.

that it is hard to prevent people from sinning in a place where the whole population, or at least a large portion of it, wants to [sin]. When you put special soldiers, military policemen, in place, they steal too. Then you need to send people [to make sure that they do not steal things]. There is no end to the matter. In Jaffa, very drastic measures were taken, and activity seemed to slow, and it appeared that [robbery and theft] had been stopped. We discovered a whole gang of people who paid for permits to enter the warehouses and steal. At this point, they were stealing from the government, because it was government property . . . Now they are stealing from the Israeli government! Now they are stealing from the Israeli army! The Jewish soldier is stealing, but it is not just him. This has been greatly exaggerated. Soldiers are not the only ones involved. Everybody is a thief! This matter truly requires that we carefully examine our characters and our actions. Apparently, we are not like how we are described in our literature, in our prayers, in the Jewish penitential prayers, in the Yom Kippur confessional – in all likelihood something is inherent within us. Yet it seems the authority of Joshua son of Nun proves insufficient, and that we need to fight against [robbery and theft] with all of our strength and policing methods. However, we would [need] unlimited [resources] because we would need to wield limitless force in Lod to protect against this . . . It would be best if we understand things for what they are and use all of our power to suppress this, because it is part of who we are! A state cannot be built or maintained by a population that steals from another population. If such a state [is created], things will not go well. This matter has exposed one of our fundamental faults. We should not cover it up. Instead, we must face it, because we know that simple methods will not allow us to uproot it. Finally, who are our soldiers? We are the ones who put on military uniforms. They are civilians in military uniform. We need to begin a long educational process that will teach respect for public property and for abandoned property. Abandoned property is not ownerless property that everybody is entitled to take. It belongs to the public.[4]

---

4   Minutes of Mapai Central Committee [meeting], 24 July 1948, file: Protocols of the Party Central Committee, 2-23-1948-1949, LPA. For a report on Ben-Gurion's statement, see 'The prime minister inveighs against the plunder of enemy property' [Hebrew], Ma'ariv, 26 July 1948.

On 16 June 1948, two days after the Palmach's Harel Brigade completed its central role in the conquest of Jerusalem's western neighbourhoods and descended from the city, Ben-Gurion invited Palmach commander Yigal Allon to talk with him about the issue of plunder. Two weeks later, when he testified before the Committee of Five, Allon stated that it had been 'a friendly impromptu conversation' that 'a stenographer [who was present] recorded'. Later in his testimony, he said:

> I became aware that a document has great significance. Now more than before people pay attention to documents. I have been in the Haganah since 1929, and we were not so meticulous about documentation. Yet lately I have had the sense that relationships are becoming more documentary in nature. A protocol of a friendly conversation.[5]

Allon saw his personal conversation with Ben-Gurion, a transcription of which is available today, as a conversation for history. Indeed, historians have marked it as illustrative of Ben-Gurionist statism.[6] Allon's comments recall those of Ya'akov Hazan, discussed above, asserting that written commands were not given. Now, Allon is dealing with a stenographer recording his 'friendly' conversation. It is clear that Allon thought that there was a political purpose behind the conversation's documentation.

It was at Ben-Gurion's invitation that Allon spoke with him about the Palmach, the conquest of Jerusalem, and the plunder. The prime minister told the Palmach commander of rumours that had reached him about the city's despoliation and how

> the news about it was being sent to all the countries in the world . . . when you descended by convoy from the city [after its conquest], there were commanders who saw what your men were transporting in the vehicles . . . this is the blackest and most bitter stain that has been cast upon us.

---

5   Minutes of Committee of Five (evening), 4 July 1948, BGA, 2.

6   For an annotated version of the conversation protocol, see Zaki Shalom, 'On relations between the political and military ranks, military discipline, and combat morality – Protocol of a conversation between Prime Minister and Minister of Defense David Ben-Gurion and General Yigal Peikowitz (Allon) in the presence of Yigael Sukenik (Yadin) 16 June 1948' [Hebrew], *Iyyunim bi-tekumat Yisrael* 12 (2002): 657–78.

In particular, Ben-Gurion directed his criticism of the pillaging at the Palmachniks:

> I promise to give you more attractive tables, because you deserve it. I ask that people find no plunder in your possession. I make this request for your benefit. Those tables will not make the People of Israel rich, but [they will make it so] we will be unable to remove this stain from upon us. Indeed, it is *for your benefit* that this thing not be in your possession. In place of every table, you will receive a better table.

Allon, in contrast, declared that 'they [the soldiers] did not take these things. They received them.' According to him, the things were given to the Palmach by 'the special institution that Etzioni [the Haganah Jerusalem District and its commander] established for distribution of military necessities. It was not an issue of robbery.' Ben-Gurion responded tersely: 'It turns out that the Jewish people is a nation of thieves.'[7]

Allon most likely reported on his meeting to Yisrael Galili. Three days later, on 19 June, the latter wrote to David Ben-Gurion and said the claim made by cabinet members and the Histadrut Executive Committee that the Harel Brigade robbed and plundered in Jerusalem needed to be looked into.[8] On 15 June, a day before his conversation with Allon, Ben-Gurion ordered that the Harel Brigade be contacted and told 'to immediately submit a detailed list of all the booty that they seized and took with them and where it could be found'.[9] Galili proposed that Ben-Gurion appoint a comrade or a committee that 'would immediately begin to look into the accusations'. Meanwhile, Galili appointed Allon to look into the issue of plunder in the ranks of Palmach, with the goal of putting a stop to it.[10] Allon argued that the Jerusalem District

---

7   Protocol of David Ben-Gurion's meeting with Yigal Allon (Peikowitz), 16 June 1948, BGA.

8   Yisrael Galili to David Ben-Gurion, 19 June 1948. Allon wrote to Ben-Gurion: 'I do not agree [with those who would treat the terms] "Palmach" and "Plunder" as synonyms.' He demanded that a committee of inquiry be established on behalf of the General Staff to look into accusations that the Jerusalem District commander made against the Palmach. Yigal Allon to David Ben-Gurion, 21 June 1948, file: Harel Brigade 12-4-53/12, YTA.

9   David Ben-Gurion to Tzvi, 15 June 1948, file: 6127/1949-109, IDF.

10   Yisrael Galili to Yigal Allon, 19 June 1948, file: Harel Brigade.

commander, David Shaltiel, had been complaining of plunder being committed by order of the brigade's commanders. In contrast, the Harel Brigade commanders cast accusing fingers at Shaltiel. Allon noted that negative occurrences were manifesting themselves on the margins of the camp and he demanded that a committee of inquiry be established on behalf of the General Staff. Perhaps unsurprisingly, Ben-Gurion did not respond to Allon's demand.[11] Ben-Gurion was not actually interested in investigating the matter; rather, he employed the plunder of Jerusalem as a political tool in his struggle against the Palmach, which he was working to dismantle at that time.

During this period, Ben-Gurion made many unfavourable comments about the Palmach in his diary. 'David [Shaltiel] is complaining that there is no discipline, they are pillaging, the commanders refuse to fight, [and] there is no military culture.'[12] In any event, Ben-Gurion refused to commission an inquiry. 'At this time, Jerusalem's defence and liberation take precedence over all else,' he wrote to David Shaltiel.[13] Allon remarked that he considered Ben-Gurion to be 'the Palmach's most serious opponent.'[14] In his book on the Harel Brigade, historian Zvika Dror addresses latent motives behind Ben-Gurion's policy:

> In the debate that took place around the dismantlement of the Palmach [General] Staff, Ben-Gurion did not hesitate to describe 'affairs' that soldiers from other units in the district, as well as citizens who were blinded by the abandoned property in Katamon, were involved in and to present them as expressions of separatist tendencies, perhaps even rebellious [tendencies] widespread in the Palmach, *to justify his plan to dismantle the General Staff.*[15]

When addressing the aforementioned conversation between Ben-Gurion and Allon, another historian, Zaki Shalom, wrote that it is

---

11   Minutes of Committee of Five (evening), 4 July 1948, 4.

12   See Ben-Gurion's diary entry for 12 June 1948: Ben-Gurion, *The War of Independence*, 507.

13   David Shaltiel, *Jerusalem 1948* [Hebrew] (Tel Aviv: Defense Ministry Press, 1981), 191.

14   Executive Committee meeting minutes, 14–15 October 1948, LMA.

15   Zvika Dror, *Har'el: Palmach Brigade in Jerusalem* [Hebrew] (Tel Aviv: ha-Kibbutz ha-me'uhad, 2005), 236, emphasis added.

'hard to understand from how he words what he says whether he was disturbed by the phenomenon of plunder itself or by the fact that it took place in Jerusalem. It should be assumed that similar events took place in other locations during the war that did not attract Ben-Gurion's attention.'[16] It is important to be precise about this point: what really mattered to Ben-Gurion was his struggle against internal opposition within the labour movement, not the plunder of Jerusalem (as we have seen, the city was seriously pillaged). There is no doubt that Palmach soldiers participated in the looting of Jerusalem. Yet they completed their role after only a short time. As was demonstrated in the first half of the book, the pillaging of the city continued for months after the Palmach departed Jerusalem, and the prime minister did nothing to stop it. In fact, as we have seen, he did not act with the requisite seriousness to stop the pillaging anywhere. This is the same Ben-Gurion who conducted the war in a dictatorial manner.

In effect, a survey of the (very) few times that Ben-Gurion referred to 'depredation' during the war reveals that for the most part, he used them to act against his opponents in the labour movement in general and the Palmach in particular. Even years after the war, he continued to connect the labour movement to the plunder of property. For example, on 4 November 1956, after the conquest of the Gaza Strip, when General Hayyim Laskov related the plunder of Gaza by Israeli soldiers, Ben-Gurion responded: 'I remember that in 1948 things were different. Then all the kibbutzim took part in the affair.'[17] Indeed, many kibbutzim pillaged and robbed, but their members were proportionally few among those involved. For example, members of labour settlements and the labour youth movements that Ben-Gurion strove to dismantle and replace with a single youth movement operated out of the Prime Minister's Office did not play a role in the despoliation of Haifa and Jaffa, for example.

Ben-Gurion's conversation with Allon was designed to leave its mark on history, and that is how things played out. Meanwhile, the many letters Sheetrit wrote, as well as the many reports he submitted with suggestions about how to curb the pillaging, have gone ignored.

---

16   Shalom, 'On relations between the political and military ranks', 659.
17   Quoted in Eyal Kafkafi, *An optional war: To Sinai and back, 1956–1957* [Hebrew] (Ramat Efal: Yad Tabenkin, 1994), 126.

It is important to remember that when the conversation between the two men took place, a major struggle was ongoing between the government and the labour movement as a whole, because the labour movement opposed how Ben-Gurion was concentrating authority in his own hands so that he could direct the war unilaterally.[18] In practice, the cabinet was not kept up to date on the war. Ben-Gurion managed the war as if he possessed a great deal of autonomy – and, in practice, he did wield almost-complete autonomy.[19] Although there is not room to discuss it at length here, it should be noted that Ben-Gurion announced that every appointment from the rank of first lieutenant (a platoon commander) and above required his approval. When discussing this topic, the Mapam newspaper journalist Benko Adar wrote: 'During the war there was unprecedented centralism.'[20] Consequently, it is hard to believe that a prime minister who got involved in the appointment of junior officers and who expressed opposition to strategies senior officers wanted to employ in battles (for example, the Battle of Latrun) simply could not find the time to handle the problem of Arab property's plunder. Perhaps this is the reason that the United States consul-general made the following remark in a dispatch to the State Department sent in mid-May 1948: 'Looting in the captured Arab areas has now been so widespread and has been regarded with such indifference by the authorities that it is difficult not to think that it is being officially tolerated.'[21]

---

18   For more on this topic, see the first section of Adam Raz, *The iron fist regime: David Ben-Gurion, the statism debate, and the controversy over Israel's nuclear program* [Hebrew] (Jerusalem: Carmel, 2019).

19   On this, see David Tal, 'The 1948 war: David Ben-Gurion's war' [Hebrew], *Iyyunim bi-tekumat Yisrael* 13 (2003): 115–38.

20   Benko Adar, *One party, two paths* [Hebrew] (Oranim: Hug Oranim Press, 2004), 287. One of Ben-Gurion's biographers wrote: 'The prime minister and minister of defence gave orders, appointed officers, visited battlefield headquarters, [and] gave instructions. From his office in "The Red House" [in the Kiryah] and the General Staff offices in Ramat Gan ("The Hill"), he dealt with every important detail from force strength to acquisition of every type and variety of weapon from throughout the world . . . Everything was under his watchful eyes. He allowed himself to get involved in every matter, from the greatest to the smallest.' Yossi Goldshtayn, *Ben-Gurion: A biography* [Hebrew] (Ramat-Gan: Bar-Ilan University Press, 2019), 705.

21   Quoted in Larry Collins and Dominique Lapierre, *O Jerusalem!* (New York: Simon & Schuster, 1972), 588. This quote does not appear in the Hebrew translation published by Schocken Press in 1978.

Once again, as we saw concerning events in Nazareth, the historian faces dilemmas: Does the protocol of a conversation or a discussion in which Ben-Gurion says that he opposes depredation (or expulsion, or village destruction for that matter) outweigh consistent, months-long disregard for the protests of his government, on the one hand, and concrete proposals for how to stop the pillaging, on the other? This I leave to the reader to decide.

There are historians who see Ben-Gurion as an exemplary democrat, and, among other things, they point to his supposed hard-line approach to the harming of Arabs, along with his opposition to expulsions, murder, and so on.[22] This argument is not difficult to make; all one need to do is gather quotes and statements from Ben-Gurion's diaries and speeches. Indeed, Ben-Gurion's diaries are an inexhaustible source, and by fastidiously assembling citations from them one can easily 'prove' any assertion.[23] Yet Ben-Gurion possessed a very permissive attitude

---

22 The following assertion made by Ben-Gurion biographer Yossi Goldshtayn displays the tremendous naivete required to believe that Ben-Gurion was an exemplary democrat: 'There is no doubt that during the war the prime minister remained true to his worldview and his perception that a civilian Palestinian population should not be expelled even during a war and even if it was known to be hostile'. When Goldshtayn finds it difficult to explain what happened in Ramle and Lydda, he places blame on the Palmach and asserts that Palmach leaders Allon and Rabin carried out the expulsion. 'Later a number of historians pointed to [what happened in Ramle and Lydda] as overwhelming proof that Ben-Gurion was involved in the plot to forcefully expel Palestinians from the country. That is not how it was. He certainly was not involved'. Goldshtayn, *Ben-Gurion*, 718. Ignoring the fact that he contradicts his earlier claim, Goldshtayn also asserts that 'following the conquest of Ramle and Lydda, when the phenomenon [the refugee problem] became more widespread and even began to have international reverberations, he [Ben-Gurion] no longer stuck to his liberal humanistic values. Instead, he began to formulate a much more uncompromising approach' (741). Rather than directly stating that Ben-Gurion strove to expel the Arabs from the country, Goldshtayn prefers to blur the truth by concealing it behind ideological terms and fine phrases like 'humanistic', 'liberal' and 'uncompromising approach'.

23 Here is the type of quotation that can be used to 'prove' the earlier assertion about the image of the army. 'War is not a philanthropic activity, but war has rules. Even during a war, there are prohibitions. Our men violated all of those prohibitions. Even the civilians are participating in the plunder. Soldiers are responsible for acts of atrocity. The commanders are responsible for these acts that besmirch our name'. Quote from diary entry for 27 November 1948, Ben-Gurion, *The War of Independence*, 853. For another book dedicated to glorifying Ben-Gurion, see Zehava Ostfeld, *An army is born: Main stages in the build-up of the army and the Ministry of Defense under the leadership of David Ben-Gurion* [Hebrew] (Tel Aviv: Defense Ministry Press, 1994), 408–9.

towards depredation and war crimes more generally, and he concentrated authority over these matters in his hands. In other words, he did not want his coalition partners examining what was happening in areas where they were fighting, expelling, and murdering Arabs and plundering their property. For example, when the cabinet members learned about atrocities taking place in northern Israel in conjunction with Operation Hiram, they pressed for the establishment of a commission of inquiry with broad authority. They pushed for this once they recognized that 'unless the committee received broad legal authority to conduct its operations, it would be a waste of time to even set it up'. Minister Pinchas Rosen made this point a few days after a decision had been made that three ministers would examine 'specific matters', as Ben-Gurion put it.[24] Ben-Gurion did not want a commission of inquiry to be established, and he implored the other ministers to continue the inquiry in accordance with the previously approved format. Yet the prime minister was acting manipulatively: the ministers could not examine what happened without the requisite authority to do so.

Currently, it is extremely difficult to research the decision-making processes pertaining to this issue, because the relevant passages in the cabinet meeting protocols that were previously available to the public have been classified.[25] As we have already seen, the state has adopted this strategy for the handling of many historical documents. According to researcher Uri Ben-Eliezer, who examined the documents in the past, 'when the cabinet turned to discuss the commission of inquiry's authority, Ben-Gurion successfully got a resolution passed stating that *he was charged with* the task of investigating allegations about the army's misconduct against Arabs in Galilee and the south'.[26] In the cabinet meeting held on 17 November 1948, the cabinet decided that it would discuss a commission of inquiry 'for military actions in the conquered territories' during its next meeting.[27] Yet we do not know what was said

24   Cabinet meeting minutes, 14 November 1948, ISA.

25   See Cabinet meeting minutes, 17 November 1948 and 5 December 1948, ISA. Sections of these protocols have been redacted.

26   Uri Ben-Eliezer, *The Making of Israeli Militarism* (Bloomington: Indiana University Press, 1998), 186, emphasis added.

27   Clause 7 of the agenda for the cabinet meeting, 17 November 1948. Today, this part of the protocol has been redacted and cannot be examined. A copy of it is in the author's possession.

during that meeting or the one that followed. We *do* know that, on 19 November, Ben-Gurion appointed Attorney General Ya'akov Shapira 'to look into whether the army and its soldiers harmed the lives of Arabs in the Galilee and the south in ways that run counter to the rules of war' during Operation Hiram.[28] To this day, the report of the commission of inquiry chaired by the attorney general remains confidential. It is important to note that even though Israeli soldiers committed numerous atrocities during Operation Hiram, only one, accused of murdering fifteen Arabs, was put on trial. The Military Court of Appeals gave the soldier, Shmu'el Lahis, a one-year prison sentence. A short time later, he was pardoned.[29]

---

28   David Ben-Gurion to Attorney-General Ya'akov Shapira, 19 November 1948, BGA. Cf. Ben-Gurion's diary entry for 19 November 1948, in Ben-Gurion, *The War of Independence*, 832. General Moshe Carmel wrote to the brigade commanders on the front lines: 'During Operation Hiram, soldiers, as well as officers, committed a number of criminal acts in the liberated territories that had absolutely no military justification . . . I have learned that in the liberated territories such actions have not completely ceased.' Moshe Carmel to the brigade commanders, 25 November 1948, file: 1137/1949-84, IDF. The materials concerning war crimes that were committed during Operation Hiram are still confidential.

29   In his opinion, Judge Gid'on Eilat stated that more grave acts of murder than the one committed by Shmu'el Lahis took place during Operation Hiram, but that he was the only one put on trial. Later, Lahis was appointed to serve as the Jewish Agency's director-general. Inbar, *Scales of justice*, 659–61. Here is a summary of the affair presented by MK Shmuel Mikunis. I include it here because it involves despoliation: 'Led by its commander, Lieutenant Shmu'el Lahis, Company Bet of the Carmeli Brigade's Twenty-Second Battalion crossed the Lebanese border. On the way towards the village of Hula (حولا), its residents came out carrying white flags to surrender. Commander Lahis brought the Arabs back to the village. After the village was searched, he assembled twenty [of the villagers] in one home and blew it up with the Arabs [still] inside it. Then he gave his soldiers the "freedom" to do "whatever they liked" with the village residents and their property.' The next day, Mikunis noted, 'Lahis did the same thing again, this time with seventeen Arab residents [in the home]'. Parliamentary question directed to the minister of defence by Shmuel Mikunis, 15 November 1948, KAJ.

Complicity in a Crime

In a meeting of the provisional government held on 23 May 1948, Bechor-Shalom Sheetrit said that if 'goodwill' was shown to the Arabs, they would return. The government needed, he asserted, 'to set a path' where there would be no inequity between Jews and Arabs.[1] Yet, three months later, after most of the Arab property that remained in the country had been looted, Ministry of Minorities director Gad Machnes said: '*Over time opinions have changed* and currently the Ministry of Minorities is doing all that it can to prevent absentee Arabs from returning to the country *based on the recognition that all of their property has been destroyed*.' Machnes made this comment during a discussion of the future of Arab-owned orchards that were now untended and desiccated. Machnes added: 'If there was a reason to protect the orchards when the conquests began, now, when 90 percent of the [irrigation] piping has been destroyed, there is not one.'[2] We are not dealing with how the policy of barring Palestinian refugees from returning to lands claimed by the State of Israel took shape here. Yet Machnes's comments shed light on how the Ministry of Minorities' policy change is inextricably tied to the plunder and destruction of Arab property.[3] In a

---

1   Cabinet meeting minutes, 23 May 1948, ISA.

2   Minutes of the Ministerial Committee on Abandoned Asset Affairs meeting, 27 August 1948, file: Abandoned Property Committee, Gimmel Lamed-17109/20, ISA, emphasis added.

3   In May, Gad Machnes wrote to Minister of Finance Kaplan: 'Arab orchards cover one hundred fifty thousand dunams . . . the departure of their owners raises a question

different discussion of the Ministerial Committee for Abandoned Asset Affairs, Justice Minister Pinchas Rosen said that the issue of moveable property was political. He assumed that the Israeli government would be held accountable for moveable property. It would be, he asserted, 'an embarrassment if the world learned that the Israeli government did nothing to protect Arab property'.[4]

Yehezkel Sahar, inspector-general of the Israeli Police, thought that the authorities were not doing enough to prevent pillaging 'in the Negev today, [and] in the Galilee tomorrow'. According to him,

> Everybody is stealing abandoned property. I tried to do something in the south. The area around Ashdod and Majdal is a rich one. Orchards, property, etc. If we do not send in the police, not even a memory will remain. The value of the property there is estimated in the hundreds of thousands of liras. Up until now, Yemenites from Sha'arayim, people from Rehovot and even notable farmers from Gadera, as well as many kibbutzim, have taken possession of abandoned Arab property. If reinforcements do not arrive, we will be unable to provide security, and everything will be taken. The Galilee is a rich area, and, if we do not send policemen there immediately, nothing will be left there in three to four weeks.[5]

Available documentation shows senior Ministry of Minorities officials modified their positions due to the widespread plunder of Arab property. In practice, the policy of destruction and depredation (though not officially agreed upon among Israeli officials) had strengthened the political line that strove to prevent *Palestinian* refugees' return. Where to and to what exactly were the Arab inhabitants supposed to return after their property, their homes, their livestock, and their orchards were either stolen or destroyed?

---

about these orchards' future. If they are not irrigated, they will be lost . . . we see a need to consult with you about this matter.' Gad Machnes to Eliezer Kaplan, 19 May 1948. Minister of Agriculture Aharon Zisling agreed with the Ministry of Minorities about this. See Summary of meeting with the minister of agriculture, 11 June 1948, file: Orchards and citrus growers, Gimmel-307/55, ISA.

4   Minutes of the Ministerial Committee for Abandoned Asset Affairs meeting, 1 October 1948, file: Administration – Abandoned Property Committee, Gimmel-2186/21, ISA.

5   Minutes of Ministry of Police meeting, 1 November 1948, file: Ministry of Police, Gimmel-304-58, ISA.

We do not have any studies about the wartime attitudes of Israeli Jews concerning Palestinian Arabs' return. Yet, based on the remarks made by representatives of Jewish groups from across the political spectrum, it is clear that the Jewish street's attitude towards Arab property disturbed them a great deal. In an August 1949 meeting of the Foreign Affairs and Defense Committee, Beba Idelsohn said,

> For more than a year I have been going around with the feeling that we have done something that we will be unable to cleanse ourselves of for generations. The final hour to figure out how we will provide [the Arabs] with a way to live equal lives has arrived.

Binyamin Mintz, a representative of the United Religious Front, said that 'if you reveal urges and you set them free, it is impossible to restrain them. Today it is Arabs and tomorrow it is Jews.' He said that he saw how the general attitude of prejudice towards Arabs was influencing his children:

> The younger generation is being educated to think that Arabs are insignificant, animals that you can just kill . . . I do not know who is dealing with those who committed acts of robbery, both soldiers and civilians, but I think that they did not punish the guilty.

Mapai leader Zalman 'Aran' Aharonowitz said that one could under-stand the gentile's attitude towards the Jew through examination of Israeli attitudes to the Arab: there 'one can see Jewish anti-Semitism directed towards Arabs manifesting itself in every Israeli child'.[6]

Plunder had two immediate social effects: first, it turned the looters into criminals in the simple sense of the term – people who violated the

---

6   Foreign Affairs and Defense Committee minutes, 29 August 1949, ISA. See the following comments made by Uri Avnery a couple of months later: 'Eighteen percent of the state's population – the Arabic speakers – already faces a typical fascist regime, with all the typical repressive measures, both direct and indirect. Robbery, murder, and expulsion are their lot . . . Only naive people will believe that these methods will only be directed towards the Arabic speakers. There is no partial freedom. There is no partial repression. A repressive regime, wherever its repression is directed, will eventually harm us all. The repression of the Jews in Europe led to the repression of all other citizens. This axiom is applicable to us as well.' Uri Avnery, *The other side of the coin* [Hebrew] (Tel Aviv: Zmora-Bitan, 1990 [1950]), 246.

law (and accepted societal norms). Second, it forcibly turned looters who acted as individuals into political collaborators. In other words, it turned them into passive proponents of a political policy that strove to remove Arab inhabitants from the State of Israel. This passive advocacy also had a long-term effect: following the Independence War, it bolstered the political line that promoted segregation of the two national communities through military rule and other means.

On the first point, Netiva Ben-Yehuda's comments, quoted above, are synoptic: those who plundered knew that they were violating an ancient social prohibition – thou shalt not steal. 'When you violate an awesome prohibition deeply rooted in your brain', wrote Ben-Yehuda, 'it will affect you for the rest of your life.'[7]

From the criminal point of view, it really makes no difference that the pillagers plundered their Arab neighbours' property, because what is really important here is that the transgressive act itself undermines the accepted social order. Since society did not collapse during the war and a radical moral and social transformation did not take place (that is to say, the authorities did not *officially* legitimize theft of Arab property), it is no surprise that there were many people who were 'resentful and disgusted by these events . . . many people demanding that the hands of looters and thieves be chopped off lest this disease spread and we be left without the means to stop it'. Ruth Lubitz, whose writings were previously quoted, made this comment when describing the Jewish population's plunder of Jaffa. She went on to note that Tel Avivians received the imposition of additional restrictions on movement in Jaffa with 'great joy'. 'Indeed, this announcement came too late', she added, but she wrote that it was received 'cordially and its reception would have been even more enthusiastic if [what had been announced] had truly been imposed and had not just existed on paper, as similar orders that had been previously issued were fated to do'.[8] Even so, it would be incorrect for readers

---

7   Netiva Ben-Yehuda, *Through the binding ropes* [Hebrew] (Jerusalem: Domino Press 1985), 285.

8   Ruth Lubitz, 'On the purity of our war' [Hebrew], *Kol Ha'am*, 30 May 1948. Different organizations protested collectively against the looting. See 'The Petah Tikvah Municipality protests against the plunder of Arab property' [Hebrew], *Kol Ha'am*, 13 May 1948: 'In response to the labour faction's suggestion, a discussion of the pillaging taking place in Haifa and in [various] Arab villages took place this evening at a municipal council meeting [in Petah-Tikvah]. Representative of the various political movements vigorously protested against the pillaging of Arab property in places that have been conquered by Jews.'

to imagine that protests against the plunder of Palestinian Arab property occurred in Jewish cities.

Moshe Smilansky, an author and publicist, also wrote in praise of measures taken to protect property:

> It took our government too long to recognize that it needed to be punctilious about protecting abandoned property, and that legal claims, not just our consciences, would force us to take responsibility for how it was robbed and stolen. Since this looting started in the presence of God and man, where has the government directed its gaze? Urban property, rural property, and agricultural property have been shamelessly stolen, and lawless people drawn from the masses and the upper classes have become rich off of it. It is good that the authorities have opened their eyes [to what is going on], even if it did so quite late. Indeed, there is not a lot left to protect. Who knows? Perhaps they will figure out who was involved and get back what was stolen.[9]

We have already noted how few military and civil cases went to trial. As a result, very few people suffered disgrace when labelled 'abandoned property offenders'. When Yosef Sprinzak told of verdicts that had been handed down in two different trials, reported in two separate news items published the same day, he 'illustrated' the Jewish authorities' attitude towards the Arab population. An officer who ordered the murder of four Arabs who had been wounded in a wartime battle was the defendant in the first trial, and a man who had sold stolen military property was the defendant in the second trial. While the first defendant received a six-month prison sentence, the second one received a three-year sentence. Sprinzak wondered what kind of effect such verdicts would have on Israeli children. 'We are not even close to being humanistic. A case cannot even be made . . . We are like all the nations.'[10]

The tens of thousands of pillaging criminals who had not stood trial benefitted from a solution that neutralized their crime and aided in quickly uprooting it from the collective Israeli conscience. In the final meeting of the Provisional State Council held in February 1949, a short time after fighting had largely ceased (but before the armistice

---

9   Moshe Smilansky, 'From our lives' [Hebrew], *Haaretz*, 26 July 1949.
10   Foreign Affairs and Defense Committee minutes, 29 August 1949.

agreements had been signed), a decision was made to grant the criminals amnesty. Ben-Gurion said:

> We now stand at the threshold of a proper democratic national life . . . in honour of this transition, the government proposes that at its final meeting the council grant amnesty to *all the citizens and residents who have failed morally and committed crimes, both those who have been sentenced and those who have yet to be sentenced,* except for those who have been accused of acts of malicious and premeditated murder . . . neither disregard for the law nor contempt for those acting in accordance with it leads us to make this proposal. On the contrary, we propose it with the hope that when a democratic government is established our legal institutions will become stronger and propriety will entrench itself throughout the land. With the beginning of Hebrew republican life's effective operation, we want all those who previously broke the law to have a chance to mend their ways and to become honest, reliable, and law-abiding citizens.[11]

The amnesty order normalized actions and crimes committed during the war by civilians and members of the defence forces.[12] It also removed the legal sanction against depredation.

---

11   Minutes of the fortieth meeting of the Provisional National Council, 'General amnesty order', 10 February 1949, ISA, emphasis added. This is the wording of the law: 'Every person in custody or in prison on the day that this order goes into effect will be released, except if he is imprisoned or in custody because he has been sentenced or been accused of murder or another crime whose maximum legal punishment is a death sentence or life imprisonment . . . a person who committed a crime prior to 10 February 1949 will not be imprisoned or arrested for it, will not be put on trial for it or will have such a trial discontinued, and will not be punished for it, except if he has been accused of murder or another crime whose maximum legal punishment is a death sentence or life imprisonment.' 'General amnesty order', 10 February 1949, file: General amnesty order, Aleph-7526/8. Following the amnesty, the decision was made to discontinue legal proceedings against many people – not just in cases of plunder and robbery but also in more serious cases such as rape. Zvi Inbar, *Scales of justice and the sword: Foundations of military law in Israel* [Hebrew] (Tel Aviv: Ma'arakhot, 2005), 628–9.

12   See Menahem Hofnung, *Israel: Security needs vs. the rule of law* [Hebrew] (Jerusalem: Nevo, 1991), 65. Zvi Zamir, commander of the Harel Brigade, later said: 'Looking back, I have no doubt that were things that should not have been allowed to happen. If they had not issued a general amnesty after the War of Independence, there would have been some Harel [Brigade] soldiers would have been put on trial and perhaps would have been sent to prison.' Amira Lam, 'Not a platter and not silver' [Hebrew], *Yedi'ot Ahronot*, 18 February 2005.

Nevertheless, the removal of legal sanction against pillaging did not fully neutralize either how society responded to it or how it judged it. One can assume that after the general amnesty, people did not look upon their neighbours as criminals in the simple sense of the term. Yet, what did they really think about the pillagers? It is hard to know; there are not enough sources available to enable a sufficiently serious response to this question (though the lack of sources might constitute part of the answer). Hagit Shlonsky, a resident of Jerusalem during its conquest, said the following about the period of looting in the city:

> One soldier wanted to make me happy, and he brought me a handkerchief and earrings. I was flattered, but he didn't tell me he had pillaged them. He just brought them to me as a gift. When I showed them to my father, he looked at me and said, 'Throw it away! How dare you take anything!' It was only then that I made a connection between those people on the street and what the soldier had given me.
>
> In our family, because my father was so outraged by the looting, we all talked about it a lot. But otherwise, *I didn't hear anybody else mention it. It took many years till people started talking and writing about it.*[13]

Looking back, it is truly difficult to know the degree to which looting was taboo in the territories claimed by the new Israeli state. Undoubtedly, the Jewish inhabitants were aware of it. Yet it is hard to know, in real time, how ubiquitous the topic of looting was in daily discourse in the Jewish street (in newspapers, as we have seen, it was almost not addressed at all). Those who have read up to this point in the book will likely answer this question in the same way its author would. Indeed, there is no doubt that history books, as well as memoirs, diaries, and other such texts, offer no mention of the plunder of Arab property. It seems to me that one should accept what Shlonsky implies: those who brought up the topic of mass plunder were rapidly silenced.[14] This seems to be what

13   Quoted in Nathan Krystall, 'The Fall of the New City', in Salim Tamari, ed., *Jerusalem 1948: The Arab Neighbourhoods and Their Fate in the War* (Jerusalem: Institute for Jerusalem Studies, 2002), 110, emphasis added.

14   Gish Amit writes: 'Consequently, the central question is not if acts of looting, confiscation, and expropriation occurred in 1948, but how the looting that nobody in

poet Ayin Hillel (the pen name of Hillel Omer) was referring to in 'The Nivozim' (The plundered), where, upon returning home, soldiers risen from the dead reveal the pus that has spread through the land and the orchards and gives off a thieving scent:

> There is a day when the dead boys will come from their graves
> To visit the fields that sprouted their blood to weigh their yield,
> And, behold, pus is there.
> At the head of streams and a Yarkon of shit, a viper speeds.
> Jerusalem is tranquil and Haifa a carcass,
> Tel Aviv's flesh is furrowed with the large silver knife,
> And, at the gate of each and every city, Bribery rides a rat . . .
> And the fragrance wafting from the abandoned orchards evokes
>   robbery's scent . . .
> It is the Disease of Israel voicelessly burning.[15]

It is important to stress, as noted in this book's introduction, that the plunder of moveable assets was substantively different from the expropriation and theft of lands and homes both during and after the war. Looting was a personal act that an individual chose to perform, and this action, in turn, affected the individual who committed it. Here, it bears emphasizing that, over the course of a few years, through the laws and regulations that it issued, the state acted as a sovereign entity and assumed control over the immoveable property that the Arabs left behind when they left the country. In other words, this was a political decision that was reached in institutions vested with the authority to make such decisions. Indeed, if we employ common democratic terminology, we can say that 'the public' participated in the decision – even if the public's representatives, rather the actual public, 'chose' to expropriate, to steal, and so on. That is to say, 'the public', whether it agreed

---

the late forties doubted had occurred became something that people did not talk about.' Gish Amit, *Ex libris: A history of theft, preservation, and appropriation at the National Library in Jerusalem* [Hebrew] (Tel Aviv: ha-Kibbutz ha-me'uhad, 2015), 83.

15   Ayin Hillel, 'The Nivozim' [Hebrew], in *The noon land: Poems* (Tel Aviv: ha-Kibbutz ha-me'uhad, 1960), 61–2. The Hebrew neologism 'Nivoz' simultaneously captures the idea of disparagement and belittlement, being wasted and being plundered. There is no English equivalent, and the Hebrew term has been maintained. On this term, see Tzi Luz, *Poetry of Ayin Hillel* [Hebrew] (Tel Aviv: ha-Kibbutz ha-me'uhad, 1996), 127.

or not, was not a participant in the decision-making process. Of course, this process was not considered a crime akin to looting. I would like to reiterate that legal expropriation was a one-time action undertaken by a sovereign entity that put it into effect through military power, policing, foreign policy, etc. *The pillaging that took place consisted of countless uncoordinated actions of individual looters who were not working together.*

There is an ongoing discussion of efforts to forget and erase Israel's Palestinian past. This topic is not this work's focus, but it is clear that the social legitimacy of efforts to expropriate land helped to blur the fundamental injustice of such activity. Sincerely expressed, the following remarks made by Kibbutz Lohamei HaGeta'ot member Avraham Tzoref raise this point:

> One day I was sitting in the abandoned orchard on the other side of the road . . . I was preoccupied with how to turn this abandoned and faltering orchard into an orchard cultivated through use of modern methods . . . suddenly, I saw a shadow cast before me. A man was standing next to me, almost close enough to touch. My surprise grew when I recognized that the stranger was not one of ours. The foreigner presented himself: 'I am Ahmad, this is my orchard.' I was shocked. After I recovered, I started to talk with the uninvited guest. He said that he now resided in Acre and that he used to live in Sumeiriya (السميرية). Suddenly, he began to explain that he knew how to fully irrigate the plots . . . It turns out that he was one of the wealthy men of Sumeiriya and one of the orchard's owners. *Until then I had known that the orchard was 'abandoned property', but I had never considered the fact that this 'abandoned property' had owners.*[16]

The social (and psychological) mechanism that made it possible for a kibbutz member to repress the existence of the previous owners of the land now in the kibbutz's possession does not touch upon the issue of individual looting. Yet perhaps Tzoref's story can teach us something about the 'forgetfulness' that over time befell both the individual pillager and the population as a whole. In any event, as we have remarked, the

---

16   Zvika Dror, ed., *Kibbutz Lohamei HaGeta'ot: A story of a place* [Hebrew] (Daliyya: Lohamei HaGeta'ot Press, 2005), 37, emphasis added.

first immediate result of the plunder was that *the granting of amnesty helped make plunder into a noncriminal offence.* Yet, what about the approach of those whom Yiftach Brigade Commander Elad Peled critically referred to as having 'furnished their homes' with stolen property?[17] How did the looting affect the way they related to social reality and themselves?

This issue leads us to the second social effect of despoliation: *the transformation of the individual looter into an adherent of a specific approach to policy.* Ephraim Kleiman, who participated in the expulsion of Bedouins from the el-'Azazme (العزازمة) tribe, had an illuminating comment to make about this:

> There is an additional aspect of the Arab's flight that few people talk about today: the fate of the property that those who fled left behind . . . regardless of whether the looting was private or public, it functioned as an additional hidden factor influencing the process that I previously described inasmuch as it created groups that had a material interest, a priori or a posteriori, in the Arab population's removal.[18]

Kleiman raises an interesting point regarding the connection between the pillage and the expulsion of the Arab population. Unlike Kleiman, however, I do not see every looter as an a priori 'supporter of expulsion'. There were certainly groups and individuals who derived financial benefit from Arab property; but *immoveable* property, not movable property, was where people really made money.

The individual looter was not necessarily an active participant, either directly or through provision of meaningful support, in expulsion operations undertaken to get Arabs to leave neighbouring cities and villages. In fact, it was more likely that he was not. Yet, in practice, *on a personal level,* he *benefitted* from the policy that set these operations in motion.[19]

---

17   Elad Peled, testimony, 30 March 2000, YRC.

18   Ephraim Kleiman, 'Khirbet Khizehs and unpleasant memories' [Hebrew], *Prozah* 25 (September 1978): 24–9.

19   It is worth mentioning that when Palestinians were expelled from specific locations, small groups carried out the expulsions. I note this because while such acts were carried out by small groups, their influence on social consciousness was nonetheless quite profound.

A statement made by Folke Bernadotte, a United Nations mediator in Palestine who was murdered by the Lehi in September 1948, makes clear that this was widely recognized. In a report dated 16 September, the day before he was murdered, Bernadotte wrote:

> There have been numerous reports from reliable sources about widespread looting, robbery, and theft, and cases where villages have been destroyed in the absence of clear military necessity. The provisional Israeli government's responsibility *for the return of private property to its Arab owners* and for compensation to be granted to owners whose property has been destroyed is clear, independent of any compensation that the provisional government is entitled to claim from the Arab states.[20]

In real time, the Jewish population did not know whether the Arab inhabitants would return or not (in fact, most decision makers did not know what would happen at the end of the war either, and there were major disagreements within the government about how to resolve the refugee 'problem'). Published throughout the world, Bernadotte's comment about the return of Arab property certainly must have sounded reasonable to the average Israeli. Yet how did such a statement affect the individual looter?

In a short and illuminating article published in the Israeli Communist Party newspaper *Kol Ha'am*, H. Kopanski argued that plunderers marked themselves when they took spoils, and that the effects of the individual plunderer's actions transcended them and had a broader social and political effect. In his opinion, plunderers are not prepared to see themselves as criminals. Therefore, they make excuses for what they did. 'That is how chauvinists makes allies and how fascists got people to collaborate in their crimes. This is how things happened throughout the world and this is how things are being done here.'[21]

Indeed, those who plundered their neighbour's property did something to themselves. But what, exactly? The first thing they did was cast

---

20 Progress Report of the United Nations Mediator on Palestine Submitted to the Secretary-General for Transmission to the Members of the United Nations 16.9.1948, UN Archive.

21 H. Kopanski, 'Movement against movement' [Hebrew], *Kol Ha'am*, 17 May 1948.

off the yoke of social prohibitions. Since the overwhelming majority of pillagers were completely unfamiliar with the world of crime and lived in accordance with societal norms, the individual plunderer needed to contend with their actions *on their own*, in their community. One can assume that some of the plunderers found it difficult to live with themselves and their community knowing that they were criminals. Then the general amnesty solved this problem for them. Besides cancelling the criminal sanction against plundering, it forced them to grant social legitimacy to the act of plunder. Under contemporary circumstances, *de facto support for the expulsion policy and/or the failure to bring back the Arab inhabitants* constituted the essence of this legitimization. In a wider sense, legitimization also obliged one to adopt a policy position that looked at Arabs through rifle sights. In this sense, the failure to enforce the prohibition against theft of Arab property for months on end functioned like a permit to plunder. In a meeting of Mapam activists in Haifa, Meir Ya'ari, for example, said that 'those who did not oppose the expulsion of Arabs are responsible for the acts of plunder'.[22] Elsewhere, he said that 'we are eventually going to pay for this. He [David Ben-Gurion] will add up the bill with us.'[23]

In my opinion, the decision to permit pillaging for months on end was part of a manipulative political strategy employed to mobilize the Jewish population in support of the far-reaching consequences of a political policy that achieved hegemony during the course of the war: the Arab population's removal from the country through destruction of their economy, their homes, and their property.[24]

---

22   'Ya'ari accuses Mapai' [Hebrew], *Herut*, 21 November 1948.

23   Minutes of conference of military personnel, 25–26 July 1948, file: (2)206.90, YYA.

24   We will not get into politological theory (theories of how politics function) here, but it is worth briefly mentioning the useful distinction that the American sociologist Robert Merton made between manifest and latent functions in Robert Merton, *Social Theory and Social Structure: Toward the Codification of Theory and Research* (Glencoe, IL: Free Press, 1949). According to Merton, 'The concept of latent function extends the observer's attention beyond the question of whether or not the behaviour attains its avowed purpose' (64). He correctly observes that in cases where scholars only treat statements made by their objects of study (in our case, the politicians/decision makers) a situation is created where, in practice, 'their inquiry is set for them by [politicians]' (65). In this way, what the historian presents as a historical 'paradox' (a gap between a politician's declared objectives, the manifest function, and the politician's actual objectives, the true function) proves indicative of his own blindness. For more,

One can say that the plunder constituted one aspect of the brutality that drained the looters of the compassion they felt towards their neighbours and converted them into a *community constituted through crime*. Since normative individuals, in contrast with professional criminals, find it difficult to live in a state of constant dissonance with their environments, they find it necessary to lie to *themselves* about their contemptuous actions. In this case, self-deception proves quite difficult: the looter is robbing people who are former neighbours, not distant enemies. In Kopanski's opinion, since 'the individual does not want to see himself stained with the mark of a robber and thief, he prefers to walk around with the symbol 'only in this way' on his lapel'.[25] Poet and essayist Yeshurun Keshet, who looked with sadness upon the social reality that resulted from the pillaging, wrote the following in his diary in June 1948:

> I am afraid that the custom of looting is gradually becoming more widespread, and it has already become part of Jerusalem's genius loci. Thirteen-year-old to fifteen-year-old boys from poor neighbourhoods whose fathers work on the black market and whose brothers are members in the separatist forces walk around with Sten guns underneath their arms.[26]

Regardless of the fact that the Irgun's symbol was a map of the Land of Israel on both sides of the Jordan River, foregrounded by a hand holding a rifle and captioned 'only in this way', it did not set policy; Prime Minister Ben-Gurion did.

Aharon Cohen, a Mapam Arab department member, pointed to the political dangers of pillaging Arab property:

> The problem is not merely a moral problem or a problem of what people will say. The looting that individuals have undertaken is a scandal. Nonetheless, this is not the main thing. First and foremost,

---

see the discussion in Adam Raz, *The iron fist regime: David Ben-Gurion, the statism debate, and the controversy over Israel's nuclear program* [Hebrew] (Jerusalem: Carmel, 2019), 16–21.

25 Kopanski, 'Movement against movement'.

26 Yeshurun Keshet, *In besieged Jerusalem: Diaries from the home front* [Hebrew] (Jerusalem: Re'uven Mas, 1973), 117.

the problem is a public-political one that is closely connected to our future destiny. Our attitude towards the Arab minority in the country serves as the first test of our defence force and our developing state's whole domestic policy... there is no need for liberal bourgeois parties to seize the reins of state power for reaction to set in. Workers' parties can also slip down the [slippery] slope of reaction too.[27]

The many examples that were provided above testify to leaders' and intellectuals' understanding of the social effects of the plunder that took place. When we remove the mobilizing pathos from the statements of Sheetrit, Buber, Hazan, Sprinzak, and others quoted in detail above, all make the same basic assertion: *the plunderer became an unwilling advocate of a policy agenda that strove to create a condition of perpetual war between Israel and the Arab world.* It seems that the idealistic youth who fought in the war, such as the pseudonymous Palmachnik 'Niv', were aware of plunder's withering effect:

You and I and most of our comrades know that even when peace arrives, we will still be asked to maintain a strong pioneering spirit and no less readiness for self-sacrifice than we do now... yet our pioneering and our devotion will not be directed towards acts of urban conquest. Then they will be directed towards acts of 'stone conquest', acts of hard grey creation. Habits tied to devotion and sacrifice that we picked up during the war will certainly aid us in becoming magnificent pioneer-builders. Meanwhile, other fundamentally rebellious and lawless habits (we should not be afraid to say this out loud) will certainly prove detrimental. How will one endure such things tomorrow if he does not take account of his customs and habits, and this lawlessness, *today*?[28]

The following comment made by politician and journalist Uri Avnery connects to what 'Niv' said: 'It is strange that people think that a man can murder, destroy and rob, and the next day, when he comes home,

27   Aharon Cohen, *Let's clarify things for ourselves (Conversations with comrades in uniform)* [Hebrew] (Tel Aviv: Mifleget ha-po'alim ha-me'uhedet be-Eretz Yisra'el, 1948), 16–17.

28   Niv [pseud.], 'Letter to a friend' [Hebrew], '*Alon ha-Palmach* 68 (3 July 1948): 29–31.

return to being the same delicate, naïve and lovely young man that he, perhaps, once was.'[29] Avnery was right: he cannot revert to his former state.

In conclusion: as a tool, or means, the plunder of property served Prime Minister Ben-Gurion's policy of removing Arab residents from the State of Israel and helped him realize it. The plunder of Arab property was only one aspect of a broader policy of Arab expulsion, and it fit together with other aspects of this policy mentioned briefly at various points in this book: the desiccation of Arab orchards through the removal or theft of irrigation pipes and motors; the burning of crops; the killing of work animals; and the physical destruction of villages. Together with the plunder of Arab property, these practices that destroyed Palestinian workers' and farmers' means of production decimated the Palestinian economy. In other words, Palestinian refugees had nothing to which to return. What differentiated the plunder of moveable Arab property from the other practices mentioned is that the expulsion of Arab residents, the burning of crops, and the destruction of buildings were practices in which only relatively small groups of people participated and which took place far from the public gaze. In contrast, an integral part of the Israeli public participated in the plunder. This made the pillagers into partners in crime, stakeholders in the non-return of the Arabs, and involuntary supporters of a specific political policy.

---

29   Avnery, *The other side of the coin*, 151.

A Brief Conclusion

One of the reasons that the Israeli Jewish population is not sufficiently aware of the plunder of Palestinian property today is the aforementioned 'conspiracy of silence'. In practice, as in the case of the military government, those who opposed the plunder (or the government) needed to keep their mouths shut. In the Knesset plenum, Finance Minister Eliezer Kaplan said:

> [I have] a few words [to say] not just to Knesset members, but also to those who are not its members: comrades, we are a small country, but the world's interest in it, including everything said and done in it, is tremendous. It is like we are in a display window and the eyes of the world are upon us: they keep tabs on us, examine us closely, [and] analyse our every step, action, and work.[1]

He was right. Those who saw the remaining Palestinian Arab population as a 'bridge' to the broader Arab world could not brag about the way that either the Jewish government (or the Jewish public) treated the Arab minority. They looted its property, and they destroyed its economy. Until 1966, 85 percent of Palestinians were under the control of a regime that instituted travel restrictions and enforced draconian prohibitions. We are not obliged to discuss the difficulty that this posed to

---

1 Minutes of the Knesset plenum, 23 November 1949, KAJ.

Prime Minister Ben-Gurion's political opponents (most of whom were in his party). Nevertheless, it is important that we remember it.

During a cabinet meeting held in mid-June 1948, Minister of Agriculture Zisling spoke prophetically in opposition to the prime minister's policy:

> Both the issue of what happened to Arab cities, villages, and property during the war and the matter of [what will happen to] Arabs after the war *place us on a most dangerous path* if we harbour any hope of alliances and peace with forces in the Middle East that could ally with us. Hundreds of thousands of Arabs who will be exiled from the Land of Israel, even if they are at fault, will be left swinging in the wind . . . their hatred for us *will grow*. Indigenous Arabs did not fight. Foreigners fought . . . Throughout the Middle East, Arabs of our land will become *an element* that will wage war against us. The Middle East will not compensate them, and they will not collect any monetary compensation. Instead, those who exploit them will profit and hundreds of thousands of Arabs, both them and their descendants, will be our enemies.[2]

As we have previously seen, among Israeli officials, Zisling was one of those most critical of the plunder of Arab property. It is fitting to revisit the comments of Minister of Minorities Bechor-Shalom Sheetrit, a man that Israelis have forgotten, at the conclusion of this book; to be a bit prosaic, *they owe him a great deal*. It is not because he emerged victorious in his struggle against Ben-Gurion and his policy, but because he fought and presented a clear voice in opposition to the dominant policy. In this sense, Sheetrit saved Zionism, or at least tried to. In a Ministry of Minorities memorandum, he wrote:

> Our victories and our sacrifices should not be stained by the taking of plunder and spoils. More than a hundred settlements were evacuated by their Arab inhabitants . . . both those who took their property or part of their property with them and those who abandoned their property and thereby tested us and set a trial before us. We need to withstand this test and prove to them and the whole world that we are

---

2   Cabinet meeting minutes, 16 June 1948, ISA, emphasis added.

a cultured people that recognizes and is prepared to assume its responsibility to protect civilian property and to maintain proper and fair relations with those who remained or will want to remain amongst us and those who will want to return to us . . . Unfortunately, criminal acts have been committed in places that we conquered that are liable to stain the Zionist movement's good name, to defile the principles that it espoused and espouses and arouse suspicions and sad thoughts about our intentions and our future government, both among Arabs and nations of the world and the best of our children and our people, both in Israel and abroad . . . Some of the finest amongst us served as a bad and embarrassing example for our masses and circles that prove hard to imagine heralding the path of booty and theft were overcome by a desire for plunder and spoils. The spirit of lawlessness hovers and all methods and means need to be employed to stop it . . . we need to restrain all the evil urges and not discount the value of interpersonal relations in the East.[3]

Sheetrit wrote the truth. This is what Buber was trying to say in the quote at the opening of part II: 'Internal redemption can only be created by gazing directly at the brutal face of truth.' I hope this book makes a modest contribution to this.

---

3   Bechor-Shalom Sheetrit, 'Memorandum of the Ministry of Minority Affairs', presented to the National Administration, 10 May 1948, file: Various reports, Gimmel-306/62, ISA.

Index